Fourth Edition

AMERICAN WAYS

AN INTRODUCTION TO AMERICAN CULTURE

MARYANNE KEARNY DATESMAN

JOANN CRANDALL

EDWARD N. KEARNY

Dedicated to Lisa Kearny, George Datesman, and Joseph Keyerleber

American Ways: An Introduction to American Culture, Fourth Edition

Copyright © 2014 by Pearson Education, Inc.

Pearson Education, 10 Bank Street, White Plains, NY 10606 USA

Staff credits: The people who made up the American Ways team, representing editorial, production, design, manufacturing, and marketing are Tracey Munz Cataldo, Rosa Chapinal, Dave Dickey, Nancy Flaggman, Barry Katzen, Amy McCormick, Lise Minovitz, Barbara Perez, Liza Pleva, Joan L. Poole, Debbie Sistino, and Jane Townsend.

Project Management: Jennifer Stem/JTS Studio, Inc.

Text composition: ElectraGraphics, Inc.

Cover design: Mary Ann Smith and Tracey Munz Cataldo

Cover photo: Mr. Bong/Fotolia

Library of Congress Cataloging-in-Publication Data

Datesman, Maryanne Kearny.
    American Ways: an Introduction to American Culture / Maryanne Kearny Datesman, JoAnn Crandall, Edward N. Kearny.—Fourth edition.
        pages cm
    Includes bibliographical references.
    ISBN 978-0-13-304702-8
    1. English language—Textbooks for foreign speakers. 2. United States—Civilization—Problems, exercises, etc. 3. Readers—United States. I. Crandall, Jo Ann. II. Kearny, Edward N. III. Title.
    PE1128.D347 2014
    428.6'4—dc23
                                2013036488

Printed in the United States

ISBN-10: 0-13-304702-4
ISBN-13: 978-0-13-304702-8

CONTENTS

What is "culture"? There are many definitions. Some would define it as the art, literature, and music of a people, their architecture, history, religion, and traditions. Others might focus more on the customs and specific behavior of a people. We have chosen to use a sociological definition of *culture* as *the way of life of a group of people, developed over time, and passed down from generation to generation.* This broad definition includes every aspect of human life and interaction. However, it would be impossible to cover every facet of American culture in a single book. We have, therefore, taken a values approach to our discussion, focusing on the traditional mainstream values that have attracted people to the United States for more than two hundred years. After explaining how these traditional values developed, we will trace how they influence various aspects of American life.

Why a book on American culture? There are many reasons. Those of us who have worked with foreign students in American universities or who have taught English to students both here and overseas repeatedly encounter questions about life in the United States. These students are frequently confused or even mystified about American values, attitudes, and cultural patterns. Even those students who have mastered enough English to take courses in an American university often find that they do not understand the cultural rules well enough to be successful as students. Many of these rules can be understood only within the broader context of American cultural patterns.

It is not only students who need the kind of information presented in this book. Foreign businesspeople, visiting scholars or government officials, and even tourists find their time in the United States more satisfying when they understand the values that underlie American behavior patterns and institutions. Newly-arrived immigrants and refugees adapt more easily to their new home when given a systematic introduction to their new country and its inhabitants.

For all of these reasons, *American Ways* is suitable for a wide audience. It has been used as a text in a number of programs for foreign students, including intensive English programs, short summer courses in the United States for foreign high school and college students, both quarter and semester courses at American universities, government programs for foreign visitors, and classes for immigrants. It has also been used in many different settings outside the United States, both as a text for students and as a reference guide—for U.S. Peace Corps volunteers, for example, and others who are teaching American culture.

What do we really learn when we study other cultures? First and foremost, we learn about our own. Until we are confronted by a different way of doing things, we assume that everyone does things the same way that we do, and thus our own culture—our values, attitudes, behavior—is largely hidden from our view. When we spend time analyzing another culture, however, we begin to see our own more clearly and to understand some of the subtleties that motivate our behavior and our opinions. By reading *American Ways*, students can begin to understand themselves and their own cultures better. To enhance this understanding, each chapter in the book is followed by a series of exercises. Some of these exercises are specifically designed to encourage students to think about their own values or patterns of behavior and to compare them with what they are learning about or experiencing in American settings. We have also included a number of exercises to encourage students to interact with and talk with Americans. In these exercises we have provided a set of carefully structured questions that students can ask Americans. The answers they receive will help students form a composite picture of American beliefs and practices as they relate to education, business, government, sports, recreation, and so on.

Some of the chapter exercises provide students with an opportunity to explore more fully an idea that has been presented or to discuss ideas with other students. You may wish to assign different exercises to different students or to small groups of students, and then ask them to share their findings and opinions with the class. If possible, small groups should include students from different countries so that, in addition to learning about American culture and their own, they are also learning about other cultures.

Perhaps this is the real goal of a course about culture: to help us become more sensitive to cultural differences and more accepting of them. However, there will always be aspects of another culture that we may not like, no matter how much we understand it. The objective of this book is not to persuade others to approve of life in the United States, but rather to help them understand it more fully.

ABOUT THE FOURTH EDITION

In revising the content of this book, we concentrated on updating events that have occurred since the third edition was published in 2005. The issues surrounding multiculturalism continue to be of great importance, as the cultural diversity of the United States continues to increase. Indeed, estimates are that by the mid-2000s, the United States will be *majority minority*. That is, the majority of Americans will be from minority groups. The traditional group of white Americans of European descent will be in the minority. Already this is the situation in the largest school systems in the country. And since the last edition of this book, the country has elected and re-elected its first African-American president, Barack Obama. His first cabinet (the heads of executive branches of the government and principal government agencies) was one of the most diverse in history, and he appointed three women to serve on the U.S. Supreme Court, one of whom is the first Hispanic Supreme Court Justice. This expanding diversity makes it increasingly difficult to describe the American culture, and it is uncertain whether the traditional mainstream culture will continue to be the dominant culture in the future.

In the fourth edition of this book, the basic conceptual framework of traditional values remains the same. However, it is not clear how future generations will interpret or change them. Chapter 12 has been largely rewritten to focus more clearly on what is happening to traditional American values and on the challenges the United States faces (some of which are global in nature). These challenges include economic decline and rising national debt, the growing gap between the wealthiest individuals and the rest of the population, and needed reform of immigration policy. Perhaps the greatest challenge is the growing polarization between the two American political parties—the Democrats and Republicans—that has led to a Congress in which little gets done. Gun violence and national security continue to be a concern, as attacks on American schools and the 2013 bombings at the Boston Marathon demonstrate.

Originally, we envisioned this book primarily for use in English language courses designed to prepare students to study in American universities. We believe students in those courses need experience presenting information and voicing their personal opinions to others; they should be encouraged to make both oral and written reports and participate in debates and formal discussions. We have written many exercises that suggest appropriate topics and activities. The fourth edition provides more explicit development of reading skills (skimming, scanning, predicting, and understanding main ideas and details) and an expanded writing section (identifying and organizing academic information into main ideas and supporting details, often preceded by discussion, research, and completion of graphic organizers). New to this edition is explicit focus on critical thinking: on assessing information, comparing alternative points of view, identifying potential problems and solutions, and being a questioning reader. There is also more attention to vocabulary in this edition, including exercises on collocation and a focus on the most important academic words (from the Academic Word List*). The book continues to offer activities such as Ask Americans, but with this addition, students will also be able to listen online to a diverse group of Americans as they answer these questions. Throughout, you will also notice the new photos, new poll data, and the exhaustive bibliography of sources that we have used in developing this edition. More than 200 new sources were consulted for the fourth edition. Of particular note is the extensive use of Pew Research Center data, and we urge teachers to have students explore this valuable continuous source of new information available online. Additionally, answers to the exercises, more teaching tips, and graphic organizers can be found in the Teacher's Manual available online.

We have been delighted to hear from many teachers about creative ways they have used *American Ways*—not only in courses that introduce American culture, but also in courses focusing on cross-cultural communication, listening/speaking, reading/writing, academic preparation, and even literature. Teachers have used the values framework to design courses where students could explore ways in which the values appear in American literature, American films, or current events, for example, focusing on materials the teacher developed from other sources and presented in addition to the text.

THE BOOK AT A GLANCE

Purpose

- To increase students' awareness and understanding of the cultural values of the United States, their own country, and, we hope, other countries
- To provide interesting cross-cultural activities for small group and class discussions, and topics for oral presentations, research, and writing projects
- To develop students' critical thinking and use of academic English

Level

High intermediate to advanced. The vocabulary level is in the range of 3,000 to 4,000 words, with emphasis on the Academic Word List.* (See page 306.) Grammatical structures are not controlled, although an effort has been made to avoid overly complex patterns.

Content

Information about traditional basic American values, where they came from, and how these values affect various institutions and aspects of life in the United States, for example, religion, business, government, race relations, education, recreation, and the family.

Types of Exercises

Pre-reading activities (previewing content and vocabulary), comprehension questions on both main ideas and details, topics for discussion and debate, critical thinking, extensive vocabulary development (with a focus on the Academic Word List and collocations), values clarification, questions for Americans, suggestions for research and oral reports, ideas for pair work and group projects, proverbs, people watching and experiments, understanding polls and the media, Internet activities, writing topics and activities to develop academic writing skills, and suggested books and movies.

Use of Text

- To orient students to American culture
- To foster cross-cultural communication
- To promote reading, writing, and discussion
- To encourage conversation
- To serve as a conceptual framework and accompany other cultural materials focusing on literature, the media, current events, and so on.

For details on the development and evaluation of the AWL, see Coxhead, Averil (2000) A New Academic Word List. TESOL Quarterly, 34(2): 213–238.

For more information about the AWL and how to use it, visit the Internet site http://www.victoria. ac.nz/lals/resources/academicwordlist/

ABOUT THE AUTHORS

Maryanne Kearny Datesman is the author of several ESL reading texts. She has taught ESL and administered programs at Western Kentucky University and American University. She has also taught at Georgetown University. In Kentucky, she established and administered a private language school and directed programs for refugees. She was co-founder of Kentucky TESOL and is a former president of WATESOL.

JoAnn (Jodi) Crandall is a professor emerita of education at the University of Maryland Baltimore County. At UMBC, she co-directed the master's program in ESOL/Bilingual Education and directed the interdisciplinary Ph.D. program in Language, Literacy, and Culture. She is a former president of TESOL and AAAL (American Association for Applied Linguistics) and a frequent speaker at national and international conferences.

Edward N. Kearny is professor emeritus of government at Western Kentucky University. He earned his Ph.D. in government from American University in 1968. He also holds a bachelor's degree in economics and a master's degree in psychology, and he has written a number of books and articles on American politics.

Acknowledgments

Our great appreciation goes to George Datesman for many hours of research, editing, help with the logistics of matching exercises with new content, and moral support, and to Lisa Kearny for help with research and contributing creative ideas for exercises and activities that would be fun to do. We also want to thank our editors at Pearson, Debbie Sistino and Joan Poole, for their considerable efforts and contributions.

We would also like to thank Averil Coxhead at the School of Language Studies, Massey University, Palmerston North, New Zealand, for allowing us the use of the Academic Word List. We wish to acknowledge the comments and encouragement we have received from many colleagues who have used this book in a wide range of settings all over the world. We would also like to thank the students we have worked with over the years for sharing their insights and perceptions of the United States with us and, in the process, helping us to better understand our own American culture.

M. K. D.

J. A. C.

E. N. K.

CHAPTER 1

INTRODUCTION: UNDERSTANDING THE CULTURE OF THE UNITED STATES

Culture hides much more than it reveals, and strangely enough what it hides, it hides most effectively from its own participants. Years of study have convinced me that the real job is not to understand foreign culture but to understand our own.

Edward T. Hall (1914–2009)

How can you define the culture of a diverse country like the United States, and what does it mean to be an American?

BEFORE YOU READ

Preview Vocabulary

A. Every chapter of **American Ways** contains many words from the Academic Word List (AWL).* Notice the AWL words in italics as you work with a partner to discuss the following questions.

1. If a country has great *ethnic diversity,* would you expect to find many people who speak different languages and have different customs?

2. Could planning a visit to another country *motivate* someone to learn a foreign language?

3. Should *immigrants* be required to learn the language of their new country before they become citizens?

4. How could you learn about the customs and *traditions* for a holiday in another country?

5. If there are more people in the United States who speak English than Spanish, which is the *dominant* language in the United States?

6. Is the climate of a country a *significant factor* in the daily lives of the people? Why?

B. There are five AWL words in the quotation by Edward T. Hall at the beginning of the chapter. Read the quotation and find the words with the following meanings. Write each word next to its meaning.

_____Convinced_____ 1. made someone think that something is true

_____reveal_____ 2. shows something that was hidden

_____Culture_____ 3. ideas, beliefs, and customs

_____Job_____ 4. work

_____Participants_____ 5. people who are taking part in an activity

See page 306 for an explanation of the AWL and how to use it. Some of these words are key to understanding the chapter reading.

Preview Content

A. Before you read the chapter, think about what you know about the "culture" of a country. Work with a partner and answer the questions.

1. What is the culture of a country? If someone asked you to describe your country's culture, which of these would you mention?

beliefs	government
cities	history
climate	holidays
customs	houses
dance	literature
food	music
geography	

Anything else? _____

2. Do you agree with the quotation by Edward T. Hall? Do people really not understand their own culture? What aspects of a country's culture are the hardest to understand?

B. Look at the pictures, charts, and graphs in this chapter, and read the headings. Then predict three topics you think this chapter will discuss.

1. _____

2. _____

3. _____

1   People are naturally curious about each other, and when we meet people from different countries, we want to know many things:

- What is life like in their country?
- What kind of houses do they live in?
- What kind of food do they eat?
- What are their customs?

2   If we visit another country, we can observe the people and how they live, and we can answer some of these questions. But the most interesting questions are often the hardest to answer:

- What do the people believe in?
- What do they value most?
- What motivates them?
- Why do they behave the way they do?

3   In trying to answer these questions about Americans, we must remember two things: (1) the immense size of the United States and (2) its great ethnic diversity. It is difficult to comprehend the size of the country until you try to travel from one city to another. If you got in a car in New York and drove to Los Angeles, stopping only to get gas, eat, and sleep, it would take you four or five days. It takes two full days to drive from New York to Florida. On a typical winter day, it might be raining in Washington, D.C., and snowing in New York and Chicago, while in Los Angeles and Miami it is warm enough to swim. It is not difficult to imagine how different daily life might be in such different climates, or how lifestyles could vary in cities and towns so far apart.

4   The other significant factor influencing American life—ethnic diversity—is probably even more important. Aside from the Native Americans who were living on the North American continent when the first European settlers arrived, all Americans came from other countries—or their ancestors did. (Incidentally,[1] some Native Americans are still members of separate and distinct Indian nations, each with its own language, culture, traditions, and even government.) In the 1500s, Spain established settlements in Florida, California, and the Southwest, and France claimed large territories in the center of the North American continent. But from the 1600s to the birth of the United States in 1776, most immigrants to the colonies that would form the United States were from northern Europe, and the majority were from England. It was these people who shaped the values and traditions that became the dominant, traditional culture of the United States.

A Nation of Immigrants

5   In 1815, the population of the United States was 8.4 million. Over the next 100 years, the country took in about 35 million immigrants, with the greatest numbers coming in the late 1800s and the early 1900s. Many of these new immigrants were not from northern Europe. In 1882, 40,000 Chinese arrived, and between 1900 and 1907 there were more than 30,000 Japanese immigrants. But by far the largest numbers of the new immigrants were from central, eastern, and southern Europe. The new immigrants brought different languages and different cultures to the United States, but gradually most of them assimilated[2] to the dominant American culture they found here.

6   In 1908, a year when a million new immigrants arrived in the United States, Israel Zangwill wrote in a play,

[1] incidentally: by the way

[2] assimilated: became part of a county or group and were accepted by other people in it

*America is God's Crucible,[3] the great
Melting-Pot where all the races of Europe
are melting and re-forming. . . . Germans
and Frenchmen, Irishmen and Englishmen,
Jews and Russians—into the Crucible with
you all! God is making the American!*

7   Since Zangwill first used the term *melting
pot* to describe the United States, the
concept has been debated. In Chapter 8 we
consider this issue in more detail, and trace
the history of African Americans as well.
Two things are certain: The dominant
American culture has survived, and it has
more or less successfully absorbed vast
numbers of immigrants at various points
in its history. It has also been changed over
time by all the immigrant groups who
have settled here.

8   If we look at the immigration patterns
of the 1900s, we see that the greatest
numbers came at the beginning and at
the end of the century. During the first
two decades of the twentieth century,
there were as many as one million new
immigrants per year, so that by the 1910
census, almost 15 percent of all Americans
had been born in another country. In
1921, however, the country began to limit
immigration, and the Immigration Act
of 1924 virtually closed the door. The
total number of immigrants admitted
per year dropped from as many as one
million to only 150,000. A quota system
was established that specified the number
of immigrants that could come from each
country. It heavily favored immigrants
from northern and western Europe and
severely limited everyone else. This system
remained in effect until 1965, with several
exceptions allowing groups of refugees
from countries such as Hungary, Cuba,
Vietnam, and Cambodia into the United
States.

9   Immigration laws began to change in
1965 and the yearly totals began to rise
again—from about 300,000 per year in
the 1960s to more than one million per
year in the 1990s. By the end of the
century, the United States was admitting
more immigrants than all the other
industrialized countries combined. In
addition to legal immigration, estimates
were that illegal immigration was adding
more than half a million more people
per year. Changes in the laws that were
intended to help family reunifications[4]
resulted in large numbers of non-
Europeans arriving, thus creating another
group of new immigrants. By the late
1900s, 90 percent of all immigrants
were coming from Latin America, the
Caribbean, and Asia.

10   In the twenty-first century, the numbers of
new immigrants have begun to approach
the percentages of the early twentieth
century. Between 1990 and 2010, the
number of foreign-born living in the
United States almost doubled from 20
million to 40 million, with about one-
third arriving since 2000. These new
immigrants accounted for about one-third
of the total growth in population and have
had an enormous impact on our country.
By the year 2010, about 13 percent of all
Americans were foreign born. Twelve
states and the nation's capital had even
higher percentages of foreign-born
residents:

- California, 27 percent
- New York and New Jersey, each over
  21 percent
- Florida and Nevada, each over 19
  percent
- Hawaii and Texas, each over 16 percent

---

[3] *crucible: a container in which substances are heated to a very high level*

[4] *reunifications: the joining of the parts of something together again*

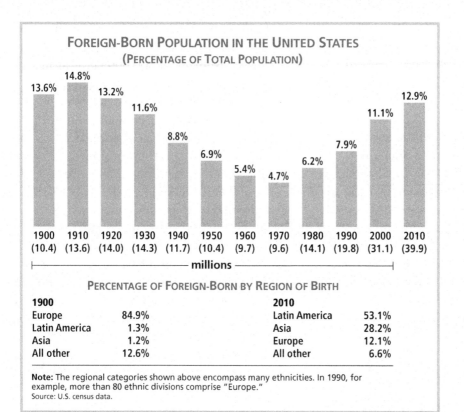

FOREIGN-BORN POPULATION IN THE UNITED STATES
(PERCENTAGE OF TOTAL POPULATION)

Year	1900 (10.4)	1910 (13.6)	1920 (14.0)	1930 (14.3)	1940 (11.7)	1950 (10.4)	1960 (9.7)	1970 (9.6)	1980 (14.1)	1990 (19.8)	2000 (31.1)	2010 (39.9)
Percentage	13.6%	14.8%	13.2%	11.6%	8.8%	6.9%	5.4%	4.7%	6.2%	7.9%	11.1%	12.9%

⊢——————— millions ———————⊣

PERCENTAGE OF FOREIGN-BORN BY REGION OF BIRTH

1900		2010	
Europe	84.9%	Latin America	53.1%
Latin America	1.3%	Asia	28.2%
Asia	1.2%	Europe	12.1%
All other	12.6%	All other	6.6%

Note: The regional categories shown above encompass many ethnicities. In 1990, for example, more than 80 ethnic divisions comprise "Europe."
Source: U.S. census data.

- Arizona, Illinois, Massachusetts, Connecticut, Maryland, and the District of Columbia, each over 13 percent

11   The twenty-first-century immigration patterns are continuing to change the color and the ethnic mix of the American population. First, the percentage of white Americans of European descent[5] continues to decrease. Few Europeans are immigrating to the United States now, and many of those who came in the early 1900s have died. Their descendants have married Americans with ancestors from other countries, and many of these second- and third-generation immigrants no longer think of themselves as Irish or German or English.

12   Second, in the early 2000s, more than half of all new immigrants were from Latin America, resulting in large concentrations of Spanish speakers around the country,

particularly in California, Florida, Texas, Arizona, and other southwestern states. Hispanics now represent the largest minority in the United States (16%), larger than the number of African Americans (13%). With their growth in numbers has come a growth in political and economic influence. Presidential candidates now consider how to win Hispanic votes, and there are more than 6,000 elected Hispanic leaders nationwide. There has been a rise in Hispanic-owned businesses and Spanish-language media. Perhaps the largest impact is in the schools, where more than 20% of the children are Hispanic.

13   The numbers of Hispanic-Americans will probably continue to grow because many of them are young adults or children. However, the number of new Hispanic immigrants has declined. In 2000, they made up more than 50% of all new immigrants, but the number fell to

[5] *descent: family origins, especially in relation to the country where one's family came from*

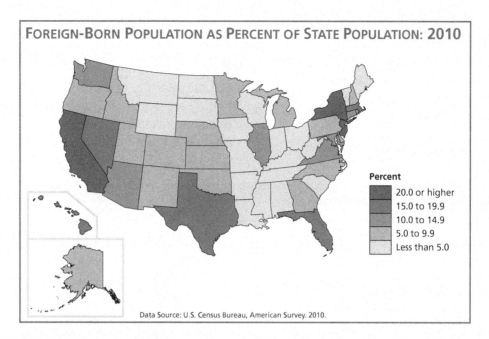

FOREIGN-BORN POPULATION AS PERCENT OF STATE POPULATION: 2010

Percent
- 20.0 or higher
- 15.0 to 19.9
- 10.0 to 14.9
- 5.0 to 9.9
- Less than 5.0

Data Source: U.S. Census Bureau, American Survey. 2010.

about 30% in 2010. Because of the poor economy, a number of immigrant residents returned to their home countries in Latin America. Due to tighter border restrictions, the number of illegal immigrants fell, and the total population of Hispanics living in the United States may have actually declined.

14 The immigrants from Asian countries are also contributing to the new American mix. According to the 2010 census, for the first time there were more Asian immigrants than Hispanic. Today, more than 35 percent of all first-generation immigrants are from Asia, and they now make up about 6 percent of the total population of the United States. If this trend continues, Asian immigrants will have an increasing impact on the American culture. As the minority non-white population of the United States continues to grow, the white majority grows smaller. In 2011, for the first time, there were more minority babies born than white majority babies. The white majority will probably fall below 50 percent sometime between 2040 and 2050. Already, several states and many of the nation's largest cities are "majority minority." This means more than half of the population are members of minority groups.

Cultural Pluralism in the United States

15 One of the critical questions facing the United States today is what role new immigrants will play in their new country. To what degree will they choose to take on the traditional American values and culture? How much will they try to maintain their own language and cultural traditions? Will they create an entirely new culture based on some combination of their values and those of the traditional American culture?

16 Historically, although the children of immigrants may have grown up bilingual and bicultural, for a number of reasons many did not pass on their language and culture. Thus, many grandchildren of immigrants do not speak the language of the old country and are simply American by culture. However, in parts of the country with established communities that share a common language or culture, bilingualism[6] and biculturalism continue.

[6] bilingualism: the ability to speak two languages equally well

This is particularly true in communities where new immigrants are still arriving. In California, for example, the test for a driver's license is given in more than thirty different languages. In general, cultural pluralism[7] is more accepted in the United States today than it was in the first half of the twentieth century, and some school systems have bilingual programs and multicultural curricula.

17 The census of 2010 recognized the increase in the diversity of the American population. There were many racial and ethnic categories to choose from, and it was possible to select more than one category.*

CENSUS 2010 SUMMARY: DIVERSITY OF THE AMERICAN POPULATION		
SUBJECT	NUMBER	PERCENT
RACE		
Total population	308,745,538	100.0
One race	299,736,465	97.1
White	223,553,265	72.4
Black or African American	38,929,319	12.6
American Indian and Alaska Native	2,932,248	0.9
American Indian, specified [1]	1,985,245	0.6
Alaska Native, specified [1]	100,522	0.0
Both American Indian and Alaska Native, specified [1]	869	0.0
American Indian or Alaska Native, not specified	845,612	0.3
Asian	14,674,252	4.8
Native Hawaiian and Other Pacific Islander	540,013	0.2
Some Other Race	19,107,368	6.2
Two or More Races	9,009,073	2.9
Two races with Some Other Race	2,464,690	0.8
Two races without Some Other Race	5,800,628	1.9
Three or more races with Some Other Race	176,026	0.1
Three or more races without Some Other Race	567,729	0.2
HISPANIC OR LATINO		
Total population	308,745,538	100.0
Hispanic or Latino (of any race)	50,477,594	16.3
Mexican	31,798,258	10.3
Puerto Rican	4,623,716	1.5
Cuban	1,785,547	0.6
Other Hispanic or Latino [2]	12,270,073	4.0
Not Hispanic or Latino	258,267,944	83.7
RACE AND HISPANIC OR LATINO		
Total population	308,745,538	100.0
One race	299,736,465	97.1
Hispanic or Latino	47,435,002	15.4
Not Hispanic or Latino	252,301,463	81.7
Two or More Races	9,009,073	2.9
Hispanic or Latino	3,042,592	1.0
Not Hispanic or Latino	5,966,481	1.9

[7] cultural pluralism: the principle that people of different races, religions, and political beliefs can live together peacefully in the same society

*For the 2010 census, people were allowed to check as many ethnic and racial categories as they wished. This chart is the U.S. government's presentation of the very complicated census information that resulted. The chart reflects the difficulties in determining ethnic and racial identities of Americans. For further information, visit the government website www.census.gov.

18 On the one hand, many Americans try to maintain their ethnic heritage and their cultural traditions. On the other hand, the number of interracial marriages is increasing, and the majority of young people believe it does not matter which race or ethnic group they marry into. Evidence of this racial acceptance was the 2008 election of Barack Obama, the first African-American president. President Obama is actually bi-racial, the son of a white mother and a black father, a native of Kenya. His ethnic heritage[8] includes an Irish great, great, great grandfather who immigrated to the United States in 1850. More and more children are born of mixed race or ethnicity. By the middle of the century, the nation will probably no longer have a white majority; some say the color of most Americans will be beige, or light brown, as a result of the mixing of races and ethnic groups.

19 In the United States, most people are very sensitive to the language used to describe racial and ethnic groups, and they try to be politically correct, or "P.C." For example, some black Americans prefer the term African-American instead of black to identify with their African heritage. The terms Native American and American Indian are used interchangeably by those native to the North American continent, while some self-identify by tribe (Navajo, Hopi, and so forth). Some Spanish speakers prefer to be called Latinos (referring to Latin America) instead of Hispanics (referring to Spain), while others prefer to be identified by their country of origin (Cuban-American or Cuban, Mexican-American, Chicano,

President Barack Obama and his family

[8] heritage: that which belongs to you because of your birth

or Mexican, etc.). Since the census uses a variety of terms, we will also use the terms white, Native American or American Indian, black or African-American, and Hispanic or Latino.

20 In spite of all this diversity, there is still a tie that binds Americans together. That tie is a sense of national identity—of being an American. Incidentally, when citizens of the United States refer to themselves as Americans, they have no intention of excluding people from Canada or Latin American countries as residents of the American continents. There is no term such as United Statesians in the English language, so people call themselves Americans. Thus, what is really a language problem has sometimes caused misunderstandings. Although citizens of Latin American countries may call the people in the United States North Americans, to many people in the United States this makes no sense either, because the term North American refers to Canadians and Mexicans as well as citizens of the United States. (NAFTA—the North American Free Trade Agreement, for example, is a trade agreement among Canada, the United States, and Mexico.) The word *American*, then, is used in this text as the nationality of the people who live in the United States of America.

Making Generalizations About American Beliefs

21 What, then, can we say about Americans? What holds them together and makes them feel American? Is it possible to make generalizations about what they believe? It is, but we must be cautious about generalizations. As we talk about basic American beliefs, we must remember that not all Americans hold these beliefs, nor do all Americans believe these things to the same degree. The ways in which some Americans practice their beliefs may also differ, resulting in a great variety of lifestyles. What we attempt to do is to define and explain the traditional, dominant cultural values that have for so many years attracted immigrants to the United States.

22 It is important to know that today there is much talk about American values and what they really are. Much of the debate is over *moral*, or religious values. In this book we are not discussing moral values. Instead, we are describing *cultural* values—the cultural engine of the country. These cultural values have defined the United States and caused people from all over the world to embrace the way of life here and eventually to identify themselves as "Americans." Indeed, by the third generation here, most immigrants have lost the language and culture of their grandparents and they think of themselves as just plain "Americans."

Immigrants being sworn in as new American citizens

23 Throughout this book we will be drawing on the wisdom of a famous observer of the American scene, Alexis de Tocqueville. Tocqueville came to the United States as a young Frenchman in 1831 to study the American form of democracy and what it might mean to the rest of the world. After a visit of only nine months, he wrote a remarkable book called *Democracy in America*, which is a classic study of the American way of life. Tocqueville had unusual powers of observation. He described not only the democratic system of government and how it operated, but also its effect on how Americans think, feel, and act. Many scholars believe that he had a deeper understanding of traditional American beliefs and values than anyone else who has written about the United States. What is so remarkable is that many of these traits of the American character, which he observed nearly 200 years ago, are still visible and meaningful today.

24 Another reason why Tocqueville's observations of the American character are important is the time when he visited the United States. He came in the 1830s, before America was industrialized. This was the era of the small farmer, the small businessman, and the settling of the western frontier. It was the period of history when the traditional values of the new country were being established. In just a generation, some forty years since the adoption of the U.S. Constitution, the new form of government had already produced a society of people with unique values. The character traits Tocqueville describes are the same ones that many Americans still take pride in today. He, however, was a neutral observer and saw both the good and the bad sides of these qualities.

25 This is a book about those traditional basic American beliefs, values, and character traits. It is not a book of cold facts about American behavior or institutions,[9] but rather it is about the motivating forces behind the people and their institutions. It is about how these traditional basic beliefs and values affect important aspects of American life: religion, business, work and play, politics, the family, and education.

26 We invite you to participate in this book. We will describe what many Americans think and believe, but you will have an opportunity to test these descriptions by making your own observations. As you read about these traditional basic values, think of them as working hypotheses[10] which you can test on Americans, on people of other nations, and on people of your nationality. Compare them with your own values and beliefs and with what is most important in your life. Through this process, you should emerge with a better understanding not only of Americans, but also of your own culture and yourself. It is by studying others that we learn about ourselves.

[9] *institutions: large organizations, especially ones dedicated to public service*

[10] *hypotheses: ideas that are suggested as an explanation for something but that have not yet been proven to be true*

AFTER YOU READ

Understand Main Ideas

Academic English organizes information into main (or most important) ideas and supporting details. That is, there are usually three or four major points presented, and the rest of the information serves to explain or support these main ideas:

- *First main idea*
    - *Supporting details*
- *Second main idea*
    - *Supporting details*
- *Third main idea*
    - *Supporting details*

When reading academic English or listening to a lecture, it is important to recognize the main points. The introduction focuses your attention on the topic. Then the main points are presented, and the conclusion reminds you of one or more central ideas. Noticing the headings in a text will help you figure out the main points the writer is presenting.

Check the predictions that you made on page 3. Did the chapter include any of the information you predicted? Then work with a partner and answer these questions about the main ideas.

1. What are two important factors that affect life in the United States?
2. What is the heading for the section that discusses the history of immigration in the United States?
3. What is cultural pluralism?
4. What is the main idea of the section headed *Making Generalizations About American Beliefs*?
5. What relationship is there between the quotation at the beginning of the chapter, the introduction (first two paragraphs), and the conclusion (paragraphs 25 and 26) of the reading?

Understand Details

Write *T* if the statement is true and *F* if it is false according to the information in the chapter.

_____ 1. One factor affecting lifestyles in the United States is the variety of climates.

_____ 2. American Indians all speak the same language.

_____ 3. The dominant American culture was established by immigrants who came from southern Europe.

_____ 4. For the first time, in the 2010 census, there were more Asian than Hispanic immigrants.

_____ 5. Zangwill believed that immigrants would lose their native cultures and become something different when they came to the United States.

_____ 6. Immigrants change American culture and are changed by it.

_____ 7. U.S. immigration policy has stayed the same for the last 100 years.

_____ 8. The English language has no adjective for *United States* and therefore uses the term *American* to refer to its people.

_____ 9. It is not possible to make generalizations about what Americans believe because they are so different.

_____ 10. Many of the characteristics of Americans that Alexis de Tocqueville observed in the 1830s are still true today.

Talk About It

Work in small groups and choose one or more of the following questions to discuss.

1. How would you compare the size and ethnic diversity of your country with that of the United States? What are some of the challenges that size (large or small) and diversity (great or limited) present to a country?

2. Should a country have immigration quotas based on country of origin? Should immigrants become citizens? Should countries allow "guest workers" (people who work there temporarily) to come? Should they allow them to become citizens?

3. How would you describe the average person in your country and what he or she believes?

4. Do you think people all over the world are basically the same or basically very different?

SKILL BUILDING

Improve Your Reading Skills: Scanning

In order to become a good reader in English, your reading speed and techniques should vary according to your purpose. For example, you may look down a page (or over several pages) to find a particular piece of information—a number, a date, a place, or the time a movie begins. This type of reading for a specific fact is called scanning.

Read the questions below. Scan the reading to find the specific information you need to answer each question.

1. Which states have the largest numbers of immigrants?

_____

2. In what year did Alexis de Tocqueville come to visit the United States?

_____

3. In 1910, what percentage of the U.S. population was foreign born?

_____

4. What was the total U.S. population according to the 2010 census?

_____

5. In what year did Israel Zangwill write a play in which he used the term

   melting pot?

_____

6. What is Obama's family tie to Ireland?

_____

Develop Your Critical Thinking Skills

Analyzing Polls

Conducting opinion polls is very popular in the United States. A newspaper, a magazine, a TV station, or a professional polling organization asks a representative group of Americans several questions to determine their opinions about topics such as politics, religion, or social issues. The pollsters usually choose men and women of different ages, occupations, and races in the same proportion that these groups are found in the population. Sometimes, however, a random sample is taken which selects people by chance.

There are three well-known polling organizations that measure public opinion on a variety of topics: Louis Harris and Associates, Gallup International Research Institutes, and the Pew Research Center. Pew also studies aspects of American life. For example, the Pew Hispanic Center recently published a report on Hispanics in the United States and how they identify themselves. As mentioned in the chapter, the terms Hispanic and Latino are generally used in the media interchangeably. In this poll, Pew found that only 24% of all Hispanics self-identify as Hispanic or Latino. When they do use these terms, 33% of them choose "Hispanic" and 14% prefer "Latino."

Read the poll and answer the questions that follow.

WHEN LABELS DON'T FIT: HISPANICS AND THEIR VIEWS OF IDENTITY

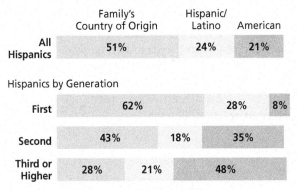

WHICH TERM DO YOU USE TO
DESCRIBE YOURSELF MOST OFTEN?

	Family's Country of Origin	Hispanic/ Latino	American
All Hispanics	51%	24%	21%

Hispanics by Generation

First	62%	28%	8%
Second	43%	18%	35%
Third or Higher	28%	21%	48%

Source: Pew Research

1. What does the phrase "country of origin" mean? What percent of all Hispanics identify themselves by their country of origin? Give some examples of these countries of origin.

2. What does "generation" mean? What do the terms "first, second, or third generation" Hispanic mean? Why did the researchers divide the group this way?

3. Who are more likely to identify with the family's country of origin—new immigrants or those who were born in the United States?

4. What percent refer to themselves as just "American?" Who are more likely to self-identify as American than by any other term—new immigrants or those born in the United States?

5. What change happens to the identity of the grandchildren of Hispanic immigrants? Why do you think this happens?

Build Your Vocabulary

Use Context Clues

There are several types of context clues that will help you guess the meaning of words you do not know. By looking at the words around an unfamiliar word, you may be able to figure out its meaning. See the four kinds of context clues below. In the examples, the vocabulary words are boldfaced. The context clues are in italics.

1. The word may be defined in the sentence. Sometimes the definition is set off by commas or dashes. Other times it is not.

EXAMPLE: There is still a tie that binds Americans together. That tie is a sense of national **identity**—*of being an American.*

EXAMPLE: A **quota** system was established that *specified the number of immigrants that could come from each country.*

2. There may be a synonym used in the same sentence.

EXAMPLE: Native Americans belong to *separate* and **distinct** Indian nations, each with its own language, culture, and even government.

3. There may be a comparison or contrast with a word (or a phrase) more familiar to you.

EXAMPLE: As the **minority** non-white population of the United States continues to grow, the white *majority* grows smaller.

4. The sentence may give an example that helps you figure out the meaning.

EXAMPLE: Tocqueville, however, was a **neutral observer** and *saw both the good and bad sides of these qualities.*

A. Use the context clues to figure out the meaning of the boldfaced words in the sentences above. Then write the correct word next to its definition.

_____ 1. a limit on the number allowed

_____ 2. a group of people whose race is different from that of most people in a country

_____ 3. someone who makes decisions based on facts, not personal feelings

_____ 4. the qualities that a group of people have that make them different from other people

_____ 5. clearly different or separate

Now fill in the blanks with some of the boldfaced words above to complete the paragraph.

What qualities give people a national _____? Do they have to
                                              1

have characteristics that are _____ from those of other countries?
                                      2

The people who are part of a _____ group may feel they have a
                                    3

set of characteristics that differ from those of the majority in their country.

B. Test your knowledge of these AWL words by matching them with their definitions.

__d__ 1. aspect   a. large organization, especially one dedicated to public service

____ 2. category   b. to start something that will continue

____ 3. concept   c. to be different

____ 4. debate   d. one part of an idea that has many parts

____ 5. establish   e. to continue in spite of difficulties

____ 6. estimate   f. group of things that all have the same qualities

_____ 7. hypothesis   g. to judge by calculating and guessing

_____ 8. incidentally   h. one of a kind

_____ 9. institution   i. an idea

_____ 10. survive   j. an explanation that is not yet proven

_____ 11. unique   k. a discussion of different opinions

_____ 12. vary   l. by the way

Understand Prefixes

Recognizing the meaning of a prefix, a group of letters added to the beginning of a word (or its root), will also help you guess the meaning of a new word. For example, the prefix mis- *means "wrong," so* misunderstand *means "not understand correctly."*

Each of the boldfaced words in the sentences below has a prefix. Identify the prefix and write its meaning. Use a dictionary, if necessary.

Example: Before the 1960s, the majority of immigrants to the United States were Europeans, but changes in immigration laws resulted in large numbers of **non-Europeans**.

Prefix: ____non____   Meaning: _____not_____

1. Estimates were that, in addition to legal immigration, **illegal** immigration was adding more than half a million more people per year.

   Prefix: _____   Meaning: _____

2. In some parts of the country with established communities that share a common language or culture, bilingualism and **biculturalism** continue. Cultural pluralism is more accepted now than it was in the first half of the twentieth century, and many school systems have developed bilingual programs and **multicultural** curricula.

   Prefix: _____   Meaning: _____

   Prefix: _____   Meaning: _____

3. People may migrate to another location in order to find work. While many people **immigrate** to the United States each year, very few Americans choose to **emigrate** to another country to live.

   Prefix: _____   Meaning: _____

   Prefix: _____   Meaning: _____

4. In the census of 2010, there were nineteen racial categories to choose from. The number of **interracial** marriages is increasing . . . and the majority of young people believe it does not matter which race they marry.

   Prefix: _____   Meaning: _____

Word Partners

Certain words and phrases tend to go together in English, for example, "ethnic diversity" or "traditional values." This is called **collocation**. *Learning these word partners will increase your ability to use new words correctly and help you express yourself as native speakers do.*

First read the sentences below. Then find the collocations to complete these sentences by matching the adjectives on the left with their noun partners on the right. Use the collocations to complete the sentences.

_c_	1. established	a. immigrants
____	2. significant	b. culture
____	3. neutral	c. communities
____	4. industrialized	d. pluralism
____	5. legal	e. hypotheses
____	6. dominant	f. countries
____	7. cultural	g. factor
____	8. working	h. observer

1. In parts of the country with _established communities_ that share a

   common language, bilingualism continues.

2. Tocqueville was a _____ who saw both the good and bad

   sides of the American character traits.

3. Ethnic diversity is a _____ affecting American life.

4. Think of the traditional values in this book as _____ that

   you can test against your own observations.

5. The United States now takes in more _____ each year than

   all other _____ combined.

6. When several cultures exist together successfully in a society, there is

   _____.

7. The _____ in the United States is becoming less white in

   the twenty-first century.

EXPAND YOUR KNOWLEDGE

Ask Americans

Interview several Americans of different ages (if possible) and ask them to complete the following statements. If there are no Americans to interview, you can ask other international students or your classmates about their view of Americans.

1. Americans are _____.

2. They like _____.

3. They don't really like _____.

4. They act _____.

5. Most Americans believe in _____.

6. The United States is a country where _____.

7. The average American is _____.

8. Americans today are worried about _____.

9. The most important thing in life to most Americans is _____.

Ask Yourself

Using the statements above as examples, complete the following statements about people from your own country.

1. People from my country are _____.

2. People from my country believe in _____.

3. My country is a place where _____.

4. The average person from my country is _____.

5. People from my country are worried about _____.

6. The most important thing in life to most people from my country is

   _____.

Think, Pair, Share

Think about the following questions and write down your answers. Then discuss your answers with a partner and share your answers with another pair of students.

1. How would you define *culture*? Look at several dictionaries to find definitions and read the first paragraph of the introduction to this book.

2. What do you think are the most important aspects of your native culture?

People Watching

Different countries have different rules for personal space, that is, when people touch, how close they stand when they are speaking to one another, how close they sit, how they behave on elevators, etc. The rules for personal space sometimes differ according to how well people know each other. People are usually not consciously aware of these rules, but they may become very uncomfortable if the rules are broken and their space is entered without permission. You can discover the rules by observing people interacting and also by testing or breaking the rules to see how other people respond.

Conduct two experiments about personal space. Follow these steps.

1. Read the rules for personal space below.

2. Make your own observations of people. Write your observations in a journal. It may be helpful to work in pairs: One person tests the rules while the other observes and records what happens.

3. Experiment with the rules. Write the responses you receive.

4. If you are not in the United States, and if you do not have an opportunity to observe Americans, you may still learn from these experiments by watching people in your own country or by observing Americans in movies or TV shows.

People in line try to avoid touching each other.

First Rule: When they are in a crowd, Americans have a bubble of space around their bodies which is about an inch thick. This bubble of space must not be broken by a stranger. If American strangers touch each other accidentally, they mutter an apology such as "Pardon me," "Excuse me," "Oh, I'm sorry," or just "Sorry."

Observation: Watch people in a crowd, standing in line, waiting in a group, or passing on a street or in a hallway. Who is touching whom? What does their relationship appear to be? What happens when people touch accidentally? How does the person touched respond? What does the one who has broken the other's bubble do? Record gestures, facial expressions, emotional responses, and words exchanged.

Experiment: See how close you can stand to someone in a crowd without touching him or her. Try breaking someone's bubble of space with a very light touch of your elbow or arm. What is the person's response? (*Warning:* This may provoke an angry response!)

Second Rule: When standing in elevators, Americans usually face the door, speak quietly, and try to avoid touching one another. If a stranger enters an elevator where there is only one other person, he or she will stand on the opposite side of the elevator. As more people get on the elevator, they occupy the corners first and then try to disperse themselves evenly throughout the available space.

Observation: Observe people in elevators. Which direction are they facing? If you are alone in an elevator and someone comes in, where does that person stand? As more people enter the elevator, where do they stand? Do the people talk to one another? How loudly do they speak? Do strangers touch? What happens in a crowded elevator when someone in the back has to get off?

Experiment: Get on an elevator where there is only one person and stand next to that individual. What is the person's reaction? In an elevator where there are a number of people, turn and face the group with your back to the door. How do the people react? Have a conversation with someone in a crowded elevator and don't lower your voice. How do you think people feel about this? Note their facial expressions.

People in an elevator avoid eye contact.

Use the Internet

Although polls are usually scientific, polling organizations also conduct informal polls online. These informal polls only reflect the views of the people who happen to visit their website and answer the poll questions. Some poll sites have interactive pages or allow you to participate in online polls. Visit these websites and compare the topics they are polling now:

www.harrisinteractive.com

www.gallup.com

www.pewresearch.org

WRITE ABOUT IT

Choose one of the following topics. Then write a short composition about it.

1. Write a short essay describing three places in your country that you would want to take someone visiting from another country. Use a graphic organizer to organize your thoughts before you write. Make notes about the names of the places, their locations, any special features, and your reasons for choosing the places.

First Place	Second Place	Third Place

2. Write a report about your country. Read the following information on regions and population growth in the United States to get ideas for your report.

The United States can be divided into different regions with different characteristics. There are a number of ways to divide and name the different regions; the map below shows the regions the U.S. Census Bureau uses. Each region contains different divisions. Notice the Mountain Division of the West Region. This is where the Rocky Mountains are located.

CENSUS REGIONS AND DIVISIONS OF THE UNITED STATES

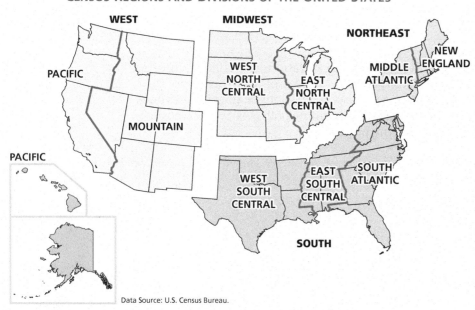

Data Source: U.S. Census Bureau.

Compare this area with the second U.S. Census map. This map shows the population density of the United States. Notice the areas that are the most highly populated in the country. Notice that the area where the mountains are has a low population density.

POPULATION DENSITY BY STATE: 2010

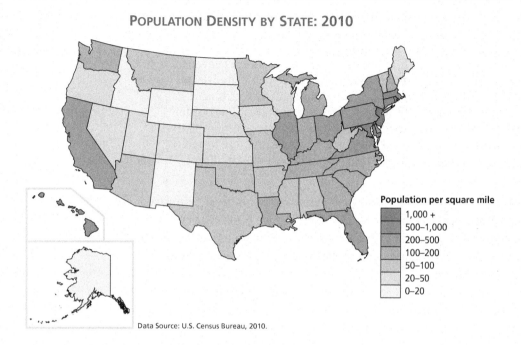

Population per square mile
- 1,000 +
- 500–1,000
- 200–500
- 100–200
- 50–100
- 20–50
- 0–20

Data Source: U.S. Census Bureau, 2010.

In 1981, Jack Garreau wrote a book entitled *The Nine Nations of North America* describing nine diverse regions of the North American continent. The book he wrote is no longer in print, but his map is of lasting interest. (It is discussed on Wikipedia and available as a Google image.) Garreau believed that the North American continent is made up of nine regions so different that each might be thought of as a separate nation. Each "nation" has a different culture, economy, political concern, and set of values:

The Empty Quarter	The Islands
Ecotopia	MexAmerica
New England	The Breadbasket
The Foundry	Quebec
Dixie	

Locate Garreau's nine "nations" on the U.S. Census map of regions and divisions. The Mountain Division has very low population density, so Garreau calls it "The Empty Quarter." "Ecotopia" is the area along the west coast from Alaska to Los Angeles, an area where people are particularly concerned about environmental issues. "New England" includes the northeastern coastal strip of Canada. "The Foundry" is the original industrial/manufacturing area from the Middle Atlantic through the East North Central Great Lakes region. "Dixie" is the old South that tried to leave the United States during the Civil War, including the South Atlantic (except for Kentucky, Maryland, and Delaware) and East South Central Divisions, and the eastern part of Texas. "The Islands" include south Florida, Puerto Rico, and the other islands of the Caribbean. "MexAmerica" includes southern California and the other states that border Mexico. "The Breadbasket" is made up of the West North Central Great Plains states and stretches from up in Canada to northern Texas. It is where much of the nation's food is grown. Quebec is the home of most French Canadians.

Write a report about the regions of your country. Where are the most populated areas? What are the major geographic regions? As you prepare your report, include some information on geographical features, natural resources, major cities, and special characteristics of each region. Use a graphic organizer to organize your ideas.

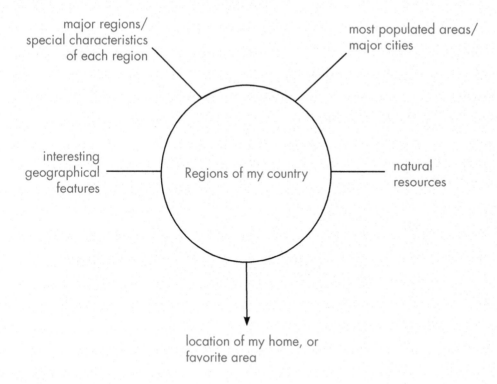

EXPLORE ON YOUR OWN

Books to Read

Sherwood Anderson, *Winesburg, Ohio*—Published in 1919, this literary masterpiece explores the hidden passions of ordinary lives in a small American town.

Richard Paul Evans, *The Road to Grace*—An advertising executive walks across the country from Seattle, Washington, to Key West, Florida.

John F. Kennedy, *A Nation of Immigrants*—President Kennedy, himself the grandson of Irish immigrants, discusses how old immigrant traditions mix with the new experiences of immigrants starting life over in America.

Barack Obama, *Dreams of My Father*—In this "Story of Race and Inheritance," President Obama reflects on his life from his birth in Hawaii to a father from Kenya and a mother from Kansas, to his enrollment in Harvard Law School.

Marco Rubio, *An American Son*—This book is a memoir by the Cuban-American U.S. Senator from Florida.

Movies to See

La Bamba—Ritchie Valens, a young 1950s rock and roll singer, rose to fame from poverty and brought the Latin American influence to his hit songs.

Last of the Mohicans—This film tells the story of Native Americans' life in 1757 and how they interacted with the British.

Sweet Land—A young woman comes to Minnesota from Norway to marry a man she has never met and faces many difficulties.

The Terminal—An eastern European immigrant who is not permitted to enter the United States decides to take up temporary residence at a JFK airport terminal.

Under the Same Moon—A young Mexican boy travels to the United States to find his mother after his grandmother passes away.

CHAPTER 2

TRADITIONAL AMERICAN VALUES AND BELIEFS

We hold these truths to be self-evident, that all men are created equal, that they are endowed by their Creator with certain inalienable rights, that among these are Life, Liberty and the pursuit of Happiness.

The Declaration of Independence (1776)

Why do so many people want to come and live in the United States? What is so attractive about the American way of life and the values of the society?

BEFORE YOU READ

Preview Vocabulary

A. Here are some key AWL words in this chapter. Look at their definitions. Put a check next to the words you already know.

_____ 1. **individual** one person, considered separately from the group

_____ 2. **achieve** to succeed in getting the result you want

_____ 3. **benefit** something that gives advantages or improves life in some way

_____ 4. **reliant** being dependent on someone

_____ 5. **constitution** a set of basic laws and principles that a democratic country is governed by

_____ 6. **ethical** relating to principles of what is right and wrong

_____ 7. **resources** a country's land, minerals, or natural energy that can be used to increase its wealth

_____ 8. **status** social or professional rank or position in relation to others

_____ 9. **welfare** money paid by the government to people who are very poor, sick, not working, etc.

_____ 10. **foundation** a basic idea or principle

B. Work with a partner. Complete each question with a word from the preceding list. Then answer the questions.

1. Why would the _____ of a country forbid titles of nobility?

   (titles such as "princess" or "sir")

2. If there are no titles of nobility, how does a society recognize people with

   high social _____.

3. Which do you think is more important to Americans, the well-being of the

   group or the _____?

4. What do immigrants have to do to _____ success in their new

   country?

5. What are some of the natural _____ found on the North

   American continent?

6. What _____ does a person get from being self-

   _____?

7. When would it not be _____ to compete with someone?

8. What country provided the language and the _____ for the

   political and economic systems of the United States?

9. What situations might cause a person to need _____?

C. Read the quotation from the Declaration of Independence at the beginning of the chapter, and find the words with the following meanings. Write each word next to its meaning.

_____ 1. the act of trying to achieve something in a determined way

_____ 2. easily noticed or understood; obvious

_____ 3. that cannot be taken away from you

_____ 4. given a good quality

Preview Content

A. Before you read, preview the chapter by looking at the illustrations and reading the headings and captions under the pictures. Work with a partner and discuss these questions.

1. What is the main idea of the quotation at the beginning of the chapter?

2. What are some reasons people want to come live in the United States? Use this graphic organizer to write down your ideas. Are any of these ideas similar? If so, draw lines connecting them.

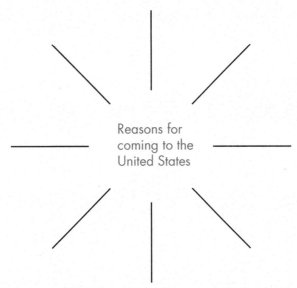

Reasons for coming to the United States

3. What is the "American Dream"? (Hint: Give a one-sentence summary of the ideas you wrote for question #2.)

4. What do you think Americans believe is the best thing about their country?

B. Think about what values and beliefs could be important to Americans. Work with a partner and make three predictions about what you will read. Write your predictions here.

1. _____

   _____

2. _____

   _____

3. _____

   _____

THE CONTEXT OF TRADITIONAL AMERICAN VALUES: RACIAL, ETHNIC, RELIGIOUS, AND CULTURAL DIVERSITY

1 From the beginning of the history of the United States there has been diversity—Native Americans throughout the North American continent, Spanish settlers in the Southwest and in Florida, French missionaries and fur traders along the Mississippi River, black slaves brought from African countries, Dutch settlers in New York, Germans in Pennsylvania, and of course the British colonists, whose culture eventually provided the language and the foundation for the political and economic systems that developed in the United States.

2 Most early Americans recognized this diversity, or pluralism, as a fact of life. The large variety of ethnic, cultural, and religious groups meant that accepting diversity was the only practical choice, even if some people were not enthusiastic about it, or were even threatened by it.

However, in time, many Americans came to see strength in their country's diversity. Today, there is widespread recognition of the value of cultural pluralism, particularly among young people.

3 When we examine the system of basic values that emerged in the late 1700s and began to define the American character, we must remember this context of cultural pluralism. How could a nation of such enormous diversity produce a recognizable national identity?

4 John Zogby, an American pollster who surveys public opinion, says that what holds the United States together is that "we all share a common set of values that make us American. . . . We are defined by the rights we have. . . . Our rights are our history, why the first European settlers came here and why millions more have come here since."

NEW WORLD COLONIES IN 1750

Source: http://web.uccs.edu/~history/index/151maps.html.

5 Historically, the United States has been viewed as "the land of opportunity," attracting immigrants from all over the world. The opportunities they believed they would find in America and the experiences that most people actually had when they arrived nurtured a unique set of values. We will examine six basic values that have become traditional American values. Three represent traditional reasons why immigrants have been drawn to America: the chance for individual freedom, equality of opportunity, and material wealth. In order to achieve these benefits, however, there were prices to be paid: self-reliance, competition, and hard work. In time, these prices themselves became part of the traditional value system. This system of values, then, consists of three pairs of benefits and the price people paid to have these benefits:

- individual freedom and self-reliance,
- equality of opportunity and competition,
- material wealth and hard work.

6 These three pairs of values have determined the unique culture of the United States and its people. Another way of thinking about these basic values involves rights and responsibilities. Americans believe that people have the right to individual freedom, equality of opportunity, and the promise of material success, but these all require substantial responsibility: self-reliance, a willingness to compete, and hard work. After examining the historical origin of each of these pairs, we will discuss the current state of these values in the United States.

Individual Freedom and Self-Reliance

7 The earliest settlers came to the North American continent to establish colonies that were free from the controls that existed in European societies. They wanted to escape the controls placed on many aspects of their lives by kings and governments, priests and churches, noblemen and aristocrats.[1] To a great extent, they succeeded. In 1776, the British colonial settlers declared their independence from England and established a new nation, the United States of America. In so doing, they defied[2] the king of England and declared that the power to govern would lie in the hands of the people. They were now free from the power of the kings. In 1787, when they wrote the Constitution for their new nation, they separated church and state so that there would never be a government-supported church. This greatly limited the power of the church. Also, in writing the Constitution they expressly forbade titles of nobility to ensure that an aristocratic society would not develop. There would be no ruling class of noblemen in the new nation.

8 The historic decisions made by those first settlers have had a profound[3] effect on the shaping of the American character. By limiting the power of the government and the churches and eliminating a formal aristocracy, the early settlers created a climate of freedom where the emphasis was on the individual. The United States came to be associated in their minds with the concept of *individual freedom*. This is probably the most basic of all the American values. Scholars and outside observers often call this value *individualism*, but many Americans use the word *freedom*. It is one of the most respected and popular words in the United States today.

9 By *freedom*, Americans mean the desire and the right of all individuals to control their own destiny without outside interference

[1] aristocrats: people who belong to the highest social class
[2] defied: refused to obey someone or do what was expected
[3] profound: important and having a strong influence or effect

from the government, a ruling noble class, the church, or any other organized authority. The desire to be free of controls was a basic value of the new nation in 1776, and it has continued to attract immigrants to this country.

10 There is, however, a cost for this benefit of individual freedom: *self-reliance.* Individuals must learn to rely on themselves or risk losing freedom. They must take responsibility for themselves. Traditionally, this has meant achieving both financial and emotional independence from their parents as early as possible, usually by age eighteen or twenty-one. Self-reliance means that Americans believe they should take care of themselves, solve their own problems, and "stand on their own two feet." Tocqueville observed the Americans' belief in self-reliance in the 1830s:

> They owe nothing to any man, they expect nothing from any man; they acquire the habit of always considering themselves as standing alone, and they are apt to[4] imagine that their whole destiny is in their own hands.

11 This strong belief in self-reliance continues today as a traditional American value. It is perhaps one of the most difficult aspects of the American character to understand, but it is profoundly important. Most Americans believe that they must be self-reliant in order to keep their freedom. If they rely too much on the support of their families or the government or any organization, they may lose some of their freedom to do what they want. Even if they are not truly self-reliant, most Americans believe they must at least appear to be so. In order to be in the mainstream of American life—to have power and/or respect—individuals must be seen as self-reliant.

12 For example, if adult children return home to live with their parents because of economic conditions or a failed marriage, most members of the family expect this to be a short-term arrangement, until the children can find a job and be self-reliant. Although receiving financial support from charity,[5] family, or the government is possible, it is usually expected to be for a short time, and it is generally not admired. Eventually, most Americans would say, people have a responsibility for taking care of themselves.

Equality of Opportunity and Competition

13 The second important reason why immigrants have traditionally been drawn to the United States is the belief that everyone has a chance to succeed here. Generations of immigrants have come to the United States with this expectation.

Immigrants on Ellis Island around 1900

[4] *are apt to: have a natural tendency to do something*

[5] *charity: an organization that gives money, goods, or help to people who are poor, sick, etc.*

They have felt that, because individuals are free from excessive political, religious, and social controls, they have a better chance for personal success. Of particular importance is the lack of a hereditary[6] aristocracy.

14 Because titles of nobility were forbidden in the Constitution, no formal class system developed in the United States. In the early years of American history, many immigrants chose to leave older European societies because they believed that they had a better chance to succeed in America. In "the old country," the country from which they came, their place in life was determined largely by the social class into which they were born. They knew that in America they would not have to live among noble families who possessed great power and wealth inherited and accumulated over hundreds of years.

15 The hopes and dreams of many of these early immigrants were fulfilled in their new country. The lower social class into which many were born did not prevent them from trying to rise to a higher social position. Many found that they did indeed have a better chance to succeed in the United States than in the old country. Because millions of these immigrants succeeded, Americans came to believe in *equality of opportunity*. When Tocqueville visited the United States in the 1830s, he was impressed by the great uniformity of conditions of life in the new nation. He wrote:

> *The more I advanced in the study of American society, the more I perceived that . . . equality of condition is the fundamental fact from which all others seem to be derived.*

16 It is important to understand what most Americans mean when they say they believe in equality of opportunity. They do not mean that everyone is—or should be—equal. However, they do mean that each individual should have an equal chance for success. Americans see much of life as a race for success. For them, equality means that everyone should have an equal chance to enter the race and win. In other words, equality of opportunity may be thought of as an ethical rule. It helps ensure that the race for success is a fair one and that a person does not win just because he or she was born into a wealthy family, or lose because of race or religion. This American concept of "fair play" is an important aspect of the belief in equality of opportunity.

17 President Abraham Lincoln expressed this belief in the 1860s when he said:

> *We . . . wish to allow the humblest man an equal chance to get rich with everybody else. When one starts poor, as most do in the race of life, free society is such that he knows he can better his condition; he knows that there is no fixed condition of labor for his whole life.*

18 However, the price to be paid for this equality of opportunity is *competition.* If much of life is seen as a race, then a person must run the race in order to succeed; a person has the responsibility to compete with others, even though we know not everyone will be successful. If every person has an equal chance to succeed in the United States, then many would say that it is every person's duty to try.

19 The pressures of competition in the life of an American begin in childhood and continue until retirement from work. Learning to compete successfully is part of growing up in the United States, and competition is encouraged by strong programs of competitive sports provided by the public schools and community groups. Competitive sports are now popular with both men and women.

---

[6] *hereditary: can be passed from an older to a younger person in the same family*

Shaking hands may be a polite acknowledgment of your competitor as well as a greeting.

20 The pressure to compete causes Americans to be energetic, but it also places a constant emotional strain on them. When they retire, they are at last free from the pressures of competition. But then a new problem arises. Some may feel useless and unwanted in a society that gives so much prestige[7] to those who compete well. This may be one reason older people in the United States sometimes do not have as much honor and respect as they have in other less-competitive societies. In fact, generally speaking, any group of people who do not compete successfully—for whatever reason—do not fit into the mainstream of American life as well as those who do compete and succeed.

Material Wealth and Hard Work

21 The third reason why immigrants have traditionally come to the United States is to have a better life—that is, to raise their standard of living. For the vast majority of the immigrants who came here, this was probably the most compelling reason for leaving their homeland. Because of its incredibly abundant natural resources, the United States appeared to be a land of plenty where millions could come to seek their fortunes. Of course, most immigrants did not "get rich overnight," and many of

them suffered terribly, but the majority of them were eventually able to improve upon their former standard of living. Even if they were not able to achieve the economic success they wanted, they could be fairly certain that their children would have the opportunity for a better life. The phrase "going from rags to riches" became a slogan[8] for the "American Dream." Because of the vast riches of the North American continent, the dream came true for many of the immigrants. They achieved material success and many became very attached to material things. *Material wealth* became a value to the American people.

22 Placing a high value on material possessions is called *materialism*, but this is a word that most Americans find offensive. To say that a person is materialistic is an insult. To an American, this means that this person values material possessions above all else. Americans do not like to be called materialistic because they feel that this unfairly accuses them of loving only material things and of having no religious values. In fact, most Americans do have other values and ideals. Nevertheless, acquiring and maintaining a large number of material possessions is still of great importance to most Americans. Why is this so?

23 One reason is that material wealth has traditionally been a widely accepted measure of social status in the United States. Because Americans rejected the European system of hereditary aristocracy and titles of nobility, they had to find a substitute for judging social status. The quality and quantity of an individual's material possessions became an accepted measure of success and social status. Moreover, as we shall see in the religion chapter, the Puritan work ethic associated material success with godliness.

[7] *prestige: the respect and importance that a person, organization, or profession has*

[8] *slogan: a short, easily-remembered phrase used in advertising or politics*

24 Americans have paid a price, however, for their material wealth: *hard work*. The North American continent was rich in natural resources when the first settlers arrived, but all these resources were undeveloped. Only by hard work could these natural resources be converted into material possessions, allowing a more comfortable standard of living. Hard work has been both necessary and rewarding for most Americans throughout their history. Because of this, they came to see material possessions as the natural reward for their hard work. In some ways, material possessions were seen not only as tangible[9] evidence of people's work, but also of their abilities. In the late 1700s, James Madison, the father of the American Constitution, stated that the difference in material possessions reflected a difference in personal abilities.

25 Most Americans still believe in the value of hard work. Most believe that people should hold jobs and not live off welfare payments from the government. There have been many efforts to reform the welfare system so that people would not become dependent on welfare and stop looking for jobs to support themselves. However, a larger question is how much hard work will really improve a person's standard of living and level of material wealth. Is it still possible to work hard and get rich in America?

26 As the United States has shifted from an industry-based economy to one that is service- or information-based, there has been a decline in high-paying jobs for factory workers. It is now much more difficult for the average worker to go from rags to riches in the United States, and many wonder what has happened to the traditional American Dream. As the United States competes in a global economy, many workers are losing their old jobs and finding that they and their family members must now work longer hours for less money and fewer benefits. When the economy weakens, everyone suffers, and there are greater numbers of the working poor—those who work hard but have low-paying jobs that do not provide a decent standard of living and may not provide health insurance and retirement benefits, and many have to rely on some outside assistance from the government or other sources.

American Values and the State of the American Dream

27 In recent years, as the economy has declined, many observers have asked if the American Dream is really dead. For the most part, the American Dream has not meant that the average American can really go from rags to riches. It has traditionally meant that by working hard, parents can enable their children to have a better life when they grow up. Every generation could be a little more prosperous and successful than their parents. While the distance between the very rich one percent and the rest of the population has dramatically increased over the last years, the overwhelming majority of Americans still believe in the ideal of the American Dream—that is, if they work hard, they and their children can have a better life. The ideal of upward mobility still exists in America. However, we must distinguish between idealism and reality in understanding the relationship between what Americans believe and how they live. Some who find that they are working longer hours for less money still hope that the American Dream will exist again, if not for them, then for their children.

28 American values such as equality of opportunity and self-reliance are ideals that may not necessarily describe the reality of American life. Equality of opportunity, for

[9] *tangible: concrete, able to be touched*

example, is an ideal that is not always put into practice. In reality, some people have a better chance for success than others. Those who are born into rich families have more opportunities than those who are born into poorer families. Inheriting money does give a person a decided advantage. Race and gender may still be factors affecting success, although there are laws designed to promote equality of opportunity for all individuals. And, of course, new immigrants continue to face challenges unique to their situation.

29 The fact that American ideals are only partly carried out in real life does not diminish their importance. Most Americans still believe in them and are strongly affected by them in their everyday lives. It is easier to understand what Americans are thinking and feeling if we can understand what these traditional American cultural values are and how they have influenced almost every facet[10] of life in the United States.

30 It is important to remember two things about these values. First, they are cultural values; they are the cultural engine that drives the United States and continues to power a nation where people from all over the world come and become "American." Secondly, putting these six values together into a system creates something new. As Aristotle said, the whole is greater than the sum of its parts. The relationship among these values—the rights and the responsibilities—creates the fabric[11] of the American society. It is this fabric that defines the American Dream—the belief that if people take responsibility for their lives and work hard, they will have the individual freedom to pursue their personal goals and a good opportunity to compete for success. These values are so tightly woven together that if any one of them is pulled out or even disturbed, the entire fabric is affected and may come apart.

31 Finally, these six cultural values—individual freedom, self-reliance, equality of opportunity, competition, material wealth, and hard work—do not tell the whole story of the American character. Rather, they form the basic structure or framework of the American culture. They enable a nation of enormous diversity to create and maintain a national identity.

32 In the next three chapters we will examine three historical factors that reinforced and helped to shape these values: the religious heritage, the frontier heritage, and the heritage of abundance. The remaining chapters will explore how these values appear in aspects of American culture: business, government, ethnic and racial diversity, education, leisure time, and the family. The final chapter will discuss the challenges facing the United States and their potential impact on the future of the country and its values.

To some, owning a beautiful house means they have achieved the American Dream.

[10] facet: one of several parts of someone's character, a situation, etc.

[11] fabric: basic structure and way of life

AFTER YOU READ

Understand Main Ideas

1. Check the predictions you made on page 30. How many of these six values did you predict—individual freedom, self-reliance, equality of opportunity, competition, material wealth, and hard work?

2. In Chapter 1, we looked at the relationship between the introduction and the conclusion, and at how the headings signaled the main ideas. Now look at the structure of Chapter 2. Reread paragraph 6 of the introduction section on page 32. What does this paragraph tell you about the structure of the reading? Notice that the six values are written as headings in the chapter. The outline below shows the structure of Chapter 2: the introduction (A), the three sections containing the six traditional values (B, C, D), and the conclusion (E). The numbers under each heading show the main ideas of each section. Work with a partner to complete the outline. (Part of it is done for you.)

A. Introduction: The Context of Traditional American Values: Racial, Ethnic, Religious, and Cultural Diversity

    1. The United States has great diversity, but it also has a national identity.

    2. What holds the United States together is a common set of

    _____.

B. Individual Freedom and Self-Reliance

    1. The early settlers came to the North American continent for individual freedom—the most basic of all the American values.

    2. The price for individual freedom is _____.

C. ___Equality of Opportunity and Competition_____

    1. Immigrants have always come for equality of opportunity—the belief that everyone should have an equal chance to ___succeed in the US___.

    2. ___A person must run the race in order to succeed.___

D. ___Material Wealth and Hard Work_____

    1. Immigrants have traditionally come for material wealth—the chance for a higher standard of ___living_____.

    2. ___People should _____ welfair___.

E. Conclusion: _____ American values _____.

1. Many Americans believe that with hard work their dreams of success can

   _____ have a better life _____.

2. Even though many of the traditional values are ideals that may not describe the reality of American life, they still influence

   _____ most American's daily lives _____.

Understand Details

Choose the best answer to complete the sentences based on the chapter.

_____ 1. Early settlers came to the North American continent and established colonies mainly because they wanted to be free from
   a. the power of kings, priests, and noblemen.
   b. the influence of their families.
   c. the problems of poverty and hunger.

_____ 2. There are no titles of nobility in the United States today because
   a. no one likes aristocrats.
   b. the church does not allow it.
   c. they are forbidden by the Constitution.

_____ 3. The price that Americans pay for their individual freedom is
   a. self-reliance.
   b. competition.
   c. hard work.

_____ 4. The American belief in self-reliance means that
   a. receiving money from charity, family, or the government is never allowed.
   b. if a person is very dependent on others, he or she will be respected by others.
   c. people must take care of themselves and be independent, or risk losing their personal freedom.

_____ 5. The American belief in equality of opportunity means that
   a. all Americans are rich.
   b. Americans believe that everyone should be equal.
   c. everyone should have an equal chance to succeed.

_____ 6. In the United States, learning to compete successfully is
   a. part of growing up.
   b. not seen as healthy by most people.
   c. not necessary, because Americans believe in equality.

7. Traditionally, immigrants have been able to raise their standard of living by coming to the United States because
   a. Americans value money more than anything else.
   b. there were such abundant natural resources.
   c. the rich have shared their wealth with the poor.

8. Americans see their material possessions as
   a. having nothing to do with social status.
   b. the natural reward for their hard work.
   c. showing no evidence of a person's abilities.

9. A belief in the value of hard work
   a. developed because it was necessary to work hard to convert natural resources into material goods.
   b. developed because the immigrants who came here had a natural love of hard work.
   c. has never been a part of the American value system because people have so much.

10. In reality, such American ideals as equality of opportunity and self-reliance
    a. do not exist because there is no equality in the United States.
    b. are always put into practice in the United States and truly describe American life.
    c. are only partly carried out in real life, but are still important because people believe in them.

Talk About It

Work in small groups and choose one or more questions to discuss.

1. Americans believe strongly in self-reliance and the freedom and independence of the individual. What are the advantages and disadvantages of being very independent? Which is more important to you, pleasing your family or having the freedom to do what you want?

2. If Americans had to pick one aspect of their country that they are most proud of, over 90 percent would choose freedom. What aspect of your country are people most proud of? How does that quality affect life there?

3. Is it healthy for a person to want to compete? Which is more important in a society—competition or cooperation? Which do you value more? Why?

SKILL BUILDING

Improve Your Reading Skills: Scanning

Read the questions below. Scan the chapter to find the specific information you need to answer each question.

1. What three types of freedoms were the early settlers seeking?
2. What happened in 1776?
3. In what year was the Constitution of the United States written?
4. What do Americans mean by the word *freedom*?

5. Why didn't a hereditary aristocracy develop in the United States?

6. Who was James Madison and what did he say in the late 1700s?

7. Who said, "We . . . wish to allow the humblest man an equal chance to get rich with everybody else"?

Develop Your Critical Thinking Skills

Using poll data to support research conclusions.

The Center for the Study of the American Dream at Xavier University conducts an annual survey of the state of the American Dream. In their 2011 survey, they found that the American Dream is still alive in spite of economic bad news and international uncertainty. Here are the results of the survey.

_____ 1. While people are worried about the economy and America's place in the world, they are still confident about their personal ability to achieve their personal American Dream.

_____ 2. Currently, the most popular definitions of the American Dream are "a good life for my family," "financial security," "opportunity," and "freedom."

_____ 3. Most Americans believe that immigration is important for keeping the American Dream alive.

_____ 4. But people have lost faith in American institutions that have protected the American Dream, including politics, business, government, and the media.

_____ 5. People also believe that the United States is losing economic power and influence in the world, and the world is looking to other countries as the standard for success.

The results of the survey are based on polls that the Center conducted. Read the following poll data and match them to the results above. Write the letter of the poll in the blank next to the result that it supports.

a. 54 percent believe that "One of America's greatest strengths is that it has always been a beacon of opportunity to the rest of the world. People still yearn to come here for a better life."

b. 63 percent believe that China's role in the world economy is more powerful than that of the U.S.

c. 83 percent have less trust in politics in general, 79 percent have less trust in big business and major corporations, 78 percent have less trust in government, and 72 percent have less trust in the media.

d. 45 percent choose "a good life for my family" as their first or second choice of how they would define the American Dream, while 34 percent choose "financial security," 32 percent choose "freedom," and 29 percent choose "opportunity."

e. 63 percent are extremely or fairly confident of reaching their American Dream in their lifetime, and 75 percent say they have already attained some measure of it.

Visit the website of the Center for the Study of the American Dream http://www.xavier.edu/americandream to learn more about their work.

Build Your Vocabulary

More AWL Words

Test your knowledge of these AWL words by matching them with their definitions.

_____ 1. accumulate a. to become smaller or less important

_____ 2. authority b. of central and underlying importance

_____ 3. convert c. the physical and mental strength that makes you able to be active

_____ 4. diminish d. to gradually get more and more money, possessions, or knowledge over a period of time

_____ 5. eliminate e. to move from one place or position to another

_____ 6. energy f. the power you have because of your official position

_____ 7. ethic g. to get rid of something completely

_____ 8. financial h. to change from one form, system, or purpose to a different one

_____ 9. fundamental i. a general idea or set of moral beliefs that influences people's behavior and attitudes

_____ 10. global j. relating to the whole world

_____ 11. promote k. relating to money

_____ 12. shift l. to help something or someone advance and be successful

Use Context Clues

Review the four kinds of context clues on pages 15 and 16 in Chapter 1. Use context clues in these sentences to choose the best meaning for the boldfaced words.

_____ 1. In 1776, the British colonial settlers declared their independence from England and established a new nation, the United States of America. In so doing, they **defied** the king of England and declared that the power to govern would lie in the hands of the people.
   a. They killed the king and members of his court.
   b. They openly resisted the king's power to govern them.

_____ 2. By *freedom,* Americans mean the desire and the right of all individuals to control their own **destiny** without outside interference from the government, a ruling class, the church, or any other organized authority.
   a. They wanted to control their own future lives.
   b. They wanted to control their Constitution.

_____ 3. To say that a person is **materialistic** is an insult. To an American, this means that this person values material possessions above all else.
   a. The person loves things.
   b. The person fears being poor.

_____ 4. John Kenneth White observes that in spite of all the changes in the nation's population, economy, and culture, the behaviors and values of Americans have remained remarkably **constant**.
   a. The behaviors and values have stayed the same.
   b. The behaviors and values have changed.

_____ 5. Because of its incredibly **abundant** natural resources, the United States appeared to be a land of plenty where millions could come to seek their fortunes.
   a. There were many natural resources.
   b. There were very few natural resources.

Word Partners

There are many verb + noun object collocations, or word partners, in English.

EXAMPLE: achieve independence

Americans expect their adult children to achieve independence and support themselves.

A. Read these word partners. Then complete the sentences that follow with the correct verb + noun object collocation.

face challenges
seek their fortunes
provide a decent standard of living
surveys public opinion
control their own destiny

1. John Zogby is an American pollster who

_____.

2. By *freedom,* Americans mean the desire and the right to

_____.

3. Millions came to the United States to

_____.

4. The working poor have low-paying jobs that do not

_____ .

5. Of course, new immigrants continue to

_____ .

Multiple Word Partners

Some English words can collocate, or partner, with only a few words; others have a
*great many collocations. For example, the verb **survey** has relatively few collocations*
with nouns:
  survey (public) opinion
  survey a group of people (teachers, voters)
  survey a piece of land or property

*When **face** is used as a verb, it has many collocations. It usually means confronting*
someone or something that is difficult or unpleasant:
  face the facts, reality, the truth, the consequences
  face the problem head-on, face the music
  face an opponent, a rival, another sports team
  face a challenge

*The verb **seek** also has many collocations. It often means to look for something you*
need or to ask someone for advice:
  seek shelter, sanctuary, comfort, help, advice, counseling
  seek your fortune, a better life, an opportunity
  seek a solution to a problem or seek a compromise
  seek the truth, seek justice, seek an answer
  seek employment, seek re-election

Choose two collocations each for **survey**, **face**, and **seek**, and then use them in
your own sentences.

Word Forms

Many words have verb and noun forms.

Verb Form	Noun Form
achieve	achievement
conceptualize	concept
emphasize	emphasis
reject	rejection
rely	reliance

Choose the correct verb or noun forms from the chart above and write them in
the following sentences. (Change the verb tenses, if necessary.)

Self-_____ is an
1
important American value. Most
Americans _____
2
the importance of eventually
becoming independent and
standing on their own two feet.
They teach this _____
3
to their children as they are
growing up, expecting them to

American children often earn spending money by selling lemonade.

_____ financial and emotional independence by the time they
4
are in their early twenties. Americans do not _____ their adult
5
children; they still love them and believe this is the best preparation for life in
the American culture.

EXPAND YOUR KNOWLEDGE

Ask Yourself

Do you agree or disagree with each of the following statements? Put a check
under the number that indicates how you feel.

+2 = Strongly agree
+1 = Agree
 0 = No opinion
−1 = Disagree
−2 = Strongly disagree

	+2	+1	0	−1	−2
1. The welfare of the individual is more important than the welfare of the group.	___	___	___	___	___
2. Our destiny is in our own hands.	___	___	___	___	___
3. People should take care of themselves, solve their own problems, and stand on their own two feet.	___	___	___	___	___
4. If I could have a better life in another country, I would go and live there.	___	___	___	___	___

5. Earning a lot of money is more important than having an interesting job.   ____ ____ ____ ____ ____

6. The government should take care of the poor and homeless.   ____ ____ ____ ____ ____

7. Life is basically a competitive race for success.   ____ ____ ____ ____ ____

8. Money and material possessions are the best indicators of high social status.   ____ ____ ____ ____ ____

9. People who work hard deserve to have a higher standard of living than others.   ____ ____ ____ ____ ____

10. If I work hard, I am sure I can be a success and get what I want in life.   ____ ____ ____ ____ ____

Ask Americans

Interview several Americans of different ages and ask them about their basic beliefs. If this is not possible, try to interview people from several different countries. Ask each one the following questions and record their answers.

1. Some people say that people achieve success by their own hard work; others say that luck and help from other people are more important. Which do you think is more important?

2. Do you agree or disagree with this statement: If you work hard in this country, eventually you will get ahead.

3. Do you think that the economic inequality in the United States today is a major problem, a minor problem, or not a problem at all?

Conduct a Poll

Read the results of the poll that follows, and then conduct a poll among your classmates asking the same questions. Compare your results with the answers that Americans gave.

How much do you think that each of the following is a cause of inequality in the U.S. today? A great deal, somewhat, not very much, not at all, or not at all sure.

CAUSES OF INEQUALITY

	Great deal/ Somewhat (NET)	A great deal	Somewhat	Not very much/ Not at all (NET)	Not very much	Not at all	Not at all sure
	%	%	%	%	%	%	%
The loss of manufacturing jobs to China, India, and other low cost countries	81	55	26	11	6	5	9
The influence of big business on government policies	78	55	23	13	7	5	9
The tax system	77	49	28	15	9	5	9
The influence of very rich people on government policy	76	56	21	16	10	6	8
The failure of the public school systems to educate many people	73	40	33	18	13	5	9
Globalization of the world economy	68	27	40	20	14	7	12

Note: Percentages may not add up to 100% due to rounding

People Watching

Rule: Americans usually stand about two and a half feet apart and at a slight angle (not facing each other directly) for ordinary conversation. They may touch when greeting each other by shaking hands (during a formal introduction) or by placing a hand briefly on the other's arm or shoulder (friends only). Some people kiss on the cheek or hug when greeting a friend. Note that the hug usually is not a full-body hug; only the shoulder and upper part of the bodies touch.

Observation: Observe people who are standing and talking. How far apart are they? Do they touch as they speak? What do you think their relationship is? Observe people greeting each other. What do they do? What is their relationship? Observe formal introductions. Do the people shake hands? Do women usually shake hands? If a man and a woman are introduced, who extends a hand first?

Experiment: Ask someone on the street for directions. When you are standing two or three feet apart and the other person seems comfortable with the distance, take a step closer. What is the person's reaction? Try standing more than two to three feet from the other person. What does the other person do? Try facing the person directly as you talk instead of standing at an angle. What happens?

Use the Internet

Many Americans interested in tracing their family history can learn when family members immigrated to the United States. Immigrants who came from Europe between 1892 and 1924 first landed on Ellis Island (in the New York harbor). There they went through Immigration. Off the coast of California is Angel Island, known as the Ellis Island of the West. From 1910 until 1940, many Asian immigrants entered the United States by first going to this island. The Statue of Liberty-Ellis Island Foundation has a museum and a website to help people do family research. The Angel Island Conservancy has just begun the process of creating a historical site on Angel Island.

Work with a partner. Visit the website http://www.ellisisland.org and click on *Ellis Island*, then *Immigrant Experience*.

You then have two choices: (1) *Family Histories* will tell you stories about individuals from different countries, or (2) *The Peopling of America* will give you a timeline that traces the history of immigration to the United States. Choose one of these, read the information, and discuss it with your partner.

Work with a partner. Visit the website http://angelisland.org/history.

How does this website compare with the Ellis Island site? How do you think it could be developed?

WRITE ABOUT IT

Choose one of the following topics. Then write a short compostion about it.

A. Write an essay about the responsibilities people in a community have to each other.

Organize your thoughts before you write. Here are a few tips.

- *Write a short plan, or outline, of your main ideas: an introduction, two or three main ideas, and a conclusion.*
- *Begin your essay by defining what you mean by the word community.*
- *Be sure to introduce each of your main points, using words such as first, second, third.*
- *Try to tie your conclusion to the introduction.*

B. Write a report about using census data to plan for the future.

How can census data help predict what the future population will be? To get some ideas for your report, read about a prediction of the future population of the United States made over 100 years ago.

In 1907, N. D. North, the Director of the Census, made a prediction about what the population of the United States would be in the year 2000. He explained this in an article in The Youth's Companion, a popular periodical of the day. According to the census of the year 1900, the population of the United States was 76,212,168. North predicted that it would grow to 311,000,000 in the year 2000, an increase of 235,000,000.

In the article, North discussed what such a large increase might mean. How would the nation feed such a larger number of people? How would the economy be affected? What would the population density look like? North observed that the only way to really measure the impact of such an enormous population would be in connection with the land area. He noted that the census of 1900 computed population density at 25.6 persons to a square mile. In the year 2000, if his prediction were accurate, the density would be 105 persons per square mile.

The UNITED STATES in A.D. 2000
BY THE HON. S. N. D. NORTH
Director of the Census

A. D. 1907   A. D. 2000

THE POPULATION REPRESENTED AS A BUILDING.

THERE ARE TWENTY-SIX PERSONS TO THE SQUARE MILE TO-DAY.

THERE WILL BE ONE HUNDRED AND FIVE PERSONS TO THE SQUARE MILE IN A. D. 2000.

North's prediction was surprisingly accurate. The census of 2010 showed a population of 308,745,538. In making his prediction, North tried to consider such factors as immigration, the birth rate, the percentage of women of child-bearing age, and the percentage of children under the age of 18. He also mentioned that people were living longer than they had before.

For your report, consider the changes in population in another country. It can be your own. If you can find a recent census and a past census, use these in your discussion. If there is no census, then think about your own city or country and discuss what you see as the changes in population and the reasons for these changes. How do you think the population will change in the future and why? Include in your report a graph or illustration such as the ones above. Use a graphic organizer like the one below to help you organize your information.

Past	Present	Future

EXPLORE ON YOUR OWN

Books to Read

Sandra Cisneros, *The House on Mango Street*—Esperanza Cordero, a girl coming of age in the Hispanic quarter of Chicago, uses poems and stories to reveal her life in a difficult environment.

Ralph Waldo Emerson, *Self-Reliance*—This is a classic essay on the American value of self-reliance and Emerson's philosophy of moral idealism.

Richard Rodriguez, *Hunger of Memory: The Education of Richard Rodriguez*—A Mexican American describes his academic success, his assimilation to middle-class America, and his loss of connection to his cultural roots.

Amy Tan, *The Kitchen God's Wife*—A Chinese immigrant mother tells her daughter about growing up in China and her life there before coming to the United States.

John Kenneth White, *The Values Divide: American Politics and Culture in Transition*—White discusses the split between conservative Republicans and liberal Democrats and the American "culture wars" of the 2000s.

Movies to See

Coming to America—An African prince goes to Queens, New York, to find a wife whom he can respect for her intelligence and independence.

The Immigrants—An immigrant endures a challenging sea voyage and gets into trouble as soon as he arrives in America.

In America—An Irish immigrant family adjusts to life in the United States.

The Joy Luck Club—This film shows the life histories of four Asian women and their relationships with their daughters who were born in the United States.

The Pursuit of Happyness—Based on a true story, this movie tells about a homeless salesman and his son trying to start a new life.

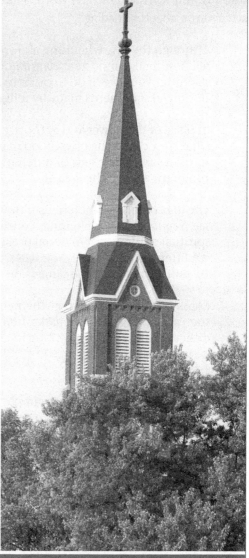

CHAPTER 3

THE AMERICAN RELIGIOUS HERITAGE

The care of every man's soul belongs to himself.

Thomas Jefferson (1743–1826)

How has religion shaped American values and what is the role of religion in the lives of Americans today?

BEFORE YOU READ

Preview Vocabulary

A. Read the following sentences from the chapter and notice the words in italics. Use context clues to help you figure out the meanings. Then choose which definition is best for the italicized word. These key AWL words will help you understand the chapter reading.

_____ 1. Although the overwhelming majority of Americans are Christians, all religions make important *contributions* to the American culture.
   a. things you give or do in order to help make something successful
   b. official statements made by religious leaders to inspire people

_____ 2. In place of the power and authority of priests, Protestants *substituted* what they called the priesthood of all believers.
   a. used something new or different
   b. fought against the idea of

_____ 3. The idea of mixing materialism (love of things) and religion may seem *contradictory*. Religion is considered to be concerned with spiritual matters, not material possessions.
   a. different or opposite
   b. similar or almost the same

_____ 4. Many businesses encourage their employees to do *volunteer* work, such as helping clean up parks, helping a child who is having difficulty in school, or working in an animal shelter.
   a. without being paid
   b. necessary or required

_____ 5. Perhaps the most *dramatic* example of the idea of self-improvement is the experience of being "born again."
   a. uncertain or undecided
   b. exciting and impressive

_____ 6. America's religious heritage seems to have encouraged certain basic values that members of many diverse faiths find easy to accept. This has helped to unite many different religious groups in the United States without requiring any to *abandon* their faiths.
   a. to leave behind or give up
   b. to try to convince others to join

B. In this chapter, there are words dealing with religion, such as *priest, soul,* and *church.* Other words have to do with wealth, such as *money, financial,* and *sum.* Look at the words below and classify them into one of two groups. Write **R** next to words dealing with *religion* and **W** next to words dealing with *wealth.*

_____ 1. bless   _____ 9. prosperity

_____ 2. faith   _____ 10. Protestant denomination

_____ 3. forgiveness   _____ 11. riches

_____ 4. fortune

_____ 5. holy

_____ 6. material success

_____ 7. missionary

_____ 8. pray

_____ 12. save and invest

_____ 13. sin

_____ 14. soul

_____ 15. spiritual

_____ 16. evangelical

Preview Content

A. **Think about these questions. Discuss them with your classmates.**

1. Read the quotation by Thomas Jefferson at the beginning of the chapter. What do you think he meant? How could this belief affect religion in the United States?

2. What do you know about religion in the United States? Do you think that the United States has the same religions as your country? Fill in the Venn diagram with the names of religions found only in your country, only in the United States, or in both countries.

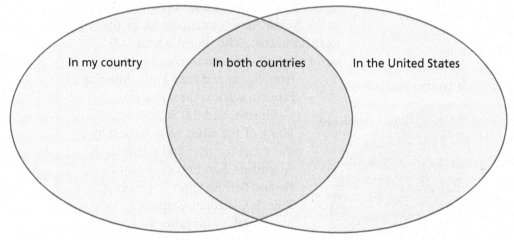

In my country   In both countries   In the United States

B. **Before you read the chapter, look at the headings of each section. Which sections do you think will have the answers to these questions? Write the heading of the section in the space below each question.**

1. How many Americans say they believe in God?

_____

2. What are the most popular religions in the United States?

_____

3. Do Americans have an official national religion?

_____

4. How has religion shaped American values?

_____

THE RELIGIOUS HERITAGE OF THE UNITED STATES: STRENGTHENING AMERICAN CULTURAL VALUES

1   The United States is and has always been a religious nation, by a number of measures. Ninety percent of Americans still say they believe in God, or a higher power/universal spirit, although their beliefs and practices are quite diverse. The majority of Americans are Christian, but all the major religions of the world are practiced in the United States. In some parts of the country, large numbers of people belong to churches and many attend worship services more than once a week. Other areas are more secular, with fewer people who are active in churches. Increasingly, young people do not belong to any church or other religious group, but most still say they believe in God. Many refer to themselves as being "spiritual," not "religious."

RELIGIOUS PREFERENCES IN THE UNITED STATES

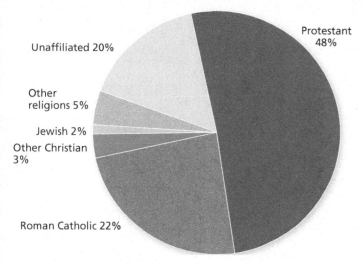

Unaffiliated 20%

Other religions 5%

Jewish 2%

Other Christian 3%

Roman Catholic 22%

Protestant 48%

2   The landscape of religion in America is complicated and constantly changing, but it has always been a very important aspect of the culture. In Chapter 2 we introduced six basic cultural values—individual freedom, self-reliance, equality of opportunity, competition, material wealth, and hard work. These values developed in and were strengthened by the nation's religious heritage. Several of these values—individual freedom, self-reliance, material wealth, and hard work—were particularly affected. In this chapter, we will first examine how the historical context shaped the nation's religious heritage and helped produce and reinforce these cultural values. Then we will look at how these values affect the religious landscape today.

3   From the beginning, religion played an important role in the history of the United States. The Catholic faith was first brought to the North American continent by the Spanish in the 1500s. For the next 300 years, Catholic missionaries and settlers from Spain and then Latin America came to what is now Florida, California, and the Southwest. Many of the cities were named by these missionaries and settlers—St. Augustine, San Francisco, Santa Fe, and San Antonio, for example. French Canadian Catholic missionaries also came with the explorers and traders from Quebec, down the Mississippi River to New Orleans. In the 1600s, European settlers began establishing colonies along the east coast of North America. Although there were some Catholics, the vast majority of the European settlers were Protestants, most from England. As the new nation formed, it was the Protestant branch of the Christian faith that had the strongest effect on the development of the religious climate in the United States.

The Development of Protestantism

4 The Protestant branch of the Christian faith broke away from the Roman Catholic Church in Europe in the sixteenth century because of important differences in religious beliefs. (The Eastern Orthodox branch of the Christian faith had separated from the Roman Catholic Church in 1054.) At the time of the Protestant Reformation, the Roman Catholic Church was the center of religious life in western European countries; the Catholic pope and the priests played the role of parent to the people in spiritual matters. They told people what was right and wrong, and they granted them forgiveness for sins[1] against God and the Christian faith.

5 The Protestants, on the other hand, insisted that all individuals must stand alone before God. If people sinned, they should seek their forgiveness directly from God rather than from a priest speaking in God's name. In place of the power and authority of priests, Protestants substituted what they called the "priesthood of all believers." This meant that every individual was solely responsible for his or her own relationship with God.

6 After the Protestants broke away from the Catholic Church, they found that they could not agree among themselves about many beliefs. Therefore, the Protestants began to form separate churches, called *denominations*. (The traditional Protestant denominations in the United States are Baptist, Methodist, Lutheran, Presbyterian, Episcopal, and United Church of Christ). There was much bitterness among some of the religious groups in the 1600s, and many Protestant denominations experienced religious persecution.[2] A number of people were even killed because of their beliefs. The result of this persecution was that many Protestants were ready to leave their native countries in order to have freedom to practice their particular religious beliefs. Consequently, among the early settlers who came to America in the 1600s, there were many Protestants seeking religious freedom.

7 In the previous chapter we noted that this desire for religious freedom was one of the strongest reasons why many colonial settlers came to America. Generally speaking, the lack of any established national religion in America appealed

Americans at worship in a Christian church

[1] sins: things someone does that are against religious laws

[2] persecution: cruel or unfair treatment, especially because of religious or political beliefs

strongly to European Protestants, whether or not they were being persecuted. A large number of Protestant denominations were established in America. At first, some denominations hoped to force their views and beliefs on others, but the colonies were simply too large for any one denomination to gain control over the others. The idea of separation of church and state became accepted.

8   When the Constitution was adopted in 1789, the government was forbidden to establish a national church; no denomination was to be favored over the others. The government and the church had to remain separate, and freedom of religion was guaranteed by the first amendment. Under these conditions, a great variety of different Protestant denominations developed and grew, with each denomination having a "live and let live" attitude toward the others. Diversity was accepted and strengthened. Today, the various Protestant denominations have completely separate church organizations, and although there are many similarities, there are also significant differences in their religious teachings and beliefs.

Self-Reliance and the Protestant Heritage of Self-Improvement

9   Protestantism has been a powerful force in shaping the values and beliefs of Americans. One of the most important values associated with American Protestantism is the value of self-improvement, an outgrowth of self-reliance. Christianity often emphasizes the natural sinfulness of human nature. However, unlike Catholics, Protestants do not go to priests for forgiveness of their sins; individuals are left alone before God to improve themselves and ask for God's guidance, forgiveness, and grace. For this reason, Protestantism has traditionally encouraged a strong and restless desire for self-improvement.

10   Perhaps the most dramatic example of the idea of self-improvement is the experience of being "born again." Individuals who have had this experience say that opening their hearts to God and Jesus Christ changed their lives so completely that it was like being born again. Many evangelicals, or religious conservatives, believe this is an important experience to have.

11   The need for self-improvement has reached far beyond self-improvement in the purely moral or religious sense. Today it can be seen in countless books that offer advice to people on how to stop smoking, lose weight, or have better relationships. Books of this type often offer advice on how to be happier and more successful in life. They are referred to as "self-help" books, and many are best sellers. They are the natural products of a culture in which people believe that "God helps those who help themselves."

Material Success, Hard Work, and Self-Discipline

12   The achievement of material success is probably the most widely respected form of self-improvement in the United States. Many scholars believe that the nation's Protestant heritage is also largely responsible for bringing this about. The idea of mixing materialism and religion may seem contradictory; religion is considered to be concerned with spiritual matters, not material possessions. How can the two mix?

13   Some of the early European Protestant leaders believed that people who were blessed by God might be recognized in the world by their material success. Other church leaders, particularly in the United States, made an even stronger connection between gaining material wealth and being blessed by God. In 1900, for example, Bishop William Lawrence

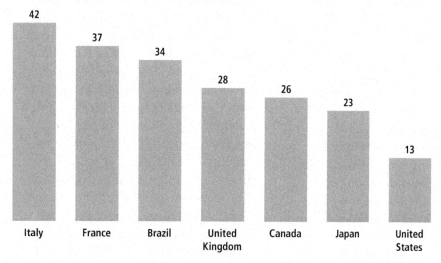

AVERAGE NUMBER OF PAID VACATION DAYS

Italy	France	Brazil	United Kingdom	Canada	Japan	United States
42	37	34	28	26	23	13

proclaimed,[4] "Godliness is in league with[5] riches. . . . Material prosperity is helping to make the national character sweeter, more joyous, more unselfish, more Christlike."

14 American religious leaders, however, never encouraged the idea of gaining wealth without hard work and self-discipline. Many scholars believe that the emphasis on these two values made an important contribution to the industrial growth of the United States. Protestant leaders viewed the work of all people as holy, not just that of priests. They also believed that the capacity for self-discipline was a holy characteristic blessed by God. Self-discipline was often defined as the willingness to save and invest one's money rather than spend it on immediate pleasures. John Wesley, the leader of the Methodist faith, told his followers, "Earn all you can, give all you can, save all you can." Encouraging people to save may also have helped create a good climate for the industrial growth of the United States, which depended on hard work and a willingness to save and invest money.

15 The belief in hard work and self-discipline in pursuit of material gain and other goals is often referred to as "the Protestant work ethic" or "the Puritan work ethic." It is important to understand that this work ethic has had an influence far beyond the Protestant church. Many religious groups in the United States share this work ethic, and even Americans who have no attachment to a particular church are influenced by the work ethic in their daily lives. Interestingly, the United States is the only industrialized country that does not have a legal requirement for workers to have a certain number of paid vacation days. Americans take an average of only two weeks of vacation time a year, while workers in other countries take as many as four, five, or even more weeks. Also, many Americans who could retire at age 65 or 66 continue to work for more years. Many Americans are proud to be called

[4] proclaimed: *said publically or officially that something is true*

[5] in league with: *working together secretly*

"workaholics," people who work long hours, often seven days a week.

Volunteerism and Humanitarianism

16   The idea of self-improvement includes more than achieving material gain through hard work and self-discipline. It also includes the idea of improving oneself by helping others. Individuals, in other words, make themselves into better persons by contributing some of their time or money to charitable, educational, or religious causes that are designed to help others. The philosophy is sometimes called *volunteerism* or *humanitarianism.*

17   Historically, some extremely wealthy Americans have made generous contributions to help others. In the early 1900s, for example, Andrew Carnegie, a famous American businessman, gave away more than $300 million to help support schools and universities and to build public libraries in thousands of communities in the United States. John D. Rockefeller, another famous businessman, in explaining why he gave a large sum from his private fortune to establish a university, said, "The good Lord gave me my money, so how could I withhold it from the University of Chicago?" Julius Rosenwald, part-owner of the Sears Roebuck company, helped pay for the building of 5,000 black schools in the rural South. In the twenty-first century, Bill Gates, Warren Buffet, and other wealthy Americans have established charitable foundations and have donated huge sums of money. Traditionally, many average Americans have also agreed that they should devote part of their time and wealth to religious or humanitarian causes. Their motivation may be part idealism and part self-improvement, a desire to be acceptable in the eyes of God and also in the eyes of other Americans.

Volunteers clean up trash.

18 The spirit of charitable giving and volunteerism continues in America today. Some religious faiths believe that it is the responsibility of their members to contribute 10 percent of what they earn to their church and other charities. Incidentally, individuals may get tax deductions for giving money to charity. This spirit of giving can be seen outside religious contexts as well. Many businesses encourage their employees to do volunteer work, such as helping clean up parks, helping a child who is having difficulty in school, or working in an animal shelter in their spare time. Parents often try to teach their children that they have a responsibility to help others. A recent *Parents* magazine had a cover story advising parents how to "raise a child who gives back." The article said that children should be taught the value of volunteering, including giving money to charity. "Volunteering boosts kids' self-esteem and teaches them to be grateful," the article promised, a good illustration of the American mixture of idealism and self-improvement.

September 11, 2001, and the National Religion

19 All Americans and many people around the world can remember exactly what they were doing at the moment they heard that terrorists had attacked the World Trade Center and the Pentagon on September 11, 2001. People in New York City and Washington, D.C., were especially devastated. Everyone knew someone who was touched by the tragedy. Immediately, there was an outpouring of love, charity, and patriotism around the country. So many people volunteered to help that officials had to limit the numbers. Millions of dollars were raised for the families of the victims, and Americans felt a huge surge of pride and love for their country. Eighty percent of them displayed

the American flag—in the windows of their houses, on their cars, even on their clothing. Crowds spontaneously sang "God Bless America," a patriotic song that is more popular (and much easier to sing) than the national anthem, along with "America the Beautiful" and "My Country 'Tis of Thee."

Firefighters stand at a memorial to those killed at the World Trade Center.

20 This mixture of religion and patriotism is an example of what some scholars have called the "national religion" of the United States. The roots of the national religion go back to colonial times. In the countries from which the American colonists emigrated, the dominant values of the nation were often supported by an organized national church. Although Americans made certain that no organized national church would exist in their young country, they have, over the years, developed a number of informal practices

that combine national patriotism with religion. The main function of this national religion is to provide support for the dominant values of the nation and comfort in times of grief. Thus, it does in an informal and less organized way what nationally organized churches did for European nations in earlier times.

21 Some observers of American society believe that the various practices that are called the national religion can have harmful effects, however. Sometimes these practices can help to create a climate in which disagreement with current national practices is discouraged or not tolerated. There have been times when citizens have disagreed with their government's

decision to wage war, for example, and other Americans accused them of being unpatriotic. This happened during the war in Vietnam, when protesters were told, "America—love it, or leave it." A similar division of opinion occurred over the U.S. decision to invade Iraq in 2003.

The Religious Landscape Today: Polarization Vs. Pluralism

22 The religious landscape in the United States is complicated and changing. In *American Grace: How Religion Divides and Unites Us*, Robert D. Putnam and David E. Campbell discuss two forces at work in the United States today: religious polarization and pluralism. There is growing polarization between evangelicals, or religious conservatives, and secular liberals. Increasingly, Americans find themselves at one end of the spectrum or another, while the number of moderates in the middle decreases. Evangelicals believe in strictly following the teachings of the Bible (as they and the church leaders interpret it) and regularly attending worship services. They are socially (and often politically) more conservative than religious moderates or liberals. They may be against abortion and gay marriage, for example, and they may believe in creationism instead of evolution. The debate between religious conservatives and liberals can grow quite heated. Some commentators have even described this split as "culture wars." However, Putnam and Campbell say there is another force at work:

> *America peacefully combines a high degree of religious devotion with tremendous religious diversity—including growing ranks of the nonreligious. . . . How can religious pluralism coexist with religious polarization? The answer lies in the fact that, in America, religion is highly fluid. . . . Religions compete, adapt and evolve as individual Americans freely move from one congregation to another, and even from one religion to another.*

Firefighters hang a giant American flag over the side of the American Express tower.

23 What American value has allowed religious pluralism to coexist with religious polarization? The fundamental American belief in individual freedom and the right of individuals to practice their own religion is at the center of religious experience in the United States. The great diversity of ethnic backgrounds has produced a climate of religious pluralism, and most of the religions of the world are now practiced here. Although the overwhelming majority of Americans are Christians, other religions and people from other cultures make important contributions to the religious landscape. There are now about as many Muslims living in the United States as there are Jews. People of Hispanic origin now make up nearly one-half of the Catholic Church here. In addition to Buddhism and Hinduism, Asian immigrants have brought with them other traditional religions of East Asia—Daoism, Confucianism, and Shintoism. And the Native American religions are still practiced and studied today, particularly for their teachings about living in harmony with nature.

24 The Census of American Religious Congregations has been tracking 236 different religions in the United States, from Albanian Orthodox to Zoroastrian, every ten years. They report in the latest census that Muslims (Islam) and Mormons (Church of the Latter-day Saints) are two of the fastest growing religious groups in the country. Between 2000 and 2010, the number of Muslims grew by 66 percent and the number of Mormons grew by 44 percent, while the number of Protestants fell by 5 percent to below 50 percent of the population for the first time. (There are also estimates of about one million Buddhists and Hindus.) Remembering that the total population of the United States is now over 310 million, here are America's top 10 religions:

1. Catholic   58.9 million
2. Baptist   27.2 million
3. Methodist   12.2 million
4. Non-denominational
   Evangelical Protestant   12.2 million
5. Lutheran   7.2 million
6. Latter-day Saints
   (Mormons)   6.4 million
7. Pentecostal   5.8 million
8. Presbyterian Reformed   5.0 million
9. Islam (Muslims)   2.6 million
10. Judaism (Jews)   2.3 million*

Source: The Association of Religion Data Archives

25 One of the most dramatic developments in recent years is the rapid rise in the number of people who say they have no religious affiliation. Almost 20 percent of adults and one third of those under 30 do not consider themselves to be a part of any particular church or faith. They

American Muslims at prayer

are referred to as the unaffiliated, or the "nones" (since they choose "none" when asked about their religious affiliation), and now number 49 million. Interestingly, 68 percent of them say that they believe in God, but they have no desire to be part of organized religion. Often they refer to themselves as being "spiritual, but not religious." They are more liberal and more secular than Americans who are affiliated with some religious group.

26 Another important development is the decline in the membership of traditional mainline Protestant churches. In the list of top ten faiths above, only four are traditional Protestant denominations (Baptist, Methodist, Lutheran, and Presbyterian). Mainline churches tend to be moderate and more liberal than the evangelicals and religious conservatives, with the exception of the Baptist Church. Most Baptists are evangelicals. (Pentecostals are evangelicals, too, but they are not generally considered as traditional mainline Protestants.)

27 There has also been a rise in the number of *non-denominational* evangelical Protestants. These churches are not affiliated with a traditional Protestant denomination and are often community churches organized by dynamic religious leaders. Some of them are "megachurches." Rick Warren's Saddleback Church in Orange County, California, which was founded in 1980, now has 100,000 members and an average weekend attendance of over 20,000. Megachurches have contemporary worship services and often focus on helping people live "happy, fulfilled Christian lives," a modern message of self-improvement. They are an example of how some American churches have evolved and adapted to meet changing needs, particularly of young people.

Religious Diversity in the United States: A Spiritual Kaleidoscope[6]

28 This chapter began with the assertion that the United States has been and still is a religious country, but that the religious landscape is complicated and changing. The historical "live and let live" tolerance of early Protestant faiths has led to a modern acceptance of diverse religions by most Americans. Although there are some who are intolerant and would disagree, the majority of Americans believe that there are many paths to God and their particular religion is not the only valid faith. The traditional lines drawn between members of different religions have broken down so that Americans frequently marry people of different faiths. This is especially true of younger Americans. More and more people work with, live near, and are friends with people of different cultures and faiths. This has created a spiritual kaleidoscope, where people move between faiths, sometimes creating their own collection of beliefs drawn from a number of different religious traditions.

29 The belief that the individual, not the organized church, should be the center of religious life has encouraged a tolerance and acceptance of all faiths by most Americans. Most also believe that religious freedom must be protected—that everyone has the right to practice his or her own religion without interference by the government or anyone else. America's religious heritage seems to have encouraged certain basic values that members of many diverse faiths find easy to accept. This has helped to unite many different religious groups in the United States without requiring any to abandon their faiths. Cultural and religious pluralism has also created a context of tolerance that further strengthens the American reality of many different religions living peacefully within a single nation.

[6] *kaleidoscope: colors or patterns that change quickly*

AFTER YOU READ

Look at the predictions you made on page 53 before reading the chapter. Did you find the information in the sections you predicted? Answer these questions:

1. How many Americans say they believe in God?

   _____

2. What are the most popular religions in the United States?

   _____

3. Do Americans have an official national religion?

   _____

4. How has religion shaped American values?

   _____

Understand Main Ideas

In Chapters 1 and 2, we discussed the importance of organizing and presenting main ideas for clear writing and formal speaking in English. Academic writing in English looks like a series of capital letter Ts:

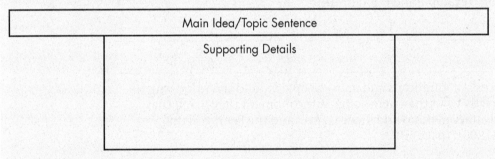

Main Idea/Topic Sentence

Supporting Details

Usually, each paragraph has a topic sentence that states the main idea of the paragraph. Often, this is the first sentence. The rest of the paragraph contains supporting details that develop or explain the main idea. There are many types of supporting details:

- *definitions*
- *facts or opinions*
- *statistics*
- *examples or illustrations*
- *descriptions*
- *quotations*

The first paragraph of this reading begins with a topic sentence supported by facts, statistics, and examples. (See page 54.) Look back at the reading and find the paragraphs that begin with the following topic sentences. Then find the details that support the main ideas stated in the topic sentence.

1. Topic sentence: Some of the early European Protestant leaders believed that people who were blessed by God might be recognized in the world by their material success. (page 56)

   Supporting detail: (quotation) _____

   _____

   _____

2. Topic sentence: American religious leaders, however, never encouraged the idea of gaining wealth without hard work and self-discipline. (page 57)

   Supporting detail: (definition) _____

   _____

   _____

3. Topic sentence: Historically, some extremely wealthy Americans have made generous contributions to help others. (page 58)

   Supporting details: (example and quotation) _____

   _____

   _____

4. Topic sentences: All Americans and many people around the world can remember exactly what they were doing at the moment they heard that terrorists had attacked the World Trade Center and the Pentagon on September 11, 2001. (page 59)

   Supporting details: (descriptions) _____

   _____

   _____

5. Topic sentence: The belief that the individual, not the organized church, should be the center of religious life has encouraged a tolerance and acceptance of all faiths by most Americans. (page 62)

   Supporting details: (example and facts) _____

   _____

   _____

Understand Details

Write **T** if the statement is true and **F** if it is false according to the information in the chapter.

_____ 1. Although there is cultural pluralism in the United States, there is no religious pluralism.

_____ 2. Protestant denominations (such as Methodist, Baptist, and Presbyterian) are part of the Roman Catholic Church.

_____ 3. No single church has become the center of religious life in the United States because the emphasis is on the individual, not a particular church.

_____ 4. Most of the settlers who came to colonial America to escape religious persecution in Europe were Catholics.

_____ 5. The Constitution of the United States separates church and state and forbids the government from ever establishing a national church.

_____ 6. Protestantism encourages a strong desire for self-improvement.

_____ 7. Some American Protestant leaders have said that people who are rich have been blessed by God.

_____ 8. The Protestant work ethic is the belief that people should share their time and their wealth to help others.

_____ 9. Evangelicals are Christians who are religiously and socially liberal.

_____ 10. The national religion of the United States is a mixture of religion and patriotism.

Talk About It

Work in small groups and choose one or more of these questions to discuss.

1. Do the majority of the people in your country belong to one particular church or religious faith? Is there a government-supported church or official religion? What are the advantages and disadvantages of having a government recognize one official religion for a country?

2. The United States does not have a national legal requirement for workers to have a certain number of paid vacation days. Does your country have such a legal requirement? Explain.

3. What is humanitarianism? Do you think that people should volunteer their time to help the poor?

4. What do you think being _religious_ means?

SKILL BUILDING

Improve Your Reading Skills: Compare and Contrast Information

In this chapter, the term "evangelical" is used to describe Americans who belong to several different religious groups. Some polls estimate that about 26 percent of Americans are evangelical. What is an evangelical, then? Reread paragraphs 10, 22, and 26 that mention evangelicals, and compare and contrast the information found there with the two definitions below. How are the definitions the same and how are they different? How do the definitions compare and contrast with information in the chapter? Summarize your findings.

The National Association of Evangelicals website www.nae.net states that evangelicals are a diverse group found in many churches, denominations, and nations. Many evangelicals rarely use the term to describe themselves. They focus instead on core theological convictions summarized by historian David Bebbington:

Conversionism: the belief that lives need to be transformed through a "born-again" experience and a life-long process of following Jesus

Activism: the expression and demonstration of the gospel in missionary and social reform efforts

Biblicism: a high regard for and obedience to the Bible as the ultimate authority

Crucicentrism: a stress on the sacrifice of Jesus Christ on the cross (crucifixion) as making possible the redemption of humanity

Wikipedia stated that evangelicals have four beliefs:

The need for personal conversion, or being "born again"

A high regard for biblical authority

An emphasis on teachings that proclaim the saving death and resurrection of the Son of God, Jesus Christ

Active expression and sharing of the gospel

Develop Your Critical Thinking Skills

Create a questionnaire with a rating scale.

In American Grace: How Religion Divides and Unites Us, Putnam and Campbell describe their measure of "religiososity," or what it means to be "religious." They used six questions, which they say can apply to any religion:

How frequently do you attend religious services?
How frequently do you pray outside of religious services?
How important is religion in your daily life?
How important is your religion to your sense of who you are?
Are you a strong believer in your religion?
How strong is your belief in God?

Choose answers for each question and give points for each answer. For example:

How frequently do you attend religious services?
every day	*5 pts.*
more than once a week	*4 pts.*
every week	*3 pts.*
every month	*2 pts.*
several times a year	*1 pt.*
never	*0 pts.*

Look at the polls that follow to get ideas for answers. When you have scores for each question, add the points to create your scale of what it means to be "religious."

UNAFFILIATED, BUT NOT UNIFORMLY SECULAR

	U.S. General Public	Unaffiliated	Affiliated
How important is religion in your life?	%	%	%
Very important	58	14	67
Somewhat	22	19	24
Not too/not at all	18	65	8
Don't know/refused	1	1	—
	100	100	100
Believe in God or universal spirit?			
Yes, absolutely certain	69	30	77
Yes, but less certain	23	38	20
No	7	27	2
Other/don't know	2	5	1
	100	100	100
Frequency of prayer			
Daily	58	21	66
Weekly/monthly	21	20	22
Seldom/never	19	59	11
Don't know	2	1	1
	100	100	100
Think of self as . . .			
Religious person	65	18	75
Spiritual but not religious	18	37	15
Neither spiritual nor religious	15	42	8
Don't know	2	2	1
	100	100	100

Source: Pew Research Center survey, June 28–July 9, 2012. Q50, Q53–54, Q52, Q97a–b.
Figures may not add to 100% due to rounding.

PROFILE OF THE "SPIRITUAL BUT NOT RELIGIOUS"

Who are the "spiritual but not religious," and how do they compare with those who reject both labels, as well as those who do consider themselves religious?

RELIGIOUS PROFILE

	Among those who identify as . . .		
	Spiritual not religious	Religious	Neither
	%	%	%
Religion			
Protestant	39	60	21
Catholic	18	25	17
Unaffiliated	32	5	52
Other	9	8	8
Don't know	2	2	3
	100	100	100
Worship attendance			
Weekly or more	19	52	6
Monthly/yearly	34	35	30
Seldom/never	47	13	64
Don't know	0	1	–
	100	100	100
Importance of religion			
Very important	31	78	7
Somewhat important	32	20	23
Not too/not at all important	36	2	69
Don't know	1	–	1
	100	100	100
Frequency of prayer			
Daily or more	44	73	11
Weekly/monthly	25	20	22
Seldom/never	31	5	66
Don't know	1	2	2
	100	100	100
Do you believe in God?			
Yes, believe in God	92	99	60
Absolutely certain	55	84	20
Fairly certain	25	13	26
Not too/not at all certain	10	1	13
Don't know how certain	1	1	2
Do not believe in God	7	1	33
Other/Don't know	2	1	6
	100	100	100
N	729	2,077	610

Source: Pew Research Center survey, June 28–July 9, 2012. Combined Q97a–b, RELIG, ATTEND, Q50, Q52, Q53–54. Based on those who think of themselves as a religious person, as a spiritual but not a religious person, and neither a religious nor a spiritual person. Figures may not add to 100% due to rounding.

Build Your Vocabulary

Use Prefixes

Some words use prefixes to create negative or opposite meanings:

connect—disconnect   patriotic—unpatriotic   significant—insignificant

Make the following words negative by adding the correct prefix. Check your answer in a dictionary.

dis-	un-	in-

1. tolerance   _____tolerance

2. affiliated   _____affiliated

3. respectful   _____respectful

4. selfish   _____selfish

5. agreement   _____agreement

6. motivated   _____motivated

Use the six words with their new prefixes in sentences.

Some prefixes add to the meaning of a word. For example, self-identify *means to identify yourself as having some particular identity. Someone may self-identify as spiritual, evangelical, or non-religious.*

Write a brief definition for each of these words:

1. Self-improvement _____

2. Self-discipline _____

3. Self-reliance _____

Use Suffixes

Some words add suffixes, or endings, to add to the meaning of a word. For example, the suffix –ism *means a set of ideas or beliefs, or the action or process of doing something.* Humanitarianism *means the belief in being humanitarian—concerned with improving bad living conditions and preventing unfair treatment of people.*

Write a brief definition for each of these words:

1. Volunteerism _____

2. Activism _____

3. Hinduism _____

4. Catholicism _____

5. Atheism _____

6. Agnosticism _____

7. Secularism _____

8. Mormonism _____

9. Judaism _____

10. Protestantism _____

Recognize Word Forms

Many adverbs end in –ly. Usually, these words are the adverb forms of words that function as adjectives.

Use the following adverbs to fill in the blanks in the sentences from the chapter. (Some have more than one possible answer.)

consequently	immediately	solely	traditionally
historically	particularly	spontaneously	

1. In Protestantism, every individual is _____ responsible for his or her own soul.

2. There was freedom of religion in the new nation. _____ there were many Protestants who came seeking religious freedom.

3. _____, some wealthy Americans, such as Andrew Carnegie in the 1900s, have made generous contributions to help others.

4. Crowds _____ sang "God Bless America" in the weeks after 9/11.

5. The Native American religions are studied today, _____ for their teachings about living in harmony with nature.

6. _____ after 9/11, there was an outpouring of love, charity, and patriotism around the country.

7. Protestantism has _____ encouraged a strong and restless desire for self-improvement.

Collocations

This chapter has many adjective + noun collocations.

Circle the one word in each of the following groups that will not form a collocation with the boldfaced word.

EXAMPLE: European / colonial / (national) / early / British **settlers**

(You can say European settlers, colonial settlers, early settlers, or British settlers, but not national settlers.)

1. **spiritual** values / beliefs / practices / banks / experiences
2. **religious** freedom / diversity / grief / persecution / climate
3. **overwhelming** grief / examples / fear / frustration / sadness

More AWL Words

Test your knowledge of these AWL words by matching them with their definitions.

_____ 1. capacity

_____ 2. adapt

_____ 3. consequently

_____ 4. display

_____ 5. function

_____ 6. fundamental

_____ 7. liberal

_____ 8. devote

_____ 9. philosophy

_____ 10. sum

a. a set of beliefs about how people should live

b. put things in a place where people can see them

c. an amount of money

d. ability to do or produce something

e. relating to the most basic parts of something

f. as a result

g. gradually change to fit a new situation

h. give time or money to help

i. the usual purpose of something

j. supporting changes in social systems that give people more equality

EXPAND YOUR KNOWLEDGE

Ask Americans

Americans have a saying, "Never discuss religion and politics." These are not "safe" topics because they may touch on personal beliefs. Most Americans, however, will be willing to talk to you if you make it clear that this is an assignment for a class you are taking. You could begin by saying: "I wonder if you could help me with an assignment I have. I'm taking a course at _____ (school) and I am supposed to interview Americans about their religious beliefs. Would you be willing to answer some questions? I won't use your name. (Show them the list of questions.) Please tell me if there are any questions you don't feel comfortable answering."

Interview several Americans and ask them questions about their religion. Choose questions from the questionnaire and rating scale you created on pages 66–67. If you cannot ask Americans, interview international students or your classmates. Compare your findings with your classmates' findings and with the poll results on page 67.

Proverbs and Sayings

There are a number of proverbs and sayings about right and wrong. For example, the golden rule, "Do unto others as you would have them do unto you," means that you should treat people the way you want them to treat you. What proverbs do you know that deal with right and wrong?

Ask Americans to explain these sayings to you. Do they know any more sayings about money? Collect as many sayings as you can and share them with your classmates.

1. A penny saved is a penny earned.
2. Early to bed and early to rise makes a man healthy, wealthy, and wise.
3. Save something for a rainy day.
4. Eat, drink, and be merry, for tomorrow you die.
5. Idle hands are the devil's workshop.

Observe the Media

Working with a partner, look at the titles of some popular American self-help books. What aspects of life do they promise to improve? What conclusions about American values can you draw from these titles?

Collect other book titles by visiting an American bookstore, checking best-seller lists or websites, and looking at ads for books in magazines and newspapers. Share your findings with the class.

Use the Internet

Work with a partner. Search the Internet and visit these websites. Discuss your findings.

1. The Committee for the Study of Religion at Harvard University sponsors a website—http://www.pluralism.org/. The website lists information about their studies of religious diversity in the United States. Go to their website and learn about their mission and what they do. How do they define pluralism? What religions do they list, and how are they practiced? Where are the religious centers for Islam, Buddhism, and Hinduism?

2. Americans volunteer in many ways: at churches, in libraries or museums, in hospitals, in animal shelters, or in schools. Former President Jimmy Carter volunteers with Habitat for Humanity. The goal of this organization is to build houses for poor people. Visit their website www.habitat.org and learn about what they do. If you are in the United States, you can find a Habitat for Humanity project near where you are.

3. The following people are highly regarded by some Americans for their religious work. Do you know who these people are and why they are important? Choose one person, do research about him or her on the Internet, and then tell a classmate about your findings.

   - Dalai Lama
   - Martin Luther King, Jr.
   - Desmond Tutu
   - Mother Teresa
   - Muhammad

WRITE ABOUT IT

The Gallup polling organization has published a book titled God Is Alive and Well: The Future of Religion in America *based on more than one million interviews, 320,000 of which were conducted in 2012. Here is the "bottom line" of what they found:*

America remains a generally religious nation, with more than two-thirds of the nation's residents classified as very or moderately religious. These overall national averages, however, conceal dramatic regional differences in religiosity across the 50 states and the District of Columbia. Residents of Southern states are generally the most religious, underscoring the validity of the "Bible Belt" sobriquet [name] often used to describe this region. Coupled with the Southern states in the high-religiosity category is Utah, the majority of whose residents are Mormon—the most religious group in America today. On the other hand, residents of New England and a number of far Western states tend to be the least religious.

RELIGIOSITY, 2011

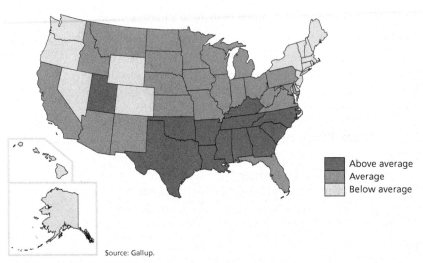

Above average
Average
Below average

Source: Gallup.

Write a report describing the religions in your country. Are there any regions where people are more religious than those of another region? If you can find one or more maps to show the distribution of religions there, include them in your report. Check on the Pew Research site and look at "The Global Religious Landscape: A Report on the Size and Distribution of the World's Major Religious Groups as of 2010." You may be able to find information about the distribution of the religions in your country there.

http://www.pewforum.org/maps

MAJORITY RELIGION, BY COUNTRY

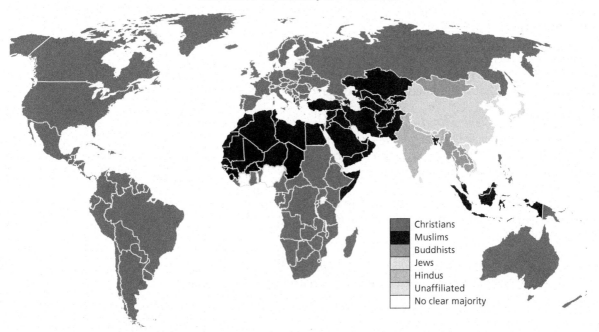

Christians
Muslims
Buddhists
Jews
Hindus
Unaffiliated
No clear majority

Review the Understand Main Ideas exercise on page 63. Use the graphic organizer for each paragraph of your composition. Write a clear topic sentence for the beginning of each paragraph and then list the supporting details below. Review the types of supporting details to get ideas of what kinds of information to use. You should have one "T" organizer for the introduction, several for your main ideas, and one for your conclusion. Try to make your conclusion refer back to your introduction. After you fill out the "T" organizers, write your composition.

Main Idea
Supporting Details

EXPLORE ON YOUR OWN

Books to Read

Ross Douthat, *Bad Religion: How We Became a Nation of Heretics*—The author believes that the United States, which does not have a national church, is losing the Christian center that has helped hold the diverse nation together.

Diana L. Eck, *A New Religious America: How a "Christian Country" Has Become the World's Most Religiously Diverse Nation*—Eck explains how the immigration of Muslims, Buddhists, Hindus, Sikhs, and other religious groups has brought religious pluralism to the United States.

Nathaniel Hawthorne, *The Scarlet Letter*—Set in early colonial times in New England, this classic story reveals the impact of an act of passion in a Puritan society.

Frank Newport, Editor, *God Is Alive and Well: The Future of Religion in America*—Newport discusses religion in America based on more than a million Gallup interviews.

Robert D. Putnam and David E. Campbell, *American Grace: How Religion Divides and Unites Us*—Putnam and Campbell discuss how personal religious ties bring a diversity of religions together in a pluralist society.

Movies to See

Doubt—The conservative principal of a Catholic school, a nun, accuses a popular, liberal priest of molesting a student.

Elmer Gantry—Elmer Gantry, a salesman, teams up with Sister Sharon Falconer, an evangelist, to sell religion in America in the 1920s.

Pay It Forward—A social studies teacher assigns his students the task of doing a favor for another person when someone else has done something for them, paying the favor forward.

Saved—In this comedy, teenagers in a religious school have difficulty deciding what is really the right thing to do.

A Simple Plan—Two brothers find a bag of stolen money and must decide what to do with it.

CHAPTER 4

THE FRONTIER HERITAGE

This ever-retreating frontier of free land is the key to American development.

Frederick Jackson Turner (1861–1932)

Why are Americans still so fascinated with life on the old western frontier, and how did the frontier shape American values?

BEFORE YOU READ

Preview Vocabulary

A. Work with a partner to answer the questions. Make sure you understand the meaning of the AWL words in italics.

1. If "spiritual" has to do with your soul, and "mental" has to do with your mind, what does *physical* have to do with?

2. If people are discussing a *controversial* topic, such as religion or politics, would you expect there to be a lot of agreement or disagreement?

3. If we say that the settlement of the western frontier had an *impact* on American culture, do we mean that it had some influence or that it was not very important?

4. If you wanted to *reinforce* your cowboy *image*, what would you wear?

5. Would someone who had a "can-do" attitude be an *optimist* or a *pessimist*?

6. Is gun control an *issue* in the United States, or do all Americans believe that everyone should have complete access to guns? What percentage of American households do you think have guns?

B. Read this paragraph from the chapter. Then use context clues and write the correct word next to its definition.

> How Americans reacted to the terrorist attacks of September 11, 2001, reveals another legacy of the frontier: Americans' willingness to take the law into their own hands to protect themselves and their families. This tendency usually appears when Americans believe the police cannot adequately protect them. For example, when the passengers fought with the terrorists on the 9/11 flight that crashed in Pennsylvania, they were hailed as heroes.

_____ 1. well enough for a particular purpose

_____ 2. described someone as being very good

_____ 3. shows something that was hidden

_____ 4. acted in response

_____ 5. a situation that exists as a result of things that happened at an earlier time

Preview Content

A. Read the quotation at the beginning of the chapter. Discuss these questions with your classmates.

1. What is a frontier?

2. Why do you think Turner says that the frontier is the "key" to understanding the development of America?

3. Which of these can be a frontier?

_____ the border between two countries

_____ an unsettled region

_____ space exploration

_____ deep-ocean exploration

_____ understanding how the mind works

_____ new or experimental medical treatments

4. What American movies about the Old West have you seen?

B. Before you read the chapter, look at the headings of each section. Examine the photos and other illustrations. Predict three values that were reinforced by the frontier experience. Write your predictions here.

1. _____

2. _____

3. _____

THE IMPACT OF THE AMERICAN FRONTIER

1   Although the American civilization took over and replaced the frontier more than a century ago, the heritage of the frontier is still evident in the United States today. Many people are still fascinated by the frontier because it has been particularly important in shaping American values. When Ronald Reagan was president in the 1980s, he liked to recall the image of life on the frontier. He was often photographed on his western ranch—chopping wood or riding his horse, and wearing his cowboy hat. More recently, in the 2000s, President George W. Bush reinforced this cowboy image by inviting members of the press to photograph him on his Texas ranch, wearing his cowboy boots and hat.

2   For many years, the frontier experience was romanticized[1] in popular movies and television shows that featured cowboy heroes fighting Indian villains. Little attention was given to the tragic story of what really happened to the Native Americans, also known as the American Indians. Today, most Americans are more aware of the darker side of the settling of the continent, when thousands of American Indians were killed and their lands were taken. When the buffalo were hunted and killed off by the white settlers, the Indians' major source of food and clothing was lost, and much of their culture was destroyed. Today, there is a renewed interest in Indian cultures, and the Smithsonian has a museum in Washington, D.C. that is dedicated to Indian culture.

3   The frontier experience began when the first colonists settled on the east coast of the continent in the 1600s. It ended about 1890 when the last western lands were settled. The American frontier consisted of the relatively unsettled regions of the United States, usually found in the western part of the country. Here, both land and life were more rugged and primitive than in the more settled eastern part. As one frontier area was settled, people began moving farther west into the next unsettled area, sweeping aside the Native Americans as they went. By settling one frontier area after another, Americans moved across an entire continent that was 2,700 miles wide. They came to believe that it was their destiny to control all the land, and eventually they did. The Native Americans were given small portions of land, called *reservations*, to control, but the United States government broke many promises and created much misery for the Indian nations.

4   While most Americans have a more balanced view of the settling of the West, many Americans still see aspects of the frontier, its people, and their beliefs as inspiring examples of traditional American values in their original and purest form. How did the frontier movement, which lasted more than two centuries, help to shape these basic American values?

5   To be sure, the frontier provided many inspiring examples of hard work as forests were turned into towns, and towns into large cities. The competitive race for success was rarely more colorful or adventurous than on the western frontier. The rush for gold in California, for silver in Montana, and for fertile land in all the western territories provided endless stories of high adventure. When it was announced that almost 2 million acres of good land in Oklahoma would be opened for settlement in April 1889, thousands of settlers gathered on the border waiting for the exact time to be announced. When it

[1] *romanticized: talked or thought about things in a way that made them seem more attractive than they really were*

The 1889 rush to claim land in Oklahoma

was, they literally[2] raced into the territory in wagons and on horseback to claim the best land they could find for themselves.

6   Although daily life on the frontier was usually less dramatic than the frontier adventure stories would lead one to believe, even the ordinary daily life of frontier men and women exemplified[3] national values in a form which seemed purer to many Americans than the life of those living in the more settled, more cultivated eastern United States.

7   Individual freedom, self-reliance, and equality of opportunity have perhaps been the values most closely associated with the frontier heritage of America. Throughout their history, Americans have tended to view the frontier settler as the model of the free individual. This is probably because there was less control over the individual on the frontier than anywhere else in the United States. There were few laws and few established social or political institutions to confine people living on the frontier. In the United States, where freedom from outside social controls has traditionally been valued, the frontier has been idealized, and it still serves as a basis for a nostalgic[4] view of the early United States, a simpler time that was lost when the country became urbanized and more

[2] literally: according to the most basic or original meaning of a word or expression

[3] exemplified: was a very typical example of something

[4] nostalgic: feeling or expressing a slight sadness when remembering happy events or experiences from the past

complex. Many people living in the West today still hold these beliefs about freedom from government controls.

Self-Reliance and the Rugged Individualist

8   Closely associated with the frontier ideal of the free individual is the ideal of self-reliance. If the people living on the frontier were free of many of society's rules, they were also denied many of society's comforts and conveniences. They had to be self-reliant. Men and women often constructed their own houses, hunted, tended their own gardens, and made their own clothing and household items.

9   The self-reliant frontiersman has been idealized by Americans who have made him the classic American male hero: the *rugged individualist*. This hero is a man who has been made physically tough and rugged by the conditions of frontier life. He is skilled with guns and other weapons. He needs no help from others and often appears in stories as alone, unmarried, and without children. Standing alone, he can meet all the dangers that life on the frontier brings and he is strong enough to extend his protection beyond himself to others.

10   There are two types of heroic rugged individualists. Each is drawn from a different stage of life on the frontier. In the early frontier, which existed before the Civil War of the 1860s, the main struggle was man against the wilderness. Daniel Boone is probably the best-known hero of this era. Boone explored the wilderness country of Kentucky in the 1760s and 1770s. On one trip, he stayed in the wilderness for two years, successfully matching his strength and skills against the dangers of untamed nature and hostile Native Americans. In 1778, Boone was captured by Native Americans who were so impressed with his physical strength and skills that they made him a member of their tribe. Later, he succeeded in making a daring escape. Boone's heroic strength is seen primarily in his ability to master the harsh challenges of the wilderness. Although he had to fight against Indians from time to time, he is admired mainly as a survivor and conqueror of the wilderness, not as a fighter.

11   The second type of heroic rugged individualist is drawn from the last phase of the western frontier, which lasted from the 1860s until the 1890s. By this time, the wilderness was largely conquered. The struggle now was no longer man against nature, but man against man. Cattlemen and cowboys* fought against farmers, outlaws, Native Americans, and each other for control of the remaining western lands. The traditions of law and order were not yet well established, and physical violence was frequent. The frontier became known as "the Wild West."

12   It is not surprising, then, that the hero drawn from this period is primarily a fighter. He is admired for his ability to beat other men in fistfights,[5] or to win in a gunfight. The principal source of his heroism is his physical prowess[6] and he is strong enough to defeat two or three ordinary men at one time. This rugged individualist is typically a defender of good against evil.

13   This hero of the Wild West is based on memories of a number of gunfighters and lawmen of the time, men such as Jesse

---

* Cattlemen were men who raised large herds of cattle as a business and needed large areas of land on which their cattle could graze before being sent to market. Cowboys usually worked for the cattlemen. They would spend most of the day on horseback rounding up the cattle or taking them on long drives to market.

[5] fistfights: fights using bare hands with the fingers curled in toward the palm

[6] prowess: great skill at doing something

James and Wyatt Earp. The Wild West hero had more impact on the American idea of heroism than Daniel Boone, the hero of the earlier wilderness frontier. It is the Wild West hero who has inspired countless western movies; until the 1960s, 25 percent of all American movies made were westerns.

American Macho Heroes

14 Through movies and television programs, this Wild West hero has helped shape the American idea of "macho," or male, strength. For the most part, almost all American male heroes on television and in movies have traditionally had the common ability to demonstrate their strength through physical violence. Once the western macho hero had been created, the model for this hero was used in other settings—for soldiers in battle, and tough detectives and policemen fighting crime. From the cowboy heroes to the Terminator, Captain America, and Jenko, these heroes can fight with their fists, guns, and other weapons. Although there are movie and TV heroes who are respected more for their intelligence and sensitivity than their physical prowess, these classic macho male heroes still dominate much of American entertainment and video games. There are now also female versions of this macho image, including Katniss Everdeen, who competes in the Hunger Games armed with just a bow and arrow.

15 The image of the rugged individualist has been criticized for overlooking many factors that played a central part in the development of the frontier. First, the rugged individualist image overstates the importance of complete self-reliance and understates the importance of cooperation in building a new nation out of the wilderness. Second, because the image has been traditionally masculine, it has overlooked the importance of pioneer women and their strength, hard work, resourcefulness, and civilizing influence on the untamed frontier.

16 Finally, the rugged individualist image is criticized because of its emphasis on violence and the use of guns to solve problems. On the frontier, men did use guns to hunt and protect themselves and their families, but western movies romanticized and glorified gunfights in the Old West. The good guys and the bad guys "shot it out" in classic westerns such as *High Noon*. Incidentally, the classic old western movies always featured the "good guys" wearing white hats, while the "bad guys" wore black hats. Gradually, however, the western hero was largely replaced in the movies by the soldier or the crime fighter—guns still blazing—and the violence in movies, and later on TV and in video games, increased.

17 Some Americans worry about the impact of these entertainment heroes on the lives and imaginations of young people. At the very least, many young people have become desensitized[7] to the sight of violence and killings. In the twenty-first century, guns became a critical issue when there were shootings in several public schools and universities. It is all too easy for teenagers to get guns, and they are much more at risk of being killed by guns than adults are. The problem is particularly bad in the inner cities, where a number of young gang members carry guns. However, several of the most shocking incidents occurred in normally peaceful suburban communities, and now many schools require students to pass through metal detectors as they enter school buildings. Other recent mass shootings in public places included the wounding of Congresswoman Gabrielle Giffords in

[7] *desensitized: made emotionally insensitive*

2011, and the killing of people in a movie theater and children in an elementary school in 2012.

18 Americans have a long history of owning guns, and many people strongly believe having a gun in their house is an important right. In fact, the right to bear arms is even guaranteed by the Second Amendment of the Constitution, although there is debate about what the founding fathers meant by this:

> *A well-regulated militia, being necessary to the security of a free state, the right of the people to keep and bear arms, shall not be infringed.*

Today, there are well over 200 million privately held guns in the United States, enough for every adult to own one, and most estimates range from 270 to over 300 million. These are guns held by private citizens and do not include those possessed by the military or the police. Most firearms (rifles, shotguns, and hand guns) are owned by Americans who enjoy hunting, target practice, or gun collecting, and these individuals usually own more than one gun. Some firearms are owned by people who want their own gun for protection of their homes and families. For example, after the terrorist attacks of September 11, 2001, the sale of guns rose. Estimates are that anywhere from 25 percent to 45 percent of U.S. households now have at least one gun.

19 How Americans reacted to the terrorist attacks of September 11, 2001, reveals another legacy of the frontier: Americans' willingness to take the law into their own hands to protect themselves and their families. This tendency usually appears when Americans believe the police cannot adequately protect them. For example, when the passengers fought with the terrorists on the 9/11 flight that crashed in Pennsylvania, they were hailed as heroes.

20 The issue of gun control is very controversial in the United States, and people on both sides of the issue have strong opinions. Many Americans favor stricter government controls on the sale of guns, and they would not consider having a gun in their home. Others who oppose gun control feel strongly enough about the issue that they have created powerful political pressure groups, such as the National Rifle Association (NRA), which has worked to prevent most gun control legislation from passing. They argue that limiting gun sales will keep law-abiding citizens, not criminals, from owning guns. On the other side are gun-control organizations such as the Brady Campaign to Prevent Gun Violence named after Jim Brady, who was shot and became paralyzed when a man tried to kill President Ronald Reagan, and a new organization founded by Gabrielle Giffords

BROAD PUBLIC SUPPORT FOR MANY GUN POLICY PROPOSALS

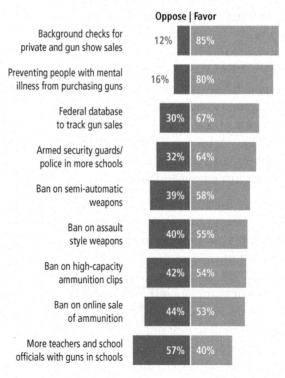

	Oppose	Favor
Background checks for private and gun show sales	12%	85%
Preventing people with mental illness from purchasing guns	16%	80%
Federal database to track gun sales	30%	67%
Armed security guards/ police in more schools	32%	64%
Ban on semi-automatic weapons	39%	58%
Ban on assault style weapons	40%	55%
Ban on high-capacity ammunition clips	42%	54%
Ban on online sale of ammunition	44%	53%
More teachers and school officials with guns in schools	57%	40%

Source: Pew Research Center Jan. 14, 2013.

and her husband Mark Kelly, Americans for Responsible Solutions. These groups are especially concerned about the sale of handguns and automatic assault rifles. They argue that American homes, particularly where there are children, are safer without guns. Interestingly, public opinion about gun control has remained about the same for over a decade, with Americans equally divided for and against it. After each mass shooting, the sale of guns rises, while those who oppose firearms (particularly automatic weapons) call for stronger gun control.

Inventiveness and the Can-Do Spirit

21 While the frontier idealized the rugged individual as the great American hero, it also respected the inventive individual. The need for self-reliance on the frontier encouraged a spirit of inventiveness. Frontier men and women not only had to provide most of their daily life essentials, but they were also constantly facing new problems and situations that demanded new solutions. Under these circumstances, they soon learned to experiment with new ways of doing things.

22 Observers from other countries were very impressed by the frontiersman's ability to invent useful new farm tools. They were equally impressed by the pioneer woman's ability to make clothing, candles, soap, and many other items needed for the daily life of her family. Lord Bryce, a famous English observer of American life, believed that the inventive skills of American pioneers enabled them to succeed at tasks beyond the abilities of most ordinary men and women in other countries. Although Americans in the more settled eastern regions of the United States created many of the most important inventions in the new nation, the western frontier had the effect of spreading the spirit of inventiveness throughout the population and helping it to become a national character trait.

23 The willingness to experiment and invent led to another American trait, a "can-do" spirit, or a sense of optimism that every

A nineteenth-century frontier family in front of their sod house

problem has a solution. Americans like to believe that a difficult problem can be solved immediately—an impossible one may take a little longer. They take pride in meeting challenges and overcoming difficult obstacles.[8] This can-do spirit has traditionally given Americans a sense of optimism about themselves and their country. Many have said that if the United States can land a man on the moon, no problem on earth is impossible. In the 1830s, Alexis de Tocqueville said that no other country in the world "more confidently seizes the future" than the United States. Traditionally, when times are hard, political leaders have reminded Americans of their frontier heritage and the tough determination of their pioneer ancestors; the can-do spirit is still a source of pride and inspiration.

Equality of Opportunity

24   The frontier is an expression of individual freedom and self-reliance in its purest (and most extreme) forms, and it is also a pure expression of the ideal of equality of opportunity. On the western frontier, there was more of a tendency for people to treat each other as social equals than there was in the more settled eastern regions of the country. On the frontier, the highest importance was placed on what people could do in their own lifetimes. Hardly any notice was taken of their ancestors. Frontier people were fond of saying, "What's above the ground is more important than what's beneath the ground."

25   Because so little attention was paid to a person's family background, the frontier offered a new beginning for many Americans who were seeking opportunities to advance themselves. One English visitor

to the United States in the early 1800s observed that if Americans experienced disappointment or failure in business, in politics, or even in love, they moved west to make a new beginning. The frontier offered millions of Americans a source of hope for a fresh start in the competitive race for success and for a better life. On the frontier, there was a continuing need for new farmers, skilled laborers, merchants, lawyers, and political leaders.

26   There were fewer differences in wealth between rich and poor on the frontier than in the more settled regions of the nation. People lived, dressed, and acted more alike on the frontier than in other parts of the United States. The feeling of equality was shared by hired helpers who refused to be called "servants" or to be treated as such. One European visitor observed, "The clumsy gait[9] and bent body of our peasant is hardly ever seen here. . . . Everyone walks erect[10] and easy." Wealthy travelers to the frontier were warned not to show off their wealth or to act superior to others if they wished to be treated politely.

27   The American frontier may not be *the key* to American development, as Frederick Jackson Turner said, but it is certainly one major factor. The frontier provided the space and conditions that helped to strengthen the American ideals of individual freedom, self-reliance, and equality of opportunity. On the frontier, these ideals were enlarged and made workable. Frontier ideas and customs were continuously passed along to the more settled parts of the United States as newer frontier regions took the place of older ones during a westward march of settlers which lasted more than two centuries. In this way, many of the frontier values became national values.

[8] obstacles: things that make it difficult for someone to succeed

[9] clumsy gait: walking in an awkward way

[10] erect: in an upright position

AFTER YOU READ

Understand Main Ideas

A. Check the predictions you made on page 79 before you read the chapter. Work with a partner. Answer these questions about the main ideas.

1. What are the three values that are traditionally associated with the frontier heritage?

2. What two new values are introduced in this chapter?

3. What are the two types of rugged individualists?

4. Describe someone with a can-do spirit.

5. What personal characteristics did the frontier settlers share?

B. In academic writing, paragraphs often begin with a topic sentence that contains the main idea. Read and highlight the first sentence of each paragraph of the reading. Then choose one main idea from each of the five main sections that you think is the most important. Write these ideas below. Compare your list with a partner's.

1. _____

2. _____

3. _____

4. _____

5. _____

Understand Details

Write **T** if the statement is true and **F** if it is false according to the information in the chapter.

_____ 1. The frontier experience began in about 1890 and is still continuing in the American West today.

_____ 2. One reason why many Americans are still fascinated by the frontier period is that it represents a time when the traditional basic American values were expressed in their purest form.

_____ 3. The settling of the frontier did little to affect the lives of the American Indians.

_____ 4. Daniel Boone is an example of the earliest type of rugged individualist hero, a man who fights against the wilderness.

_____ 5. The primary qualities of the American macho hero are intelligence, sensitivity, and caring for others.

_____ 6. It is difficult for the average American to buy a gun, so very few people own them.

_____ 7. Members of the NRA (and many gun owners) believe the right to own a gun is guaranteed in the United States Constitution.

_____ 8. The can-do spirit came from the willingness of the pioneers to work together on a cooperative project for the good of all.

_____ 9. On the frontier, family name and ancestry were more important than what a person could do.

_____ 10. On the frontier, the rich and the poor rarely mixed, and social class was more important than in the more settled regions.

Talk About It

Work in small groups and choose one or more of the following questions to discuss.

1. What effect do you think seeing violence on TV or in movies has on children? What happens when people become desensitized to violence?

2. What qualities should a true hero have? Who are some of your own personal heroes? Why do you admire and respect these people?

3. Would you have a gun in your own home? Why or why not?

4. If you were going to live in the wilderness for a week, what ten things would you take with you? Why?

5. Some Americans are nostalgic for the Old West, and there may be a period of your country's history that is romanticized in a similar way. If you could travel back in time to anywhere in the world, what place and what period in history would you like to visit? Why?

SKILL BUILDING

Improve Your Reading Skills: Scanning

Scanning is looking for a specific piece of information. Scan the chapter to find these dates. Write what happened next to the date to complete the timeline. Some are done for you.

1600s: _Settlers established colonies on the East Coast_ _____

1760s and 1770s: _____

1778: _Boone was captured by Native Americans_ _____

1860s: _____

April 1889: _____

1890 _____

Until 1960s: <u>*25 percent of all American movies made were Westerns*</u>

1980s: _____

2001: _____

Develop Critical Thinking Skills

Evaluating Pros and Cons: *Some consider space to be the final frontier, but spending money on space exploration has become controversial. Should we continue to support the international space station? Should we go to the moon again or plan to visit Mars? What are the benefits that have come from space exploration? What scientific discoveries have been made? Should we continue to send astronauts into space, or should we concentrate on unmanned missions? Think about the pros and cons of space exploration and fill out the chart below. You may wish to do some research on the Internet to get ideas.*

Pros of Space Exploration	Cons of Space Exploration

Build Your Vocabulary

Use Context Clues

Review the four kinds of context clues on pages 15–16 of Chapter 1. Use context clues to choose the correct words to fill in the blanks.

desensitized	fascinated	nostalgic	romanticize
exemplified	fists	obstacles	

1. In many action movies, the heroes are expected to be able to fight with their

   _____.

2. Some people prefer to _____ life on the frontier; they do not

   want to look at its negative aspects.

3. If you are reading a book that is so interesting that you can't put it down, you

   are _____ by the book.

4. Frontier people were good examples of the American national values; these

   people _____ these values.

5. In order to succeed, people living on the frontier had to overcome many

   difficulties and _____, such as clearing the land for farming.

6. Americans like to remember the days on the frontier; they feel

   _____ about the Old West.

7. Some Americans worry that their children are becoming

   _____ to the violence and killing on television. It doesn't

   seem to bother their children.

More AWL Words

Test your knowledge of these AWL words in the chapter by matching the words
with their definitions.

_____ 1. area   a. someone who is still alive after almost being
                          killed

_____ 2. automatic   b. to keep someone in a place that they cannot leave

_____ 3. aware   c. something that tests strength, skill, or ability

_____ 4. challenge   d. someone paid to discover information

_____ 5. classic   e. easily noticed or understood; obvious

_____ 6. confine   f. the act of working with someone to achieve
                          something

_____ 7. consist   g. realizing that a problem exists

_____ 8. construct   h. to build something large

_____ 9. cooperation   i. designed to operate by itself

_____ 10. deny   j. a fairly large area of a state

_____ 11. detective   k. a single thing in a set, group, or list

_____ 12. evident   l. to be made of a number of things

_____ 13. feature   m. to say that something is not true

_____ 14. item   n. considered important, with a value that lasts for a
                          long time

_____ 15. phase   o. one of the stages of a process

_____ 16. region   p. something you notice because it seems interesting

_____ 17. survivor   q. a particular part of a country or city

Word Partners

Match the word partners to form collocations. Then use the correct collocations in the paragraph.

_____ 1. unsettled   a. fathers

_____ 2. law-abiding   b. spirit

_____ 3. can-do   c. individualism

_____ 4. founding   d. citizens

_____ 5. physical   e. region

_____ 6. rugged   f. prowess

Many Americans believe that when the _____ wrote the
                                              1
Constitution, they meant to ensure the right of the people to own guns. They

would argue that _____ should be allowed to keep guns in their
                          2
homes. The frontier strengthened the tradition of owning guns because it was an

_____, and settlers needed guns for hunting and protection. They
          3
had to be tough, and part of the frontier legacy is the _____ and
                                                                  4
_____ of Western movie heroes. Frontier settlers were also known for
          5
their inventiveness and their _____ .
                                        6

Proverbs and Sayings

Ask Americans, if possible, to explain these proverbs and sayings about succeeding on your own or being tough. What similar proverbs and sayings are there in your culture?

1. Pull yourself up by the bootstraps.
2. If at first you don't succeed, try and try again.
3. Actions speak louder than words.
4. Life is what you make it.
5. Every problem has a solution.
6. When the going gets tough, the tough get going.

Ask Yourself

Do you agree or disagree with each of the following statements? Put a check under the number that indicates how you feel.

+2 = Strongly agree

+1 = Agree

 0 = No opinion

−1 = Disagree

−2 = Strongly disagree

	+2	+1	0	−1	−2
1. I love action movies that have a lot of gunfights.	____	____	____	____	____
2. A real man should be able to defend himself well and even win in a fistfight.	____	____	____	____	____
3. Intelligence and sensitivity in a man are more important than physical strength.	____	____	____	____	____
4. Watching fights in movies and on TV shows probably doesn't hurt children.	____	____	____	____	____
5. Having a gun in your home is a good way to protect yourself against robbers.	____	____	____	____	____
6. I believe people should not own guns and there should be strict laws controlling the sale of them.	____	____	____	____	____
7. Every problem has a solution.	____	____	____	____	____
8. What you do is more important than who your ancestors were.	____	____	____	____	____

Your teacher will place the numbers +2, +1, 0, −1, −2 around the room with the zero in the middle. As the teacher reads the above statements, walk to the number that reflects your opinion. Explain your choice.

Ask Americans

Read the statements from the previous exercise to several Americans. If this is not possible, try to interview people from several different countries. Ask them if they agree or disagree with each statement. Write their opinions in your notebook.

Think, Pair, Share

Think about this question, and write your answer. Then share it with a partner and with another pair of students.

> *In 2003, Arnold Schwarzenegger was elected Governor of California in a special election. During his campaign, he frequently referred to his movie role as "the Terminator" and talked about how he was going to clean up the state government. He was re-elected in 2006 and served as governor until 2011. Some people nicknamed him "the Governator." Based on the information in this chapter, why do you think this image appealed to Californian voters?*

People Watching

> *Americans are very conscious of space and have a strong sense of territory—that is, the idea that a particular space belongs to them. Children may have a special place to play with their toys; Mom may have her own desk; Dad may have a workshop. Observe Americans at home, in a public place, or in a social situation to see how they use space. (Watch TV shows, if you are not in the United States.) If someone has been sitting in a particular chair and gets up, does the person tend to come back to the same chair? When someone asks, "Is that seat taken?" what does that person mean?*

Conduct the following experiment and record the results in your journal.

Rule: When an American sits down at a table where a stranger is sitting alone, the American will choose a seat across from the other person or at least one chair away. The space is divided in half between them, and personal belongings must be kept on each person's respective side of an imaginary boundary line.

Observation: Observe people sitting in a public place where there are tables, such as a cafeteria or library. What happens when a stranger sits down at a table where a person is sitting alone? If someone sits down next to a stranger, what happens? How do the people acknowledge each other's presence? Does the person who was sitting there first move his or her belongings?

Experiment: Choose a table where a stranger is sitting alone and sit down in the next chair. What happens? Sit across from someone at a table and put some personal belongings (such as books) on the table in front of you. Push them toward the other person so that they are more than halfway across the table. What is the person's reaction?

Observe the Media

Work in small groups and choose one of the following activities to do together.

1. Cowboys and the Old West are frequently used in advertisements for blue jeans, SUVs, trucks, cars, and other American products. What image do they have? Why does this image help sell this or that product? Collect examples of ads in magazines or newspapers that use cowboys or western themes. Make a collage and share it with your classmates. Explain what the message is to the people who may buy these products.

2. Watch American TV shows or movies that have male heroes. Compare the heroes of several shows. How do they compare with the description of *American macho* presented in this chapter? What personality traits do they have? Compare the heroes of several shows. Reread the section on page 83 for help with descriptions.

Use the Internet

Choose one of these topics and do research on the Internet.

1. The rush to the West to find gold or silver created a number of very wealthy towns with hotels, opera houses, and beautiful houses. Today, many of these cities are "ghost towns." Some towns have no people living in them; in others only a few people remain. Choose one of these ghost towns and find information about it. Answer the questions, and then write a summary of what you learned about the town.

Restored Western ghost town in Cody, Wyoming

Bodie or Calico, California	Pinos Altos, New Mexico
Gold Hill or Silver City, Utah	Goldfield, Nevada
Shakespeare Ghost Town, New Mexico	

   • Why did people come to the town?

   • What can be seen there today?

   • What did you find most interesting about the town?

2. From May 1804 until September 1806, Meriwether Lewis and William Clark traveled from St. Louis, Missouri, to the Oregon coast, and back again. Work with a partner to find out more about this historic trip. Do an online search for "Lewis and Clark Expedition." Answer these questions.

   • Who was the U.S. President who ordered the expedition?

   • What territory had the United States purchased from France in 1803?

   • What was the purpose of the expedition?

   • Who was Sacajawea?

   • What route did Lewis and Clark follow?

   • What important discoveries did they make?

WRITE ABOUT IT

CIVILIAN FIREARMS OWNERSHIP, 2006 OR LATEST YEAR AVAILABLE

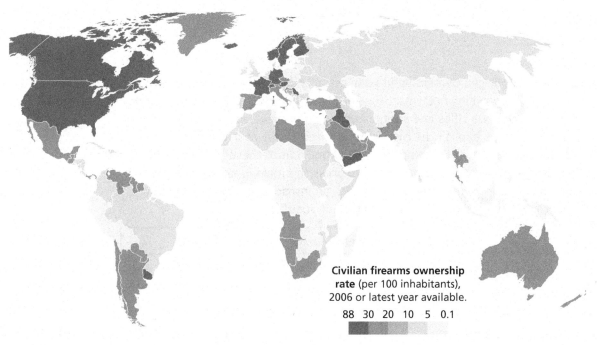

Civilian firearms ownership **rate** (per 100 inhabitants), 2006 or latest year available.

88 30 20 10 5 0.1

TOP TEN COUNTRIES WITH CIVILIAN FIREARMS OWNERSHIP

(per 100 people)

- United States — 88.8
- Yemen — 54.8
- Switzerland — 45.7
- Finland — 45.3
- Serbia — 37.8
- Cyprus — 36.4
- Iraq — 34.2
- Uruguay — 31.8
- Sweden — 31.6
- Norway — 31.3

TOTAL CIVILIAN FIREARMS HOLDINGS, SELECTED COUNTRIES

(in millions)

- United States — 270
- India — 46
- China — 40
- Germany — 25
- France — 19
- Brazil — 15
- Mexico — 15
- Russian Federation — 13
- Yemen — 12
- South Africa — 6
- England and Wales — 3
- Colombia — 3
- Ukraine — 3

Civilian Firearms Ownership: A United Nations Map of the World

This map shows the rate of civilian (or private) gun ownership in countries around the world. It indicates how many firearms are owned per 100 inhabitants in each country, not counting the military or police. The first bar graph below the map lists the top ten countries with the highest per capita (per 100 people) rate, and the other bar graph shows the total number of guns owned in selected countries. How does the United States rank by each measure? Notice that Switzerland, Finland, Sweden, and Norway are also on the top ten list. Why does the second bar graph compare the number of guns in the United States with India and China? Why is gun ownership so high in the United States?

This chapter has explored the profound influence of the historical frontier period on the values and beliefs of Americans. It includes an explanation of how the gun culture of the United States evolved on the frontier and continues today. Reread the parts of the chapter that talk about how Americans feel about guns, paragraphs 9, 12–14, 16–18, and 20. What do these paragraphs tell you about why the rate of gun ownership is so high in the country today?

Write a report about gun ownership in your country. Include information about the laws concerning owning firearms, how people feel about guns, whether there are as many handguns as rifles and shotguns, how guns are used, and any historical information that helps explain the ownership of firearms in your country. Use a graphic organizer to plan your composition. Fill out one of these "T"s for each paragraph. Write a clear topic sentence to express the main idea, and then list the supporting details. Remember to start with an introduction and end with a conclusion that refers back to the introduction, if possible.

Main Idea
Supporting Details

EXPLORE ON YOUR OWN

Books to Read

Stephen E. Ambrose, *Undaunted Courage: Meriwether Lewis, Thomas Jefferson and the Opening of the American West*—This book is a best-selling account of the expedition by Lewis and Clark through the American West in the early 1800s, as they traveled from St. Louis, Missouri, to the Pacific Ocean.

Dee Brown, *Bury My Heart at Wounded Knee: An Indian History of the American West*—In this best-selling book, Brown presents a documented historical account of the systematic destruction of the American Indian during the last half of the 1800s.

Willa Cather, *O Pioneers!*—A classic novel written in 1913 about the physical hardships of the frontier and the enormous changes it brought to the United States.

Larry McMurtry, *Lonesome Dove*—A best-selling novel about life, love, and adventure on the American frontier.

O. E. Rölvaag, *Giants in the Earth: A Saga of the Prairie*—This is the classic story of a Norwegian pioneer family's struggles as they try to make a new life on the American frontier.

Movies to See

Bowling for Columbine—In this controversial documentary, filmmaker Michael Moore explores the roots of America's fascination with guns and violence.

Dances with Wolves—A soldier sent to a remote western Civil War outpost makes friends with wolves and Indians, eventually falling in love with a white woman raised by the Indians.

Far and Away—A young Irishman who loses his home after his father's death decides to go to America to begin a new life and eventually goes to live on the frontier.

High Noon—In this classic movie, a sheriff who must face a returning deadly enemy finds that his own town refuses to help him.

True Grit—A young girl hires Rooster Cogburn, a Deputy U.S. Marshal, to hunt for the murderer of her father.

Native American dancing with rings—Hopi hoop dance

CHAPTER 5

THE HERITAGE OF ABUNDANCE

For millions of people throughout this world, during the past three centuries, America has symbolized plenty, wealth, and abundance of goods.

David Potter (1910–1971)

How did the abundance of natural resources affect the development of American values and how is abundance being redefined today?

BEFORE YOU READ

Preview Vocabulary

A. Read the following sentences from the chapter and notice the words in italics. These key AWL words will help you understand the chapter. Use context clues to help you figure out the meanings. Then choose which definition is best for the italicized word.

_____ 1. In the aristocratic European nations the settlers left behind, the material wealth and comforts of the ruling classes were *guaranteed* by their birth.
   a. certain to happen
   b. unlikely to happen

_____ 2. Unlike many countries where the love of material things was seen as a vice, a mark of weak moral character, in the United States it was seen as a virtue, a positive *incentive* to work hard, and a reward for successful efforts.
   a. encouragement
   b. discouragement

_____ 3. It was not until the twentieth century that Americans began to think of themselves more as *consumers* than producers.
   a. someone who buys and uses products and services
   b. someone who makes things to sell

_____ 4. Advertising *techniques* were so successful that over time they began to be used to change Americans' attitudes, behavior, and beliefs.
   a. new products and inventions
   b. special ways of doing something

_____ 5. *Technological* devices that can engage us 24 hours a day have increased the pace of life in the United States, and they have changed the way we receive and exchange information.
   a. based on modern knowledge about science and computers
   b. expensive, old pieces of equipment

_____ 6. Big Data is an extraordinary knowledge *revolution* that is sweeping, almost invisibly, through business, academia, government, health care, and everyday life.
   a. a complete change in ways of thinking, methods of working
   b. a very expensive action that people do not like

_____ 7. In order to be valuable and useful, Big Data has to be managed. One way is to rely on *experts* to analyze large amounts of data and then tell us what is important.
   a. people who have special knowledge or skills
   b. people who enjoy using the Internet

_____ 8. Diamandis, Kotler, and others detail the ways that Americans can join with individuals around the world to find *innovative* solutions for providing clean water, enough food, and adequate shelter to everyone.
   a. methods that have been used successfully for many years
   b. new, different, and better methods

_____ 9. Americans viewed the material wealth and abundance of the United States as an ever-*expanding* pie that would continue to grow so that all people could get a bigger piece of a bigger pie.
   a. becoming larger
   b. becoming smaller

B. Read the quotation by David Potter at the beginning of the chapter. Find the words with the following meanings. Write each word next to its meaning.

_____ 1. periods of 100 years

_____ 2. represented an idea or quality

_____ 3. products

_____ 4. enough, or more than enough

_____ 5. a large quantity of something

Preview Content

A. Think about the David Potter quotation and discuss the questions with your classmates.

1. Do you agree with David Potter? Why or why not? What is the source of American abundance?

2. What are the advantages and disadvantages of having abundance? List the positive and negative aspects in the chart.

American Abundance	
Plus +	Minus –

3. Think about your daily activities. What do you throw away every day?

4. How do you use the Internet? How many communication devices do you have?

B. Read the headings in the chapter and look at the illustrations. Write three topics that you predict will be covered in this chapter.

1. _____

2. _____

3. _____

A HISTORY OF ABUNDANCE

1 Although the population of the United States accounts for only about 5 percent of the total population of the world, Americans use up more than 20 percent of the world's energy per year, generating about four and a half pounds of trash and garbage per person each day.

WHAT HAPPENS TO STUFF WE THROW AWAY?

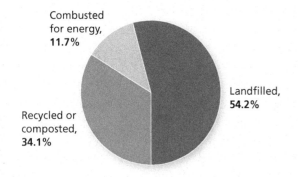

Combusted for energy, **11.7%**

Landfilled, **54.2%**

Recycled or composted, **34.1%**

Based on the 2010 Municipal Solid Waste Characterization Report

Only a country that has great abundance could afford to throw so much away. America has sometimes been criticized as a "throw-away" country, a land where there is so much abundance that people are sometimes viewed as wasteful. Scholars like David Potter, an American historian, believe that the abundant material wealth of the United States has been a major factor in the development of the American character.

2 This abundance is the gift of nature. In what is now the continental United States, there are more than 3 million square miles of land. When the European settlers first arrived in the seventeenth and eighteenth centuries, much of this land was rich, fertile farmland, with an abundance of trees and animals. There were relatively few Native Americans living on this land, and they had neither the weapons nor the organization necessary to keep the European settlers out. Never again can human beings discover such a large area of rich, unfarmed land, with such a small population and such great undeveloped natural resources.

3 But it would be a mistake to say that the abundant natural resources of North America were the only reason why the United States became a wealthy nation. The beliefs, determination, and hard work of the early settlers were equally important.

4 In the aristocratic European nations the settlers left behind, the material wealth and comforts of the ruling classes were guaranteed by their birth. Therefore, as Tocqueville said, the wealthy took these things for granted and assumed they would always have their wealth and social status. The poor people in those aristocratic nations also did not concern themselves with wealth, since they knew that they had little hope of becoming wealthy or changing their status.

5 In the early years of the United States, however, wealth and social position were not permanently determined at birth. The idea of equality of opportunity in America made the level of material wealth of both the rich and the poor much less certain. At any time, the rich might lose some of their wealth and the poor might increase theirs. Therefore, all classes in American society thought about protecting their material possessions and looked for ways to acquire more. Tocqueville believed that this was not so much a matter of greed; rather, it was a matter of their insecurity. People might be naturally insecure if their material wealth, and that of their children, could change so rapidly either upward or downward during a lifetime, or even a single generation. Tocqueville concluded that it was extremely important both to rich Americans and poor Americans to increase their personal wealth and material

comforts. Therefore, the entire population joined in the task of increasing the nation's material abundance as quickly as possible.

6 Tocqueville visited the United States fifty years after the nation had won its independence from England. He was impressed with the great progress made in such a short time. Although the country was still in an early stage of development, and there was not much money available for investment, the United States had already made great progress in both trading and manufacturing. It had already become the world's second leading sea power and had constructed the longest railroads in the world. Tocqueville worried, however, about the effect of all this material success. In such a society, materialism could be made into a moral value in itself rather than a means to an end.

7 Tocqueville's concern, to a large extent, became a reality. In the process of creating a land of abundance, Americans began to judge themselves by materialistic standards. Unlike many countries where the love of material things was seen as a vice or a mark of weak moral character, in the United States it was seen as a virtue, a positive incentive to work hard, and a reward for successful efforts.

8 Traditionally, the people of the United States have been proud of their nation's ability to produce material wealth so that they could maintain a high standard of living. This helps to explain why Americans use materialistic standards not only to judge themselves as individuals, but also to judge themselves as a nation. And the opportunity to share in the good life has attracted immigrants to the United States for generations.

From Producers to Consumers

9 The emphasis on producing wealth and maintaining a high standard of living developed over a period of time. In the 1700s and 1800s, most Americans thought of themselves more as producers than consumers. As farmers they produced food and many of their own household goods, and later as factory workers they produced manufactured goods. It was not until the twentieth century that Americans began to think of themselves more as consumers than as producers. This image change is probably due to the coming of mass advertising, made possible by the beginning of radio broadcasts in the 1920s and the spread of television programming in the 1950s. In the 1920s, businesses agreed to pay for, or sponsor, radio programs that would run short commercials advertising their products. Companies were able to reach large numbers of Americans at one time to convince them to buy their products; the emphasis was now on consuming.

10 The development of mass advertising continued with television, and by the end of the 1960s, scholars had begun to study the effect of mass advertising on American society. Historian David Potter observed that mass advertising in the United States had become so important in size and influence that it should be viewed as an institution, such as the school or the church. One effect of advertising was that sponsors had some control over the content of television programs. If businesses did not like the content, they could withdraw their sponsorship. A second effect was that advertising techniques were so successful that over time they began to be used to change Americans' attitudes, behavior, and beliefs. For example, the government ran ads to urge teenagers not to use drugs; charities had ads to ask for donations; and politicians paid to advertise their campaigns. In the 2012 presidential election, candidates spent a total of more than $900 million on TV ads alone, with most of the money spent in states where the race was competitive.

11 Advertising money follows the consumer as well as the voter. Today, almost all homes in the United States have at least one television set (the average household has more than two), and the family TV is in use about eight hours a day. Some estimates are that the average American sees about 50,000 commercials a year. When popular events such as the Super Bowl are on, mass advertising may reach 50 million or more viewers during a single program. In addition to radio and television, there are ads in magazines and newspapers, and marketers try to reach people outside their homes with ads everywhere. By 2007, many Americans felt mass advertising was out of control. A *New York Times* article, "Anywhere the Eye Can See, It's Likely to See an Ad," talked about the (then) new video screens in New York taxicabs and public elevators, and the new, ever-changing digital billboards. New York City's Times Square is the best-known and most spectacular example of American outdoor advertising, with its huge digital billboards that have ads showing 24 hours a day.

Times Square, New York—the city that never sleeps

12 And then came the Internet. By 2008, more than 75 percent of homes in the United States had a computer, and over the next few years, Americans abandoned their desktops for laptops, tablets, and smartphones. Over 80 percent of adults 18 and older now use the Internet, and the numbers continue to grow. This use of digital media has had a profound effect on advertising: it has changed the emphasis from mass advertising to target marketing. That is, advertisers are now creating ads for individual users on the Internet, using digital information about their use of digital media. Perhaps mass advertising has reached the point when most consumers simply ignore most of the ads, and businesses have learned that they can reach consumers better by appealing to their individual buying habits and other aspects of their lives. Some aspects that target marketers consider are geographic location and climate, gender, age, income, and education, as well as people's values, attitudes, and lifestyles.

What American Consumers Like

13 People in the advertising business, and others who study American society, are interested in the question: *What does the American consumer like?* Max Lerner, a well-known scholar who has studied American society, has said that American consumers are particularly fond of three things: comfort, cleanliness, and novelty.

14 Lerner believes that the American love of comfort perhaps goes back to the frontier experience, where life was tough and there were very few comforts. This experience may have created a strong desire in the

pioneers and their children for goods that would make life more comfortable. Today, the Americans' love of comfort is seen in the way they furnish their homes, design their cars, and travel. How Americans choose a new mattress for their bed is an example of the American love of comfort. Many Americans will go to a store where beds are set up and lie down on several mattresses to see which is the most comfortable.

Bath time for the family dog

15 Cleanliness is also highly valued by Americans. Perhaps their Puritan heritage has played some role in their desire for cleanliness. The Puritans, a strict Protestant church group whose members were among the first settlers of America, stressed the need to cleanse[1] the body of dirt and of all evil tendencies, which for them included sexual desire. The saying "Cleanliness is next to godliness" reflects the belief of most Americans that it is important to keep not only their bodies, but also their clothes, their houses, their cars, and even their pets clean and smelling good. Indeed, many Americans are offended by anyone who does not follow their accepted standards of cleanliness.

16 Marketing to American consumers requires an awareness of their desire for cleanliness. In his book, *The Power of Habit: Why We Do What We Do in Life and Business,* Charles Duhigg tells of Proctor & Gamble's (P&G) experience marketing Febreze, a spray that makes things smell good. Febreze actually destroys the molecules of odors, and P&G was sure it would be a great seller. Their ads focused on how their product could eliminate, not just cover up, bad smells—even pet smells. To their shock, the product didn't sell. After analyzing the behavior of potential customers, they discovered that people didn't want to be reminded that their houses smelled bad and therefore needed Febreze. P&G changed their ad campaign completely. Instead of marketing it as a cleaning product, they presented it as a reward for when the cleaning was finished: "Who wants to admit their house stinks? . . . On the other hand, lots of people crave a nice smell after they've spent thirty minutes cleaning. . . . Within a year, customers had spent more then $230 million on the product." Sometime later, P&G began reminding customers that Febreze also gets rid of odors.

17 Along with cleanliness and comfort, Americans love having things that are new and different. Perhaps this love of novelty is reinforced by their pride in their inventiveness. Americans have always

[1] cleanse: to make something completely clean

been interested in inventing new products and improving old ones. Advertisements encourage people to get rid of old products and try new ones, whether the old ones still work or not. And if they cannot afford to buy something now, advertisers encourage consumers to charge it on a credit card—"Buy now—pay later."

18　In addition to the three qualities that Lerner mentions, there is a fourth quality that American consumers like very much—convenience. In the late 1900s, there was a dramatic increase in such labor-saving devices as automatic washing machines, clothes dryers, dishwashers, food processors, microwave ovens, garbage disposals, and power lawn mowers. Today, all of these, and many more, are found in a typical suburban home. The American desire for convenience also created the concept of *fast-food* restaurants such as McDonald's and KFC, which are now found in every city and almost every small town in the United States, and are now exported all over the world. For those who prefer to prepare their food at home, American grocery stores are full of convenience foods that are packaged and ready to cook, or are even precooked.

19　Like microwaves and dishwashers, fast-food restaurants and convenience foods save the American consumer time that would otherwise be spent fixing meals or cleaning up. These conveniences, however, do not cause Americans to be less busy. Women now make up more than one-half of the American workforce, and the majority of mothers with children under the age of eighteen work outside the home. With both parents employed, children eat a lot of take-out food, a significant contributor to childhood obesity.[2] These conveniences reflect not so much a leisurely lifestyle as a busy one in which even minutes of time are too valuable to be wasted. Alexis de Tocqueville was one of the first to see in this a curious paradox[3] in the American character. He observed that Americans were so busy working to acquire comforts and conveniences that they were unable to relax and to enjoy leisure time when they had it. Today, as in Tocqueville's time, many Americans have what one medical doctor has called "the hurry sickness."

An Abundance of Technology

20　Technological devices that can engage us 24 hours a day have increased the pace of life in the United States, and they have changed the way we receive and exchange information. For example, computers and other digital devices have changed our television viewing habits. By 2003, the majority of American homes had either cable or satellite TV. Consequently, in addition to the broadcast networks—ABC, CBS, NBC, and Fox—most Americans can now choose from hundreds of TV channels. There is everything from 24-hour news to movies, children's programs, reality shows, sports, and games, and there are many specialty channels that focus on cooking, home improvement, music, travel, history, drama, comedy, public affairs, entertainment news, and lifestyles. There are also public TV networks offering educational and cultural programs, supported by contributions from viewers, donations from private companies and foundations, and government grants.

21　The result of all these choices is that the TV viewing audience has become more fragmented, with a smaller percentage watching any given program. This means that mass advertisers must also use other ways to reach the buying public. Some companies pay for product placement in

---

[2] obesity: *the condition of being too heavy in a way that is dangerous to your health*

[3] paradox: *a situation that seems strange because it involves two ideas or qualities that are opposite or very different*

TV shows and movies—the hero drinking a Coke, for example, and many companies are doing target marketing. Most large companies do extensive market research to find individuals who are most likely to buy their products. They then focus on delivering their ads to these individuals, often using the Internet and other direct-marketing techniques.

22 Advertising money is going to the Internet also because more and more Americans are online instead of watching TV at all. Increasingly, Americans are using their computer, smartphone, tablet, or other digital device—instead of television—to get their news and entertainment. This is especially true of the Millennials, young people who came of age at the start of the new millennium, the year 2000. Because they are such a desirable market group, advertising money is especially targeting them on the Internet. Traditional sources of news such as TV, newspapers, and news magazines have lost advertising revenue with serious consequences. Many big city papers have gone out of business because there are not enough readers to attract the advertisers needed to pay publishing costs. Some news magazines have gone to online publishing only. The problem is that much of the advertising money in papers and news magazines traditionally went to support the covering of news events. News reporters worked on stories for months to gather and analyze details of complicated and important stories. With a loss of advertising revenue, news organizations have had to downsize, employing fewer staff reporters. As a result, in American media it is sometimes difficult to get in-depth coverage and analysis of news in the United States and around the world.

23 The Internet and the 24-hour cable news networks have created a desire for instant reporting and explanation of news events, sometimes leading to factual mistakes or the wrong interpretation of what is happening. Sometimes the news can be superficial and even silly. A great deal of time and attention is paid to the lives of celebrities, for example, resulting in a mixture of news and entertainment sometimes called "newsertainment" or "infotainment." However, the Internet can also be a source of valuable news reports by eyewitnesses of events around the world, although it may be difficult to verify the accuracy of videos taken on iPhones. Another aspect of the Internet is that individuals can customize, or personalize, the news they receive about current events, and they can set up their own news sites or blogs. Increasingly social media such as Facebook, Twitter, Tumblr, Pinterest, and others are informing and shaping the opinions of their users, as more and more Americans spend more and more time online.

The majority of American families have access to the Internet.

An Abundance of Knowledge: Big Data

24 The first time most Americans heard the term *Big Data* was probably during the 2012 presidential election. President Obama's campaign had purchased huge quantities of digital information on prospective voters. This Big Data, collected from many sources and then carefully analyzed, allowed the Obama team to run the presidential campaign in a whole new way, with such a deep understanding of their potential voters that they could win them over vote by vote. In doing this, the campaign "overturned the long dominance of TV advertising in U.S. politics and created something new in the world: a national campaign run like a local ward election, where the interests of individual voters were known and addressed," according to *MIT Technology Review*.

25 Rick Smolan and Jennifer Erwitt have written a large "coffee table" book called *The Human Face of Big Data*. Smolan and Erwitt say that some people define Big Data as more information than can fit on a personal computer. Others say that it is more than just the quantity of the information—it is also the tools that allow us to see patterns and make use of the knowledge. "Big Data is an extraordinary knowledge revolution that is sweeping, almost invisibly, through business, academia, government, health care, and everyday life," the authors state. Here are some startling facts they reveal about this revolution:

> The average person today processes more data in a single day than a person in the 1500s did in an entire lifetime.

> According to BabyCenter.com, today one in three children born in the United States already have [sic] an online presence (usually in the form of a sonogram[4]) before they are born. That number grows to 92 percent by the time they are two. . . . with a third of all children's photos and information posted online within weeks of their birth.

> Each of us now leaves a trail of digital exhaust,[5] an infinite stream of phone records, texts, browser histories, GPS data, and other information that will live on forever.

26 This supply of Big Data about us raises important personal questions. What happens to all this information? What will it mean to have a complete digital record of our lives from before birth to death? How will this information about us be stored? Who owns our personal information, and who decides how it can be used? Some of these questions are already being debated. For example, who owns the photos we post or store on the Internet? There are also questions about how the government and law enforcement agencies can use our personal information. What can governments do with it? What about the police? And, of course, there is already a concern about criminals and terrorists having access to knowledge about us. Identity theft[6] on the Internet is a big problem, and there are worries that terrorists could get control of important national infrastructure, such as defense[7] networks or power systems.

27 Big Data also raises larger questions about how humanity uses all this new information. Until the coming

---

[4] *sonogram: an image of an unborn baby inside its mother's body*

[5] *exhaust: a gas or stream that is produced when a machine is working*

[6] *identity theft: a crime in which someone steals personal information about another person, such as a bank account number, and uses this information to deceive other people and get money or goods*

[7] *defense: the act of protecting something or someone from attack or destruction*

of computers, the human race often suffered from a lack of knowledge; now many believe we have too much of it. Every 18 months computing power doubles, and the amount of knowledge we have is increasing exponentially. (1+1=2+2=4+4=8+8=16, and so on.) This incredible[8] limitless[9] supply of information is a double-edge sword—it cuts both ways. That is, it has both positive and negative effects. On the positive side, it enables us to solve important problems and can bring many benefits to humanity. On the negative side, it can overwhelm us and may even cause us to make poor decisions. Brain research reveals that when we try to process too much information, the decision-making part of our brain actually shuts down. We then focus on the last piece of information and forget important facts that came before. Research shows that we then make bad decisions that are more affected by our emotions. What we should do is stop, do something else, and let our subconscious[10] mind sort through the data for us. Our subconscious mind evaluates the data, sees connections, and makes creative use of the knowledge. When we return to the task, our brains can then see what is important and enable us to make good decisions.

28   In order to be valuable and useful, Big Data has to be managed. One way is to rely on experts to analyze large amounts of data and then tell us what is important. The problem is that there is so much data that it overwhelms even the experts. We no longer just load information into a computer and tell it what to do. Now computers talk to each other and generate their own new information. This has created new ways of processing data some call "crowdscience,"[11] or "citizenscience." In *Reinventing Discovery: The New Era of Networked Science*, Michael Nielsen explains how scientists can collaborate online to solve complex problems. And they can multiply their efforts by engaging the general public to sort through masses of information. For example, Galaxy[12] Zoo enables people to classify galaxies on their smartphones, enlarging what Nielsen calls the collective intelligence. In fact, a citizen scientist discovered a whole new classification of galaxies.

Redefining American Abundance

29   The United States has always come from a culture of abundance, not scarcity. Bono, the rock star/activist, observed that Americans avoided the "curse of natural resources" that some developing nations now face. Americans learned how to develop the enormous natural resources on their continent and use them "not just to build a modern society but also to feed and supply the world." Now Americans are redefining their abundance as a powerful supply of ideas that can help bring solutions to the problems of the world. In *Abundance: The Future Is Better Than You Think*, Peter H. Diamandis and Steven Kotler say that scarcity of resources is a matter of perspective and accessibility. It you have a tree full of oranges and you pick all the fruit that you can reach, you have run out of your source of oranges. But if someone invents a ladder, you have access to a new supply.

[8] *incredible: difficult to believe*

[9] *limitless: without a limit or end*

[10] *subconscious: the part of your mind that has thoughts and feelings that you do not always realize that you have*

[11] *crowdscience—a group of people work together to solve a scientific problem or do scientific research. The group may be a few people, or it may involve thousands.*

[12] *galaxy—any of the large groups of stars that make up the universe*

30 A good example of this is the development of the controversial technology of "fracking." This allows drilling companies to get oil and natural gas from underground supplies in the United States that had not been previously accessible. The supplies of gas and oil are so vast that in 2012, the International Energy Agency projected that by 2020 the United States would become the world's leading oil producer. However, environmental groups are afraid of what this technique will do to the water supply and the ecology of the areas where this is being done.

31 Diamandis, Kotler, and others detail the ways that Americans can join with individuals around the world to find innovative solutions for providing clean water, enough food, and adequate shelter to everyone. Diamandis and Kotler refer to the populations of the world who lack basic necessities as "the rising billion." With the spread of mobile phones around the world, anyone anywhere will have the opportunity to join in creating a world of shared abundance. They define abundance:

> Abundance is not about providing everyone on this planet with a life of luxury[13]—rather it's about providing all with a life of possibility. To be able to live such a life requires having the basics covered and then some. . . . Today most poverty-stricken Americans have a television, telephone, electricity, running water, and indoor plumbing.

32 Definitions of poverty and abundance may be relative, as Diamandis and Kotler suggest. But there is probably universal agreement about the basics that everyone needs: clean water, enough food, and adequate shelter. The sharing of Big Data and networking technology gives us the tools to meet these basic needs and bring "a life of abundant possibility" to all. This will not happen automatically. There are many obstacles to overcome—pollution of the environment, scarcities of food and clean water, and bad decisions by government leaders or even human greed—but the good news is that there are individuals around the world who are dedicated to making it happen.

33 We began by explaining where the American ideal of abundance came from historically, and how it has affected the development of the United States. In contrast to most nations, Americans have traditionally believed that the wealth of their country was like an ever-expanding pie. Instead of the rich getting a larger piece and the poor getting a smaller one, the pie would continue to expand to provide large pieces for everyone. Most important, there would always be enough pie for all. The belief in the continuing heritage of abundance made Americans an optimistic people with confidence that human problems could be solved. It greatly reduced the conflict between the rich and poor that has torn many other nations apart. Perhaps most important, the belief in an always growing abundance gave strong support to such basic national values as freedom, self-reliance, equality of opportunity, competition, and hard work. It seemed to Americans that their high standard of living was a reward for practicing these values.

34 Today, some Americans worry that their economic pie may not continue to expand. But individuals like Diamandis and Kotler say that the revolution in Big Data and new tools to use and share the knowledge are the new face of American abundance. We will simply make more pies.

[13] luxury: very great comfort and pleasure, such as you get from expensive food, beautiful things, etc.

AFTER YOU READ

Understand Main Ideas

Check the predictions you made on page 101 before reading the chapter. Write your predictions that were correct:

_____

_____

_____

Work with a partner and answer these questions about the main ideas of each section of the chapter. Skim the sections for the main ideas if you do not remember them.

1. *A History of Abundance:* What three values were strengthened by the abundant natural resources of the United States?

2. From *Producers to Consumers:* What caused Americans to change from thinking of themselves mainly as producers to thinking of themselves mainly as consumers?

3. *What American Consumers Like:* What four things do American consumers like?

4. *An Abundance of Technology:* What changes have new technologies brought in American TV-viewing habits and in the way Americans access entertainment and information?

5. *An Abundance of Knowledge: Big Data:* What is Big Data and why is it important? What two kinds of questions does it raise?

6. *Redefining American Abundance:* What is the new definition of American abundance, and how can it benefit the rest of the world?

Understand Details

Write the letter of the best answer according to the information in the chapter.

_____ 1. Which of the following statements is <u>not</u> true?
   a. The European settlers found a North American continent that was rich in undeveloped resources.
   b. The values of the American people inspired them to develop a wilderness continent into a wealthy nation.
   c. The American government discouraged them from developing the natural resources.

_____ 2. Tocqueville believed that in a nation such as the United States, where wealth and social position are not determined by birth,
   a. the rich are not worried about keeping their wealth.
   b. everyone is worried about either acquiring wealth or holding on to it if they have it.
   c. people worry about money so much because they are basically very greedy.

_____ 3. Americans probably think of themselves more as consumers than producers because
   a. few people are still farmers.
   b. they are influenced by mass advertising.
   c. they are concerned about competing on the international market.

_____ 4. Advertisers are now creating ads for individual users on the Internet, using digital information about their use of digital media. This means that
   a. advertisers create personal ads for you by following what you do on the Internet.
   b. advertisers use media experts to design digital ads.
   c. advertisers use mass media technology to reach as many people as possible.

_____ 5. The spread of cable and satellite TV has meant that
   a. more Americans watch the networks ABC, NBC, CBS, and Fox than other channels.
   b. there is a virtually unlimited variety of television programs available.
   c. the number of people watching one program at the same time has increased dramatically.

_____ 6. Another aspect of the Internet is that individuals can customize, or personalize, the news they receive about current events, and they can set up their own news sites or blogs. This means that
   a. the Internet offers no real way for people to share news and their opinions about news.
   b. most people are interested in general news and there are few individual differences.
   c. people can choose to receive only news that interests them personally.

_____ 7. Which of these is implied, but not stated directly, in the _What American Consumers Like_ section of the chapter?
   a. Fast food is as healthy as home-cooked food.
   b. Most of the cooking is done by women.
   c. Men use credit cards more than women.

_____ 8. Based on information in the _What American Consumers Like_ section, which one of these statements is true?
   a. Americans like new products and want to improve old ones.
   b. When buying a chair, most Americans would be more concerned about its beauty than its comfort.
   c. At first, Febreze did not sell well because Americans are not concerned about how their houses smell.

_____ 9. The view that a country's economy is an ever-expanding pie
   a. is held by most nations in the world today.
   b. is a belief held by Americans and reinforced by their experiences.
   c. is a belief that a country's food supply will continually expand.

_____ 10. Fracking is a new technique that allows drilling companies to get oil and natural gas from underground supplies in the United States that had not been accessible. This means that

 a. oil and gas supplies have always been easy to reach in the U. S.

 b. oil and gas companies are not permitted to use the fracking technique.

 c. the fracking technique gives companies the opportunity to reach oil and gas they could not get to before.

Talk About It

Work in small groups and choose one of these questions to discuss.

1. Which do you think is more important for economic growth: a good supply of natural resources or the values of the people in the society? Give examples.

2. What are the basic necessities of life? Do we have a responsibility to make sure everyone has them?

3. What do you think of fast-food restaurants? Are convenience foods (canned goods, frozen food, pre-cooked dinners, etc.) popular in your country?

4. What personal information do you put on the Internet? Who owns your personal information? Who should be able to use it and how?

SKILL BUILDING

Improve Your Reading Skills: Highlighting

For successful academic reading, use strategies for identifying and remembering the main points. One strategy is to highlight the first sentence in each paragraph as you read. The first sentence is often the topic sentence and states the topic, or main idea, of the paragraph.

Practice this strategy. Highlight the first sentence of each paragraph in the _What American Consumers Like_ section of the chapter. In your notebook, copy the seven sentences to make a one-paragraph summary of the section.

Develop Your Critical Thinking Skills

Reread the quotation from Diamandis and Kotler: "Abundance is not about providing everyone on this planet with a life of luxury—rather it's about providing all with a life of possibility. To be able to live such a life requires having the basics covered and then some. . . ."

Evaluate this definition of abundance. In what ways do you agree or disagree with it? Be prepared to participate in a classroom discussion about this issue.

Build Your Vocabulary

Opposites

Match the words with opposite meanings. Then fill in the sentence blanks with the correct words.

_____	1. abundance	a.	expand
_____	2. consumer	b.	wealth
_____	3. downsize	c.	downward
_____	4. mass	d.	vice
_____	5. positive	e.	scarcity
_____	6. poverty	f.	private
_____	7. public	g.	poor
_____	8. rich	h.	producer
_____	9. upward	i.	targeted
_____	10. virtue	j.	negative

1. Unlike many countries where the love of material things was seen as a

   _____, a mark of weak moral character, in the United States it

   was seen as a _____, an incentive to work hard, and a reward

   for successful efforts.

2. Tocqueville thought that Americans might be insecure if their

   material wealth could change so rapidly either _____ or

   _____ during a lifetime.

3. Mass advertising reinforces the American's self-image as a

   _____.

4. The United States comes from a culture of abundance, not

   _____.

5. _____ television has no commercials, and programs are paid

   for by donations and government grants.

6. Today most _____-stricken Americans have a television, telephone, electricity, running water, and indoor plumbing.

7. With a loss of advertising revenue, news organizations have had to

    _____, employing fewer staff reporters.

Technology Words

There are a number of words and phrases in the chapter that deal with technology. Some of these words apply to television; others relate to the Internet, and some relate to both. In the Venn diagram that follows, write the words that apply to these three categories. Write the words that only apply to television in one circle, the words that only apply to the Internet in the other circle, and the words that apply to both in the area that overlaps. Look on the Internet for any words you do not know.

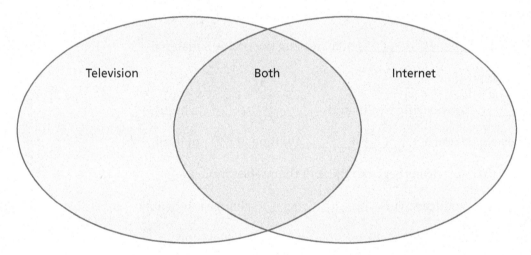

Advertisements	Facebook	Sponsor
Blog	Mass marketing	Targeted marketing
Cable	Movies	Tumblr
Channel	Network	Twitter
Commercials	News	Video
Data	Online	Viewer
Digital	Pinterest	Website
Entertainment	Satellite	World Wide Web

More AWL Words

Test your knowledge of these AWL words by filling in the blanks in these sentences from the chapter.

concluded	generation	institution	task
consumers	image	maintaining	technique
emphasis	insecure	period	

People might be naturally _____ if their material wealth, and that
₁

of their children, could change so rapidly either upward or downward during a

lifetime, or even a single _____. Tocqueville _____
₂ ₃

that it was extremely important both to rich Americans and poor Americans

to increase their personal wealth and material comforts. Therefore, the entire

population joined in the _____ of increasing the nation's material
₄

abundance as quickly as possible.

The _____ on producing wealth and _____ a high
₅ ₆

standard of living developed over a _____ of time. It was not until
₇

the twentieth century that Americans began to think of themselves more as

_____ than producers. This _____ change is probably
₈ ₉

due to the coming of mass advertising, made possible by radio and television.

Television used the same _____ that radio had developed. Historian
₁₀

David Potter observed that mass advertising in the United States became so

important in size and influence that it should be viewed as an _____
₁₁

such as the school or the church.

EXPAND YOUR KNOWLEDGE

Conduct an Experiment

*In the chapter, there is information about how advertisers target people they want to
have as customers. Newspaper editor Arthur Brisbane says that there are several things
an ad must accomplish to be successful:*

"A good advertisement must do five things and do them all. If it fails in one, it fails in all.
It must make people see it, read (listen/watch) it, understand it, believe it, want it."

Choose one (or more) of these activities to count the ways advertising is part of your life. Write your findings in your notebook. Then report your findings to the rest of the class.

1. Count the number of TV commercials you see in one hour.
2. Count the number of billboards or other outdoor advertising messages you see in a day.
3. Count the number of advertisements you see on the Internet in one hour.
4. Count the number of advertising messages you see on people's clothing in one day.

People Watching

1. Observe what Americans throw away. Visit a fast-food restaurant and count the containers that are thrown away from one person's meal. How much food is wasted? How does this compare with people eating in fast-food restaurants in your country?

2. Visit a supermarket and note the kinds of convenience or packaged foods available. Be sure to check all the departments. Here are some examples of what you may find: salad in a bag, fruit already cut up and ready to eat, rice and pasta boxed dinners, ready-to-cook meat and poultry dishes, and frozen dinners. Notice what Americans are buying at the grocery store. How does this compare with grocery shoppers in your country? Notice the different varieties of the same type of products. How many kinds of milk do you count? How many kinds of bread? How many kinds of rice? Record your observations in your journal.

A family enjoys eating at a fast-food restaurant.

Think, Pair, Share

Think about current environmental problems and possible solutions. For these words and phrases, write **P** for the environmental problems, and **S** for the solutions.

_____ endangered species   _____ conserving energy

_____ trash and garbage   _____ protecting wildlife

_____ recycling   _____ air pollution

_____ wastefulness   _____ global warming

What other environmental problems and solutions can you think of? Write your answers below and share them with your partner.

_____

_____

_____

Ask Americans / Create a Poll

All countries must now consider their energy needs and how to meet them in the future. The United States is no exception. This chart is based on a poll that asked Americans about their government's policy for addressing the nation's energy supply.

Create your own poll by writing questions for each item, and then ask Americans to answer your questions. Compare your results with this poll.

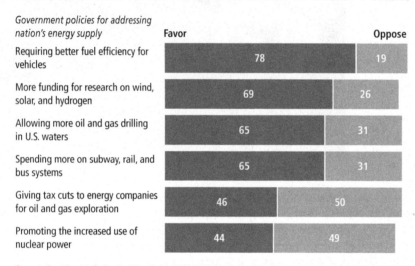

PUBLIC CONTINUES TO SUPPORT BROAD RANGE OF ENERGY POLICIES

Government policies for addressing nation's energy supply

Policy	Favor	Oppose
Requiring better fuel efficiency for vehicles	78	19
More funding for research on wind, solar, and hydrogen	69	26
Allowing more oil and gas drilling in U.S. waters	65	31
Spending more on subway, rail, and bus systems	65	31
Giving tax cuts to energy companies for oil and gas exploration	46	50
Promoting the increased use of nuclear power	44	49

Source: Pew Research Center Mar. 7–11, 2012. Q43.

Small-Group Project

An interesting example of Big Data is the phenomenon of YouTube. It started in 2007 and by 2012 there were 60 hours of video uploaded every minute and more than 4 billion page views per day, with the numbers continuing to rise at a faster and faster pace. An article in Time *magazine proclaimed, "There's never been an object like YouTube in human history." Modern life generates huge quantities of video, and most of it is created by amateurs, not professionals. Before YouTube, there was no central place for videos to be gathered and stored. One of Google's main challenges is to keep the site from crashing because of all these videos. Another challenge is how to organize the videos so that people can find what they want to see. YouTube is using a type of crowdsourcing by having its users do the organizing of the videos themselves. This process is evolving.*

Work in a small group to look at how YouTube organizes videos. Visit YouTube and look for a type of video that you want to see. What words do you use to describe this type of video? How does YouTube organize videos? Is it easy to find the videos you want on YouTube? How would you organize YouTube videos to make the site easier to use?

Use the Internet

Choose one of the topics below and do research on the Internet:

1. Learn more about what Diamandis and Kotler have to say about abundance: "We think it's critically important for you to have access to this ongoing evidence for abundance. Therefore, we've created five different ways for you to stay plugged in, interact with the authors, and join an ongoing conversation about radical advances in energy, food, water, health, education, technophilanthropy, DIY [Do It Yourself] innovation, and all the rest." Visit their websites to learn more: http://www.AbundanceHub.com

2. In spite of all the abundance in the United States, you may be surprised to learn that hunger is still a problem. Many Americans do not make enough money to provide adequate food for their families. Also, because of poverty, many Americans do not have access to fresh fruits and vegetables in their neighborhoods, and so they eat a lot of cheap fast food. Childhood obesity is a problem, as well as hunger. Learn about a documentary film that was made about the problem. Search on the Internet for the film "A Place at the Table." Find more information at websites such as www.takepart.com or www.magpictures.com/aplaceatthetable/

3. If you are interested in the protection of endangered species, visit websites such as www.worldwildlife.org or the U.S. government site www.fws.gov/endangered/

WRITE ABOUT IT

In this chapter, there was a discussion of advertising and what Americans like to buy. What happens to all the "stuff" that people buy? What happens to the old electronic products (phones, computers, etc.) when people buy new ones? The Environmental Protection Agency (EPA) is the government agency that is in charge of what happens to Americans' trash and garbage.

How Americans Dispose of Trash and Garbage

Information from the EPA website

http://www.epa.gov/epawaste/nonhaz/municipal/index.htm

Municipal Solid Waste (MSW)—more commonly known as trash or garbage—consists of everyday items we use and then throw away, such as product packaging, grass clippings, furniture, clothing, bottles, food scraps, newspapers, appliances, paint, and batteries. This comes from our homes, schools, hospitals, and businesses.

Each year EPA produces a report on MSW generation, recycling, and disposal. In 2010, Americans generated about 250 million tons of trash and recycled and composted over 85 million tons of this material, equivalent to a 34.1 percent recycling rate. On average, we recycled and composted 1.51 pounds of our individual waste generation of 4.43 pounds per person per day.

EPA encourages practices that reduce the amount of waste needing to be disposed of, such as waste prevention, recycling, and composting.

- *Source reduction,* or waste prevention, is designing products to reduce the amount of waste that will later need to be thrown away and also to make the resulting waste less toxic.

- *Recycling* is the recovery of useful materials, such as paper, glass, plastic, and metals, from the trash to use to make new products, reducing the amount of new raw materials needed.

- *Composting* involves collecting organic waste, such as food scraps and yard trimmings, and storing it under conditions designed to help it break down naturally. This resulting compost can then be used as a natural fertilizer.

Recycling and composting prevented 85.1 million tons of material from being disposed of [in] 2010, up from 15 million tons in 1980. This prevented the release of approximately 186 million metric tons of carbon dioxide equivalent into the air in 2010—equivalent to taking 36 million cars off the road for a year. Learn more about how *common wastes and materials,* including food and yard wastes, paper, metals, and electronics, contribute to MSW generation and how they can be recycled.

MSW RECYCLING RATES, 1960–2010

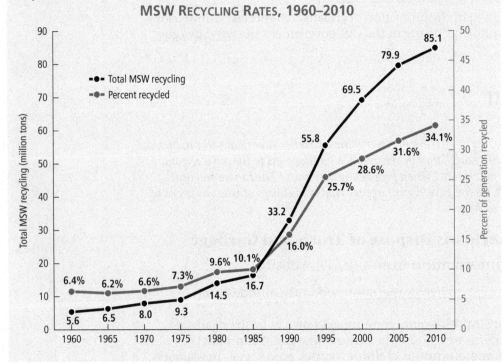

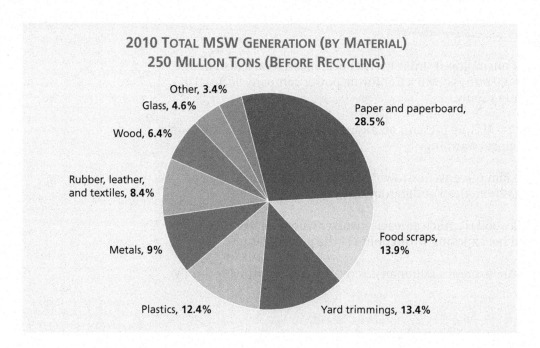

**2010 TOTAL MSW GENERATION (BY MATERIAL)
250 MILLION TONS (BEFORE RECYCLING)**

Other, **3.4%**

Glass, **4.6%**

Wood, **6.4%**

Rubber, leather, and textiles, **8.4%**

Metals, **9%**

Plastics, **12.4%**

Yard trimmings, **13.4%**

Food scraps, **13.9%**

Paper and paperboard, **28.5%**

The EPA is trying to teach Americans to reduce, reuse, and recycle. It is clear that Americans are doing better at recycling. Write a report about how your country deals with trash and garbage. Do research on the Internet and share your own personal experiences.

EXPLORE ON YOUR OWN

Books to Read

Rachel Carson, *Silent Spring*—This best-selling book published in 1962 was one of the first to warn of environmental problems and the dangers of chemical pollution.

Peter H. Diamandis and Steven Kotler: *Abundance: The Future is Better Than You Think*—This book details ways that technology, innovators, technophilanthropists, and ordinary people are finding solutions to some of the world's worst problems.

Al Gore, *Earth in the Balance: Ecology and the Human Spirit*—In this best seller, the former vice president calls on Americans to rethink their relationship with the environment or face terrible consequences.

Eric Schlosser, *Fast Food Nation: The Dark Side of the All-American Meal*—A disturbing look at the fast-food industry in the United States and how it affects American food production, health, and popular culture.

Rick Smolan and Jennifer Erwitt, *The Human Face of Big Data*—A large, "coffee table" picture book that illustrates how huge quantities of information are affecting our lives.

Movies to See

Erin Brockovitch—An unemployed single mother becomes a legal assistant and almost single-handedly brings down a California power company accused of polluting a city's water supply.

An Inconvenient Truth—Al Gore presents an award-winning documentary movie about the effects of global warming.

Promised Land—The film presents one town's experience with fracking, a process for getting natural gas from deep underground.

Silkwood—Karen Silkwood is a nuclear reactor worker who may have been murdered to prevent her exposing wrongdoing at the power plant.

The Truman Show—An insurance salesman discovers that his entire life is a TV show.

THE WORLD OF AMERICAN BUSINESS

The business of America is business.

President Calvin Coolidge (1872–1933)

What effect does business have on American values? Do Americans see business owners and leaders as heroes or as villains?

BEFORE YOU READ

Preview Vocabulary

A. Here are some key AWL words in Chapter 6. Look at their definitions. Put a check next to the words you already know.

_____ 1. **ultimate**   the best or most perfect example of something

_____ 2. **aid**   help or advice given to someone who needs it

_____ 3. **alternative**   something you can choose instead of something else

_____ 4. **cycles**   events that happen again and again

_____ 5. **overseas**   happening abroad

_____ 6. **policy**   an official way of doing something

_____ 7. **priorities**   things that are most important and need your attention before anything else

_____ 8. **submitting**   agreeing to obey

_____ 9. **theoretically**   supposed to be true

B. Work with a partner. Read these sentences from the chapter. Fill in the blanks with words from the preceding list.

1. _____, if one business tries to take unfair advantage of its customers, it will lose to a competing business which treats its customers more fairly.

2. Gaining success and status through competition is often seen as the American _____ to systems where social rank is based on family background.

3. Entrepreneurs often began as common people themselves; without the _____ of inherited social title or inherited money, they became "self-made" millionaires.

4. A final characteristic of entrepreneurs that appeals to most Americans is their strong dislike of _____ to higher authority.

5. The site keeps track of everyone's contribution online, and all who participate in the process get a percent of the profits from the sales; such websites offer the _____ form of collaboration.

6. Some American businesses that had moved their operations

   _____ are now returning, and manufacturing is coming back.

7. Americans' respect for their business institutions rises and falls in

   _____, going back to the Industrial Revolution of the 1800s.

8. Traditionally, Republicans have been in favor of a laissez-faire, or hands-off

   _____, and Democrats have favored more regulations and

   safeguards.

9. *MetLife*'s most recent study of the American Dream shows a significant shift

   in _____.

Preview Content

A. Read the questions and discuss them with your classmates.

1. Read the quotation by President Calvin Coolidge at the beginning of the chapter. What do you think the quotation means? Do you agree? Why is business so important to Americans?

2. What does it mean to "go from rags to riches"?

3. What is an entrepreneur?

4. What are the advantages and disadvantages of starting and running your own business? Write some ideas in a pro-and-con chart.

B. Preview the chapter by reading the headings and looking at the illustrations. Predict what the chapter is about. Put a check by the ideas you predict will be discussed in the chapter.

_____ the natural resources of the United States

_____ what Alexis de Tocqueville said about business in the 1830s

_____ the role of entrepreneurs in American business

_____ how to start your own business

_____ what Americans think they can do to get rich

_____ what Americans think of corporate CEOs

_____ what products the United States exports to other countries

_____ differences in wealth or social class

_____ how the American Dream has changed

_____ changes American business faces

THE CHARACTERISTICS OF AMERICAN BUSINESS

1. It is essential to become familiar with two words in order to understand the meaning of *business* to Americans: They are *private* and *profit*. Businesses are directly or indirectly owned and operated by private individuals (or groups of individuals) in order to make a profit. In contrast to these privately owned, for-profit businesses, there are also (1) public, government-owned-and-operated institutions, and (2) nonprofit organizations, such as churches, charities, and educational institutions. These organizations and institutions should not be confused with businesses. However, in recent years a new type of business called "for purpose" or "for benefit" has appeared, a form of for-profit charity. We will discuss these new benefit corporations later in the chapter.

How Business Competition Reinforces Other Values

2. The statement by President Coolidge in the 1920s, "The business of America is business," still points to an important truth today—that business institutions are at the heart of the American way of life. One reason for this is that Americans view business as being more firmly based on the ideal of competition than most other institutions in society. Since competition is seen as the major source of progress and prosperity by most Americans, competitive business institutions have traditionally been respected. Competition is seen not only as a value itself; it is also the means by which other basic American values such as individual freedom, self-reliance, equality of opportunity, and hard work are protected.

3. Competition protects the freedom of the individual by ensuring that there is no monopoly of power. In contrast to one all-powerful government, many businesses compete against each other for profits. Theoretically, if one business tries to take unfair advantage of its customers, it will lose to a competing business that treats its customers more fairly. Where many businesses compete for the customers, they cannot afford to give them inferior products or poor service.

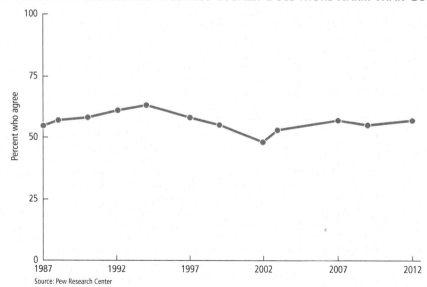

GOVERNMENT REGULATION OF BUSINESS USUALLY DOES MORE HARM THAN GOOD

Source: Pew Research Center

4   A contrast is often made between business, which is competitive, and government, which is a monopoly. Because business is competitive, many Americans believe that it may be even more supportive of freedom than government, even though government leaders are elected by the people and business leaders are not. Many Americans believe that competition is vitally important to preserving freedom. So closely is competitive business associated with freedom in the minds of most Americans that the term *free enterprise*, rather than the term *capitalism*, is most often used to describe the American business system.

5   Competition in business is also believed to strengthen the ideal of equality of opportunity. Americans compare business competition to a race open to all, where success and status go to the swiftest[1] person, regardless of social class. Gaining success and status through competition is often seen as the American alternative to systems where social rank is based on family background. Business is therefore viewed as an expression of the idea of equality of opportunity rather than the aristocratic idea of inherited privilege.

6   Business competition is also seen by most Americans as encouraging the value of hard work. If two businesspeople are competing against each other, the one who works harder is likely to win. The one who spends less time and effort is likely to lose. Because businesspeople must continually compete against each other, they must develop the habit of hard work in order not to fail.

7   Americans are aware that business institutions often do not live up to the ideals of competition and the support of freedom, self-reliance, equality of opportunity, and hard work. Americans sometimes distrust the motives of businesspeople, believing that they are capable of putting profit before product safety or a cleaner environment. Therefore, most Americans believe businesses need some government regulation, although they may disagree on how much. Even with these flaws,[2] however, most Americans believe that business comes closer than other institutions to encouraging competition and other basic values in daily practice.

The Dream of Getting Rich

8   There is a second reason why business institutions have traditionally received respect in the United States. One aspect of the great American Dream is to rise from poverty or modest wealth to great wealth. In the United States, this has usually been accomplished through successful business careers. Most of the great private fortunes in the nation have been built by people who were successful in business, many of whom started life with very little. Indeed, today about 35 percent of the Forbes 400 (the 400 wealthiest Americans) were raised poor or middle class. Careers in business still offer the best opportunity for the ambitious individual to become wealthy, although many of the wealthiest Americans have inherited fortunes from their family.

9   Alexis de Tocqueville observed the great attractiveness of business careers for Americans as early as the 1830s. He wrote that Americans strongly preferred business to farming because business offered the opportunity to get rich more quickly. Even those who were farmers were possessed with a strong business spirit. They often ran small businesses to add to the money they made from farming. Tocqueville also

---

[1] *swiftest: quickest and fastest*

[2] *flaws: mistakes, marks, or defects*

Longwood Mansion, Natchez, Mississippi, is an example of the opulent lifestyle many Americans hope to have.

noticed that American farmers were often more interested in buying and selling land for a profit than in farming it. Thus, even in Tocqueville's day, when most Americans were still farmers, the seeds of a business civilization had already been planted.

10 Not only is business seen as the easiest way for individuals to become rich, it is also seen as generally benefiting the entire nation. Through competition, more people gain wealth and the nation prospers. By contrast, a government-run system of production and distribution of goods is seen as inferior. It is distrusted because of the monopoly of power held by the government, which eliminates competition. Most Americans would probably prefer to limit government's control over businesses and let the free enterprise system, or the free market, work on its own. However, there is a great debate about the role of the government

vs. business in providing services such as health care and retirement benefits. The United States is one of the few industrialized countries in the world that does not have universal health care guaranteed and managed by the government. Health care in the United States has been tied to employment since the 1940s, although the government's role has been increasing in the 2000s. The Affordable Care Act (passed in 2009 and implemented 2010-2015) has the goal of enabling all Americans to have access to affordable health insurance. However, this plan (known as Obama Care) has been controversial from the start, with opposition from many business leaders and conservative politicians.

11 As for retirement, since the 1980s most businesses have switched from offering pensions to retired workers to offering them 401K retirement accounts for

saving and investment. This has allowed employees access to their retirement funds while still working, and it has resulted in many workers spending this money and not saving enough for their retirement. This is a growing problem in the United States. In the future, as these workers face retirement without adequate savings, the government retirement benefits may also be reduced. Both individuals and companies now contribute money into the government Social Security System (and Medicare, the government health care system for retirees), but there is serious concern that as the aging population grows, there will not be enough money to fund these benefits. We will examine this problem more in the next chapter on government.

The Entrepreneur as Business Hero

12 Because of the many beliefs that connect business to the wealth and the traditional values of the United States, people who are successful in business have sometimes become heroes to the American people. Entrepreneurs provide examples of traditional American values in their purest form for a number of reasons. The first reason is that they succeed in building something great out of nothing. The people who, more than 100 years ago, built up the nation's great industries, such as steel, railroads, and oil refining, were usually entrepreneurs. They started with very little money or power and ended up as the heads of huge companies that earned enormous fortunes.

13 The fact that these early entrepreneurs built great industries out of very little made them seem to millions of Americans like the heroes of the early frontier days, who went into the vast wilderness of the United States and turned forests into farms, villages, and small cities. The entrepreneur, like the earlier hero of the frontier, was seen as a rugged individualist who reinforced the values of freedom, self-reliance, and hard work. The nineteenth-century entrepreneurs often began as common people themselves; without the aid of inherited social title or inherited money, they became "self-made" millionaires. They were thus perfect examples of the American idea of equality of opportunity in action.

14 The strong influence of the success stories of the early entrepreneurs can be found in the great popularity of the novels of Horatio Alger, which were published in late-nineteenth and early-twentieth-century America. About 17 million copies of these books were sold to the American public. The central theme of Alger's novels is that in the United States a poor city boy or a poor farm boy can become a wealthy and successful businessman if he works hard and relies on himself rather than others. This is because the United States is a land of equality of opportunity where everyone has a chance to succeed.

15 In Alger's first published novel, *Ragged Dick*, a poor city boy who shines shoes for a living becomes Richard Hunter, a successful and wealthy businessman. The hero rises "from rags to riches" and fulfills the American Dream. Dick succeeds only partly because he lives in a land of equality of opportunity. His success is also due to the fact that he practices the American virtues of self-reliance and hard work. According to Alger, Dick "knew that he had only himself to depend upon, and he determined to make the most of himself . . . which is the secret of success in nine cases out of ten." Dick was also a hardworking shoe-shine boy, "energetic and on the alert for business." This quality marked him for success, explained Alger, because in all professions, "energy and industry are rewarded."

The Corporate CEO/CFO

17 In contrast to business entrepreneurs who are seen as creating something new, there are the leaders of existing large business corporations— the CEO (Chief Executive Officer) and the CFO (Chief Financial Officer) who manage the businesses. The great entrepreneurs of the late nineteenth century built huge business organizations that needed new generations of business leaders to run them in the twentieth century. These leaders, sometimes referred to as "organizational men or women," now run large American corporations. They are powerful and often acquire great personal wealth, but they do not usually have the hero image of entrepreneurs because they are managing businesses that someone else started. Although most Americans admire the earning power of entrepreneurs and would probably not want to put a limit on their income, they are less generous in their view of CEOs. Indeed, many highly paid CEOs have come under severe attack for their multi-million-dollar-a-year salaries and their self-serving management decisions.

16 Although few Americans today read Horatio Alger's stories, they continue to be inspired by the idea of earning wealth and success as entrepreneurs who "make it on their own." A final characteristic of entrepreneurs that appeals to most Americans is their strong dislike of submitting to higher authority. Throughout their history, Americans have admired entrepreneurs who conduct their business and their lives without taking orders from anyone above them. Americans have great respect for those who can say, "I am my own boss." Many American workers still dream of one day having their own business and being their own boss.

18 In her book *Pigs at the Trough: How Corporate Greed and Political Corruption Are Undermining America*, Arianna Huffington details how certain CEOs took huge sums of money from the corporations they were managing and spent it on themselves. She describes how John Rigas, the CEO of Adelphia, a large cable company, borrowed $3.1 billion from the company when it was in financial trouble and spent it outrageously:

He spent $13 million to build a golf course in his backyard, $150 million to buy the Buffalo Sabres hockey team, $65 million to fund a venture capital[3] group run by his son-in-law, thousands to maintain his three private jets, and $700,000 for a country club membership.

19 It is not just the greed of some corporate leaders; it is the effect their decisions have had on the employees of their companies, their stockholders, and the society at large. The early 2000s saw a number of other corporate scandals, when CEOs and other corporate officers received huge sums of money from companies that were failing. One of the worst examples was the Enron Corporation, which left thousands of employees out of work and destroyed their retirement savings. What angered Americans was not only the outrageous greed of the corporate executives, but also their lies to the stockholders, their criminal mismanagement of the business, and their cruel treatment of their own employees.

20 For most of the twentieth century, there were many good-paying manufacturing jobs. Many of these factory jobs did not require a college degree, and large numbers of average Americans could earn enough money to have a comfortable middle class existence. However, the realities of the global economy caused some American businesses to make significant changes. In order to make products that were cheap enough to compete in the global market, many companies moved their factories overseas. Companies could no longer afford to pay Americans those high wages. Second, some companies downsized to become more competitive. Old, giant corporations such as IBM laid off thousands of workers, downsizing to become more efficient, as well as more competitive. Third, some companies reduced the number of full-time employees and replaced them with part-time workers so they did not have to pay health insurance or retirement benefits. Finally, some companies started outsourcing[4] work to other countries. Telephone customer support is a good example of outsourcing. Today, when an American calls about a problem with a product or to inquire about the status of an order, the person answering the call may be in India or the Philippines, rather than the United States.

21 In the twenty-first century, in addition to watching CEOs send their good-paying jobs overseas, Americans were hit by an economic recession. Most of the wealth held by the middle class was in the homes they owned. The value of their homes had increased dramatically in the late 1990s and the 2000s creating a "housing bubble."[5] When the bubble burst, middle class homeowners were devastated. Suddenly their homes were worth half of what they had been, and at the same time, many people lost their jobs. To make matters worse, American financial institutions went into a crisis. The banking system was in danger of collapsing[6] and the government had to loan them money so they would not fail. The government also gave loans to two American automobile companies, Chrysler and General Motors, to keep them from collapsing. The decision was made that some companies were simply "too big to fail."

---

[3] *venture capital: money that is lent to people so that they can start a new business*

[4] *outsourcing: hiring employees in another country instead of using workers where the business is located*

[5] *bubble: a successful or happy time, especially in business*

[6] *collapsing: suddenly failing to work*

The Middle Class vs. the One Percent

22 By 2010, many middle-class Americans were really angry. Their incomes had remained the same (adjusted for inflation) for 25 years. They were discouraged about finding a good job and paying the mortgage[7] on their home. Many people took money out of their retirement accounts to survive. And they learned that what they had left in their investment retirement accounts had declined along with the stock market fall of 2008. The Huffington Post reported that their Real Misery Index was the highest it had ever been. The Misery Index combines data on unemployment, credit card debt, and inflation of essentials such as gas, food, medical costs, and housing. In some locations, large numbers of homes went into foreclosure because the owners could no longer afford the mortgage payments, and the banks took back the houses.

23 But not all Americans were miserable. The gap between the very rich and the rest of the population had been growing since the late 1980s. Now it was clear that the very rich one percent had gotten even richer during the economic crisis. Some corporate CEOs had made fortunes downsizing companies and buying others that were in financial trouble. Banks and other financial institutions were selling financial products that few people understood. It seemed to some that the business institutions that had brought America jobs and new products and services were now just making money off of money. And people suddenly realized that because of the tax structure, investment income was taxed at a lower rate than earned income. Warren Buffet, one of the richest Americans, said that his secretary paid a higher tax rate than he did. This became an issue in the 2012 presidential election because Mitt Romney, the Republican candidate, had made a fortune with his corporation that downsized American companies. Also, most of his income came from investments that were taxed at the lower rate, and much of his money was in off-shore bank accounts, outside the United States.

24 Then the economy started to improve. As the stock market recovered and rose higher and higher, so did the anger of the working class Americans. In the fall of 2011, some people started a movement called Occupy Wall Street, demanding that the rich pay "their fair share" of taxes. They camped out in the park near the Wall Street stock exchange in New York City, and the demonstrations spread to other cities. Eventually cold weather and other factors put a stop to most demonstrations, but the anger continued.

More and more business on the New York Stock Exchange is done electronically.

[7] mortgage: money borrowed from a bank to buy a house and paid back over a number of years

25 It was not just the working class Americans who were disturbed. News commentators began asking if the American Dream was dead, and books about how to save or restore the American Dream appeared. Huffington sounded the alarm in her book *Third World America: How Our Politicians Are Abandoning the Middle Class and Betraying the American Dream*. Huffington, herself an immigrant from Greece, said she wrote the book as a warning about what could happen. In 1980, when she came to the United States to find "a better life," that was the phrase everyone associated with America—a better life. "Upward mobility has always been at the center of the American Dream—a promise that if you work hard and play by the rules, you'll do well, and your children will have the chance to do even better." But in the last few years, Huffington said she saw that the middle class was "getting the short end of the stick." Washington had rushed to the rescue of Wall Street but had forgotten about Main Street. Our political system is broken, she observed, and our economic system "has been reduced to recurring episodes of Corporations Gone Wild."

26 Americans' respect for their business institutions rises and falls in cycles, going back to the Industrial Revolution of the 1800s. At times, business leaders are seen as greedy and corrupt villains; at other times, they are hailed as heroes. This is not the first time that Americans have questioned the motives of business leaders. In the late 1800s, for example, some business leaders were known as "robber barons" because of their corrupt practices and their disregard for others. This caused the government to pass laws to regulate business practices. Now, when there are business scandals, the government responds with more rules and regulations. Traditionally, Republicans have been in favor of a laissez-faire, or hands-off policy, and Democrats have favored more regulation and safeguards. The one factor that does not change is the strong belief in the value and importance of the American Dream.

Redefining the American Dream

27 Why does the American Dream of a better life persist in a bad economy or in the midst of other troubles? And why does it seem to encourage and inspire many Americans instead of discouraging and depressing them? Huffington says that, when writing her book *Third World America*, she was again and again struck by the resilience,[8] creativity, and acts of compassion[9] that she discovered taking place all over America.

28 First, many Americans truly are resilient. Perhaps part of this trait comes from their frontier heritage, where people believed they could pull themselves up by their bootstraps in times of trouble. The strong belief in self-reliance and individual freedom has led many Americans to redefine the American Dream for themselves. MetLife, a large American company that provides insurance, annuities, and employee benefits, has been doing an annual study of the American Dream for more than five years. Their most recent study shows a significant shift in priorities. It reveals the rise of what they call the "Do-It-Yourself" (DIY) American Dream and a portrayal of Americans as "resilient and adaptive." Faced with economic hardship, Americans now say that having close relationships with their friends and family is more important than acquiring additional material possessions. They are more content with what they

---

[8] *resilience: the ability to quickly become strong, healthy, or happy after a difficult situation*

[9] *compassion: sympathy for people who are suffering and a desire to help them*

already have, and they are seeking a better balance between their work and their personal lives. The study concludes that for most Americans now, "Achieving a sense of personal fulfillment is more important toward realizing the American Dream than accumulating material wealth."

29 Second, creativity is highly valued in American society. Gary Shapiro, president and CEO of the Consumer Electronics Association (which is responsible for the world's largest annual technology trade show), believes that innovation in business is critical. In *The Comeback: How Innovation Will Restore the American Dream*, Shapiro says that throughout history, our great innovators have been the real drivers of American economic success. American innovation is what creates new jobs and even whole new industries that never existed before. "Most importantly," Shapiro concludes, "innovation moves us forward as a nation, pushing us to succeed and strive for a better tomorrow. In short, innovation is the American Dream."

30 Richard Florida, author of *The Rise of the Creative Class*, believes that the role of innovation and creativity is rising in the United States today, and not just in the field of technology. Based on his analysis of census data, Florida estimates that nearly one-third of the American workforce now belong to "the creative class." They either create new ideas, technology, or content in fields such as science, education, design, the arts, and entertainment, or they engage in solving complex problems, in fields such as business, law, finance, and health care. These creative workers tend to cluster on the east and west coasts, in high-tech centers, and near major research universities and institutions. They have a strong, positive impact on the economic future of these areas.

31 Third, the compassionate nature of Americans and their search for meaning are a part of the redefinition of the American Dream. In *Abundance: The Future Is Better than You Think*, Peter Diamandis and Steven Kotler talk about the DIY (Do-It-Yourself) innovator. They say that the marriage of self-reliance and technology has helped shape the DIY innovator into a force for spreading abundance and a force for good. DIY innovators now have the technical tools to turn their visions of a better world into real businesses that can solve real problems. For example, Chris Anderson, the editor in chief of *Wired* magazine leads a nonprofit online community called DIY Drones. Using crowdscience techniques, his group of DIY innovators learned to build drones[10] for about $300.00 apiece, instead of the military's price of $35,000 to $250,000. Now they are looking at using drones to carry supplies into places where monsoons wash out roads, or areas with no roads at all. Another company, part of what Diamandis and Kotler call the Maker Movement, has a network of drones and recharging stations housed in shipping containers and spread throughout Africa. Smartphones are used to place orders in villages that are in remote locations, and then drones deliver the orders. Drones such as the Quad Copter can carry everything from medicine to replacement parts for farm machinery at a cost less than six cents per kilogram-kilometre.

32 Ebay's first president Jeff Skoll, Facebook founder Mark Zuckerberg, and Pay Pal founder Elon Musk are part of a new group of billionaires that Diamandis and Kotler call the *technophilanthropists*. They have made their fortunes in new fields of technology and now they are changing the face of philanthropy in the United States. Traditionally, philanthropists have

[10] *drone: an airplane or piece of equipment that does not have a person inside it, but is operated by radio*

started giving their money to charity toward the end of their lives. However, many of these technophilanthropists were billionaires before the age of 30, and they turned to philanthropy right afterward. Skoll says that they are full of the energy and confidence "that come from building global businesses at such a young age. They want to tackle audacious goals like nuclear proliferation[11] or pandemics[12] or water." They think big and believe that they can find solutions to "impossible" problems such as providing clean, safe drinking water to everyone on the planet. Because of their young age, they think they can really make a difference in their lifetime, solving enormous social problems.

33 A number of the technophilanthropists are DIY social entrepreneurs. Diamandis and Kotler say these are individuals who "combine the pragmatic, results-oriented methods of a business entrepreneur with the goals of a social reformer." Some social entrepreneurs start benefit corporations where profits are spent bringing about social change. These benefit corporations are established to solve particular social problems; they raise profits but use the money for projects often done by nonprofit organizations. The Center for Association Leadership says that the newly emerging benefit corporations are blurring the traditional line between for-profit corporations and nonprofit organizations. Benefit corporations must commit to providing social or environmental benefits, "while still showing a healthy bottom line." They are "devoted to what is known in the business community as the triple bottom line: people, planet, and profit," and they must publicly report on their social and environmental performance. They are also a potential source of financial support for nonprofit organizations, and their profit structure allows benefit corporations to continue their work without constantly having to look for outside funding.

34 Jeff Skoll, the first president of eBay, says social entrepreneurs are intensely enthusiastic people who are anxious to reach their goals. They go beyond what charities usually do to bring about change. He describes social entrepreneurs this way:

> By nature, entrepreneurs aren't satisfied until they do change the world, and let nothing get in their way. Charities may give people food. But social entrepreneurs don't just teach people to grow food—they're not happy until they've taught a farmer how to grow food, make money, pour the profits back into the business, hire ten other people, and in the process, transform the entire industry.

The Future of American Business

35 In good economic times and bad, a number of Americans still try to start their own business. Many of these hopeful entrepreneurs have regular jobs, and they run their business venture on the side, in their spare time. The government encourages small business start-ups through the Small Business Administration (SBA), because they are the creators of most new jobs in the United States and employ more than half of all American workers. The SBA defines a small business as one that employs fewer than 500 people, but the vast majority of them (over three-quarters) have no employees at all—only the self-employed owner. About half of all small businesses are home-based, and the Internet plays an important role. Surprisingly, more than 99 percent of all American firms *with* employees are small businesses, with half of them employing 10–99 people. In the United States, there are over 23,000,000 small businesses and

---

[11] *nuclear proliferation: the spread of nuclear weapons*

[12] *pandemic: an illness or disease that affects the population of a very large area*

only about 18,500 large firms employing more than 500 workers.

36   The Internet has given individuals the tools to collaborate on almost everything, and many Americans who have business ideas find support there. Sites such as www.quirky.com will even help you develop an idea for a new invention. You submit an idea, and they ask their online crowd of people to vote on whether they think it's an invention worth bringing to life. If your idea is chosen, you participate in a crowdsourcing process of designing, engineering, financing, manufacturing, and then distributing your product. The quirky site keeps track of everyone's contribution online, and all who participate in the process get a percentage of the profits from the sales, even a fraction of a percent. Such websites offer the ultimate form of collaboration.

37   The Internet provides the global connections that allow businesses, large and small, to interact with potential customers everywhere, at any time. The United States remains one of the largest markets in the world, and it will undoubtedly continue to be a major player in the global economy. The World Bank ranks the United States fourth in the world for ease of doing business, behind Singapore, Hong Kong, and New Zealand. And the diverse multicultural American workforce will continue to be an asset in coming years.

38   Some American businesses that had moved their operations overseas are now returning, and manufacturing is coming back. However, much of the new manufacturing uses robotics[13] and requires fewer workers, and the workers must have higher-level skills. American education systems and business communities are trying to collaborate to help provide workers with the new skills necessary for future employment. Significant changes will be necessary.

39   Although the institution of American business has certainly undergone enormous changes in recent decades, it has remained one of the most important institutions in the United States. In many ways, the business of America is still business.

---

[13] *robotics: the study of how robots (machines that do the work of a person) are made and used*

AFTER YOU READ

Understand Main Ideas

Check the predictions you made on page 125 before reading the chapter. How many of your predictions were correct? Look at the headings in the chapter and work with a partner to complete the outline of the main ideas.

A. The Characteristics of American Business: private, for-profit

B. How Business Competition Reinforces Other Values

    1. Competition protects individual _____ *freedom* _____

    2. Competition strengthens _____

    3. Business competition encourages _____

C. The Dream of Getting Rich

    1. Careers in business offer _____

    2. Americans distrust _____

D. The Entrepreneur as Business Hero

    1. Entrepreneurs are respected because _____

    2. The early entrepreneurs may be compared to _____

    3. Americans were influenced by Horatio Alger's _____

    4. Americans also respect entrepreneurs' dislike of _____

E. The Corporate CEO/CFO

    1. CEOs do not create new businesses, they _____

    2. Americans have lost respect for CEOs because _____

F. The Middle Class vs. the One Percent

    1. Middle class Americans became discouraged about _____

    2. They were angry because _____

    3. Books were written about _____

G. Redefining the American Dream

    1. Americans are _____

    2. There is a high value placed on _____

3. They are compassionate and are searching for _____

4. The technophilanthropists are _____

H. _____

1. Many Americans still choose to _____

2. The Internet _____

Understand Details

Write **T** if the statement is true and **F** if it is false according to the information in the chapter.

_____ 1. Most American businesses are directly or indirectly owned by the government.

_____ 2. Most Americans believe that business supports ideals and values that are important to the country.

_____ 3. Americans believe that competition among businesses is good for the economy but it does little to protect the freedom of the individual.

_____ 4. To succeed in American business, Americans believe that family background and social position are more important than anything, including hard work.

_____ 5. Most Americans believe that success in business offers the best chance to fulfill the dream of being wealthy.

_____ 6. A CEO may be admired since he or she started a successful business from practically nothing.

_____ 7. Some American companies moved their factories overseas because they could not afford to pay the high wages expected in the United States.

_____ 8. Most American companies pay their workers good retirement pensions, so people do not have to worry about having enough money when they stop working.

_____ 9. There are many more large corporations in the United States than small businesses.

_____ 10. Even in bad economic times, many Americans still try to start their own small businesses.

Talk About It

Work in small groups and choose one or more of these questions to discuss.

1. What qualities should a good businessperson have in order to be successful? Are these the same personal qualities that you would like your own boss to have?

2. How do you find out about job openings in your country? How important are family and personal connections?

3. Who do you admire more: people who start their own business from nothing, or those who save a big corporation that is in trouble? Why?

SKILL BUILDING

Improve Your Reading Skills: Scanning

Scan the chapter to look for these names. Then identify each person with a short phrase.

EXAMPLE: Alexis de Tocqueville *observed Americans' attraction to business in the 1830s.*

1. Calvin Coolidge _____

2. Arianna Huffington _____

3. Mark Zuckerberg _____

4. Warren Buffet _____

5. Gary Shapiro _____

6. Jeff Skoll _____

7. Chris Anderson _____

8. Horatio Alger _____

9. Richard Florida _____

10. Mitt Romney _____

Develop Your Critical Thinking Skills

Analyze a Reading

Read the following article from the website of the Small Business Administration (SBA) and analyze what it says. Write answers to these questions:

1. Who do you think the intended readers are, and why?

2. The article has a heading that reads "Small business is BIG!" What information is given that supports that claim?

3. What do you think are the most important and convincing facts in this article?

SMALL BUSINESS, BIG IMPACT!

One thing is for sure, as a small business owner you are not alone! There are millions of small businesses across the United States traveling the same road as you each and every day. Although your business operates in its own unique fashion, the cumulative impact of the small business sector is enormous.

SMALL BUSINESS IS BIG!

- The 23 million small businesses in America account for 54 percent of all U.S. sales.
- Small businesses provide 55 percent of all jobs and 66 percent of all net new jobs since the 1970s.
- The 600,000 plus franchised small businesses in the U.S. account for 40 percent of all retail sales and provide jobs for some eight million people.
- The small business sector in America occupies 30–50 percent of all commercial space, an estimated 20–34 billion square feet.

Furthermore, the small business sector is growing rapidly. While corporate America has been "downsizing," the rate of small business "start-ups" has grown, and the rate for small business failures has declined.

- The number of small businesses in the United States has increased 49 percent since 1982.

Since 1990, as big business eliminated four million jobs, small businesses added eight million new jobs.

Build Your Vocabulary

Same or Different

Read these sentences, which contain AWL words in bold. Look at the list of words after each sentence. Write the letter of the one word that has a different or opposite meaning from the boldfaced word.

_____ 1. A government-run system of production and **distribution** of goods is seen as inferior.
   a. sharing   b. giving   c. supplying   d. collecting

_____ 2. The people who, more than 100 years ago, built up the nation's great industries, such as steel, railroads, and oil **refining**, were usually entrepreneurs.
   a. purifying   b. selling   c. cleaning   d. improving

_____ 3. The strong influence of the success stories of the early entrepreneurs can be found in the great popularity of the novels of Horatio Alger, which were **published** in late-nineteenth and early-twentieth-century America.
   a. produced   b. printed   c. hidden   d. created

_____ 4. Jeff Skoll, the first president of eBay, says social entrepreneurs are **intensely** enthusiastic people who are anxious to reach their goals.
a. strongly   b. seriously   c. mildly   d. deeply

_____ 5. Even in a bad economy, the American Dream makes people feel encouraged and inspired, not discouraged and **depressed**.
a. happy   b. unhappy   c. sad   d. miserable

More AWL Words

Test your knowledge of these AWL words in the chapter by matching the following words with their definitions.

_____ 1. acquire		a. to support an idea
_____ 2. aware		b. a difference between things that are compared
_____ 3. benefit		c. an official rule or order
_____ 4. capable		d. understanding what is happening
_____ 5. contrast		e. main idea in a piece of writing
_____ 6. creative		f. having the skills needed to do something
_____ 7. decline		g. something that supplies information
_____ 8. energy		h. social or professional position
_____ 9. enormous		i. something that improves your life
_____ 10. financial		j. relating to money
_____ 11. global		k. physical and mental strength
_____ 12. guarantee		l. to buy or obtain something
_____ 13. regulation		m. a group of people who play a game or sport together
_____ 14. reinforce		n. producing or using new ideas
_____ 15. source		o. a formal written promise that something will be done or will happen
_____ 16. status		p. extremely large
_____ 17. team		q. affecting the whole world
_____ 18. theme		r. to decrease in quantity or importance

Idioms and Popular Phrases

The chapter contains several idioms and popular phrases that add color to the language. Look at the explanations below, and then read the sentences taken from the chapter. Find the phrase in italics for each of these meanings and write the letter of the sentence next to the correct meaning.

__a__ 1. do what is right and expected

_____ 2. warn that something bad will happen

_____ 3. get the worst deal

_____ 4. take care of yourself and help yourself, be self-reliant

_____ 5. keep a record

_____ 6. work toward completing or achieving something

_____ 7. change completely

_____ 8. profit after expenses, after all the numbers are added/subtracted

   a. "Upward mobility has always been at the center of the American Dream—a promise that if you work hard and *play by the rules,* you'll do well, and your children will have the chance to do even better."
   b. But in the last few years, Huffington said she saw that the middle class was *"getting the short end of the stick."*
   c. Perhaps part of this trait comes from their frontier heritage, where people believed they could *pull themselves up by their bootstraps* in times of trouble.
   d. Huffington *sounded the alarm* in her book about how American politicians are abandoning the middle class and betraying the American Dream.
   e. The quirky site *keeps track of* everyone's contribution online, and all who participate in the process get a percent of the profits from the sales, even a fraction of a percent.
   f. They want to *tackle* audacious *goals* like nuclear proliferation or pandemics or water.
   g. They're not happy until they've taught a farmer how to grow food, make money, pour the profits back into the business, hire ten other people, and in the process, *transform* the entire industry.
   h. Benefit corporations must commit to providing social or environmental benefits, "while still showing a healthy *bottom line.*"

EXPAND YOUR KNOWLEDGE

Ask Yourself / Ask Americans

Do you agree or disagree with each of the following statements? Put a check under the number that indicates how you feel.

+2 = Strongly agree

+1 = Agree

 0 = No opinion

–1 = Disagree

–2 = Strongly disagree

	+2	+1	0	–1	–2
1. I admire a person who is his or her own boss more than someone who must answer to others.	___	___	___	___	___
2. I would like to own my own business.	___	___	___	___	___
3. I think we should work to live, not live to work.	___	___	___	___	___
4. A teacher has more prestige than a businessperson.	___	___	___	___	___
5. Companies should offer loyal employees lifetime employment.	___	___	___	___	___
6. Corporate CEOs deserve as much money as they can get.	___	___	___	___	___
7. The place where I live is more important to me than where I work.	___	___	___	___	___
8. I would take a job I liked for less pay over a job I didn't like for more pay.	___	___	___	___	___
9. I would work on an assembly line in a factory if the pay were good.	___	___	___	___	___
10. All things considered, a government-run system is better for a country and its people than capitalism.	___	___	___	___	___

Ask several Americans to respond to these statements, if possible. If there are no Americans available, ask people from other countries.

People Watching

Who works in the United States? What ages? Men, women, teenagers, the elderly? What kind of jobs do they do? To answer these questions, if you are in the United States, look around you in various businesses open to the public: restaurants, banks, stores, drugstores, supermarkets, clubs, dry cleaners, doctors' offices, theaters, and so on. If you are near a university, check to see who is working in the library and the cafeteria. (If you are not in the United States, you may gather information from Americans you know, or you can observe people in your country.)

Observe people working in at least ten different places and record your results in this chart.

Kind of Job	Gender of Worker	Age of Worker	Other Observations
1.			
2.			
3.			
4.			
5.			
6.			
7.			
8.			
9.			
10.			

Proverbs and Sayings

Americans have a strong "sense of time." They think of it as a resource—something to be used, saved, spent, shared, etc. How they talk about time is an indication of how they feel about it.

Add to the list of time expressions below by asking Americans for suggestions, by listening to conversations, and by watching TV.

1. A stitch in time saves nine.
2. Time is money.
3. Time and tide wait for no man.
4. I don't have time for that today.
5. Can you give me a few minutes of your time?
6. We lost a lot of time on that.

Small-Group Discussion

Read the following explanation about how different cultures structure time, and then discuss the questions with members of your small group. When you have finished, report your group's findings to the rest of the class.

> *Edward T. Hall has described two basic types of cultures, with regard to the ways those cultures deal with time. He calls these "monochronic" and "polychronic" cultures. In monochronic cultures, people do one thing at a time. In polychronic cultures, people do many things at a time. For example, in a monochronic culture, when someone has a business appointment, that person expects to have the complete attention of the other party until the appointment has ended. On the other hand, in a polychronic culture, a person who has a business appointment expects there to be many others waiting and being dealt with at one time, sometimes both in person and on the phone.*

1. How are activities scheduled in your country?
2. Is your culture monochronic or polychronic?
3. Which best describes the United States?
4. Which would best describe the following situations?

   a. You arrive at the airport an hour before your flight to find that there are large crowds pushing their way to the counter. Whoever pushes hardest gets to the front and gets waited on. The ticket agent behind the counter serves several people at once, focusing attention on the one who has made himself or herself most noticed.

   b. The doctor has told you that he will meet you at the hospital at 10:00 A.M. to take care of a minor problem. You have difficulty finding transportation, but finally arrive at 10:45. The doctor is seeing another patient and sends word that he will not be able to see you now until he can "squeeze you in" around his other appointments. You will probably have to wait until late afternoon.

5. What other monochronic or polychronic situations can you think of?

Use the Internet

Work with a partner and do research on the Internet. Look for information about one of these super-rich business leaders.

Bill Gates

Ted Turner

Oprah Winfrey

Michael Bloomberg

Jeff Bezos

Sergey Brin

Laurene Powell Jobs

Melissa Mayer

Small-Group Project

Work in a group to create a small business.

- Decide on a name and describe what business the company will conduct.
- Choose a slogan for your business.
- List what the qualifications of the employees will be and what benefits the company will offer.

- Make up an advertisement for the business and, if possible, videotape it.
- Present your company to the rest of the class.

WRITE ABOUT IT

Choose one of the following topics. Then write a short composition about it.

1. Compare the way American businesses operate with the way businesses operate in your country. For example, compare a typical transaction at a shop. How do the activities differ? Consider these points:

   a. When the employees work

   b. Who the employees are and how long they have worked there

   c. Whether the shopkeeper waits on one person or several people at a time

   d. If the customer bargains or there is a set price

   e. If the employees know the customers

   f. What the relationship is between the employees and their employer

2. Most businesses in America require those applying for a job to submit a résumé, a summary of their work experience, education, and qualifications. Write a résumé for a job that you would like to have. Describe the position you want, and then write a résumé to convince an employer to hire you. As you write, consider the following advice from Jerrold G. Simon, EdD, a psychologist and career development specialist at Harvard Business School, who advises people to "sell themselves" in their résumé:

   The most qualified people don't always get the job. It goes to the person who presents himself more persuasively in person and on paper. So don't just list where you were and what you did. This is your chance to tell how well you did. Were you the best salesman? Did you cut operating costs? Give numbers, statistics, percentages, and increases in sales or profits.

EXPLORE ON YOUR OWN

Books to Read

Horatio Alger, *Ragged Dick; Or, Street Life in New York with the Boot Blacks*—Horatio Alger wrote this classic story of "rags to riches" about a young boy who works hard and eventually becomes a middle-class gentleman.

F. Scott Fitzgerald, *The Great Gatsby*—In this classic American novel about a self-made man, Jay Gatsby's pursuit of wealth causes his fall.

Chrystia Freeland, *Plutocrats: The Rise of the New Global Super-Rich and the Fall of Everyone Else*—Freeland looks at the economic elites who threaten the democratic, politically open society of the United States and the American Dream.

Arianna Huffington, *Third World America: How Our Politicians Are Abandoning the Middle Class and Betraying the American Dream*—Huffington, herself an immigrant from Greece, warns about what could happen if the government does not protect the middle class.

Gary Shapiro, *The Comeback: How Innovation Will Restore the American Dream*—Shapiro says that throughout history, our great innovators have been the real drivers of American economic success.

Movies to See

9 to 5—In this popular comedy, three women who are tired of being treated badly by their boss decide to capture him and make changes at their workplace.

Class Action—A lawyer who is suing an auto company over a safety defect faces his daughter, who is the attorney representing the company.

Trading Places—A rich stockbroker and a street-smart beggar find themselves trading places as part of a bet by two old millionaires.

Up in the Air—A businessman makes his living traveling around the country firing people for different companies.

Wall Street—A young and impatient stockbroker is willing to do anything to get to the top, including trading on illegal inside information.

CHAPTER 7

GOVERNMENT AND POLITICS IN THE UNITED STATES

A wise and frugal Government shall restrain men from injuring one another, [and] shall leave them otherwise free to regulate their own pursuits of industry and improvements.

Thomas Jefferson (1743–1826)

What role do Americans think their government should play in their lives? How do American values affect how the United States government functions?

BEFORE YOU READ

Preview Vocabulary

A. Read the following sentences from the chapter and notice the words in italics. These key AWL words will help you understand the chapter reading. Use context clues to help you figure out the meanings. Then choose which definition is best for the italicized word.

_____ 1. The way in which the national government is organized in the U.S. Constitution provides an excellent *illustration* of the American suspicion of governmental power.
   a. example that shows the truth very clearly
   b. argument against an idea

_____ 2. The judicial branch both *interprets* the law and determines whether the law is constitutional—that is, whether the law is permitted under the U.S. Constitution.
   a. explains
   b. rejects

_____ 3. The Senate has certain powers over foreign treaties and *military* actions.
   a. relating to law
   b. relating to war

_____ 4. This requires the president to have "the advice and *consent* of the Senate" before taking certain action on the international front.
   a. permission to do something
   b. a careful plan for action

_____ 5. The Bill of Rights guarantees the right of a fair criminal *procedure* for those accused of breaking laws.
   a. punishment
   b. method

_____ 6. After a *series* of legal challenges, the U.S. Supreme Court decided about a month after the election that the Florida state legislature had a right to stop recounting the ballots and certify the electoral votes.
   a. events that are related and have a particular result
   b. events that break the law and have consequences

_____ 7. The Great *Depression* of the 1930s greatly weakened the businessperson's position as the American ideal of the free individual, and big business lost respect.
   a. a time when there was not much business activity and many people had no jobs
   b. a time when there was much corruption and greed among business leaders

_____ 8. The widespread unemployment and other economic hardships of the Depression gave rise to the *assumption* that individuals could not be expected to rely solely on themselves in providing for their economic security.
   a. promise that something will happen in the future
   b. belief (that you think is true although you have no proof)

_____ 9. There is an *ideological* divide over the role and size of the national government—Republicans have traditionally believed that big government is not only inefficient, it also endangers individual rights and freedoms, while Democrats have called for more government regulation of financial institutions and corporate polluters and higher taxes on upper income Americans to fund social programs.
   a. based on a particular set of beliefs or ideas
   b. based on historical differences

_____ 10. Still, it is individuals, their rights, their interests, and their ambitions, not those of the nation as a whole, that are the *focus* of attention.
   a. the most important part
   b. the most difficult part

B. There are four AWL words in the quotation by Thomas Jefferson at the beginning of the chapter. Read the quotation and find the words with the following meanings. Write each word next to its meaning.

_____ 1. acts of trying to get something

_____ 2. prevent someone from doing something

_____ 3. to control an activity by rules

_____ 4. hurting

Preview Content

A. Before you read, preview the chapter by looking at the illustrations and reading the headings and the captions under the pictures. Work with a partner and answer these questions.

1. Do you agree with the quotation by Thomas Jefferson? Paraphrase (rewrite) the quotation in your own words.

2. In the United States, who has more power, the president or Congress? Why do you think so?

3. What are the two major political parties in the United States? What is the main difference in their beliefs?

B. Make a graphic organizer about government. Write the word *government* in the center of a piece of paper. Then draw lines out from the center, as you did on page 29. Write all the things you think a government should do for its people.

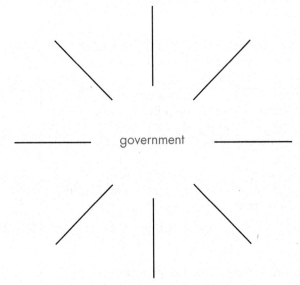

government

C. Predict five topics that will be discussed in this chapter. Write your predictions here.

1. _____

2. _____

3. _____

4. _____

5. _____

1   The ideal of the free individual has had a profound effect on the way Americans view their government. Traditionally, there has been a deep suspicion that government is the natural enemy of freedom, even if it is elected by the people. The bigger and stronger the government becomes, the more dangerous many Americans believe it is to their individual freedom.*

The Signing of the Declaration of Independence, a painting by John Trumbull

2   This suspicion of strong government goes back to the men who led the American Revolution in 1776. These men believed the government of Great Britain wanted to discourage the freedom and economic opportunities of the American colonists by excessive taxes and other measures that would ultimately benefit the British aristocracy and monarchy. Thomas Paine, the famous revolutionary writer, expressed the view of other American revolutionists when he said, ". . . Government even in its best state is but a necessary evil; in its worst state, an intolerable[1] one . . . "

The Organization of the American Government

3   The way in which the national government is organized in the U.S. Constitution provides an excellent illustration of the American suspicion of governmental power. The provisions of the Constitution are more concerned with keeping the government from doing evil than with enabling it to do good. The national government, for example, is divided into three separate branches. This division of governmental power is based on the belief that if any one part or branch of government has all, or even most of the power, it will become a threat to the freedom of individual citizens.

4   The legislative or lawmaking branch of the government is called the *Congress*. Congress has two houses—the Senate, with two senators from each state regardless of the size of its population, and the *House of Representatives*, consisting of a total of 435 representatives divided among the fifty states by population. (In the House, states with large populations have more representatives than states with small populations, while in the Senate, each state has equal representation.) The

---

*It is important to note that all 50 states have state governments, and within the states there are local governments at the city and/or county level, all of which have their own laws, police, and court systems. According to the Constitution, states have all powers not given to the national (or federal) government. If there is a conflict between a state law and a national law, the national law prevails.

[1] intolerable: too difficult, bad, or annoying to accept or deal with

president, or chief executive, heads the executive branch, which has responsibility to carry out the laws. The *Supreme Court* and lower national courts make up the judicial branch. The judicial branch settles disputes about the exact meaning of the law through court cases. It both interprets the law and determines whether the law is *constitutional*—that is, whether the law is permitted under the U.S. Constitution.

5   If any one of the three branches starts to abuse[2] its power, the other two may join together to stop it, through a system of *checks* and *balances.* The Constitution is most careful in balancing the powers of the legislative and executive branches of the government because these two (Congress and the president) are the most powerful of the three branches. In almost every important area of governmental activity, such as the power to make laws, to declare war, or to conclude treaties with foreign countries, the Constitution gives each of these two branches enough power to prevent the other from acting on its own.

6   Observers from other countries are often confused by the American system. The national government may seem to speak with two conflicting voices, that of the president and that of Congress. For example, a treaty with a foreign government signed by the president dies if the Senate refuses to *ratify* it—that is, if the Senate doesn't vote to accept it. The Senate has certain powers over foreign treaties and, with the House, military actions. This requires the president to have "the advice and consent of the Senate" before taking certain actions on the international front. The Senate also must approve all the members of the president's cabinet, such as the Secretary of State and the Secretary of Defense.

7   On the other hand, the president may prevent a bill passed by Congress from becoming law. When both houses of Congress have agreed on a piece of legislation or a resolution, it is sent to the president. The president has ten days to act, not counting Sundays. At that point, there are four possibilities:

1. The president agrees with the bill, signs it, and it becomes law.

2. The president disagrees with the bill, vetoes it, and sends it back to the Congress with his or her reasons for refusing to sign it. If two-thirds of both the House and the Senate vote to override the president's veto, the bill becomes law.

3. The president may take no action and after ten days (not counting Sundays), the bill becomes law without his signature.

4. If the Congress adjourns[3] before the ten-day period is over, and the president has neither signed nor vetoed the bill, it is defeated. This is called a *pocket veto.* Presidents sometimes do this with bills they do not like but do not want to go on record as having vetoed.

8   Although the American system of divided governmental power strikes many observers as inefficient and even disorganized, most Americans still strongly believe in it for two reasons: (1) It has been able to meet the challenges of the past, and (2) it gives strong protection to individual freedoms.

9   In addition to dividing government powers into three branches, the Constitution includes a *Bill of Rights* that is designed to protect specific individual rights and freedoms from government interference. Some of the guarantees in the Bill of Rights concern the freedom of expression. The government may not interfere with an individual's freedom of speech or freedom

[2] *abuse: to deliberately use power or authority for the wrong purpose*

[3] *adjourns: stops meeting for a short time*

of religious worship, or the right to assemble (get together). The Bill of Rights also guarantees the right of a fair criminal procedure for those accused of breaking laws. These rights are sometimes called "due process." They include provisions that someone accused of a crime must be charged with the crime and is presumed innocent until proven guilty. The accused has the right to an attorney, and there must be a trial declaring someone guilty before punishment is given. Thus, the Bill of Rights is another statement of the American belief in the importance of individual freedom.

The Election of the President and the Congress

10   The president and both houses of Congress have almost complete political independence from each other because they are all chosen in separate elections. For example, the election of the Congress does not determine who will be elected president, and the presidential election does not determine who will be elected to either house of Congress. This system is quite different from the way a parliamentary system of government chooses a prime minister. Another difference is that there are only two important political parties in the United States: the Democrats, who are traditionally liberal or progressive, and the Republicans, who are more conservative. In parliamentary systems, there may be a number of significant political parties that must agree to form a government, while in the United States this is not the case. The president, the representatives, and the senators are all chosen by the American citizens in elections.

11   Because the elections of the president and members of the two houses of Congress are separate from each other, it is quite possible in the American system to have the leader of one political party win the presidency while the other major political party wins a majority of the seats in Congress. Thus, the Republicans may control one house, while the Democrats may control the other. During the late 1900s, while most of the presidents were Republican, the Democrats often controlled one or both of the houses of Congress. In 1994, the reverse happened: While Bill Clinton, a Democrat, was president, the Republicans won control of both the House of Representatives and the Senate. Then in the early 2000s, for a time, the Republican Party controlled the presidency (George W. Bush) and both houses of Congress. The presidency of Barack Obama (a Democrat) has again seen divided government; after the first two years, in both of his terms the House was controlled by the Republicans, and the Senate was controlled by Democrats.

12   In order to understand what is happening in Washington, it is important to know not only the party of the president, but also which parties control the House and the Senate. Because both the House of Representatives and the Senate must agree on all legislation before it goes to the president, legislation may pass one house but be blocked in the other. Furthermore, the party in control of the House or Senate has the potential of changing every two years. Members of the House of Representatives are elected for two-year terms, while senators serve six-year terms. The Senate terms are staggered[4] so that only one-third of the senators run for re-election each time the House elections are held, every two years.

13   Presidential elections are held every four years, on the first Tuesday in November.

[4] staggered: arranged so that their terms of office (time serving as a senator or representative) do not all begin and end at the same time

When the Constitution was written, the founding fathers had a disagreement about how the president should be elected. Some did not want the members of Congress to choose the president, and others were afraid to leave the choice entirely to the voters. The result was a compromise—the electoral college, a system for indirectly electing the president. The system persists today. In presidential elections, people are actually voting for representatives called *electors*, and it is these electors who officially choose the president. With the electoral college system, the winner of the plurality[5] (the highest number) of each state's popular votes gets all of that state's electoral votes, in most cases. (There are several exceptions.) The number of each state's electoral votes is equal to the total number of their representatives in the House and the Senate. Though the number of electoral votes varies according to each state's population, it is still possible for a person to be elected president without getting the highest number of the popular, or individual, votes.

14 Although Americans were aware of the electoral college system, the average voter did not give it much thought until the election of 2000. There had been only three previous instances of presidents ever losing the popular vote but winning the electoral vote, and it seemed a remote possibility. The last time it had happened was in 1888, when Benjamin Harrison won the presidency, even though Grover Cleveland had the majority of popular votes. All through the 1900s, the presidents who were elected had won at least a plurality, (the highest number of the popular votes), in addition to winning the electoral votes. However, in the election of 2000, Al Gore, the Democratic candidate, won more popular votes than George W. Bush, the Republican candidate, but Bush

won the most electoral votes and became president. (In the 2004 election between George W. Bush and John Kerry, the electoral college was not an issue, because Bush won both the popular vote and the electoral vote.)

15 The result of the election of 2000 sent shock waves through the American political system. One reason was that the vote was incredibly close, and several states had to count their votes a second time. The state with the most controversial results was Florida, where the governor of the state was Jeb Bush, George W. Bush's brother. Although Gore had won the popular vote nationwide, whoever won the twenty-five Florida electoral votes would win the election. The recounts of the votes in Florida showed Bush winning by fewer than 1,000 votes out of almost six million votes cast. After a series of legal challenges, the U.S. Supreme Court decided about a month after the election that the Florida state legislature had the right to stop recounting the ballots and certify the electoral votes. The Supreme Court ruled that a state has the ultimate right to determine how its electors are chosen.

The Ideal of the Free Individual

16 In the late 1700s, most Americans expected the new national government created by the Constitution to leave them alone to pursue their individual goals. They believed the central purpose of government was to create the conditions most favorable to the development of the free individual.

17 Before the Civil War of the 1860s, the American ideal of the free individual was the frontier settler and the small farmer. President Thomas Jefferson expressed this ideal when he said, "Those who labor in

[5] *plurality: the number of votes received by the winning person in an election where there are three or more people trying to be elected*

the earth are the chosen people of God, if ever he had a chosen people. . . ." Jefferson glorified farmers for being free individuals who relied on no one but themselves for their daily needs. Being dependent on none but themselves, farmers, he believed, were the most honest of citizens. Throughout his life Jefferson favored a small, weak form of government, which he believed would encourage the development of a nation of free, self-reliant farmer citizens.

18 From the end of the Civil War until the Great Depression of the 1930s, the successful businessperson replaced the farmer and the frontier settler as the ideal expression of the free individual. The prevailing view of Americans was that government should not interfere in business. If it were to do so, it would threaten the development of free individuals whose competitive spirit, self-reliance, and hard work were developing the United States into a land of greater and greater material prosperity.

19 Government, therefore, remained small and inactive in relation to the great size of the nation and the amount of power held by business corporations. Some government regulations were in place during this period, but these had only a small impact on business practices. From the 1870s until the 1930s, business organizations and ideas dominated American government and politics. During much of this time, the Republican Party was in power, and it strongly supported these policies.

The Development of Big Government

20 Traditionally, Republicans have favored letting businesses compete with little or no government regulation: Let the free enterprise system regulate itself in the marketplace. On the other hand, Democrats have traditionally favored using government to regulate businesses, protect consumers and workers, and also to solve social problems. Not surprisingly, it was a Democratic president who presided over the creation of "big government."

21 The Great Depression of the 1930s greatly weakened the businessperson's position as the American ideal of the free individual, and big business lost respect. The Depression also created the need for emergency government action to help the needy on a scale never before seen in the United States in peacetime. As a result, the idea that government should be small and inactive was largely abandoned. Moreover, the ideal of the free individual underwent some very important changes.

22 The widespread unemployment and other economic hardships of the Depression gave rise to the new assumption[6] that individuals could not be expected to rely solely on themselves in providing for their economic security. This new assumption, in turn, led to a large and active role for the national government in helping individuals meet their daily needs. The Democratic Party, led by President Franklin Roosevelt, brought about a number of changes in the 1930s, which he referred to as a "New Deal" for Americans.

23 Even with the return of prosperity after the Depression and World War II (1941–1945), the growth of government's role in helping to provide economic security for individuals did not end. It continued in the prosperous postwar years, and it was greatly expanded during the presidency of another Democrat, Lyndon Johnson, in the 1960s. Roosevelt's New Deal grew into what some saw as a permanent "welfare state" that provided payments for retired persons, government checks for the unemployed, support for families

---

[6] assumption: something you think is true although you have no proof

with dependent children and no father to provide income, health care for the poor and the elderly, and other government benefits. Johnson called the new welfare programs "The Great Society."

The Controversy over Entitlements

24 The development of big government, and the establishment of government social programs, is not without controversy. On the one hand, some Americans fear that economic security provided by the government will weaken self-reliance, an ideal that is closely associated in the minds of Americans with individual freedom. At worst, it presents a danger to individual freedom by making an increasing number of Americans dependent on the government instead of on themselves. In this way, the strong traditions of individualism and self-reliance have made Americans less accepting of social programs than the citizens of other democracies such as those in Western Europe, which have more extensive social programs than those of the United States.

25 A Pew Research study reveals the contrast between European and American attitudes:

WHICH IS MORE IMPORTANT

	Nobody in need	Freedom to pursue life's goals
U.S.	35	58
Britain	55	38
Germany	62	36
France	64	36
Spain	67	30

American opinions continue to differ considerably from those of Western Europeans when it comes to views of individualism and the role of the state. Nearly six-in-ten (58%) Americans believe it is more important for everyone to be free to pursue their life's goals without interference from the state, while just 36% say it is more important for the state to play an active role in society so as to guarantee that nobody is in need.

26 Americans generally are not in favor of European-style socialism that guarantees benefits for all who are needy. Indeed, some consider socialism a potentially dangerous, foreign economic system. Some conservatives have accused President Obama of being a socialist for some of his liberal stands. On the other hand, most Americans believe that their national government should provide some kind of "safety net" to take care of people in certain circumstances such as temporary loss of employment, damages from a natural disaster such as a hurricane, and of course retirement. It is interesting that the term for these benefits has changed. We used to make a distinction between welfare benefits and entitlements. Programs such as unemployment benefits, food stamps, and Medicaid (health care for the poor), were known as "welfare." Social Security and Medicare (health care for the retired) were seen as "entitlements," because working Americans and their employers pay into these systems. Therefore, when workers retire, they consider that they have paid for these benefits and they are entitled to them. Now the term welfare is almost never used, and all these government benefits are referred to as entitlements.

27 While most Americans would believe that the national government should provide them with some support, if they should need it, they may disagree about how much support and for how long. Democrats generally favor more generous support from the government than Republicans do. Republicans believe in a smaller role for the government and a greater emphasis on individual responsibility. During the 2012 election,

Republican presidential candidate Mitt Romney was overheard saying that 47 percent of Americans were dependent on government support and saw themselves as victims who could not take care of themselves:

> There are 47 percent of the people who will vote for the president no matter what . . . who are dependent upon government, who believe that they are victims. . . . These are people who pay no income tax . . . and so my job is not to worry about those people. I'll never convince them that they should take personal responsibility and care for their lives.

28 In fact, about half of all American households have someone who receives some aid from the federal government. However, this number includes people who are retired and are receiving Social Security and Medicare benefits, now about 14 percent of the population, plus another 2 percent who are receiving other Social Security benefits. Most Americans believe that they have earned the right to having Social Security and Medicare when they retire, but the problem is that these benefits now take about one-third of the federal budget.

29 As the population ages, there are fewer younger workers and their employers paying Social Security taxes into the system, and more retired workers taking money out. Americans are living longer in retirement, and their medical expenses are rising. Because older Americans are more likely than young people to vote, politicians pay particular attention to their needs. They want the older Americans' votes. However, as budget deficits[7] grow, the reality is that some adjustments to all entitlements are likely to be needed, including Social Security and Medicare.

The Role of Special Interest Groups

30 Over time, practically all social and economic classes of Americans have seen the need to take advantage of, or to protect themselves from, the actions of government, especially the national government. To accomplish this, Americans with similar interests have formed special interest groups to more effectively influence the actions of government. These special interest groups are often called "lobbying[8] groups" or "pressure groups." Although lobbying groups have existed throughout the nation's history, they have grown significantly in both numbers and power since the late 1900s.

31 The National Rifle Association (mentioned in Chapter 4) is an example of a powerful and effective lobby. Its members are mostly people who own guns for hunting, target practice, and personal protection. The NRA, however, receives a great deal of money from business corporations that manufacture guns. Because of the attitudes and interests of its members, the NRA strongly opposes almost all government restrictions on the sale of all handguns, rifles, shotguns, and even semi-automatic and assault weapons. Even though most of the general public favors some gun control measures, the NRA has always been able to block the passage of most gun-control legislation. (See poll on page 167.)

---

[7] *deficit: the difference between the amount of money that a government spends and the amount that it takes in from taxes and other activities*

[8] *lobbying: trying to influence the government or someone with political power so that they make laws favorable to you*

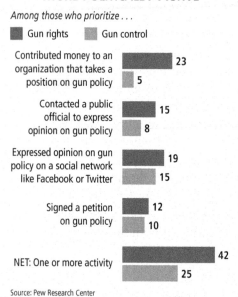

GUN RIGHTS PROPONENTS MORE POLITICALLY ACTIVE

Among those who prioritize . . .

■ Gun rights　■ Gun control

Contributed money to an organization that takes a position on gun policy
- 23
- 5

Contacted a public official to express opinion on gun policy
- 15
- 8

Expressed opinion on gun policy on a social network like Facebook or Twitter
- 19
- 15

Signed a petition on gun policy
- 12
- 10

NET: One or more activity
- 42
- 25

Source: Pew Research Center

32　Those who are concerned about the right to own guns are more likely to be politically active. The public sees both parties as being supportive of their views on gun control/gun rights—conservative Republicans are more concerned about their right to own guns, and liberal Democrats are more likely to favor stricter gun control laws.

33　Although few interest groups have been as successful as the NRA, most well-organized interest groups have achieved a large measure of success. By organizing into groups which put pressure on government officials, people can gain more rewards and avoid more government restrictions than if they tried to do it as individuals.

34　With this principle in mind, business interest groups have multiplied in recent decades so that most major trades, businesses, and even professions have their lobbyists in Washington. There are influential lobbies representing labor unions, farm groups, teachers, doctors, lawyers, and specific industries such as oil and natural gas, pharmaceuticals, and biotechnology. Interest groups representing ethnic groups such as African Americans, Native Americans, Mexican Americans, and Jewish Americans have also expanded. There are also interest groups representing a variety of ideals or causes that want government support. These include groups pressing for a clean environment and those promoting greater protection for consumers. As one congressman exclaimed, "Everybody in America has a lobby!"

35　The political tendency of recent decades is for the size of the government to bring about an increase in the number and size of interest groups, and for the greater demands made on the government by interest groups to increase the size of the government. Groups such as the AARP (American Association of Retired Persons) not only demand new government programs, regulations, and benefits for their members, they also strongly resist any

Interest groups represent a variety of populations in the United States.

attempts to reduce existing programs that they believe protect their interests, such as Social Security and Medicare. The result of this continuing cycle can be referred to as "interest group government." No single interest dominates government and politics as business groups did before the Great Depression. Instead, government and politics are based on reaching compromises with a large number of groups and pleasing as many as possible.

The New Individualism: Interest-Group Government

36 Interest-group government can be seen as expressing a new form of American individualism. Unlike the old frontier or business individualism, individuals do not claim to succeed on their own, but rather by forming groups to influence the government. Still, it is individuals, their rights, their interests, and their ambitions, not those of the nation as a whole, that are the focus of their attention. The interest group is no more than a tool to achieve the goals of the individual by influencing the government.

37 Although many Americans have benefited in some way from government-sponsored programs, some experts believe that interest-group government is harmful to the United States. The effect on politicians is enormous. First, interest groups often focus on one issue that is more important to their members than all others. For example, some people feel very strongly that abortion should not be legal in the United States. They may choose to vote for candidates primarily because of their stand on the abortion issue. Generally, because their members feel so strongly, lobby groups are able to promise that their members will vote for a candidate if he or she promises to support their issue once elected. The NRA gives members of Congress grades for their voting record on gun control, and it has been particularly effective in re-electing or defeating senators and representatives.

38 Second, members of special interest groups contribute large sums of money to election campaigns. Because candidates must rely mostly on private, not public, funding, they are often forced to depend on special interest groups for their campaign funds. Candidates at all levels of government—national, state, and local—must spend enormous amounts of their time raising funds for their re-election. For example, because members of the House of Representatives are elected every two years, they engage in continual fundraising. Senators and presidential candidates are also pressured. The situation has become so bad that many people are agreeing with the statement, "We have the best government that money can buy!" There have been efforts to reform the system, but the Supreme Court's *Citizens United* decision in 2010 ruled that corporations, individuals, and labor unions could make unlimited contributions to political campaigns through Super PACs (Political Action Committees). In the presidential election of 2012, Super PACs spent over $524 million, according to the Federal Election Commission.

The Political Landscape in the 2000s: Red States vs. Blue States

39 In reporting the results of presidential elections, TV news reports show the map of the United States with red states (awarding the state's electoral votes to the Republican candidate), and blue states (giving the electoral votes to the Democratic candidate). These colors have come to symbolize the deep divisions in America. In Obama's first national speech at the Democratic Convention in 2004, he offered his vision of a country where we are not red states or blue states—we are one people—the United States of America. But the divisions persist.

40 In *Barack Obama and the New America: The 2012 Election and the Changing Face of Politics*, Alan Abramowitz says the American voters are strongly divided

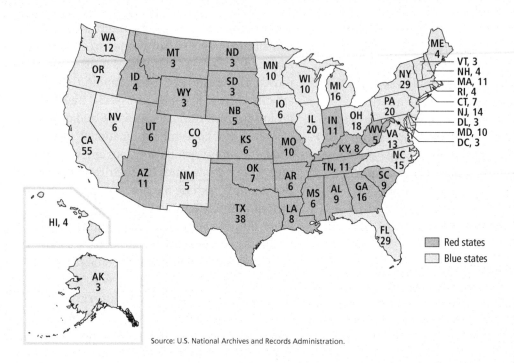

WA 12, OR 7, ID 4, MT 3, ND 3, SD 3, WY 3, NV 6, UT 6, CO 9, NB 5, KS 6, MN 10, IO 6, MO 10, WI 10, MI 16, IL 20, IN 11, OH 18, KY, 8, ME 4, VT, 3, NH, 4, MA, 11, RI, 4, CT, 7, NJ, 14, DL, 3, MD, 10, DC, 3, NY 29, PA 20, WV 5, VA 13, NC 15, CA 55, AZ 11, NM 5, OK 7, AR 6, TN, 11, SC 9, MS 6, AL 9, GA 16, TX 38, LA 8, FL 29, HI, 4, AK 3

Red states
Blue states

Source: U.S. National Archives and Records Administration.

along party lines. In an unusually partisan election, over 90 percent of the Democrats voted for Obama, and over 90 percent of the Republicans voted for Romney. Even the Independents, now about one-third of the electorate, were split 50/50 Obama/ Romney. Also, more than 90 percent of voters chose their House or Senate representatives according to their party. Abramowitz says that this unusual degree of party loyalty reflects the deep divisions in American society:

A close examination of the voting patterns in 2012 demonstrates the existence of three major divisions between Democrats and Republicans—a racial divide between a Democratic Party increasingly dependent on votes from non-whites and an overwhelmingly white Republican Party, an ideological divide over the role and size of government, and a cultural divide over values, morality, and lifestyle.

41 *First, the racial divide.* Barack Obama's winning the presidency in 2008 was truly a historical event. For the first time ever, the United States had an African-American president. The Democrats had traditionally had more support from non-white Americans than the Republicans, but this election brought people of all races together behind a candidate that promised "hope and change"—an America where the ultimate American Dream could come true. Some believed that it was a fluke,[9] something that happens only by chance or luck. But Obama captured the imagination of millions of Americans. Young voters were energized for the first time since the anti-war movements of the 1960s and early 1970s, and also for the first time, social media played an important role. Obama built a grass-roots organization where his campaigners came to know potential voters personally, and many Americans felt like they were part of history. Well over a million people stood outside in the freezing weather on the Washington, D.C., Mall in January, 2009, to watch Obama's inauguration on huge TV screens.

42 Obama's re-election in 2012 proved that his winning in 2008 was not a fluke. Obama lost a number of white voters, but

[9] *fluke: something that only happens because of chance or luck*

his coalition of non-white voters held. By 2012, 28 percent of the voting public were non-white: African Americans, Hispanics, Asian Americans, and other non-whites. Republicans were greatly surprised by Obama's victory and realized that it reflected a new reality in the United States: In spirit, the country has already become the multi-racial, multicultural country the demographers predicted for 2050. We do not have to wait thirty or forty years to see the political effects of being a majority-minority country—the demographic shift is already affecting elections. The Republican Party is in search of a new direction. Because the Republican Party hopes to attract new voters, it will have to appeal to Hispanics, African Americans, Asian Americans, and other non-white voters. The color of the electoral map is also changing, as Democratic Hispanic populations in states such as New Mexico, Colorado, and Nevada are starting to turn these red states blue.

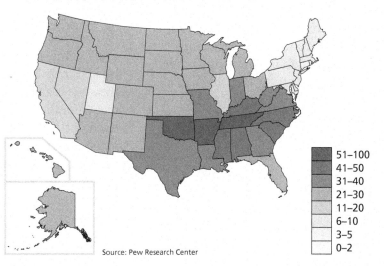

PERCENTAGE OF EACH STATE'S POPULATION THAT AFFILIATES WITH EVANGELICAL PROTESTANT TRADITION

51–100
41–50
31–40
21–30
11–20
6–10
3–5
0–2

Source: Pew Research Center

43   *Second, the ideological divide over the role and size of the national government.* Republicans have traditionally believed that big government is not only inefficient, it also endangers individual rights and freedoms. In 2012, the Tea Party* pushed the Republican Party more to the very conservative right, insisting that government spending is the cause of all economic problems and demanding severe budget cuts. Romney campaigned on a plan to reduce huge budget deficits through significant cuts in social programs; the elimination of many health, safety,

and environmental regulations; and the repeal of the Obama health care law, while cutting taxes on upper income households and corporations. Obama and the Democrats called for more government regulation of financial institutions and corporate polluters, higher taxes on upper income Americans to fund social programs, and full implementation of the new health care law.

44   *Third, the cultural divide over values, morality, and lifestyles.* Republicans have increasingly built an alliance with religious conservatives of all faiths, particularly evangelical Christians. Republicans have become associated with traditional values and lifestyles, such as limiting access to abortions and opposition to gay marriage and other rights for homosexuals. They have also been against some birth control methods, including the "morning after" pill. In the meantime, the Democratic Party has moved further left on these issues. Obama allowed gays to serve openly in the military, and he called for gays' right to marry and other minority rights in his second inaugural address.

The Tea Party is a very conservative grass-roots movement originally organized by people who were worried about growing government debt (the amount of money owed). The name refers to the Boston Tea Party when American colonists threw tea into the Boston Harbor to protest the British tax on tea.

45 The country as a whole has become more liberal on these social issues, with a majority now favoring gay marriage and the right to abortion in early months of a pregnancy. Most young people are more liberal and less religious than their parents, so the demographics favor the Democrats in the future. Other lifestyle differences include the legalization of marijuana and the passage of laws recognizing gay marriage in a number of states. A look at the red state/blue state map shows the Democratic strength in the liberal Northeast and West coast states and the big cities, while Republicans find their supporters in the more conservative South and in rural areas.

Finding the Way Forward

46 Both the Republicans and the Democrats truly believe that they have the roadmap that will lead the United States to a safe and prosperous future. Republicans believe the country's economic difficulties are due to a spending problem, while Democrats believe it is an income problem. Republicans believe that dependence on entitlements seriously weakens individual freedom and responsibility. They believe that Americans are living beyond their means, borrowing money they need to run a larger and larger government, and creating a terrible financial burden for their children and grandchildren.

47 Democrats are concerned about the widening gap between those who are very, very wealthy and those who are very, very poor. They believe that the government can protect individual freedom by passing laws that ensure equal access to health care and jobs for all Americans, and by showing the way forward with government programs that will engage private businesses in cooperative projects to rebuild needed infrastructure, roads and bridges, and create partnerships between schools and businesses to provide the educated workforce of the future.

48 In *Our Divided Political Heart: The Battle for the American Idea in an Age of Discontent*, E.J. Dionne, Jr. urges Americans to look back at their history to understand who they are as a people. They must recognize that from the beginning, Americans have lived with a tension between two core values: their love of individualism and their respect for community. These two values work together to give the nation balance, and both values interact with the important value of equality.

49 Obama has spoken about this need for balance between the individualism of private business and the community of common government:

> From our first days as a nation, we have put our faith in free markets and free enterprise as the engine of America's wealth and prosperity. More than citizens of any other country, we are rugged individualists, a self-reliant people with a healthy skepticism of too much government.
>
> But there has always been another thread running throughout our history—a belief that we are all connected; and that there are some things we can only do together, as a nation. . . . The America I know is generous and compassionate; a land of opportunity and optimism. We take responsibility for ourselves and each other; for the country we want and the future we share.

50 Obama is expressing a belief in the role traditional American values play in the nation and its government. The twenty-first century will continue to offer challenges to the United States citizens and its government leaders. Hopefully, the six basic cultural values—individual freedom, self-reliance, equality of opportunity, competition, material wealth, and hard work will continue to guide and direct the United States and its people in the future.

AFTER YOU READ

Understand Main Ideas

Check the predictions you made on page 152 before reading the chapter. Next to each of your predictions, write the number of the paragraph where you found the information you predicted.

Work with a partner and answer these questions about main ideas from each section of the chapter. Skim the sections for the main ideas if you do not remember them.

1. *A Suspicion of Strong Government:* Why are Americans suspicious of a strong government?

2. *The Organization of the American Government:* What are the four possible things that can happen once Congress sends a bill to the president?

3. *The Election of the President and the Congress:* What is the Electoral College? How does it work?

4. *The Ideal of the Free Individual:* What effect did the two ideals of the free individual have on the development of the government before the Great Depression of the 1930s? Why?

5. *The Development of Big Government:* What major effect did the Great Depression have on the government?

6. *The Controversy over Entitlements:* What are entitlements and why are they controversial?

7. *The Role of Special Interest Groups:* What are special interest groups? Why are they formed and whom do they represent?

8. *The New Individualism: Interest-Group Government:* How do special interest groups affect how the government operates?

9. *The Political Landscape in the 2000s: Red States vs. Blue States:* What are the traditional beliefs of the Republican and the Democratic parties? What are three important differences?

10. *Finding the Way Forward:* What do the two political parties believe should happen in the future? What is the balance needed between their two ideologies?

Understand Details

Write the letter of the best answer according to the information in the chapter.

_____ 1. Americans do not want to have a strong national government because
   a. they are afraid of their political leaders.
   b. they are afraid it will put limits on their individual freedom.
   c. they are much more concerned with national glory.

_____ 2. The Constitution of the United States
   a. gives by far the most power to Congress.
   b. gives by far the most power to the president.
   c. tries to give each branch enough power to balance the others.

_____ 3. The president of the United States
    a. has the power to make official treaties with foreign governments without the approval of Congress.
    b. can veto a law that has been passed by Congress.
    c. is elected if his political party wins most of the seats in Congress.

_____ 4. The Bill of Rights
    a. explains the rights of Congress and the rights of the president.
    b. guarantees citizens of the United States specific individual rights and freedoms.
    c. is part of the Declaration of Independence.

_____ 5. The American ideal of the free individual
    a. was exemplified by the farmers and the frontier settlers in the late 1700s and early 1800s.
    b. was exemplified by the businessman before the Civil War of the 1860s.
    c. caused the national government to grow in size and strength during the late 1800s.

_____ 6. The number of electoral votes a candidate receives
    a. is determined by who wins the total popular vote nationwide.
    b. is determined by the electoral votes of the states the candidate wins.
    c. is equal to the number of seats each state has in the House of Representatives.

_____ 7. Which of these statements is _true_ about the 2000 presidential election?
    a. George W. Bush became president in 2000 because he won a plurality of votes nationwide.
    b. The Supreme Court played a major role in the 2000 election.
    c. Jeb Bush played an important role in the election because he was governor of California.

_____ 8. Stronger gun-control laws are favored by
    a. the National Rifle Association.
    b. most of the American people.
    c. very few Americans.

_____ 9. Which statement about lobby groups is _not_ true?
    a. They have become less powerful in recent years.
    b. They try to influence the government and public opinion.
    c. They have caused the government to get larger.

_____ 10. Which statement about the traditional beliefs of the political parties is _false_?
    a. The Democrats believe that government should play a major role in solving society's problems.
    b. The Republicans believe that business and the free market can solve society's problems.
    c. The Republicans and the Democrats basically agree about the role of government and they have the same political beliefs.

Talk About It

Work in small groups and choose one or more of these questions to discuss.

1. How is the government of your country organized? Which system do you think works better, one that has separate elections for the different branches and divides the power, or a parliamentary system? Why?

2. What personal qualities do you think political leaders should have? What kind of leader do you admire?

3. How do lobby groups affect the operation of a government? Who do you think is more trustworthy—business or government leaders?

4. Look at the following poll about gun control policy proposals in the United States. Why do you think it is so difficult for Americans to agree on what gun control policy should be? What are the limits on gun ownership in your country? Compare the policies in your country with what is proposed in the United States.

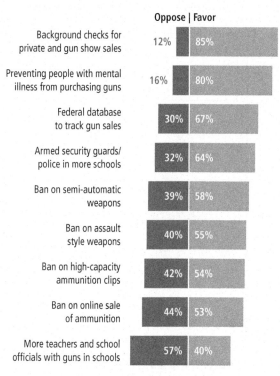

BROAD PUBLIC SUPPORT FOR MANY GUN POLICY PROPOSALS

Oppose | Favor

Proposal	Oppose	Favor
Background checks for private and gun show sales	12%	85%
Preventing people with mental illness from purchasing guns	16%	80%
Federal database to track gun sales	30%	67%
Armed security guards/ police in more schools	32%	64%
Ban on semi-automatic weapons	39%	58%
Ban on assault style weapons	40%	55%
Ban on high-capacity ammunition clips	42%	54%
Ban on online sale of ammunition	44%	53%
More teachers and school officials with guns in schools	57%	40%

Source: Pew Research Center Jan. 9–13, 2013.

SKILL BUILDING

Improve Your Reading Skills: Note Taking

Fill in this graphic organizer with information about how the U.S. government is organized. Take notes about each branch and fill in the boxes with your notes. First, write the names of the three branches of government. Then write who the people are in each branch. Finally, write what the responsibilities are for each branch. When you have finished, share your notes with a partner.

BRANCHES OF GOVERNMENT

Branch	People	Responsibilities
Executive	_____ Cabinet	_____ _____ _____ _____ _____
_____	Congress Senate and _____ 100 _____ 435 _____	Enact laws _____ _____ _____ _____
_____	Supreme Court 9 Justices	_____ _____ _____ _____ *Note: There are many possible responses for responsibilities.*

Develop Your Critical Thinking Skills

One of the sections in this chapter is The Controversy over Entitlements. *Reread that section and think about why there is a controversy over entitlements in the United States. Then consider this: The Pew Research Center asked Americans if they had ever received any of six different government benefits or services. They found that 27% had received unemployment benefits, 26% had received Social Security, 22% had received Medicare, and 8% had received welfare benefits. Pew then studied different demographic groups and reported on how many benefits each group had received. The results are in the chart that follows.*

TOTAL NUMBER OF BENEFITS RECEIVED BY SELECTED DEMOGRAPHIC GROUPS

% in each group who received each number of government benefits in their lifetimes

	No Benefits	One Benefit	Two Benefits	Three or More
All	45	23	17	15
Men	51	23	15	12
Women	39	22	19	19
White	44	23	19	14
Black	36	20	17	27
Hispanic	50	27	12	11
Republican	48	21	19	12
Democrat	40	23	17	20
Independent	47	24	17	11
Family income				
<$30,000	30	21	21	29
$30–49,999	44	21	21	15
$50–99,999	57	26	11	6
$100,000+	61	25	10	4
Community type				
Rural	38	22	20	20
Suburban	47	23	16	14
Urban	46	23	17	14

Note: Based on total sample, N = 2,511. Whites and blacks include only non-Hispanics. Hispanics are of any race. "Don't know/Refused" responses not shown.

Work with a partner to use information from these different sources—the chapter section and the poll—to make generalizations about who is most likely to receive government benefits in the United States. Be sure your generalizations include all the demographic categories: sex, race, political party, family income, and community type. Take notes, and then share your findings with another pair of students. Include answers to these questions:

Who is more likely to receive more than one benefit: a man or a woman?

Who is more likely to receive benefits: someone living in a city or someone living in a rural area?

What impact do you think age has on who is likely to receive benefits?

What impact does income have on who is likely to receive benefits?

What is the relationship between the positions that the Republican Party and the Democratic Party have on entitlements and the people who are actually receiving them?

Build Your Vocabulary

More AWL Words

Test your knowledge of these AWL words by matching the words and definitions.

_____ 1. area   a. in a noticeable or important way

_____ 2. challenge   b. a particular subject or range of activities

_____ 3. conclude   c. existing or happening in many places or situations

_____ 4. core   d. basic structures or systems a country needs

_____ 5. considerably   e. a length of time with a beginning and an end

_____ 6. grades   f. something that tests strength, skill, or ability

_____ 7. impact   g. particular

_____ 8. infrastructure h. the most important or central part

_____ 9. period   i. to continue doing something, even though it is difficult

_____ 10. persist   j. happening before

_____ 11. previous   k. the effect or influence that an event has on something

_____ 12. specific   l. marks (numbers or letters) that show how well you have done

_____ 13. widespread   m. to complete successfully

Fill in the blanks with the correct words to complete these sentences:

1. E.J. Dionne, Jr., urges Americans to look back at their history to understand who they are as a people. They must recognize that from the beginning, Americans have lived with a tension between two _____ values: their love of individualism and their respect for community.

2. The NRA gives members of Congress _____ for their voting record on gun control, and it has been particularly effective in re-electing or defeating senators and representatives.

3. Republicans believe that the government can protect individual freedom by passing laws that ensure equal access to health care and jobs for all Americans, and by showing the way forward with government programs that will engage private businesses in cooperative projects to rebuild needed _____ roads and bridges, and create partnerships between schools and businesses to provide the educated workforce of the future.

4. Some government regulations were in place during this period, but these had only a small _____ on business practices.

5. In almost every important _____ of governmental activity, such as the power to make laws, to declare war, or to _____ treaties with foreign countries, the Constitution gives each of these two branches enough power to prevent the other from acting on its own.

Which Word Doesn't Belong?

This chapter contains a number of words that have to do with government and politics. Look at each group of words, and decide which one does not belong with the boldfaced word. Circle the words that do not belong. Then, on a separate piece of paper, use each one in a sentence.

EXAMPLE: **parties:** Republican, Democrat, (NRA)

1. **executive branch:** president, cabinet, bureaucracy, Congress, policy, veto
2. **legislative branch:** Congress, Supreme Court, Senate, House of Representatives, bill
3. **judicial branch:** national courts, Supreme Court, judges, vice president

4. **elections:** candidate, vote, veto, plurality, electoral college, convention
5. **politics:** party, campaign, lobby, fund-raisers, strategy, Bill of Rights

Collocations

This chapter contains many verb + noun object collocations. Read the sentences below. Fill in the blanks with the missing nouns to complete the collocations.

| ballots | bill | disputes | law | term | treaty |

1. The Supreme Court both *interprets* a _____ and determines whether it is constitutional.

2. The president may *veto* a _____ he doesn't like and send it back to Congress.

3. The Senate has to *ratify* a _____ that the president has signed.

4. If an election is very close, a candidate may request that the officials *recount* the _____.

5. The president *serves* a _____ of four years.

6. The judicial branch *settles* _____ about the exact meaning of the law through court cases.

EXPAND YOUR KNOWLEDGE

Group Project

Work in a small group to create the profile of a perfect candidate for public office.

- First decide what office your candidate is running for.
- Then describe what the person would look like (female or male, age, appearance) and what qualifications he or she would have.
- Think about how you would run the campaign.
- What kinds of advertisements would you create? What activities and appearances would you have?
- Make a poster for your candidate, perhaps with a collage of pictures that illustrate the issues your candidate is supporting in the campaign. Look on the Internet or in newspapers and magazines for ideas.
- When you have finished, present your candidate to the rest of the class.

Ask Yourself / Ask Americans

Who do you trust? Look at the list below, and put a check next to the people you would trust. Put two checks next to your top three choices. Share your list with a group of classmates. Then compare your opinions with the poll results that follow.

Advertising practitioners	Journalists
Bankers	Lawyers
Business executives	Medical doctors
Car salespeople	Members of Congress
Chiropractors	Nurses
Clergy	Pharmacists
College teachers	Police officers
Dentists	Psychiatrists
Engineers	Senators
HMO Managers	State governors
Insurance salespeople	Stockbrokers

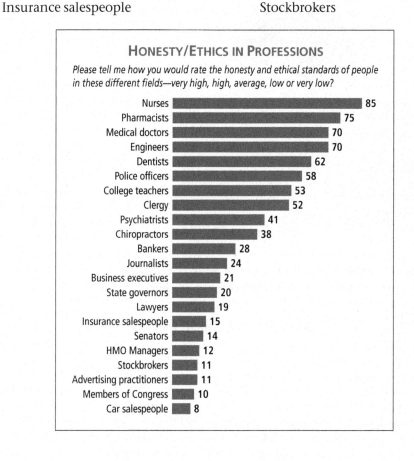

HONESTY/ETHICS IN PROFESSIONS

Please tell me how you would rate the honesty and ethical standards of people in these different fields—very high, high, average, low or very low?

Profession	Rating
Nurses	85
Pharmacists	75
Medical doctors	70
Engineers	70
Dentists	62
Police officers	58
College teachers	53
Clergy	52
Psychiatrists	41
Chiropractors	38
Bankers	28
Journalists	24
Business executives	21
State governors	20
Lawyers	19
Insurance salespeople	15
Senators	14
HMO Managers	12
Stockbrokers	11
Advertising practitioners	11
Members of Congress	10
Car salespeople	8

Use the Internet

Work with a partner to find information about how governments spend their money.

> *Reread paragraphs 28 and 29 of the chapter. In the United States, a large percentage of the budget is for mandatory programs (those that must be paid). Mandatory expenditures include the interest on the public debt and entitlement programs such as Medicare (medical benefits for the elderly) and Medicaid (medical benefits for the poor). The rest of the budget is discretionary spending (the government has a choice about how to spend this money). This includes defense and all other expenditures. The graph below shows the percentages of federal spending in 2010 by the American government. Note that the interest on the federal debt is almost 6 percent.*

2010 FEDERAL SPENDING

- Social Security, **20.4%**
- National Defense, **20.1%**
- Medicare, **13.1%**
- Medicaid/CHIP, **8.1%**
- Interest, **5.7%**
- Low-Income Assistance, **5.3%**
- Everything else, **27.4%**

Use the Internet to look for information about the budget of your country, or choose another country. What has the largest percentage of expenditures? What percentage is spent on defense? How much is spent on social welfare, such as health care and education? What can you tell about the priorities of a people by looking at the budget of their country?

People Watching

> *As mentioned in Chapter 3, Americans sometimes say that it is dangerous to talk about two topics: religion and politics. It is also often difficult to know what you should say to people when you first meet them. The questions you might ask others from your country may not be appropriate or acceptable in another society or culture.*

Ask a number of Americans of different ages, of both sexes, and of different ethnic or racial backgrounds, if possible, to look at the following questions. Ask them whether these are polite, acceptable questions that they would ask someone themselves. Record each person's reaction to each question. If they say certain questions are unacceptable, ask them why. How would it make someone feel if you asked one of these questions? Are there some circumstances when it would be all right to ask a question and other circumstances when it would not be all right? Which questions are acceptable in your country and which are not? Compare your findings with those of your classmates.

1. What is your name?

2. What do you do for a living?

3. Where are you from? or Where do you live?

4. Do you like your job?

5. How much do you make?

6. Are you a Republican or a Democrat? Why?

7. Are you married? Why, or why not?

8. Do you have children? Why, or why not?

9. How old are you?

10. What is your religion?

WRITE ABOUT IT

Choose one of the following topics. Then write a short compostion about it.

1. Write a letter to the president of the United States about an issue that interests or concerns you. You might write about health care, global warming, or oil drilling in the Arctic wilderness. Use persuasive techniques:

   a. Begin with a fact or statistic that is an attention-getter.

   b. Order your arguments so that you end with your strongest point.

   c. Anticipate the other side of the argument and deal with those points.

   d. End on a strong, positive note.

2. In 1960, President John F. Kennedy appointed his brother Robert Kennedy to be attorney general of the United States. In 1992, President Bill Clinton announced that he wanted to appoint his wife Hillary to an important government position, perhaps a cabinet-level post. Polls showed, however, that two-thirds of the American public disapproved of Hillary Clinton's having a major post, and Clinton was forced to reconsider. Why do you think Americans accepted the appointment of a president's brother but not his wife? What do you think about any president appointing a spouse or family member to government office? Write a "letter to the editor" (of a newspaper) expressing your opinion.

EXPLORE ON YOUR OWN

Books to Read

E.J. Dionne, Jr., *Our Divided Political Heart: The Battle for the American Idea in an Age of Discontent*—Dionne explores the effects of an extreme form of individualism that endangers the constructive role of government and community.

Nancy Gibbs and Michael Duffy, *The Presidents' Club: Inside the World's Most Exclusive Fraternity*—Two journalists examine the relationships between sitting presidents and their predecessors.

Barack Obama, *The Audacity of Hope: Thoughts on Reclaiming the American Dream*—Writing before his election, Obama calls for a new kind of politics based on shared values that bring us together.

Larry J. Sabato, Editor, *Barack Obama and the New America: The 2012 Election and the Changing Face of Politics*—A series of articles examines what happened in the election and what it means for the country.

Robert Penn Warren, *All the King's Men*—This classic American novel is about the rise and fall of a fictional southern politician who resembles Huey P. Long, a governor of Louisiana.

Movies to See

All the President's Men—Tells how reporters Woodward and Bernstein uncovered the details of the Watergate scandal that led to President Nixon's resignation.

The American President—A romantic comedy about a widowed U.S. president who falls in love with a lobbyist.

The Candidate—A candidate for the U.S. Senate from California has no hope of winning, so he is able to run his campaign any way he chooses.

The Ides of March—In the final days of a presidential primary, there is a scandal that threatens the campaign.

Milk—This movie is based on the true story of the gay rights activist and politician Harvey Milk, the first openly gay person to be elected to public office in California.

CHAPTER 8

ETHNIC AND RACIAL DIVERSITY IN THE UNITED STATES

So in this continent, the energy of Irish, Germans, Swedes, Poles and all the European tribes, of the Africans, and of the Polynesians—will construct a new race, a new religion, a new state.

Ralph Waldo Emerson (1803–1882)

In the United States, how do immigrants from different countries and people of different ethnicities get along together?

BEFORE YOU READ

Preview Vocabulary

A. Work with a partner to answer the questions. Make sure you understand the meaning of the AWL words in italics.

1. If a country tries to *accommodate* new immigrants, is it trying to help them succeed or trying to prevent them from entering the country?

2. If there is *discrimination* against a minority group, how might the people be treated differently?

3. Is a *federal* government program one at the state level or at the national level?

4. If you are *inclined* to do something, are you likely or unlikely to do it?

5. Is *instruction* usually given by a teacher or by a student?

6. When public *facilities* were segregated in the South, did blacks and whites go to different schools and sit in separate areas of restaurants and movie theaters?

7. Do most people live in *residential* or commercial (business) areas?

8. If an ethnic minority wants to *retain* its culture, are families more likely to continue speaking their native language at home or to speak English?

9. If a law has a *bias,* does it treat everyone equally?

10. How many generations back can you *trace* your ancestry?

B. The following words refer to positive or negative situations or conditions. Write a plus sign (+) next to the positive and write a minus sign (−) next to the negative connotation.

_____ accommodation	_____ enrich
_____ inspire	_____ prejudice
_____ civil rights	_____ inequality
_____ integrated	_____ resources
_____ degrade	_____ inferior
_____ poverty	_____ segregation
_____ despair	_____ slavery
_____ discrimination	

Preview Content

Before you read, think about what you know about the racial and ethnic diversity of the United States. Discuss the questions with your classmates.

1. Read the quotation by Emerson at the beginning of the chapter. How did people from so many different countries create the American culture in the United States?

2. Skim the first paragraph of the reading. What does *assimilation* mean? What group had the strongest influence on shaping the dominant American culture? Why do you think so?

3. Why do you think some immigrants from some countries might have more success in the United States than others have?

4. What do you know about the history of African Americans in the United States?

In 1899, a Native American speaks to a history class at Hampton Institute, a historically black college in Virginia.

1 The population of the United States includes a number of different ethnic groups coming from many races, nationalities, and religions. The process by which these many groups have been made a part of a common cultural life with commonly shared values is called *assimilation*. Scholars disagree as to the extent to which assimilation has occurred in the United States. As we mentioned in Chapter 1, some have described the United States as a "melting pot" where various racial and ethnic groups have been combined into one culture. Others are inclined to see the United States as a "salad bowl" where the various groups have remained somewhat distinct and different from one another, creating a richly diverse country.

2 The truth probably lies somewhere between these two views. Since 1776, an enormous amount of racial and ethnic assimilation has taken place in the United States, yet some groups continue to feel a strong sense of separateness from the culture as a whole. Many of these groups are really *bilingual and/or bicultural*. That is, they consider themselves Americans, but they may also wish to retain the language and sometimes the cultural traditions of their original culture.

3 People of Hispanic origin were on the North American continent before settlers arrived from other European countries in the early 1600s. In Florida and the Southwest, Spanish and Latin American settlements were established centuries before the thirteen colonies joined together to form the United States in the late 1700s. Because of their long history and the continued influx of newcomers into the established communities, many Hispanics, or Latinos, have taken a special pride in maintaining their cultural traditions and the use of the Spanish language.

4 Generally speaking, over the years whites from different national and religious backgrounds have been gradually assimilated into the larger American culture, with some exceptions. For example, American Jews are one group who have traditionally retained a strong sense of group identity within the larger culture. This may be a result of the long history of persecution in the Christian countries in Europe, the weaker forms of discrimination and anti-Jewish feeling that have sometimes existed in the United States, and their own strong feeling of ethnic pride. Yet along with their own group identity, most American Jews have a strong sense of being a part of the larger American culture.

The Establishment of the Dominant Culture

5 The first census of the new nation, conducted in 1790, counted about 4 million people, most of whom were white. Of the white citizens, more than eight out of ten traced their ancestry back to England. African Americans made up a surprising 20 percent of the population, an all-time high. There were close to 700,000 slaves and about 60,000 "free Negroes." Only a few Native Americans who paid taxes were included in the census numbers, so there is no accurate count of the total Native American population.

6 It was the white population that had the greater numbers, the money, and the political power in the new nation, and therefore this majority soon defined what the dominant culture would be. At the time of the American Revolution, the white population was largely English

in origin, Protestant, and middle-class. Such Americans are sometimes referred to as "WASPs" (white Anglo-Saxon Protestants); however, many people now consider this an insulting term. Their characteristics became the standard for judging other groups. Those having a different religion (such as the Irish Catholics), or those speaking a different language (such as the Germans, Dutch, and Swedes), were in the minority and would be disadvantaged unless they became assimilated. In the late 1700s, this assimilation occurred without great difficulty for most immigrants. According to historians Allan Nevins and Henry Steele Commager, "English, Irish, German, . . . Dutch, Swedish—mingled[1] and intermarried with little thought of any difference."

7 The dominant American culture that grew out of the nation's early history, then, was English-speaking, western European, Protestant, and middle-class in character. It was this dominant culture that established what became the traditional values described by Tocqueville in the early 1830s. Immigrants with these characteristics were welcome, in part because Americans believed that these newcomers would probably give strong support to the basic values of the dominant culture, such as freedom, equality of opportunity, and the desire to work hard for a higher material standard of living.

The Assimilation of Non-Protestant and Non-Western Europeans

8 As is the case in many cultures, the degree to which a minority group was seen as different from the characteristics of the dominant majority determined the extent of that group's acceptance. Although immigrants who were like the earlier settlers were accepted, those with significantly different characteristics tended to be viewed as a threat to traditional American values and way of life.

9 This was particularly true of the immigrants who arrived by the millions during the late nineteenth and early twentieth centuries. Most of them came from poverty-stricken nations of southern and eastern Europe. They spoke languages other than English, and large numbers of them were Catholics or Jews.

10 Americans at the time were very fearful of this new flood of immigrants. They were afraid that these people were so accustomed to lives of poverty and dependence that they would not understand such traditional American values as freedom, self-reliance, and competition. There were so many new immigrants that they might even change the basic values of the nation in undesirable ways.

11 Americans tried to meet what they saw as a threat to their values by offering English instruction for the new immigrants and citizenship classes to teach them basic American beliefs. The immigrants, however, often felt that their American teachers disapproved of the traditions of their homeland. Moreover, learning about American values gave them little help in meeting their most important needs, such as employment, food, and a place to live.

12 Far more helpful to the new immigrants were the "political bosses" of the larger cities of the northeastern United States, where most of the immigrants first arrived. Those bosses saw to many of the practical needs of the immigrants and were more accepting of the different homeland traditions. In exchange for their help, the bosses expected the immigrants to keep them in power by voting for them in elections.

[1] mingled: met and talked with a lot of different people socially

Immigrant boys study in night school because they work during the day.

13 Many Americans strongly disapproved of the political bosses. This was partly because the bosses were frequently corrupt;[2] that is, they often stole money from the city governments they controlled and engaged in other illegal practices. Perhaps more important to disapproving Americans, however, was the fact that the bosses seemed to be destroying such basic American values as self-reliance and competition.

14 The bosses, it seemed, were teaching the immigrants to be dependent on them rather than to rely on themselves. Moreover, the bosses were "buying" the votes of the immigrants in order to give themselves a monopoly of political power in many larger cities. This practice destroyed competition for political office, which Americans viewed as an important tradition in politics just as it was in other facets of American life.

15 Despite these criticisms, many scholars believe that the political bosses performed an important function in the late nineteenth and early twentieth centuries. They helped to assimilate large numbers of new immigrants into the larger American culture by finding them jobs and housing, in return for their political support. Later the bosses also helped the sons and daughters of these immigrants find employment, but the second generation usually had the advantage of growing up speaking English.

16 The fact that the United States had a rapidly expanding economy at the turn of the century made it possible for these new immigrants, often with the help

[2] corrupt: dishonest

of the bosses, to better their standard of living in the United States. As a result of these new opportunities and new rewards, immigrants came to accept most of the values of the larger American culture and were in turn accepted by the great majority of Americans. For white ethnic groups, therefore, it has generally been true that their feeling of being a part of the larger culture—that is, *American*—has usually been stronger than their feeling of belonging to a separate ethnic group—Irish, Italian, Polish, etc.

The African-American Experience

17 The process of assimilation in the United States has been much more successful for white ethnic groups than for non-white ethnic groups. Of the non-white ethnic groups, Americans of African descent have had the greatest difficulty in becoming assimilated into the larger culture. African Americans were brought to the United States against their will to be sold as slaves. Except for the American Indian tribes who inhabited the United States before the first white settlers arrived, other ethnic groups came to America voluntarily—most as immigrants who wanted to better their living conditions.

18 The enslavement of African Americans in the United States was a complete contradiction of such traditional basic American values as freedom and equality of opportunity. It divided the United States into two increasingly different sections: the southern states, in which black slavery became the basis of the economy, and the northern states, which chose to make slavery against the law.

19 A minority of whites in the North insisted that slavery and freedom could not exist together in a free country and demanded that slavery be abolished,[3]

even if this meant war with the South. A much larger number of northern whites believed that freedom and equality of opportunity needed to be protected for white people only, but they were afraid that black slavery would eventually take away their economic freedom. If, for example, the slave system of the South were allowed to spread into the frontier regions of the West, poor and middle-income whites could no longer look to the western frontier as a land of equality and opportunity where people could better their position in life. Rather, whites would have to compete with unpaid slave labor, a situation that they believed would degrade their work and lower their social status.

20 Abraham Lincoln was able to become president of the United States by appealing to both the white idealists who saw slavery as an injustice to African Americans and to the larger numbers of northern whites who saw slavery as a threat to themselves. Lincoln's argument was that if black slavery continued to spread westward, white freedom and equality would be threatened. Lincoln also believed that basic ideals such as freedom and equality of opportunity had to apply to all people, black and white, or they would not last as basic American values.

21 When Lincoln won the presidency in 1860, the southern states left the Union and tried to form a new nation of their own based on slavery. A Civil War (1861–1865) between the North and South resulted, which turned out to be the bloodiest and most destructive of all the nation's wars. When the North was finally victorious, black slavery ended in the United States.

22 Back in the 1830s, Tocqueville predicted trouble between blacks and whites in the United States:

[3] *abolish: officially end a law or system*

Martin Luther King, Jr., addresses followers at a civil rights protest.

These two races are fastened to each other without intermingling; and they are unable to separate entirely or to combine. Although the law may abolish slavery, God alone can obliterate[4] the traces of its existence.

23 Although slavery was abolished in the 1860s, its legacy[5] continued and African Americans were not readily assimilated into the larger American culture. Most remained in the South, where they were not allowed to vote and were legally segregated from whites. Black children were not allowed to attend white public schools, for example, and many received an inferior education that did not give them an equal opportunity to compete in the white-dominated society. Many former slaves and their families became caught in a cycle of poverty that continued for generations. Although conditions were

much worse in the segregated South, blacks continued to be the victims[6] of strong racial prejudice in the North as well.

The Civil Rights Movement of the 1950s and 1960s

24 This state of affairs remained unchanged until after World War II. Over one million African Americans had served in segregated units during the war. After the war was over, black leaders began to lead a civil rights movement for equality with whites. In 1948, President Harry Truman ordered that the military be fully integrated. Then in 1954, the United States Supreme Court declared that racially segregated public schools did not provide equal educational opportunities for black Americans and were therefore illegal. Incidentally, Thurgood Marshall, Chief Counsel for the National Association

[4] *obliterate: to destroy something so that almost nothing remains*
[5] *legacy: a situation that exists as a result of things that happened at an earlier time*
[6] *victims: people who suffer bad treatment even though they have done nothing to deserve it*

for the Advancement of Colored People (NAACP) argued the case before the court, and in 1967 he became the first African-American Supreme Court Justice.

25 Black leaders throughout the United States were greatly encouraged by the 1954 decision to desegregate the schools. They decided to try to end racial segregation in all areas of American life. The most important of these leaders was Martin Luther King Jr., a black Protestant minister with a great gift for inspiring[7] people. From the late 1950s until his assassination[8] by a white gunman in 1968, King led thousands of people in nonviolent marches and demonstrations against segregation and other forms of racial discrimination. King's goal was to bring about greater assimilation of black people into the larger American culture. His ideals were largely developed from basic American values. He wanted greater equality of opportunity and "freedom now" for his people. He did not wish to separate his people from American society, but rather to gain for them a larger part in it.

26 Some black leaders, such as Malcolm X, urged a rejection of basic American values and complete separation of blacks from the white culture. Malcolm X believed that American values were nothing more than "white men's values" used to keep blacks in an inferior position. He believed that blacks needed to separate themselves from whites, by force if necessary, and build their own society based on values that they would create for themselves. Because he saw Christianity as a "white" religion, Malcolm turned to a faith based on Islam, and he became a leader of the "black Muslim" faith (founded in 1930). The great majority of American blacks, however, shared Martin Luther King's Protestant religious beliefs and his goal of assimilation rather than separation. Most African Americans continued to look to King as their leader.

27 Largely as a result of King's activities, two major civil rights[9] laws were passed during the 1960s, which brought about great changes in the South. One law made it illegal to segregate public facilities. The other law made it illegal to deny black people the right to vote in elections.

28 The civil rights laws of the 1960s helped to bring about a significant degree of assimilation of blacks into the larger American culture. Most important, the laws eventually helped to reduce the amount of white prejudice toward black people in all parts of the country. A federal program called affirmative action required employers to actively seek black workers and universities to recruit black students. As a result of the civil rights laws and affirmative action, the number of African Americans attending the nation's colleges and universities, holding elective public office, and earning higher incomes increased dramatically in the late 1960s and 1970s. Today, African Americans are sports and entertainment heroes, university professors, medical doctors, lawyers, entrepreneurs, and reporters. There is now a sizable black middle class, and there are a number of wealthy African Americans.

29 African Americans are active politically and voted in large numbers in the elections of 2008 and 2012. They are now mayors of major cities and members of Congress; they hold offices in all levels of government—local, state, and national. In 2008, Barack Obama became the first black American president, truly a dream come

[7] inspiring: encouraging people to achieve something great

[8] assassination: the murder of an important person

[9] civil rights: rights that every person should have, such as the right to vote or to be treated fairly by the law, whatever his or her sex, race, or religion

true for many who had worked in the civil rights movement. Congressman John Lewis, himself a black civil rights leader, reflected on what Obama's election meant to him personally:

When we were organizing voter-registration drives, going on the Freedom Rides, sitting in, coming here to Washington for the first time, getting arrested, going to jail, being beaten, I never thought—I never dreamed—of the possibility that an African American would one day be elected President of the United States. My mother lived to see me elected to the Congress, but I wish my mother and father both were around. They would be so happy and so proud, and they would be so gratified. And they would be saying that the struggle, and what we did and tried to do, was worth it.

Diversity in the Twenty-first Century

30 The civil rights movement benefited not only African Americans, but all minorities in the United States—American Indians, Hispanics, Asians, and others. Racial discrimination in employment and housing was forbidden by law. The civil rights laws also advanced the rights of women, and these laws have reinforced the ideal of equality of opportunity for all Americans. Recently, sexual orientation entered the picture. President Obama called for equality for gays in his second Inaugural Address and for laws that permit them to marry. Public opinion polls showed that a majority of Americans agreed with him. The Congress that took office that year was the most diverse ever, although it was not as diverse as the nation as a whole. Among its 535 members, it included 98 women, 43 African Americans, 31 Latinos, 12 Asian-Americans or Pacific Islanders, seven openly gay or bisexuals, two Muslims, one Buddhist, and one Hindu.

31 Although African Americans represent about 13 percent of the population, they are still grossly underrepresented in Congress, and the same is true of Hispanics. The median income of a married black or Hispanic man working full-time is still significantly less than that of a married white man. Segregation and discrimination are against the law, but residential patterns create largely segregated neighborhood schools, particularly in many urban areas. Whites are more likely than blacks and Hispanics to live in the suburbs, where the neighborhood schools are usually in better condition and offer a better education. Many blacks and other ethnic minorities in the inner city are trapped in cycles of

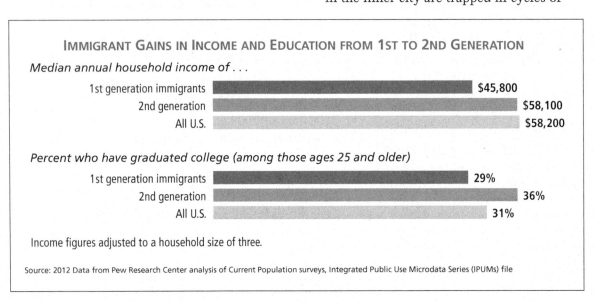

IMMIGRANT GAINS IN INCOME AND EDUCATION FROM 1ST TO 2ND GENERATION

Median annual household income of . . .

1st generation immigrants	$45,800
2nd generation	$58,100
All U.S.	$58,200

Percent who have graduated college (among those ages 25 and older)

1st generation immigrants	29%
2nd generation	36%
All U.S.	31%

Income figures adjusted to a household size of three.

Source: 2012 Data from Pew Research Center analysis of Current Population surveys, Integrated Public Use Microdata Series (IPUMs) file

poverty, unemployment, violence, and despair. Blacks are the most frequent victims of violent crime, and as many as one in five young males may have a criminal record. A larger percent of black and Hispanic children than white children live in poverty and may have only one parent at home.

32 On the other hand, Americans continue to believe strongly in the ideal of equality of opportunity and to search for ways to give everyone an equal chance at success. The American Dream still attracts immigrants and inspires people of all races and ethnic backgrounds. In reality, some immigrant groups have more success than others. As one would expect, history shows that immigrants who come with financial resources, a good educational background, and the necessary work skills are likely to do the best. For example, immigrants from the Middle East tend to have a higher socioeconomic level than the average white American. So do Asians, as a group. Those who come without financial resources and a strong educational background do not do as well. However, studies show that the second generation does significantly better than the first. The adult children of immigrants have a higher standard of living:

> *A new analysis of the 20 million adult U.S.-born children of immigrants finds they are substantially better off than immigrants themselves; they have higher incomes, more are college graduates and homeowners, and fewer live in poverty. Among Latinos and Asian Americans, the second generation are more likely than immigrants to speak English, have friends outside their racial and ethnic group, and think of themselves as "a typical American."*

33 Sonia Sotomayor, the first Hispanic Supreme Court Justice, is an inspiring example of the success some Hispanic Americans have achieved. In her book, *My Beloved World,* she describes being born into and growing up in a world that was "a tiny microcosm of Hispanic New York City." Her grandparents, aunts, uncles, and cousins lived in a few square blocks of the South Bronx:

> *My playmates were my cousins. We spoke Spanish at home, and many in my family spoke virtually no English. My parents had both come to New York from Puerto Rico* in 1944, my mother in the Women's Army Corps, my father with his family in search of work as part of a huge migration from the island, driven by economic hardship.*

34 Sotomayor's father died when she was a child and her family had a difficult time financially. They lived in low-income housing and both she and her brother worked part-time jobs during the school year and full-time in the summer to help with the family's finances. She knew little of the world outside her neighborhood as a child, and the Perry Mason TV show inspired her to want to become an attorney. Sotomayor was an excellent student, but she was surprised by the number of great universities that offered her admission and even full scholarships. She says for the next several years, she "lived the day-to-day reality of affirmative action." As a Hispanic minority woman, she benefited from the affirmative action law that was just beginning to cause universities to recruit minority students. Out of many offers, she chose Princeton, and then went to Yale for her law degree.

35 Today, immigrants with all kinds of backgrounds and skill levels find their way to the United States. Some of them are highly educated, and they may find employment in fields such as technology, medicine, and science. Others may come from poor rural or urban areas and have

---

People who live in Puerto Rico are citizens of the United States.

a limited education. Many of these are young people who risk their lives to come without documentation to do agricultural or construction work. Others find work taking care of children or cleaning homes or buildings. Often, they are paid less than a documented worker would be. However, what they are able to earn in dollars and send back to their countries can support many family members there. Many of these individuals do not want to become U.S. citizens; their only wish is to be able to work here. Americans are trying to find ways to accommodate these workers, while still protecting the interests of U.S. citizens.

A Universal Nation

36 It is important to remember that the dominant culture and its value system established by the early settlers had its roots in white, Protestant, western Europe. In the late 1800s and early 1900s, millions of immigrants came from eastern and southern Europe, bringing cultural traditions perceived by the dominant culture as quite different. By the 1920s, Americans had decided that it was time to close the borders to mass immigration, and the number of new immigrants slowed to a trickle.[10] In spite of the worries of those in the dominant culture, the new immigrants did assimilate to life in the United States. They greatly enriched the cultural diversity of the nation, and they ultimately did not cause major changes to its system of government, its free enterprise system, or its traditional values.

37 In 1965, the United States made important changes in its immigration laws, allowing many more immigrants to come and entirely eliminating the older laws' bias in favor of white European immigrants. As a result, the United States now takes in large numbers of new immigrants who are non-white and non-European. The majority are from Asia and Latin America. In addition to the large numbers of legal immigrants, for the first time the United States has significant numbers of immigrants without legal documentation. Many worry about what the impact will be on American society. Can the American economy offer these new immigrants the same opportunities that others have had? What will be the effect on the traditional value system that has defined the United States for over 200 years?

38 Many Americans see wonderful benefits for their country. Ben Wattenberg, a respected expert on American culture, believes that the new immigration will be of great help to the nation. According to Wattenberg, something very important is happening to the United States: It is becoming the first universal nation in history. Wattenberg believes that the United States will be the first nation where large numbers of people from every region on earth live in freedom under one government. This diversity, he says, will give the nation great influence and appeal to the rest of the world during the twenty-first century.

39 Perhaps the United States will be described not as a "melting pot" or a "salad bowl," but as a "mosaic"—a picture made up of many tiny pieces of different colors. If one looks closely at the nation, the individuals of different colors and ethnic groups are still distinct and recognizable, but together they create a picture that is uniquely American. *E pluribus unum*—the motto of the United States from its beginning—means "one composed of many." Out of many, one.

---

[10] *trickle: a movement of people or things into a place in very small numbers or amounts*

AFTER YOU READ

Understand Main Ideas

Working with a partner, write the answer to each of the pre-reading questions on page 179. Then make up seven more questions about other main ideas, one question for each of the seven sections. Answer these questions, and then share them with another pair of students.

Understand Details

Write the letter of the best answer according to the information in the chapter.

_____ 1. Scholars who see the United States as a "salad bowl" emphasize
    a. the great extent of racial and ethnic assimilation in the United States.
    b. the many differences between different racial and ethnic groups in the United States.
    c. the rapid growth of the population of the United States.

_____ 2. In American society, there are some members of ethnic groups (such as some Jews and Hispanics) that are bicultural; they feel that
    a. they are fully assimilated into American society.
    b. they do not belong at all to American society.
    c. they belong to American society, but at the same time they also have another separate identity.

_____ 3. Which of the following was not a characteristic of the dominant American culture during the early decades of the nation's history?
    a. Catholic
    b. western European
    c. middle-class

_____ 4. Which of the following was true about the political bosses in northeastern cities during the late nineteenth and early twentieth centuries?
    a. They were more afraid of new immigrants than were other Americans.
    b. They were more cruel to new immigrants than were other Americans.
    c. They were more helpful to new immigrants than were other Americans.

_____ 5. Today ethnic groups in the United States
    a. have no feeling of belonging to an ethnic group (such as Irish, Italian, or Polish) whatsoever.
    b. consider themselves as part of the American culture in varying degrees, often depending on how similar their culture is to the majority.
    c. feel much more a part of their ethnic group than part of the American culture.

_____ 6. What was the <u>main</u> reason most northern whites disliked slavery?
   a. It went against their religious beliefs.
   b. It went against the U.S. Constitution.
   c. It threatened their own economic opportunities.

_____ 7. After the Civil War, African Americans in the South lived in a social system where
   a. many continued to be slaves.
   b. segregation was legal.
   c. there was racial discrimination, but no laws separated them from whites.

_____ 8. In 1954, the U.S. Supreme Court declared
   a. African Americans could not legally be denied their right to vote for racial reasons.
   b. racially segregated public schools are illegal.
   c. no one may be denied freedom of speech, press, or religion.

_____ 9. On which of the beliefs listed below did Malcolm X <u>disagree</u> with Martin Luther King?
   a. Black people should be assimilated into the larger American society.
   b. Black people were not treated fairly by the larger American society.
   c. Black people should have freedom and equality.

_____ 10. Which of these statements about race and ethnicity in America is <u>true</u>?
   a. Most young African Americans today have no interest in learning about the black culture and they identify fully with the white culture.
   b. Racial prejudice, segregation, and discrimination are at an all-time high in the United States today.
   c. Using the word mosaic to describe the American culture suggests a positive image.

Talk About It

Work in small groups and choose one or more of these questions to discuss.

1. What are the advantages and disadvantages to being a part of a multicultural society in the twenty-first century?

2. What is your country's policy on immigration? Would you want to be an immigrant in your country? Why or why not?

3. Should a country discourage people from segregating themselves by minorities? What are the advantages and disadvantages to people living in segregated communities?

4. This chapter describes the dominant American culture as being white, English-speaking, Protestant, and middle-class. How would you describe the dominant culture of your country, if there is one?

SKILL BUILDING

Improve Your Reading Skills: Scanning

Scan the chapter to find these dates. Write what happened next to the date to complete the time line about racial and ethnic diversity in the United States.

early 1600s: _____

1790: _____

1861–1865: _____

late 1800s and early 1900s: _____

1920s: _____

1950s and 1960s: _____

1965: _____

2008 and 2012: _____

Develop Your Critical Thinking Skills

This chapter has three definitions or descriptions of the diversity of the United States: *melting pot, salad bowl,* and *mosaic.* Reread the part of the chapter where each of these appears and write a brief definition for each. Evaluate these as definitions and explain how they are different. Would you rather live in a country that is described as a "melting pot," a "salad bowl," or a "mosaic"? Why? Share your answers with a partner.

Build Your Vocabulary

Definitions

Match the word with its definition. Then fill in the sentence blanks with the correct form of the word.

_____ 1. abolish   a. to meet and talk together

_____ 2. assassination   b. dishonest

_____ 3. civil rights   c. to officially end a law or system

_____ 4. corrupt   d. someone who suffers bad treatment

_____ 5. registration   e. to encourage someone to achieve something great

_____ 6. inspire   f. the murder of an important person

_____ 7. legacy   g. rights that every person should have

_____ 8. mingle   h. recording names on an official list

_____ 9. mosaic   i. to destroy something so that nothing remains

_____ 10. obliterate   j. a situation that exists as a result of things that happened at an earlier time

_____ 11. trickle   k. a picture made by fitting together small pieces of colored stones, glass, or paper

_____ 12. victim   l. a movement of people or things into a place in very small numbers or amounts

1. Although slavery had ended in the North by the late 1700s, it was not

   _____ in the rest of the country until the 1860s.

2. Black people in the 1950s and early 1960s did not have the same

   freedom and equality as whites in the South; they had to fight for their

   _____.

3. Martin Luther King, Jr., was able to _____ his followers to

   demonstrate against segregation.

4. King was the most important black leader in America from the late 1950s

   until his _____ by a white gunman in 1968.

5. Unfortunately, the _____ of slavery continues in the United

   States, and there are still problems between the races.

6. When John Lewis was organizing voter- _____ drives,

   he never dreamed that one day an African American would be elected

   president.

7. People who come to the United States from many different countries

   have _____, and many have married persons of a different

   national origin.

8. Often, it is the poor minorities who live in the inner cities who are the

   _____ of crime.

9. Perhaps the United States is really more of a _____ than a melting pot or a salad bowl.

10. Immigration by white Europeans has now slowed to a _____; the majority of the immigrants now come from Asia, Latin America, or the Caribbean.

11. Few people would really want to _____ the rich diversity of cultures living together in the United States.

12. Many of the big city political bosses of the late 1800s and early 1900s were _____; they stole money from the city governments.

More AWL Words

Test your knowledge of these AWL words Read the sentences below and notice the boldfaced AWL words. Then use context clues and write the correct AWL word next to its definition.

1. Some are **inclined** to see the United States as a salad bowl where the various groups have remained **somewhat** distinct and different from one another, creating a richly diverse country.

2. The **process** by which these many groups have been made a part of a common cultural life with commonly shared values is called *assimilation*.

3. Many Americans strongly disapproved of the political bosses. **Despite** these criticisms, many scholars believe that the political bosses performed an important **function**.

4. In 1948, President Harry Truman ordered that the military be fully **integrated**.

5. Some immigrants risk their lives to come to the United States without **documentation** to do agricultural or **construction** work.

6. In 1965, the United States made important changes in its immigration laws, allowing many more immigrants to come, and entirely **eliminating** the older laws' **bias** in favor of white European immigrants.

7. Segregation and **discrimination** are against the law, but **residential** patterns create largely segregated neighborhood schools, particularly in many urban areas.

_____ 1. have an opinion about whether something is good or bad that influences how you deal with it

_____ 2. working on new buildings

_____ 3. even though something else exists or is true

_____ 4. the practice of treating a person or group differently from another in an unfair way

_____ 5. official papers that are used to prove that something is true

_____ 6. getting rid of something completely

_____ 7. job

_____ 8. influenced toward a particular action or opinion

_____ 9. have all the races together, not segregated

_____ 10. a series of actions

_____ 11. relating to homes

_____ 12. more than a little, but not very

EXPAND YOUR KNOWLEDGE

Think, Pair, Share

Do you agree or disagree with these statements? Draw a circle around your response, and then share your answers with a partner and another pair of students.

1. I would emigrate to another country if I could have a better life there for myself and my family.   agree   disagree

2. Foreigners who come from any country in the world are welcomed in my country.   agree   disagree

3. My government should encourage refugees from other countries to settle in my country.   agree   disagree

4. My family would not object if I chose to marry someone of another nationality.   agree   disagree

5. My family would not object if I chose to marry someone of another race.   agree   disagree

6. It is important to maintain your own language and cultural traditions even if you have left your country.   agree   disagree

7. People are really basically the same all over the world.   agree   disagree

8. People who are very different from the dominant culture (race, religion, or ethnic background) have as high a status as anyone else in my country.   agree   disagree

9. Every person in the world should learn to speak at least one foreign language.   agree   disagree

10. I believe that my children will have a higher standard of living than I had growing up.   agree   disagree

Ask Americans

If possible, ask several Americans to tell you about their ethnic backgrounds. Or, ask immigrants in your own country about their backgrounds. Ask them the following questions. Then report your findings to the class.

1. What nationalities were your ancestors?
2. When did your ancestors immigrate to America?
3. Does anyone in your family still speak the language of the "old (original) country"?
4. Does your family maintain contact with any relatives in the old country?
5. What family customs or traditions from the old country do you observe?
6. Have you or any of your family members done any genealogy research to learn about your family history?

Observe the Media

Work in small groups to discuss these questions.

1. How are ethnic and racial minorities and women represented in the media?
2. If you are in the United States, watch national and local news broadcasts and count the number of women and minorities reporting the news. If you are not in the United States, observe the media in the country where you are. What percentages do you find?
3. Watch TV commercials and count the racial and ethnic minorities. How do the numbers compare with the news reporters? What conclusions can you draw from these observations?

Think, Pair, Share

Read the following information about choosing racial identity on the census form. Then answer the questions and share your answers with a partner.

The 2010 census had several choices for race including:
White
Black, African American, or Negro
American Indian or Alaska Native
(and other choices such as Chinese, Filipino, Japanese, etc.)

Americans could choose one race or more—as many as they wanted to—to describe their racial identity. (The census reported numbers of people of one race, or more than one race.) When asked to declare his race on the 2010 census, President Obama chose to check the box Black, African American, or Negro instead of checking multiple boxes. For Obama, the son of a white mother and an African father, the question of his racial identity has been a lifelong struggle. His choice on the census reveals his decision to identify with African Americans.

What do you feel defines your identity? Is it your race? Your ethnic background? The color of your skin? The language you speak? Your cultural heritage? What does identity mean to you?

Have a Debate

Unlike most countries, the United States does not have an official language. While English is widely understood to be the main language of government, commerce, and most education, the people who wrote the Constitution purposely did not declare any one language as the official language.

Look at the chart of languages below. What can you conclude about the number and variety of languages spoken in the United States?

LANGUAGES SPOKEN AT HOME: 1980, 1990, 2000, AND 2007

Characteristic	1980	1990	2000	2007	Percentage change 1980–2007
Population 5 years and older	210,247,455	230,445,777	262,375,152	280,950,438	33.6
Spoke only English at home	187,187,415	198,600,798	215,423,557	225,505,953	20.5
Spoke a language other than English at home[1]	23,060,040	31,844,979	46,951,595	55,444,485	140.4
Spoke a language other than English at home[2]	**23,060,040**	**31,844,979**	**46,951,595**	**55,444,485**	**140.4**
Spanish or Spanish Creole	11,116,194	17,345,064	28,101,052	34,547,077	210.8
French (incl. Patois, Cajun, Creole)	1,550,751	1,930,404	2,097,206	1,984,824	28.0
Italian	1,618,344	1,308,648	1,008,370	798,801	−50.6
Portuguese or Portuguese Creole	351,875	430,610	564,630	687,126	95.3
German	1,586,593	1,547,987	1,383,442	1,104,354	−30.4
Yiddish	315,953	213,064	178,945	158,991	−49.7
Greek	401,443	388,260	365,436	329,825	−107.1
Russian	173,226	241,798	706,242	851,174	391.4
Polish	820,647	723,483	667,414	638,059	−22.2
Serbo-Croatian	150,255	70,964	233,865	276,550	84.1
Armenian	100,634	149,694	202,708	221,865	120.5
Persian	106,992	201,865	312,085	349,686	226.8
Chinese	630,806	1,319,462	2,022,143	2,464,572	290.7
Japanese	336,318	427,657	477,997	458,717	36.4
Korean	266,280	626,478	894,063	1,062,337	299.0
Vietnamese	197,588	507,069	1,009,627	1,207,004	510.9
Tagalog	474,150	843,251	1,224,241	1,480,429	212.2

[1] The languages highlighted in this table are the languages for which data were available for the four time periods: 1980, 1990, 2000, and 2007.
[2] The total does not match the sum of the 17 languages listed in this table because the total includes all the other languages that are not highlighted here. Note: Margins of error for all estimates can be found in Appendix Table 2 at <www.census.gov/population/www/socdemo/ language/appendix.html>. For more information on the ACS, see <www.census.gov/acs/www/>. Source: U.S. Census Bureau, 1980 and 1990 Census, Census 2000, and 2007 American Community Survey.

Organize a debate on whether or not a country should have an official language, or languages. Have one team argue in favor of an official language and the other team argue against it. When planning your arguments, consider the following questions.

1. Why do you think the founding fathers omitted the designation of an official language?

2. What are the possible consequences of having one official language to speakers of other languages?

3. Do you think that most immigrants recognize the value of knowing the language of their new country?

New immigrants study English in community education classes.

Use the Internet

Choose one of these topics to research on the Internet.

1. Working in small groups, choose an ethnic group in the United States to research online. For example, you might choose Turkish Americans, Korean Americans, Ethiopian Americans, Nigerian Americans, Peruvian Americans—any group you wish. Decide what questions you want answered. These might include the following:

   Where do they live in the United States?

   How many of them live here?

   What festivals do they have?

   What are some typical foods?

   Are there native-language newspapers?

   Are there special schools?

   What kinds of websites are there for this group?

   When you have finished your research, make a report to the rest of the class on what you learned. Begin by giving your classmates clues and having them guess which group you have chosen. You could use the clues for a scavenger hunt and have the last clue direct them to the group's home country on a world map.

2. A Smithsonian museum in Washington, D.C., is dedicated to the cultures of the American Indian. Visit its website, www.nmai.si.edu, and write a report on what you learn about the museum.

3. In 2013, Rosa Parks made history for a second time when she became the first black woman to be honored with a full-length statue in the U.S. Capitol's Statuary Hall. President Obama and leaders of Congress were there for the presentation of the statue. Look online and learn about this interesting woman. Who was Rosa Parks? What was her important role in the civil rights movement?

WRITE ABOUT IT

Choose one of the following topics. Then write a short composition about it.

1. Describe a time when you or a friend or a family member experienced discrimination. Write it as a narrative, following chronological order, with an explanation. You could use either the past or the present tense. Include information such as the following:

    Where this occurred

    What happened

    Who was involved

    What the result was

    How each of the people involved felt

    What can be done to eliminate discrimination and prejudice

2. Write a letter to the president of the United States or to the leader of your country proposing a new immigration policy. Explain how many people should be admitted each year, from what countries, on what basis, and what should be done once they have arrived. Support your opinions carefully. Offer solutions to any problems that might be anticipated. (If you write about the United States, you may wish to do research about what is happening to the children of immigrants who came without legal documents and the "Dream Act.")

EXPLORE ON YOUR OWN

Books to Read

Julia Alvarez, *How the Garcia Girls Lost Their Accents*—Four sisters from the Dominican Republic adjust to life in the United States and try to integrate their old culture into their new one.

Langston Hughes, *Let America Be America Again*—The African-American poet examines the ideals of the American dream of freedom, the value of hard work, and the reality of the limitations that some Americans face.

Sonia Sotomayor, *My Beloved World*—In this memoir, the first Hispanic Supreme Court Justice tells about her journey from a Bronx housing project into the university world.

Rachel L. Swarns, *American Tapestry: The Story of the Black, White, and Multiracial Ancestors of Michelle Obama*—This book is based on extensive research on several generations of the First Lady's family.

Ronald Takaki, *Strangers from a Different Shore*—The author presents a history of Asian Americans using personal experiences mixed with historical facts.

Movies to See

America America—In this story of the early life of a Greek immigrant, positive first impressions of America are soon compromised by reality.

American History X—A former neo-nazi skinhead tries to prevent his younger brother from going down the same wrong path that he did.

Freedom Riders—This film tells the story of the Civil Rights movement interstate busing protest campaign.

The Help—During the Civil Rights movement of the 1960s, a young author writes a book about African-American maids' views about their white employers and their daily lives.

Lincoln—This movie focuses on the president's last months in office during the Civil War as he tries to hold the country together while abolishing slavery.

CHAPTER 9

EDUCATION IN THE UNITED STATES

Americans regard education as the means by which the inequalities among individuals are to be erased and by which every desirable end is to be achieved.

George S. Counts (1889–1974)

Who pays for education in the United States and how does that affect what is taught in American schools?

BEFORE YOU READ

Preview Vocabulary

A. Read the following sentences from the chapter and notice the words in
italics. These key AWL words will help you understand the chapter reading.
Use context clues to help you figure out the meanings. Then choose which
definition is best for the italicized word.

_____ 1. Parents who live in large cities may send their children to Catholic
or other religious schools because they believe that these schools are
safer and have higher *academic* standards than the public schools.
a. relating to education
b. relating to danger

_____ 2. Although the amount of money spent per child is not always the best
indicator of the quality of education the child receives, it certainly is
an important factor.
a. increase
b. sign

_____ 3. Many of the new jobs in the United States either require a college
education, even a graduate degree, or are low-paying jobs in the
service *sector* of the economy—such as in fast-food restaurants, small
stores, and hotels.
a. information
b. part, area, or segment

_____ 4. In a test case in 1896, the Supreme Court of the United States stated
that racial segregation in public schools and other public facilities in
the southern states did not *violate* the Constitution.
a. protect
b. disobey or do something against

_____ 5. The Supreme Court of the United States invented what is called the
"separate but equal" doctrine to *justify* racial segregation in public
schools and other public facilities in the southern states.
a. to give a reason for something
b. prevent something from happening

_____ 6. The public schools in the inner city were composed *predominantly*
of African-American students and often shared the neighborhood
problems of high crime rates and other forms of social disorder.
a. mostly or mainly
b. definitely or exactly

_____ 7. There are some bilingual programs in areas where there is a large
concentration of one language group, particularly Spanish speakers.
a. academic achievement
b. large amount of something in one place

_____ 8. The goal of the American education system is to teach children how to learn and to help them reach their *maximum* potential.
   a. largest possible
   b. minimum

_____ 9. These standards are not only in line with college and career requirements, but they also ensure that students who move from one state to another during school will be taught and *assessed* with the same standards.
   a. given scholarship money after careful examination
   b. had a judgment made after careful examination

B. Read these two sentences from the chapter and notice the words in italics. Then use context clues and write the correct word next to its definition.

1. Americans *regard* education as the *means* by which the inequalities among individuals are to be *erased* and by which every desirable end is to be *achieved*.

2. Toqueville *eventually* decided that the tendency of public education to encourage people to *seek* a higher *status* in life was in *harmony*, not in *conflict*, with the customs of American society.

_____ 1. agreement, working together

_____ 2. got rid of something so that it did not exist anymore

_____ 3. social position

_____ 4. think about

_____ 5. finally

_____ 6. a method or system

_____ 7. gotten, reached

_____ 8. look for

_____ 9. disagreement or argument

Preview Content

A. Think about the George S. Counts quotation at the beginning of the chapter. In small groups, discuss how education can erase inequalities. Make a list of some examples.

B. Discuss these questions with your classmates.

1. What are the differences between public and private schools? Which are better? Why?

2. What qualities do you think American universities are looking for when they decide who will be admitted?

Education often takes place in an informal setting.

3. What do you know about the system of education in the United States? Work with a partner to fill in the K-W-L chart with what you *know* about education in the United States and what you *want* to know. Then, as you read the chapter, fill in what you have *learned*.

K	W	L
What We <u>Know</u> About Education in the United States	What We <u>Want</u> to Know About Education in the United States	What We Have <u>Learned</u> About Education in the United States

C. Read the headings in the chapter and look at the illustrations. Write five topics that you predict will be covered in this chapter.

1. _____

2. _____

3. _____

4. _____

5. _____

THE ESTABLISHMENT OF PUBLIC SCHOOLS IN AMERICA: TOCQUEVILLE'S OBSERVATIONS

1   As might be expected, educational institutions in the United States reflect the nation's basic values, especially the ideal of equality of opportunity. From elementary school through college, Americans believe that everyone deserves an equal opportunity to get a good education.

2   From the beginning, when Americans established their basic system of public schools in 1825, they reaffirmed[1] the principle of equality by making schools open to all classes of Americans and by financing the schools with tax money collected from all citizens. Those who favored public schools believed that these institutions would help reduce social-class distinctions in the United States by educating children of all social classes in the same "common schools," as they were known at the time.

3   When Alexis de Tocqueville arrived in the United States in 1831, he found a great deal of enthusiasm about the new and growing public elementary schools. The mayor of New York City gave a special dinner for Tocqueville during which a toast[2] was offered in honor of "Education—the extension of our public schools—a national blessing."

4   Because he was a French aristocrat, Tocqueville at first shared the fears of some wealthy Americans who believed that universal education would be a danger rather than a national blessing. He eventually decided, however, that the tendency of public education to encourage people to seek a higher status in life was in harmony, not in conflict, with the customs of American society. The ideal of equal opportunity for all regardless of family background was much stronger in the United States than in France.

5   Tocqueville also noted that American public education had a strong practical content that included the teaching of vocational[3] skills and the duties of citizenship. Thus, public education not only gave Americans the desire to better themselves, but it also gave them the practical tools to do so. Moreover, the material abundance of the United States provided material rewards for those who took full advantage of the opportunity for a public education.

6   During the next century and a half, public schools in the United States were expanded to include secondary or high schools (grades 9–12) and colleges and universities, with both undergraduate and graduate studies.

The Educational Ladder

7   Americans view their public school system as an educational ladder, rising from elementary school to high school and finally college undergraduate and graduate programs. Most children start school at age five by attending kindergarten, or even at age three or four by attending preschool programs. Then usually there are five to six years of elementary school, two to three years of middle school, and four years of high school. (School systems may divide the twelve years a bit differently, usually depending upon school-age population, but all do have twelve years of elementary, middle school, and senior high school.)

[1] reaffirmed: formally stated an intention or belief again, especially as an answer to a question or doubt

[2] toast: the action of drinking wine or other drink in order to thank someone, wish someone luck, or celebrate something

[3] vocational: training or advice relating to the skills needed to do a particular job

Most school systems have kindergarten as well.

8 After high school, the majority of students go on to college.* Undergraduate studies lead to a bachelor's degree, which is generally what Americans mean when they speak of a "college diploma." Students may also receive an associate degree for two years of study at a community college. Some of these associate degrees are in vocational or technical fields.

9 The bachelor's degree can be followed by professional studies, which lead to degrees in such professions as law and medicine, or graduate studies, which lead to master's and doctoral degrees. The American public schools are free and open to all at the elementary and secondary (high school) level, but the public colleges and universities charge tuition[4] and have competitive entrance requirements.

10 The educational ladder concept is an almost perfect reflection of the American ideal of individual success based on equality of opportunity and on "working your way to the top." In the United States, there are no separate public educational systems with a higher level of education for the wealthy and a lower level of education for the masses. Rather, there is one system that is open to all. Individuals may climb as high on the ladder as they can. The abilities of the individuals, rather than their social class, are expected to determine how high each person will go.

11 Although the great majority of children attend the free public elementary and high schools, about 10 percent choose to attend private schools. The majority of these are religious schools that are associated with particular churches and receive financial support from them, though parents must also pay tuition. A major purpose of these schools is to give religious instruction, which cannot be done in public schools, but that is not always the reason that parents send their children to these schools. Parents who live in large cities may send their children to Catholic or other religious schools because they believe that these schools are safer and have higher academic standards than the public schools. The public schools in many of these cities have encouraged parents and community

Harvard University in Cambridge, Massachusetts

* The word college is used in several different ways. It is generally used instead of university to refer to the education after high school, as in the expressions "go to college" and "get a college education." It is also used to refer to the school, as in "Where do you go to college?" Often, people use the word college to refer to a small school that does not offer graduate degrees or to a two-year community college. University is used for large schools that offer both undergraduate and graduate degrees. Universities often call the divisions within them colleges, as in the College of Arts, Humanities, and Social Sciences of the University of Maryland, Baltimore County.

[4] tuition: the money you pay for being taught at a school or college

members to establish charter schools[5] in an attempt to keep these children in the public schools.

12 There are also some elite[6] private schools that serve mainly upper-class children. For these private schools, students must pay such high tuition costs that only wealthier families can afford them, though scholarships are usually offered to some talented, less affluent children who cannot pay the tuition. Parents often send their children to these schools so that they will associate with other upper-class children and maintain the upper-class position held by their parents, in addition to getting a good education.

13 Unlike private religious schools, elitist private schools do conflict with the American ideal of equality of opportunity. These schools often give an extra educational and social advantage to the young people whose families have the money to allow them to attend. However, because these schools are relatively few in number, they do not displace the public school as the central educational institution in the United States. But attending a good private school does give students an advantage when competing with public school graduates for admission to the best universities in the nation. Thirty-five percent of the students admitted to Harvard, for example, graduated from a private school.

14 There is another area of inequality in the American education system. Because of the way that schools are funded, the quality of education that American students receive in public schools varies greatly. Traditionally, the largest percentage of the money for schools came from the local level (cities and counties), primarily from property taxes. School districts that had middle-class or wealthy families had more tax money to spend on education. Therefore, wealthier school districts had beautiful school buildings with the most up-to-date technology and the latest science equipment, and poorer school districts had older buildings with less modern equipment. Today, the states pay the largest amount for funding elementary and secondary schools, and the federal government pays an average of ten percent of the cost. However, the amount a local district spends on the schools still has a huge impact, and students living in low-income communities go to schools with the least resources and often the least experienced teachers.

15 Although the amount of money spent per child is not always the best indicator of the quality of education the child receives, it certainly is an important factor. Some believe that all schools, public or private, religious or not, should be eligible for public school funding. They would support a system of vouchers,[7] which parents could use to help pay tuition at any school of their choice. Some states are now experimenting with voucher systems.

Attending an American University

16 Money is also increasingly a factor in receiving a college education. All university students must pay tuition expenses in the United States, and the cost of an education is rising much more rapidly than is the average family income. Because tuition is much lower at public universities than at private ones, wealthy

---

[5] charter schools: schools to which the state, local, or federal government (or private organization) has given money and special permission to operate but that are operated by parents, private companies, etc., rather than by the public school system

[6] elite: limited to wealthy people with a high social status

[7] vouchers: types of tickets that can be used instead of money for a particular purpose

students have more choices. There are a number of financial aid programs in the form of loans and scholarships available at both public and private schools. About 80 percent of college students have some form of student aid. However, the expenses of buying books and living away from home make it increasingly difficult for many students to attend even the less expensive public universities. The majority of students must work during their college years to help meet costs, and sometimes their work schedule reduces the number of courses they can take and increases the time it takes them to complete a college degree. Most young people graduate from college with significant debt from student loans.

17 A growing number of students cannot afford to go away to college and pay the tuition and living expenses for a public or private university. They choose instead to attend community college programs for two years in their hometowns, paying much less in tuition. These two-year colleges offer a wide range of programs. Some offer two-year degrees called associate degrees. Students may also take their first two years of college at a community college and then transfer to a state university. Community colleges feed into the state university systems and offer educational opportunities to large numbers of students who ordinarily would not be able to attend a university. The popularity of community colleges continues to grow. Now a number of the community colleges offer four-year bachelor degree programs through state systems.

The differences in yearly cost among public two- and four-year colleges and private four-year colleges is significant:

	Public two-year (in-state)	Public four-year (in-state)	Private four-year
Tuition & fees	$ 3,131	$ 8,655	$29,056
Room, board, books, etc.	$12,453	$13,606	$14,233
Total cost	$15,584	$22,261	$43,289
Net price (after scholarships, grants, aid)	$ 4,350	$ 5,750	$15,680

Source: The College Board's Trends in College Pricing 2012 and Trends in Student Aid 2012 reports.

18 Despite its costs, the percentage of Americans seeking a college education continues to grow. In 1900, less than 10 percent of college-age Americans entered college. Today, over half of all Americans have taken some college courses, and many have attended for four years or more. There are more than 20 million students attending college now, and there are roughly 3,000 different colleges and universities to choose from. Today, many parents who were not able to attend college when they were young have the satisfaction of seeing their sons and daughters attend. About half of the students enrolled in college today are the first generation of their family to attend.

19 As we have seen in earlier chapters, the American definition of success has traditionally been one of acquiring wealth and a good standard of living. It is not surprising, therefore, that Americans value education for its monetary[8] value. The belief has been widespread in the United States that the more schooling people have, the more money they will earn when they leave school. The belief is strongest regarding the desirability of certain undergraduate university degrees, or a professional degree such as medicine or law following the undergraduate degree. Both undergraduate and graduate degrees

[8] monetary: relating to money

in science, technology, engineering, and math (STEM) fields offer high salaries. In the United States, there are not enough graduates with STEM degrees to fill the jobs now available, so employment prospects in these fields are excellent. The monetary value of graduate degrees in "nonprofessional" fields such as literature, art, music, history, or philosophy, however, is not as great.

TRENDS IN COLLEGE TUITION PRICES

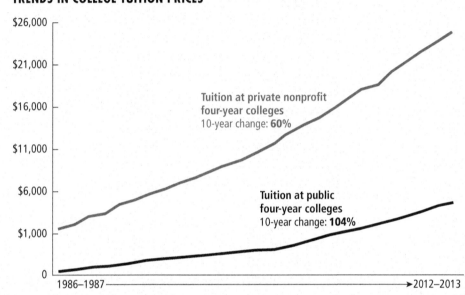

Tuition at private nonprofit four-year colleges
10-year change: **60%**

Tuition at public four-year colleges
10-year change: **104%**

Source: The College Board's *Trends in College Pricing 2012*.
Note: Tuition for public four-year colleges is for in-state students.

20 In recent years, there has been a change in the job market in the United States. In the past, it was possible to get a high-paying factory job without a college education. Workers with skills learned in vocational schools, training programs, or on the job could do work that did not require a college education. These were among the jobs that new immigrants were often able to obtain. Increasingly, however, the advent[9] of new technologies has meant that more and more education is required to do much of the work. Many of the new jobs in the United States either require a college education, even a graduate degree, or they are low-paying jobs in the service sector of the economy—such as in fast-food restaurants, stores, and hotels. New manufacturing jobs often require a knowledge of robotics, for example.

21 Because of the importance of higher education, many adults combine working with taking classes at a college. Many public and private colleges and universities are making it easier for students to take classes through *distance learning*, using the Internet to provide materials and lectures as well as to engage students in discussion. Some students who are living on campus or commuting to classes take at least part of their coursework by distance learning, but it is also possible for a student to obtain both undergraduate and graduate degrees without ever being on a college campus.

22 An exciting new trend is the growth of MOOCs—Massive Open Online Courses— where thousands of people can participate in courses taught by some of the most important scholars in the United States. It began with a few professors at elite American universities, but it is becoming much more frequent, and other universities around the world are joining in. The focus has been on the learning experience, not on earning college

[9] *advent: the time when something first begins to be widely used*

credits, though some are exploring ways of providing certificates for successfully passing the examinations that go with the courses.

Educating the Individual

23 American schools tend to put more emphasis on developing critical-thinking skills than they do on acquiring quantities of facts. American students are encouraged to ask questions, think for themselves, and express their own opinions in class, a reflection of the American values of individual freedom and self-reliance. The goal of the American education system is to teach children how to learn and to help them reach their maximum potential.

24 The development of social and interpersonal skills may be considered as important as the development of intellectual skills. To help students develop these other important skills, schools have added a large number of extracurricular[10] activities to daily life at school. These activities are almost as important as the students' class work. For example, in making their decisions about which students to admit, colleges look for students who are "well-rounded." Grades in high school courses and scores on pre-college tests like the Scholastic Aptitude Test (SAT) are very important, but so are the students' extracurricular activities. It is by participating in these activities that students demonstrate their special talents, their level of maturity and responsibility, their leadership qualities, and their ability to get along with others.

25 Some Americans consider athletics, frequently called *competitive sports*, the most important of all extracurricular activities. This is because many people believe it is important for all young people, young men and young women, to learn how to compete successfully. Team sports such as American football, basketball, baseball, and soccer are important because they teach students the "winning spirit." At times, this athletic competition may be carried to such an extreme that some students and their parents may place more importance on the high school's sports program than its academic offerings.

26 Student government is another extracurricular activity designed to develop competitive, political, and social skills in students. The students choose a number of student government officers who compete for the votes of their fellow students in school elections. Although these officers have little power over the central decisions of the school, the process of running for office and then taking responsibility for a number of student activities if elected is seen as good experience in developing their leadership and competitive skills, and in helping them to be responsible citizens.

27 Athletics and student government are only two of a variety of extracurricular activities found in American schools. There are clubs and activities for almost every student interest—art, music, drama, debate, foreign languages, photography, volunteer work—all aimed at helping the student to become more successful in later life. A number of school districts now require all students to engage in community service—tutoring, meeting with the elderly in nursing homes, cleaning up community parks, etc.—as a requirement for high school graduation. Many parents watch their children's extracurricular activities with as much interest and concern as they do their children's intellectual achievements in the classroom.

The Standards Movement

28 In the late 1900s, international comparisons of education revealed that,

---

[10] extracurricular: sports or other activities that you do in addition to your usual classes

in general, American students did not perform as well in math, science, and other subjects as students from many other developed countries. Some believed this was because American standards for education might not be high enough. Unlike the situation in many other countries, traditionally, local community school districts have had responsibility for determining school curricula and selecting textbooks, with only limited state and national supervision. However, since the 1990s, both the state and the federal government have become more involved in determining school standards. The federal government has set national goals for education that include standards for early childhood, elementary, secondary, and adult education. Even teacher education programs have to meet federal and state standards. Most major educational associations, such as national associations of teachers of science, math, or language arts, have also evaluated the current curricula and criteria for certification and developed new standards.

29 To ensure that standards are met, the federal government now requires annual testing in reading and mathematics in most elementary and middle grades; states also may require students to pass a series of examinations in such subjects as reading, writing, mathematics, and civics before they can graduate from high school. While most states have already set standards, at least for mathematics and reading, for all students, more recently the governors of 45 states, the District of Columbia, and four U.S. territories, created a new set of standards for mathematics and English language arts. Only Alaska, Minnesota, Nebraska, Texas, and Virginia have remained outside. These Common Core Standards focus on concepts and procedures that are needed for entry into college or the workforce. These standards are not only in line with college and career requirements, but they also ensure that students who move from one state to another during school will be taught and assessed with the same standards.

30 Standardized tests are not without controversy, however. In the early 2000s, the federal government began a program called No Child Left Behind (NCLB), with the goal of holding schools and teachers accountable for student progress. Schools were given grades to measure the progress of their students on standardized tests. Parents were given the opportunity to remove their children from schools with low or failing grades and send them to schools with better grades. However, several problems have occurred. The emphasis on standardized testing takes a lot of classroom time. Estimates are that preparing for or taking these standardized tests can consume up to 20 percent of the school year. Some teachers are spending more time "teaching to the test" than making sure students understand important concepts. A number of educators fear that the American tradition of asking questions and thinking for oneself is being replaced by memorization of facts to be tested.

31 One of the strongest critics of emphasizing standardized testing is Diane Ravitch, who was originally a strong supporter of NCLB. In her book, *The Death and Life of the Great American School System: How Testing and Choice are Undermining Education,* Ravitch explains why she believes NCLB has failed. When local schools are given a failing grade (because the students have failed to improve enough on the tests), parents can choose to have their students transfer to a better school, but they do not. Parents want to have their children attend a school in their home neighborhood. Ravitch says that after 10 years of NCLB, we should be able to see dramatic improvement in our schools and

the progress of our students, but we do not:

> By now, we should be able to point to sharp reductions of the achievement gaps between children of different racial and ethnic groups and children from different income groups, but we cannot. . . . Many children continue to be left behind . . . and they are the same children who were left behind 10 years ago.

32 Ravitch believes that it is the responsibility of our public schools to provide equality of educational opportunity to all students, regardless of race, ethnicity, or income, and if they are unable to reach equality of educational attainment, we must give them special help. We cannot afford to leave any of our children behind, without the education they need to compete for good jobs and a decent standard of living—without a chance to achieve the American Dream.

Inequalities in the American Education System

33 The most significant departure from the ideal of equality of opportunity in education occurred in the education of African Americans. As we saw in the previous chapter, after the Civil War in the 1860s, the southern states developed a social and legal system that segregated the former black slaves from the white population in all public facilities, including schools. Blacks had separate schools that were inferior to the white schools by almost any measure.

34 The *Brown versus the Board of Education* Supreme Court decision of 1954 ended legal segregation in the southern schools, but segregation continued until the Civil Rights Acts of the mid-1960s. During the late 1960s and the 1970s, a series of court decisions forced the nation

Before segregation ended, black students often attended schools with crowded, substandard classrooms and inadequate resources.

to take measures to integrate all of its public schools, in both the South and the North. Although there had been no legal segregation in the North, the neighborhood schools of both the North and the South reflected the makeup of the races who lived in the neighborhood. These residential patterns resulted in a number of segregated schools in the North, particularly in big cities. Many public schools in the inner city were composed predominantly of African-American students and often shared the neighborhood problems of poverty, high crime rates, and other forms of social disorder. These schools were clearly unequal to those in the predominantly white, middle-class neighborhoods in the suburbs.

35 For the next twenty years, the courts required Americans to try to achieve racial balance in the public schools. The most controversial method used to deal with unequal neighborhood schools was the busing of schoolchildren from their home neighborhoods to schools in more distant neighborhoods in order to achieve a greater mixture of black and white children in all schools. Black children from the inner city were bused to schools in predominantly white, middle-class neighborhoods, and students living in the middle-class neighborhoods were bused into the poorer black neighborhood schools. Most students did not like it, and neither did their parents, who wanted their children to attend neighborhood schools. Busing continued through the 1970s and the 1980s with mixed success, and it has been largely abandoned. Most school districts now allow children to attend school in their own neighborhood, even if it is predominantly black or white.

36 In addition to trying to end segregation, the federal government created assistance programs for the neediest children. These

included special reading instruction, smaller classes, early childhood programs, and some economic assistance. As a result, according to Paul Barton of the Educational Testing Service, the racial achievement gap was cut in half in the 1970s and 1980s. However, since the 1980s, the gap has remained almost unchanged.

37 At the college level, during the 1970s there was a growth in affirmative action programs. Because African Americans and other minorities had experienced discrimination in the past, colleges and universities tried to actively recruit minority students. The goal was to have the student population reflect the percentages of minorities in the population of the state or country as a whole. All minority students were recruited, Hispanics as well as blacks. In the previous chapter, we mentioned that Supreme Court Justice Sonia Sotomayor experienced the benefits of affirmative action, with admission to and scholarship offers from many top universities.

38 Over the years, there have been challenges to the use of affirmative action in determining college admissions. In 2003, the Supreme Court ruled that the University of Michigan could consider a student's ethnic or racial heritage during its decision-making. As Justice Sandra Day O'Conner wrote in the Supreme Court decision, "Effective participation by members of all racial and ethnic groups in the civic life of our nation is essential if the dream of one Nation, indivisible, is to be realized."

39 In 2013, the Supreme Court considered another challenge to affirmative action brought by Abigail Fisher, a white honor roll student who had been denied admission to the University of Texas at Austin in 2008. The University guaranteed admission to the top ten percent of all

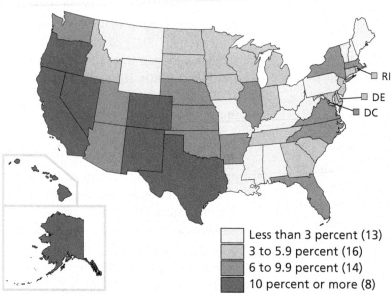

☐	Less than 3 percent (13)
☐	3 to 5.9 percent (16)
☐	6 to 9.9 percent (14)
☐	10 percent or more (8)

Source: U.S Department of English, National Center for Education Statistics

graduating Texas high school students regardless of race, but it considered race and ethnicity as factors for all other students. Fisher was in the top 12 percent of her class and claimed that minority students with lower qualifications were admitted instead of her, violating her constitutional rights. The Supreme Court ruled that universities should try to achieve diversity with "race-neutral policies." These complex legal issues cause Americans to ask themselves how to provide equality of educational opportunity to all students—white, black, Hispanic, Asian, and other minorities.

The Increasing Responsibilities of Public Schools

40 Americans place the weight of many of their ideals, hopes, and problems on the nation's public school system. Some observers believe they have placed more responsibilities on the public schools than the schools can possibly handle. For example, public schools are often expected to solve student problems that result from the weakening of family ties in the

United States. Rising divorce rates and births to single mothers have resulted in an increasing number of children in the public schools who are raised by only one parent. Studies have shown that these children are more likely to have problems at school than are children raised in families with two parents.

41 The education of the new immigrant children provides the public school system with some of its greatest challenges. Many of the children come from countries where they have not had strong educational preparation, and their academic skills are below grade level. Others have come from school systems with standards similar to, or even more advanced than, the American schools, and their academic adjustment is much easier. However, all these children must learn English. This means that they are trying to learn new concepts at the same time that they are struggling to learn a new language. Studies show that it takes five to seven years in order for them to be able to compete with English-speaking American children on an equal basis in

classes where English is the language of instruction. There are some bilingual programs in areas where there is a large concentration of one language group, particularly Spanish speakers. However, there are more than 400 languages spoken in the United States, and some school districts report that 100 or more different languages are spoken by children in their schools. It is not uncommon for five or six different native languages to be spoken by the students in one classroom.

42 It is obvious that children who are not native speakers of English are going to be at a disadvantage when taking standardized tests. Many are not going to be able to compete with native speakers on these tests. Under the No Child Left Behind program, their lower scores may affect the rating of their school, and they affect the overall average test scores of American students. Thus, school districts with high concentrations of non-native speakers of English may have lower test scores than districts that do not. Unfortunately, many of these school districts are the ones that have limited financial resources and may not be able to provide students with all the extra support that they need. In general, during times of economic downturns, there is less money going to the public schools from the state and local governments that fund them. (As stated before, the national government only provides an average of 10 percent of the funding for American elementary and secondary schools.)

43 The limitations on school funding create fewer problems for wealthier Americans. In the last few years, the testing scores of high-income students have gone up while the scores of black students, Hispanic students, and low-income students have remained unchanged. Some reading scores have actually gone down. The lowest scores are in school districts—such as Detroit (Michigan) and Washington, D.C.—where poverty and racial segregation are most concentrated. The inner-city public school system in Washington, D.C. has the largest achievement gap of any city in the nation between white and black students. And yet, in the area surrounding the city are seven of the ten wealthiest counties in the country, with some of the best schools and highest concentrations of adults with advanced college degrees.

44 In a controversial book entitled *Coming Apart: The State of White America, 1960–2010*, Charles Murray describes the widening gap between what he sees as a new upper class and a new lower class. Murray says that members of the new upper class live in certain super zip codes in the United States, where the income and education levels are high, and the people are often the leaders and decision makers of the country. Four cities are the centers of power: "It is difficult to hold a nationally influential job in politics, public policy, finance, business, academia, information technology, or the media and not live in the areas surrounding New York, Washington, D.C., Los Angeles, or San Francisco."

45 Murray worries that these elite Americans are isolated from the rest of the country and do not understand the problems of the middle class. They are economically secure and often some of the wealthiest people in the country. During the economic recession, their incomes went up while the rest of Americans saw their incomes fall. They have their own subculture. Generally, they are married, religious, socially liberal, physically fit, and very concerned about their children's education. They want to send their children to the right preschool, so that they can go to the right elementary school and the right high school, so that they can get admitted to one of the most

prestigious universities, particularly Harvard, Princeton, or Yale. Interestingly, all the present Supreme Court Justices have law degrees from either Harvard or Yale, and all the U.S. presidents from George H. W. Bush through President Obama (Presidents George H. W. Bush, Bill Clinton, George W. Bush, and Barack Obama) have degrees from either Harvard or Yale.

Twenty-first Century Challenges to American Education

46 We began by observing that the public schools in the United States reflect the ideal of equality of opportunity. When they began in the early 1800s, there was a belief that if children from all classes attended the same schools, there would be fewer social class distinctions. From the beginning, of course, the reality was that the schools were not open to all. In many parts of the country, African Americans could not attend public schools. After the Civil War, the Supreme Court tried to justify segregated schools by saying that they could be "separate but equal." Justice John Marshall Harlan believed that the decision violated the nation's highest law and its basic values. "Our Constitution is color-blind," he said, "and neither knows nor tolerates classes among its citizens." Then, in 1954, the Supreme Court held that laws that forced black students to go to racially segregated schools violated the U.S. Constitution because such schools could never be equal. The opinion of the Court was that "to separate [black school children] from others . . . solely because of their race generates a feeling of inferiority . . . that may affect their hearts and minds in a way unlikely ever to be undone."

47 And now, in the 2000s, we find that American schools are once again largely segregated, this time not by law, but because of residential patterns and the love of local neighborhood schools. Now we find that the children of new immigrants may also be in schools where there are a majority of minority students. And we learn that the high school graduation rate for both African Americans and Hispanics is below that of white students. How will we address these critical problems? What does the future hold? On the one hand, local schools reflect residential patterns where there is significant segregation. On the other hand, however, neighborhoods are becoming increasingly integrated as minorities settle in the suburbs. Another factor is that young people are marrying other races and ethnic groups at an increasingly rapid rate. More and more children are born of mixed race/ethnicity.

48 The impact of the enormous number of new immigrants cannot be overstated. From 1980 to 2010, the percentage of foreign-born Americans more than doubled. One in four school children lives with a parent who was born outside the United States. Forty-five percent of the students in U.S. schools are a member of a racial or ethnic minority group. This has caused schools to examine the curricula and try to make it more inclusive. Many schools have adopted history or social studies textbooks that include more information about African Americans, Hispanic Americans, and other minorities, and literature texts that include poetry and fiction written by Americans of all ethnic backgrounds.

49 The challenge is to find ways to give all students, in whatever schools they are attending, the very best education possible. Most Americans would probably agree that there should be minimum core standards that all school districts meet, but there should also be flexibility to account for local diversity. There has always been an effort to find a balance between educational standards and the unique

TOP TEN SPOKEN LANGUAGES IN LEP STUDENTS' HOMES

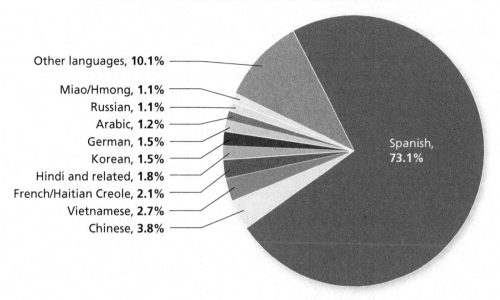

Other languages, **10.1%**
Miao/Hmong, **1.1%**
Russian, **1.1%**
Arabic, **1.2%**
German, **1.5%**
Korean, **1.5%**
Hindi and related, **1.8%**
French/Haitian Creole, **2.1%**
Vietnamese, **2.7%**
Chinese, **3.8%**

Spanish, **73.1%**

Note: Refers to limited English proficient (LEP) students, ages 5 to 18, currently enrolled in school. LEP students are those who reported speaking English less than "very well."
Source: MPI analysis of the 2009 American Community Survey.

circumstances of local neighborhood schools. Americans of all races, ethnic groups, and levels of income care deeply about the education of their children. And the majority of parents want their children to attend their neighborhood school. If it is not a good school, they want to see it improved, not closed.

50 In contrast to many other countries, the local school district has always had a great deal of control over neighborhood schools. Americans are often suspicious of the federal government telling them how to run their local schools. Many school districts are administered by local school boards elected by the people in the district. There are often public school board meetings where parents debate what is happening in the schools—sometimes about what is being taught or what books are being used.

51 American public schools have generally served the United States well by educating a diverse population and working to bring people together. Americans face increased challenges now as they struggle to find ways to provide all students equality of educational opportunity. And they are now debating how to bring equality of achievement to more young people. The future wellbeing of America depends on it.

AFTER YOU READ

Understand Main Ideas

Read the predictions you made on page 204 before reading the chapter. If you have not already done so, complete the L (What We Have Learned) part of the chart you started on page 204 before you read the chapter. With your partner, make up five questions about main points in the chapter and ask another pair of students to answer the questions. Then share your K-W-L chart with the other pair of students.

Understand Details

Write the letter of the best answer according to the information in the chapter.

 1. In the beginning of the chapter, it is implied that some wealthier Americans opposed the first public schools in the United States because
   a. they cost too much money.
   b. they would weaken social-class barriers.
   c. people who did not pay for their education would not value it.

 2. Tocqueville finally concluded that public education in the United States would
   a. give Americans not only the desire but also the means to better their position in life.
   b. not provide any practical training in vocational skills.
   c. not work because people would be prevented from rising to a higher class by the aristocracy.

 3. Which of these statements is <u>false</u>?
   a. American high school students have the choice of going to a free public school or a private one where they must pay tuition.
   b. The American education system is based on strong principles of equality of opportunity—all students should have an equal opportunity to get a good education.
   c. After twelve years of school, American students receive a bachelor's degree diploma at graduation.

 4. Which of these statements is <u>true</u>?
   a. Most of the money to pay for American public schools comes from state and local taxes.
   b. Religious schools that serve middle-class students receive money from the national government, but elite private schools do not.
   c. The national Department of Education determines the curriculum for all schools and sets the standards for high school graduation and college admission.

_a___ 5. From 1900 to 2000, the percentage of young Americans who take at least some college courses
   a. increased enormously, from less than 10 percent to over 50 percent.
   b. increased slightly, from about 10 percent to about 20 percent.
   c. stayed about the same, at around 20 percent.

_b___ 6. What the majority of Americans probably value most about higher education is
   a. its cultural value.
   b. its monetary value.
   c. its moral value.

_c___ 7. Which of the following would not be considered an extracurricular activity?
   a. a school baseball team
   b. the student government of a school
   c. a classroom research project

_c___ 8. In 1896, the U.S. Supreme Court said that racially segregated schools and other public facilities
   a. violated the principle of equality.
   b. violated the U.S. Constitution.
   c. did not violate the principle of equality or the U.S. Constitution.

_b___ 9. Which of these statements about American schools is <u>false</u>?
   a. Public schools that are mainly black or mainly white today usually are the result of the racial makeup of neighborhoods.
   b. African Americans are the fastest growing minority in the schools today.
   c. In some school districts, 100 different languages may be spoken.

_c___ 10. Which of these statements about multiculturalism in the United States is <u>true</u>?
   a. In the United States, all immigrant children attend bilingual programs until they learn English very well and are allowed to attend regular classes with native speakers.
   b. In the United States, there are almost no uniform standards for any schools.
   c. Multicultural education discusses history from the perspectives of all the ethnic groups involved, not just the Anglo-American.

Talk About It

Work in small groups, and choose one or more of these questions to discuss.

1. Should universities be free or have very low tuition? Why or why not?

2. Are most schools in your country coeducational? What are the advantages and disadvantages of having boys and girls in the same classroom?

3. Is it possible for college teachers and students to be friends? What do you think the role of a teacher should be?

4. What should the requirements for entering a university be? Should extracurricular activities in high school or personal characteristics be considered? Why, or why not?

SKILL BUILDING

Develop Your Critical Thinking Skills

In this chapter, there are references to two important goals of education: teaching students facts, and teaching them creative thinking skills. These two approaches to teaching can be summed up in the question, "Are students vessels to be filled or lamps to be lit?" Which do you think is more important—learning a large quantity of facts or learning to think creatively? Why?

Do some research to support your opinion. Reread the last three sections of the chapter, concentrating on paragraphs 23, 24, 28, 29, 30, 41, and 49. Think about your own experience and consider these questions.

- Which approach is used more in your country?
- How do the college admission standards in the United States compare to those in your country?
- Which approach prepares students better for the world of work?
- How do you teach a large quantity of facts to students?
- How do you teach creative thinking?

Think of three more questions raised by this contrasting approach and then share your opinions and your questions with other students in a small group.

Build Reading Skills: Types of Supporting Details

Usually, each paragraph has a topic sentence that states the main idea of the paragraph. Often, this is the first sentence. The rest of the paragraph contains supporting details that develop or explain the main idea. There are many types of supporting details:

- *definitions*
- *facts or opinions*
- *statistics*
- *examples or illustrations*
- *descriptions*
- *quotations*

Look back at the reading and find the paragraphs that begin with the following topic sentences. Then find the details that support the main ideas stated in the topic sentence. Write at least one detail for each sentence, and identify the type of detail that it is.

1. Despite its costs, the percentage of Americans seeking a college education continues to grow.

_____

_____

2. In the late 1900s, international comparisons of education revealed that, in general, American students did not perform as well in math, science, and other subjects as students from many other developed countries.

_____

_____

3. One of the strongest critics of emphasizing standardized testing is Diane Ravitch, who was originally a strong supporter of NCLB.

_____

_____

4. The impact of the enormous number of new immigrants cannot be overstated.

_____

_____

Build Your Vocabulary

Vocabulary Check

Use the words in the box to complete the sentences.

attainment	elite	facilities	obvious	tuition	vocational
displace	extracurricular	isolated	remove	violated	zip codes

1. In 1954, the Supreme Court ruled that segregation denied black children an equal opportunity to an education; segregation _____ the Constitution.

2. In the past, many students who went to competitive schools such as Harvard received their high school education at _____ private schools for the rich.

3. Sports, clubs, and other _____ activities held after school help students get a well-rounded education.

4. Ravitch believes that it is the responsibility of our public schools to provide equality of educational opportunity to all students, regardless of race, ethnicity, or income, and if they are unable to reach equality of educational _____, we must give them special help.

5. Murray says that members of the new upper class live in certain super

   _____ in the United States, where the income and education

   levels are high, and the people are often the leaders and decision makers of

   the country.

6. However, because these schools are relatively few in number, they do

   not _____ the public school as the central educational

   institution in the United States.

7. Murray worries that these elite Americans are _____ from

   the rest of the country and do not understand the problems of the middle

   class.

8. At the university level, there is no free system of public education;

   even universities supported by public funds charge students

   _____.

9. It is _____ that children who are not native speakers of

   English are going to be at a disadvantage when taking standardized tests.

10. Before the civil rights laws were passed, segregation of public

    _____ was legal in the South.

11. Parents were given the opportunity to _____ their children

    from schools with low or failing grades and send them to schools with

    better grades.

12. Some American high schools offer _____ education to

    prepare students for jobs right after school; these students do not attend

    college.

EXPAND YOUR KNOWLEDGE

Ask Americans

Find out how Americans feel about education. Ask several Americans the following questions and record their answers. If you cannot interview Americans, interview a classmate and share the responses with another student.

1. Where do you think your child would get the best education—public school, private school, or charter school? And why?

2. How do you feel about the American education system? What would you do to improve it, if anything?

3. How does the quality of American education compare to other countries? Is there a difference between the quality at the high school level compared to the university level?

4. Are drugs and/or violence problems in the schools in your neighborhood? How should we protect children in schools? Should there be armed guards?

5. How important is a college education? What is the value of a college education? What difference does it make in a person's life? Is it worth the cost?

6. What do you think about ebooks? Should they replace paper textbooks? Why or why not?

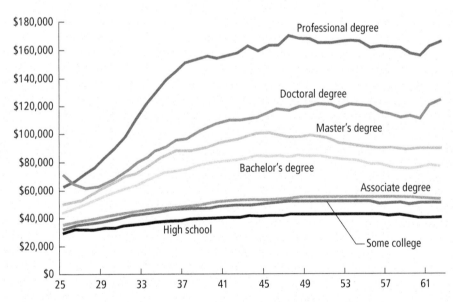

MEAN EARNINGS BY AGE, 2009

Source: 2009 American Community Survey (ACS) Integrated Public Use Micro Sample.
Notes: Estimated for full-time, full-year workers. Plots show a 3-year moving average.

Think, Pair, Share

What should be taught in public schools? What should be the priorities? Read the following list of areas that are covered in American schools, and decide which are the most important.

Arrange the items in order from most important to least important by renumbering the sentences. Then share your list with a partner and with another pair of students.

_____ 1. Developing students' moral and ethical character

_____ 2. Teaching students how to think

_____ 3. Preparing students who do not go to college for a job or career after graduation

_____ 4. Helping students to become informed citizens so that they will be adequately prepared to vote at age eighteen

_____ 5. Preparing students for college

_____ 6. Developing students' appreciation of art, music, and other cultural pursuits

_____ 7. Other (your opinion) _____

Small-Group Project

Some American parents are so dissatisfied with the public schools that they are educating their children at home. Homeschooling now provides education for an increasing number of American children, and the trend is growing. Some public school educators agree that the current model for public schools needs to be changed, and some have begun to create—or to work with a company or a private business—alternative or charter schools, experimenting with class size, grouping, schedules, and curriculum. Perhaps most dramatic, these alternatives to traditional public or private schools are sometimes transforming the roles of the teachers and the students, giving students much more power to decide what they want to learn.

Plan an ideal school. With your group, decide whether it would be homeschooling or an alternative school. Name your school, and then describe it in detail. Decide on school colors and a motto for your school. You may include these points in your description:

- Who would the students be (age, social class, ethnicity)?
- What kind of a building would you use?
- Would the school have a special emphasis (science, music)?
- What would the teachers be like (age, experience, roles)?

- How many students would be in a class?
- Who would determine the curriculum?
- What about tests and homework?
- How would discipline be maintained?
- What would be the role of the parents?
- What special activities would the students have?
- What would a typical day be like?
- What do you think others would say about this school?

When your description is complete, share your new school with the rest of the class.

People Watching

Find the answers to the following questions. Then compare your answers with those of your classmates.

1. When is the right time to ask a question in an American classroom? Watch others and notice the following. (If you have difficulty finding the answers to these questions, ask a fellow student, or ask the teacher to explain when it is the right time for questions.)

    a. Is the teacher talking when students ask questions?

    b. How do students indicate that they have a question to ask?

    c. How does the teacher indicate that he or she is ready for questions? Does the teacher ask, "Are there any questions?" Does the teacher pause and look up from notes or from the chalkboard?

    d. What other signals does a teacher send to indicate that questions are invited?

2. One of the most difficult things for students to understand is when an interview or an appointment with a teacher or professor is over. How do you know when you should leave? Watch a teacher and student in an interview or appointment, if possible, and see which of these are used to indicate the appointment is over. If you cannot observe a teacher and student, perhaps you can watch another similar situation, such as a job interview, a meeting with a counselor, or an appointment with a doctor. Look for the following:

    a. The teacher moves noticeably in the chair—maybe closer to the desk or toward the door.

    b. The teacher says, "Well . . ." or "It has been nice talking to you" or "I think you understand now. . . ."

    c. The teacher turns his or her attention to other business such as papers on the desk or a schedule of appointments.

    d. The teacher moves the chair back from the desk.

Ask Yourself / Ask Americans

Schools around the world differ in their expectations of students. In some schools, students are expected only to listen and remember what their teachers say; in others, they are expected to ask questions. It's important to know these differences if you are going to be successful in a school in another country.

Respond to the following statements. Write **T** (True) or **F** (False) in the first column to indicate how you think students should behave in your country. Then ask an American (preferably a student) for his or her opinion, and record those answers in the second column.

	You	American Student
1. Students should not ask questions; they should only answer them.	_____	_____
2. Students should rise when the teacher enters the classroom.	_____	_____
3. Asking a teacher questions challenges his or her authority.	_____	_____
4. Students should never address teachers by their first names.	_____	_____
5. Students should memorize everything their teachers assign; education is primarily memorizing books and teachers' lectures.	_____	_____
6. Male and female students should attend the same classes.	_____	_____

What differences do you notice in the responses? Compare your answers with others in the class.

Use the Internet

Work with a partner and do one of these activities.

1. Some people predict that of the 6,000 languages currently spoken in the world, about half will not be spoken by the next century. Use the Internet to find information about languages in danger of becoming extinct. Then discuss these questions in small groups.

   a. Why should anyone care if a language is "dying"?

   b. What can be done to help maintain or revitalize a language that is in danger of being lost?

   c. How important do you think it is to preserve languages?

2. American Indian languages are among the most endangered in the world. Many of the 155 languages have not been written. Even those that have been written may have very few people who still speak the language. Use the Internet to find information about Native American languages spoken in the United States and the number of their speakers. Then work with a partner and answer these questions.

   a. How many speakers are there of the most widely spoken languages, Navajo and Ojibwa?

   b. In what states do most of these people live? (What are the five most common states?)

   c. How many languages have twenty speakers or fewer?

3. There are a lot of sources for instruction online. The chapter mentions MOOCs, massive online open courses. Do some research to find out more about MOOCs. Also, look at the free courses offered online by the Khan Academy at http://www.khanacademy.org/

WRITE ABOUT IT

Choose one of the following topics. Then write a short composition about it.

1. What are the advantages and disadvantages of working while attending college?

2. What do you think the real value of a college education is? Is it monetary? Is it intellectual? Is it social? Write an essay explaining your views.

3. The English language has always been friendly to *borrowing* from other languages. Given the closeness of so many Spanish-speaking countries to the United States, and the presence of Spanish-speaking peoples in the Southwest before the colonists moved there from the East Coast, it is not surprising that a number of Spanish words have entered English, especially the English spoken in the United States. Look at this list of words borrowed from Spanish.

alcove	broncos	chaps	patio	siesta	tango
alfalfa	burrito	desperado	poncho	stampede	tornado
alligator	cafeteria	lasso	rodeo	taco	vanilla
avocado	canyon	macho			

What do you notice about these words? How many words relate to food? How many words relate to the life of the cowboy or to the West? (Note: The word for the fair that brings horseback riding, cow roping, and other cowboy feats to many western towns each year is *rodeo*.) Were there any words that surprised you?

Compare borrowings in English with those in other languages that you know. What similarities or differences do you see? Write a report about your findings.

EXPLORE ON YOUR OWN

Books to Read

Lawrence Blum, *High Schools, Race, and America's Future: What Students Can Teach Us About Morality, Diversity, and Community*—This book describes a high school course on race and racism taught in a racially, ethnically, and economically diverse high school, with insights about how the course relates to students' daily lives.

Jonathan Kozol, *Savage Inequalities: Children in America's Schools*—Kozol takes a disturbing look at the differences in public schools attended by rich children versus those attended by poor children and the consequences of the inequalities.

Arthur Levine and Diane Dean, *Generation on a Tightrope: A Portrait of Today's College Student*—Levine and Dean give an account of a generation that is sophisticated about technology but has limited preparation for the world of work.

Charles Murray, *Coming Apart: The State of White America, 1960–2010*—Murray describes the widening gap between what he sees as a new upper class and a new lower class.

Diane Ravitch, *The Death and Life of the Great American School System: How Testing and Choice are Undermining Education*—Ravitch explains why she believes the No Child Left Behind government education program has failed.

Movies to See

The Blindside—This movie is based on a true story of a homeless teen who is taken in by a wealthy family and becomes the star player on the high school football team.

The Interrupters—This is a documentary film that tells the story of three violence interrupters who try to protect their Chicago communities from the violence they once used themselves.

Lean on Me—This film is based on the true story of Joe Clark, a dedicated, but extremely tough, principal of a terrible inner-city school that he is determined to improve.

Stand and Deliver—A dedicated teacher inspires his disadvantaged Latino students to learn calculus to pass an advanced placement exam and build up their self-esteem.

Waiting for "Superman"—This documentary analyzes the failures of the American public education system by following several students trying to gain admission to a charter school.

CHAPTER 10

HOW AMERICANS SPEND THEIR LEISURE TIME

The form and type of play and sports life which evolve in any group or nation mirror the development in other segments of the culture.

American Academy of Physical Education

How do Americans' values affect how they spend their leisure time?

BEFORE YOU READ

Preview Vocabulary

A. Read these sentences from the chapter. Then use context clues to figure out the meanings of the AWL words in italics.

1. The form and type of play and sports life which *evolve* in any group or nation mirror the development in other segments of the culture.

2. The competitive ethic in organized sports contains *elements* of hard work and physical courage. Hard work is often called "hustle," "persistence," or "never quitting" in the sports world, while physical courage is referred to as "being tough" or "having guts."

3. "The Bible says leisure and lying around are morally dangerous . . . sports keep us busy. . . . There are probably more really *committed* Christians in sports, both collegiate and professional, than in any other occupation in America."

4. Some people are particularly concerned about the injuries that high school players get in football games. The pressure to "hit hard" and win high school games is *intense*.

5. In the past, teams and most players stayed in one city and *bonded* with the fans. Now professional sports are more about money and less about team loyalty.

6. Many worry about the amount of sex and violence that children are *exposed* to as they watch TV, play games, and explore the Internet.

7. Mississippi officials *attribute* the drop in childhood obesity to a local focus on the issue, a 2007 law that mandated more physical education, and a decision by the state school board to put more fruits, vegetables, and whole grains on menus.

8. First Lady Michelle Obama started a campaign to fight childhood obesity by stressing children's health and fitness. She *advocated* for federal legislation requiring schools to offer healthier lunches, and she is encouraging kids to exercise more.

Now write the correct AWL word next to its definition.

_____ 1. willing to work very hard at something

_____ 2. parts or features of a whole system

_____ 3. develop by gradually changing

_____ 4. to say that an event is caused by something or someone

_____ 5. very strong

_____ 6. shown, faced with

_____ 7. acted and spoke out in support of

_____ 8. developed a special relationship

B. Classification: Recreational activities are usually not competitive and are done for fun, relaxation, and, sometimes, self-improvement. Sports are more organized and usually involve competition and rules of how to play.

Write **S** if the word or phrase concerns sports and **R** if it has to do with recreation.

_____ 1. team

_____ 2. hobby

_____ 3. handicrafts

_____ 4. hustle

_____ 5. gold medal

_____ 6. do-it-yourself projects

_____ 7. professional tennis

_____ 8. going to the theater

_____ 9. video games

_____ 10. skiing

Preview Content

A. Think about the quotation by the American Academy of Physical Education at the beginning of the chapter. Then discuss these questions with your classmates.

1. How do you think Americans like to spend their leisure time?
2. What are the advantages and disadvantages of playing competitive sports?
3. What do you know about Americans' eating habits? What is "junk food"?
4. What is the impact of television and video games on children?
5. How has technology impacted leisure time?

B. Read the headings in the chapter and look at the illustrations. Write five topics that you predict will be covered in this chapter.

1. _____

2. _____

3. _____

4. _____

5. _____

SPORTS AND AMERICAN VALUES

1 Most social scientists believe that the sports that are organized by a society generally reflect the basic values of that society and attempt to strengthen them in the minds and emotions of its people. Therefore, organized sports may have a more serious social purpose than spontaneous, unorganized play by individuals. This is certainly true in the United States, where the three most popular organized sports are American football,* basketball, and baseball, with soccer gaining in popularity.

2 Traditionally, Americans have seen organized sports as an example of equality of opportunity in action. In sports, people of different races and economic backgrounds get an equal chance to excel. For this reason, notes sociologist Harry Edwards, Americans have viewed organized sports as "a laboratory in which young men, regardless of social class, can learn the advantages and rewards of a competitive system." Although Edwards specifically mentions young men, young women also compete in organized sports without regard to their race or economic background. The majority of American football and basketball players, both college and professional, are African-American, and about one-third of professional baseball players are Hispanics or Latinos. Women's sports have grown in popularity in the United States, and they now have more funding and stronger support at the college level than in the past. The Olympics provide evidence of the increased interest in women's organized sports. American women have won gold medals for several team sports—softball, basketball, and soccer.

3 The American ideal of competition is also at the very heart of organized sports in the United States. Many Americans believe that learning how to win in sports helps develop the habits necessary to compete successfully in later life. This training, in turn, strengthens American society as a whole. "It is commonly held," says one sports writer, "that the competitive ethic taught in sports must be learned and ingrained[1] in youth for the future success of American business and military efforts." In fact, about two-thirds of American boys play organized sports outside of school, and more than half of the girls do, too.

4 Amateur athletics, associated with schools and colleges, are valued for teaching young people traditional American values. The competitive ethic in organized sports contains elements of hard work and physical courage. Hard work is often called "hustle," "persistence," or "never quitting" in the sports world, while physical courage is referred to as "being tough" or "having guts." Slogans are sometimes used to drive home the competitive virtues for the young participants:

> Hustle—you can't survive without it.
>
> A quitter never wins; a winner never quits.
>
> It's easy to be ordinary, but it takes guts to excel.

5 In the process of serving as an inspiration for traditional basic American values, organized sports may be considered as part of "the national religion," a mixture of patriotism and national pride on the one hand, with religious ideas and symbols on the other (see Chapter 3). Billy Graham, a famous American Protestant religious leader, once observed: "The Bible says

---

*Generally, in the United States, when the word "football" is used, it refers to the American game of football. What is known as football in other countries is called "soccer" in the United States.

[1] ingrained: attitudes or behavior that are firmly established and therefore difficult to change

leisure and lying around are morally dangerous . . . sports keep us busy. . . . There are probably more really committed Christians in sports, both collegiate and professional, than in any other occupation in America." On the other hand, in recent years there have been a number of examples of professional sports stars behaving very badly, and there have been significant scandals in college sports as well.

Competition Carried to an Extreme?

6   Although sports in the United States are glorified by many, there are others who are especially critical of the corrupting power of sports when certain things are carried to excess. An excessive desire to win in sports, for example, can weaken rather than strengthen traditional American values.

7   Critics have pointed out that there is a long tradition of coaches and players who have done just this. Vince Lombardi, a famous professional football coach, was often criticized for stating that winning is the "only thing" that matters in sports. Woody Hayes, another famous football coach, once said: "Anyone who tells me, 'Don't worry that you lost; you played a good game anyway,' I just hate." Critics believe that such statements by coaches weaken the idea that other things, such as fair play, following the rules, and behaving with dignity when one is defeated, are also important. Unfortunately, many coaches still share the "winning is the only thing" philosophy.

8   There is, however, also a tradition of honorable defeat in American sports. Sociologist Harry Edwards, for example, has pointed out:

American football is a rough sport that sometimes causes injuries.

The all-important significance of winning is known, but likewise, there is the consoling[2] "reward" of the "honorable defeat." Indeed, the "sweetness" of winning is derived . . . from the knowledge of having defeated a courageous opponent who performed honorably.

9 When the idea of winning in sports is carried to excess, however, honorable competition can turn into disorder and violence. In one baseball game, the players of two professional teams became so angry at each other that the game turned into a large-scale fight between the two teams. The coach of one of the teams was happy about the fight because, in the games that followed, his team consistently won. He thought that the fight had helped to bring the men on his team closer together. Similarly, a professional football coach stated, "If we didn't go out there and fight, I'd be worried. You go out there and protect your teammates. The guys who sit on the bench, they're the losers." Both coaches seemed to share the view that if occasional fights with opposing teams helped to increase the winning spirit of their players, so much the better. Hockey coaches would probably agree. Professional hockey teams are notorious[3] for the fights among players during games. Some hockey fans seem to expect this fighting as part of the entertainment.

10 There are some who criticize this violence in sports, particularly in football, which may be America's favorite spectator sport. From time to time articles appear in newspapers or magazines such as *Sports Illustrated*, one of the nation's leading sports magazines, criticizing the number of injuries that have resulted from the extreme roughness of the game, increased by a burning desire to defeat one's opponent. In recent years, there has been a lot of attention paid to head injuries—brain concussions that cause problems as athletes age. There is evidence that these injuries cause brain damage that can be severe, even resulting in dementia.[4] People are particularly concerned about the injuries that high school players get in football games. The pressure to "hit hard" and win high school games is intense. In some parts of the country, especially in the South, boys start playing tackle football in elementary school, bringing the risks of competitive pressure to nine- and ten-year-olds. Concussions are also a problem for soccer players, particularly for girls (when "heading") because their necks are not as strong as boys.

11 Most Americans would probably say that competition in organized sports does more to strengthen the national character than to corrupt it. They would probably say that eliminating competition in sports and in society as a whole would lead to laziness rather than hard work and accomplishment. One high school principal, for example, described the criticism of competitive sports as "the revolutionaries' attempt to break down the basic foundations upon which society is founded." Comments of this sort illustrate how strong the idea of competition is in the United States, and how important organized sports are as a means of maintaining this value in the larger society.

12 Another criticism of professional sports is that the players and the team owners get too much money, while fans have to pay more and more for tickets to the games. Basketball, baseball, and football stars get multi-million-dollar contracts similar to rock singers and movie stars. Some have asked whether these players are really athletes or entertainers. Furthermore,

[2] *consoling: making someone feel better when he or she is feeling sad or disappointed*

[3] *notorious: famous or well-known for something bad*

[4] *dementia: loss of the ability to think normally*

players are often traded to other teams, or choose to go as free agents, and a whole team may move to another city because of money. In the past, teams and most players stayed in one city and bonded with the fans. Now professional sports are more about money and less about team loyalty.

13 College football and basketball programs are also affected by big money. The teams of large universities generate millions of dollars, and there is enormous pressure on these sports programs to recruit top athletes and have winning seasons. The pressure is on the young athletes as well. There are some high school students who would not be able to afford college if they did not get a sports scholarship. Once they are in college, it is often difficult to balance the demands of daily sports practice and the season game schedule with the need to study. Some colleges have a better rate of athletes graduating than others. In addition to the danger of failing academically, there is another reason why some athletes do not finish college. The very best football and basketball players are often recruited by professional teams while they are still in school. Some students may choose to give up studying for a college degree for the chance to earn big money and early success as a pro.

14 Another problem facing organized sports is the use of performance-enhancing drugs.[5] With the pressure to win so strong, a number of athletes have turned to these drugs. Although the use of most performance-enhancing drugs is illegal, it has now spread from professional sports down to universities and even high schools and middle schools. The use of these drugs puts the health of the athletes in danger, and it is ethically wrong. It goes against the American values of equality of opportunity and fair competition. But

by 2004, the problem had become so significant that President George W. Bush mentioned it in his State of the Union address:

> Athletics play such an important role in our society, but, unfortunately, some in professional sports are not setting much of an example. The use of performance-enhancing drugs like steroids in baseball, football, and other sports is dangerous, and it sends the wrong message—that there are shortcuts to accomplishment, and that performance is more important than character.

The use of these drugs has called into question the achievements of some baseball players and their records for homeruns, etc., and several players have been denied admission to the Baseball Hall of Fame.

15 The case of cyclist Lance Armstrong and his use of performance-enhancing drugs has received intense international attention. Armstrong was widely respected in the United States (although many overseas were suspicious) for his seven Tour de France wins and his charity work fighting cancer. The U.S. Post Office was even an official sponsor of his cycling races. It was a shock to many Americans when the evidence of his drug use was revealed, and he was stripped of his cycling victories.

Recreational Activities

16 Unlike organized sports, what is generally called recreation in the United States is not expected to encourage competition. For this reason, recreation is much more spontaneous and serves the individual's needs away from the competitive world of work. Nevertheless, much can be learned about the values of Americans from an examination of the kinds of recreation in which they engage. Many recreational

---

[5] *performance-enhancing drugs: drugs such as steroids that some athletes use illegally to improve their strength or endurance*

activities are organized at the local level and are paid for (in part) by local governments. Local Parks and Recreation organizations often offer a wide range of activities to community members. There is usually a Parks and Recreation department that operates a recreation center that has fitness equipment and offers classes, and it maintains outdoor facilities. These may include public parks, playgrounds, soccer and baseball fields, basketball and tennis courts, golf courses, walking and bike trails, and swimming pools. These facilities are open to all at little or no cost. During good weather, many communities sponsor outdoor activities and festivals that feature events such as food tasting, outdoor concerts, county fairs, contests, and races. Often, these are attended by whole families and groups of friends.

17 Some Americans prefer recreation that requires a high level of physical activity. This is true of the most popular adult recreational sports: jogging or running, tennis, and skiing. It would seem that these Americans carry over their belief in hard work into their world of play and recreation. The expression "We like to work hard and play hard" is an example of this philosophy.

18 Physical fitness is a way of life for these Americans. Some of them regularly work out at community gyms or private sports clubs—lifting weights, swimming, playing squash or racquetball; participating in aerobic exercise classes; or using exercise bikes, treadmills, rowing machines, or stair-steppers. Some choose to do long-distance running and may participate in a marathon race. In addition to the famous Boston and New York marathons, there are races in many other cities and even in small towns, drawing from several hundred to thousands of participants. Few of the runners expect to win—most just want to finish the race, and over a half a million people do finish a marathon each year. The number of people participating in marathon races has gone down dramatically, but the number finishing them has gone up.

19 Most races are open to all, young and old alike, even those in wheelchairs, and many encourage walkers as well as runners. Charity races are also very popular. Participants ask people to sponsor them by contributing to the charity if they finish the race. The distances vary from 5K to 10K to full marathons and often include social events. The Race for the Cure to raise money for breast cancer research draws women who are breast cancer survivors and their friends and family, and those who participate to honor a loved one who has (or had) the disease.

20 The interest that Americans have in self-improvement, traceable in large measure to the nation's Protestant heritage (see

Serious runners train hard for their races.

Chapter 3), is also carried over into the recreation habits of some people. It is evident in the joggers who are determined to improve the distance they can run, or the people who spend their vacation time learning a new sport such as sailing or scuba diving. The self-improvement motive, however, can also be seen in many other popular forms of recreation that involve little or no physical activity.

Many Americans enjoy rock climbing, white-water rafting, and motorcycling.

21   Interest and participation in cultural activities, which improve people's minds or skills, are also popular. Millions of Americans go to symphony concerts, attend live theater performances, visit museums, hear lectures, and participate in artistic activities such as painting, performing music, or dancing. Many Americans also enjoy hobbies such as weaving, needlework, candle making, wood carving, quilting, and other handicrafts.[6] Community education and recreation programs offer a wide range of classes for those interested in anything from using computers to gourmet cooking, learning a foreign language, writing, art, self-defense, yoga, and bird-watching.

22   The recreational interests of Americans also show a continuing respect for the self-reliance, and, sometimes, the adventure and danger of frontier life. While some choose safe pastimes such as handicrafts, gardening, or DIY (Do It Yourself) projects like building bookcases in their den, others are ready to leave home and take some risks. Adventure travel has grown to be a multi-billion-dollar business. Millions of Americans have bought mountain bikes to explore the wilderness on their own. Many others are choosing to go white-water rafting, mountain climbing, rock climbing, skydiving, helicopter skiing, and bungee jumping. U.S. park officials complain about the number of people who take life-threatening risks in national parks and have to be rescued. "It is as if they are looking for hardship," one park official stated. "They seem to enjoy the danger and the physical challenge."

23   Not all Americans want to "rough it" while they are on their adventure holidays, however. There are a number of travelers who want "soft adventure." Judi Wineland, who operates Overseas Adventure Travel, says, "Frankly, it's amazing to us to see baby boomers seeking creature comforts." On her safari trips to Africa, she has to provide hot showers, real beds, and night tables. The Americans' love of comfort, mentioned in Chapter 5, seems

[6] *handicrafts: skills needing careful use of your hands, such as sewing or making baskets*

to be competing with their desire to feel self-reliant and adventurous. Others simply enjoy being outdoors in the United States fishing, birding, or observing other wildlife. More than 90 million Americans a year participate in these activities.

Health and Fitness

24 In spite of all these opportunities to be physically active, however, many Americans are not physically fit, or even try to be. The overall population is becoming more overweight, due to poor eating habits and a sedentary[7] lifestyle. Government studies estimate that fewer than half of Americans exercise in their leisure time. Experts say that it is not because Americans "don't know what's good for them"—they just don't do it. By mid-2000, the Centers for Disease Control (CDC) sounded the alarm— almost two-thirds of Americans were overweight, and more than one in five were obese. The CDC reported that obesity had become a national epidemic. After smoking, obesity was the number two preventable cause of death in the United States. The government began a campaign to urge people to lose weight and get more exercise. But by 2011, the numbers were worse: More than one-third of American adults were obese. Incidentally, the obesity rate is higher in some states than others. The map above shows the percent of obese people in each state.

25 It's not that Americans lack information on eating well. Newspapers and magazines are full of advice on nutrition, and diet books are best-sellers. Indeed, part of the

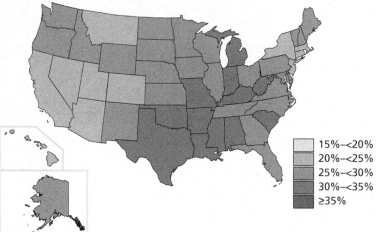

PREVALENCE OF SELF-REPORTED OBESITY AMONG U.S. ADULTS
BEHAVIORAL RISK FACTOR SURVEILLANCE SYSTEM, 2011

15%–<20%
20%–<25%
25%–<30%
30%–<35%
≥35%

Source: Center for Disease Control.

problem may be that there is too much information in the media, and much of it is contradictory. For thirty years, the government encouraged people to eat a diet high in carbohydrates and low in fat to avoid health risks such as heart disease and certain types of cancer. Many Americans ate low-fat, high-carbohydrate foods and gained weight. Then in the early 2000s, high-protein, low-carbohydrate diets became popular.

26 Many Americans have tried a number of diets, searching for the magic one right for them. Some overweight people say the diet advice is so confusing that they have just given up and eat whatever they want. Since 1994, the government has required uniform labeling so that consumers can compare the calories, fat, and carbohydrates in the food they buy. More than half of Americans say they pay attention to the nutritional content of the food they eat, but they also say they eat what they really want when they feel like it. For example, they may have switched to skim milk but still buy fancy, fat-rich ice cream. As one American put it, "Let's face it—if you're having chips and dip as a snack, fat-free potato chips and fat-free

[7] sedentary: doing or requiring much sitting

sour cream just don't taste as good as the real thing."

Nutrition label from a small bag of chips

27 Experts say that it is a combination of social, cultural, and psychological factors that determine how people eat. A *Newsweek* article on America's weight problems referred to "the culture of overindulgence"[8] seemingly ingrained in American life. "The land of plenty seems destined to include plenty of pounds as well," they concluded. Part of the problem is that Americans eat larger portions[9] and often go back for second helpings, in contrast to how much people eat in many other countries.

28 Another factor is Americans' love of fast food. Although the fast-food industry is offering salads on its menus, most Americans still prefer "junk food." They consume huge quantities of pizza, hamburgers, French fries, and soft drinks at restaurants, not only because they like them, but also because these foods are often the cheapest items on the menu. Another significant factor is Americans' busy lifestyle. Since so many women are working, families are eating a lot of fast food, frozen dinners, and restaurant takeout. Some experts believe that Americans have really lost control of their eating; it is not possible to limit calories when they eat so much restaurant and packaged food. It takes time to prepare fresh vegetables and fish; stopping at a fast-food chain for fried chicken on the way home from work is a much faster alternative. Often, American families eat "on the run" instead of sitting down at the table together.

29 First Lady Michelle Obama started a campaign to fight childhood obesity by stressing children's health and fitness. Her program is called "Let's Move," and it focuses on better nutrition as well as increased physical activity. She advocated for federal legislation requiring schools to offer healthier lunches, and she is encouraging kids to exercise more. At the White House, she planted a garden with the help of kids from D.C. inner city schools and called attention to the fact that many poor inner city neighborhoods do not have grocery stores that sell fresh fruits and vegetables. Many have only small neighborhood stores that sell chips and sodas and other "junk food" that is high in calories and low in nutritional value. Often, both children and adults who live in poverty have higher rates of obesity than the general population.

30 There is evidence of some improvement in the rates of childhood obesity. Mississippi is among the most obese states in the nation, according to the Centers for Disease Control and Prevention (CDCP), but its rate of childhood obesity has dropped in recent years. The state made important changes in the time for exercise and the type of food served in the public schools:

> Mississippi officials attribute the drop to a local focus on the issue, a 2007 law that mandated more physical education and a decision by the state school board to put more fruits, vegetables, and whole grains on menus.

[8] *overindulgence: the habit of eating or drinking too much*

[9] *portions: the amount of food for one person, especially when served in a restaurant*

31 Not everyone thinks that having the government mandate exercise programs or school lunch menus is a good idea, but it does seem to be helping. The problem of childhood obesity is truly alarming: Nearly one in three children in the United States is overweight or obese. The numbers are even higher in the African-American and Hispanic communities, where nearly 40 percent of the children are overweight or obese.

First Lady Michelle Obama has created a program to fight childhood obesity.

The Impact of Television, Video Games, and the Internet

32 Ironically, as Americans have gotten heavier as a population, the image of a beautiful woman has gotten much slimmer. Marilyn Monroe, a movie star of the 1950s and 1960s, would be overweight by today's media standards. Television shows, movies, and TV commercials feature actresses who are very slender.[10] Beer and soft drink commercials, for example, often feature very thin girls in bikinis. As a result, many teenage girls have become insecure about their bodies and so obsessed[11] with losing weight that some develop eating disorders such as anorexia or bulimia.

33 Another irony is that although television seems to promote images of slender, physically fit people, the more people watch TV, the less likely they are to exercise. Television has a strong effect on the activity level of many Americans. Some people spend much of their free time lying on the couch watching TV, channel surfing,[*] and eating junk food. They are called "couch potatoes," because they are nothing but "eyes." (The small marks on potatoes are called *eyes*.) Couch potatoes would rather watch a baseball game on TV than go play softball in the park with friends, or even go to a movie. Cable and satellite TV bring hundreds of stations into American homes, so there is an almost limitless choice of programs. Americans spend more of their leisure watching TV than doing any other activity.

34 Another challenge is the effect of all this technology on children. Some worry that American children and young people are spending too much time watching television, using the Internet, and playing video games. One effect is that channel surfing and surfing on the web shorten a child's attention span. Also, research shows that multitasking is really switching rapidly from one task to another, and it is not really doing several tasks at the same minute. There is evidence that the brains of children and young people are being rewired by these activities. There is an effect on both their minds and their bodies. Clearly, they are not getting enough exercise. The government estimates that eight to 18-year-olds spend an average of 7.5 hours a day using entertainment media, including TV, computers, video games, cell phones, and movies. Only one-third of high school students get the recommended levels of physical activity.

[10] *slender: thin, graceful, and attractive*

[11] *obsessed: thinking about a person or a thing all the time and being unable to think of anything else*

[*] *Constantly clicking the remote control to change from channel to channel. (Note also the term "surf the web" that means to go from site to site, and surfing refers to the sport of riding the waves on a special board.)*

LEISURE TIME ON AN AVERAGE DAY

Other leisure activities, **17 minutes**

Relaxing and thinking, **17 minutes**

Playing games, using computer for leisure, **25 minutes**

Participating in sports, exercising, recreation, **19 minutes**

Reading, **18 minutes**

Socializing and communicating, **38 minutes**

Watching TV, **2.7 hours**

Total leisure and sport time = **5.0 hours**

Note: Data include all persons age 15 and over. Data include all days of the week and are annual averages for 2010.
Source: Bureau of Labor Statistics, American Time Use Survey.

35 Others worry more about the quality of what children are watching on TV, the content of video games, and what they are seeing on the Internet. Many worry about the amount of sex and violence that children are exposed to as they watch TV, play games, and explore the Internet. Americans face a constant dilemma[12]— how to balance the right to free speech with the need to protect children and maintain standards of decency.[13] Because Americans place such a high value on individual freedom, particularly freedom of speech, they have traditionally been very hesitant to censor,[14] or even restrict, the flow of information by any means of communication. True censorship occurs when the government sets the standards; most Americans would prefer that the entertainment industry regulate itself, and the movie industry does have a rating system for films. The Entertainment Software Rating Board (ESRB) "assigns the age and content ratings for video games and mobile apps, enforces advertising and marketing guidelines for the video game industry, and helps companies implement responsible online privacy practices."

"On the Internet, nobody knows you're a dog."

36 On the one hand, some people believe that the federal government should regulate the Internet to protect children. There have been instances where adults have met children or teenagers over the

[12] dilemma: a situation in which you have to make a difficult choice between two or more actions

[13] decency: basic accepted behavior, especially moral and sexual behavior

[14] censor: to examine books, movies, or letters to remove anything that is offensive

Internet and have persuaded them to meet in person. In several instances, teenagers have been kidnapped. Parents have great fear about their children meeting strangers on the Internet and about their possible exposure to pornography. It is against the law to send pornography through the U.S. mail, and some wish it were outlawed on the Internet as well. (Child pornography is already against the law.) But it is not just children who can get into trouble on the Internet. Many adults have been the victims of scams where they are tricked into giving personal information that allows criminals to steal money from their bank accounts, or even their whole identity. The anonymity of the Internet is valued by many, but it also has hurt a number of people. Most alarming is the cyberbullying of some teenagers that has been so hurtful that the victims have committed suicide.

37 On the other hand, many Internet users believe that government regulation could threaten the growth and vitality of the Internet. Some would argue that the lack of regulation has permitted the Internet's explosive growth and the development of new technologies to deliver it. Wireless technology now allows Americans to access the Internet just about anywhere, including, ironically, many fast-food restaurants. Many people are happy that technology has made it possible for them to communicate with just about anyone anywhere. However, this 24/7 access (24 hours a day, 7 days a week) has a huge impact on leisure time and Americans' ability to relax. Joe Robinson, in his book *Work to Live: Reclaim Your Life, Health, Family, and Sanity*, states, "The line between work and home has become so blurred that the only way you can tell them apart is that one has a bed." Robinson and others are trying to get American companies to offer more vacation time. The majority of Americans work more than forty hours a week, and many only get one or two weeks a year of paid vacation time. When the economy has a downturn, many are afraid to take the short amount of vacation time they have. The U.S. Travel Association reports that the average American vacation is now 3.8 days; people are taking more long-weekend trips, and fewer one- or two-week-long trips.

38 Robinson has organized the Work to Live campaign, with the goal of changing the national labor laws so that everyone would be entitled to at least three weeks of vacation per year. He says that our founding fathers Thomas Jefferson and John Adams "believed that democracy was at risk if all attention in society was focused only on making money. It's hard to be an engaged citizen, not to mention a parent or actual human, when the overwork culture abducts you from all other responsibilities in life." He argues that Americans would be even more productive if they could have a month of vacation like most Europeans do.

39 Vacation time renews the spirit and gives people the energy and vitality to lead productive lives. Leisure time in the United States offers something for everyone; the only complaint that most Americans have is that they do not have enough of it. Americans, like people everywhere, sometimes choose recreation that just provides rest and relaxation. Watching television, going out for dinner, and visiting friends are simply enjoyable ways to pass the time. However, as we have seen, millions of Americans seek new challenges involving new forms of effort even in their leisure time. "Their reward," states *U.S. News & World Report*, "is a renewed sense of vitality,"[15] a sense of a goal conquered and confidence regained in dealing with life's "ups and downs."

[15] *vitality: great energy and cheerfulness, and the ability to continue working effectively*

AFTER YOU READ

Understand Main Ideas

Review the predictions you made on page 231 before you read the chapter. Were your predictions correct? Write the number of the paragraph where you found the information next to each prediction.

Understand Details

Write the letter of the best answer according to the information in the chapter.

_____ 1. Organized sports in a society
   a. are a poor reflection of the values of that society.
   b. are a good reflection of the values of that society.
   c. are leisure activities and games which tell us very little about the social values of a country.

_____ 2. Which of the following ideals is at the very heart of organized sports in the United States and is, therefore, the most important ideal expressed in organized sports?
   a. self-reliance
   b. self-denial
   c. competition

_____ 3. Which of these statements is not true?
   a. Billy Graham, a Protestant religious leader, has criticized sports for having a negative effect on the morals of young Americans.
   b. Most Americans would probably agree that organized sports are an important way for young people to learn to compete.
   c. Organized sports are an example of the "national religion," the mixing of national pride and religious values.

_____ 4. Vince Lombardi, a famous professional football coach, expressed the view that
   a. sports help boys grow into men.
   b. a good football player makes a good soldier.
   c. winning is the only thing that matters.

_____ 5. Leading sports publications such as *Sports Illustrated* have stated that
   a. sports are good in general, but excessive violence in sports should be stopped.
   b. sports corrupt the American spirit and should be replaced with noncompetitive activities.
   c. many aspects of American culture, such as music and art, have been replaced by the love of sports.

_____ 6. Some of the most popular forms of recreation in the United States, such as jogging, reflect the attitude that
   a. Americans like the challenge of adventure sports.
   b. contact with nature is good for the soul of man.
   c. it is good to work hard and to play hard.

_____ 7. Which of these statements is <u>not</u> true?
   a. Many Americans like to spend their leisure time learning new skills in order to improve themselves.
   b. The American respect for self-reliance can be seen in the popularity of adventure travel, where people often have to rough it.
   c. Because of their active lifestyles, the number of people who weigh more than they should is decreasing.

_____ 8. According to the chapter, why do so many Americans have poor eating habits?
   a. They are unaware of the dangers of high-fat diets.
   b. The foods that they buy in the stores have no labels that give nutritional information.
   c. They are too busy to cook, and they eat a lot of fast food.

_____ 9. Which of these statements is <u>not</u> true?
   a. The majority of American homes have TV systems that can get fifty channels or more.
   b. Most Americans have such a busy lifestyle that they watch very little TV.
   c. American children watch a lot of television, and play a lot of video games.

_____ 10. Which of these statements <u>is</u> true?
   a. Most Americans are not concerned about the level of violence on television.
   b. The federal government censors programs on TV to maintain high standards of decency.
   c. Some children's television programs are educational and have much less violence than adult programs.

Talk About It

Work in small groups and choose one or more of the following questions to discuss.

1. What is your favorite sport, and why? Have you ever played on a team? Explain.

2. What are popular forms of recreation in your country? What do you like to do in your leisure time?

3. How would you compare the day-to-day level of physical activity of people in your country with that of Americans?

4. Do you think college sports teams are really like professional teams? Should the players be paid? Why or why not?

5. What is the most violent sport? Have you ever been at a sports event where there was fighting? Explain.

SKILL BUILDING

Improve Your Reading Skills: Scanning

Scan the chapter for these names and terms. Then identify each with a short phrase.

1. junk food: _____

2. couch potato: _____

3. Vince Lombardi: _____

4. channel surf: _____

5. Michelle Obama: _____

6. cyberbullying: _____

7. Lance Armstrong: _____

8. Judi Wineland: _____

9. CDC: _____

10. Joe Robinson: _____

Develop Your Critical Thinking Skills

Work with a partner and find examples of how Americans' traditional values affect organized sports and other ways Americans spend their leisure time. Put the examples into the correct categories. First match the examples with the values they illustrate, and then look for additional examples in the chapter. Answers may be used more than once.

_e,h_ 1. individual freedom   _____ 4. competition

_____ 2. self-reliance   _____ 5. material wealth/the American Dream

_____ 3. equality of opportunity   _____ 6. hard work

a. both boys and girls play organized sports

b. hustle and persistence, never quitting

c. great emphasis on winning in sports

d. many blacks on professional basketball teams

e. Americans free to pursue a great variety of individual interests in their leisure time

f. love of adventure travel in the wilderness, roughing it

g. many children have smartphones and other digital devices

h. professional sports team members free to change teams as free agents

i. emphasis on children playing competitive sports

j. popularity of do-it-yourself projects

k. buying teenagers cell phones and computers

l. having very little vacation time

Build Your Vocabulary

Opposites

Read the sentences below that contain pairs of opposites in parentheses. Choose the correct words and write them in the sentence blanks.

1. Baseball, football, basketball, and soccer are popular (**individual/team**)

   _____ sports.

2. Slogans are sometimes used to drive home the competitive (**vices/virtues**)

   _____ for the young participants: A quitter never wins; a

   (**winner/loser**) _____ never quits.

3. When the idea of winning in sports is carried to excess, honorable

   competition can turn into (**order/disorder**) _____ and

   violence.

4. There are some who (**criticize/praise**) _____ this violence

   in American sports, particularly in football, which is probably America's

   favorite (**participant/spectator**) _____ sport.

5. (**Amateur/Professional**) _____ athletics, associated with

   schools and colleges, are valued for teaching young people traditional

   American values.

6. Most Americans would probably say that competition in organized sports

   does more to (**corrupt/strengthen**) _____ the national

   character than to (**corrupt/strengthen**) _____ it.

7. Some Americans prefer recreation that requires a high level of (**physical/**

   mental) _____ activity such as jogging, tennis, and skiing.

8. The overall population is becoming overweight due to poor eating habits and a (**sedentary/active**) _____ lifestyle.

9. Another irony is that although television seems to promote images of (**obese/slender**) _____, physically fit people, the more people watch TV, the less likely they are to exercise.

10. Unfortunately, most experts would probably say that the 1990s brought few (**positive/negative**) _____ changes in children's programming.

More AWL Words

Test your knowledge of these AWL words by matching them with their definitions.

comment	guidelines	item	overseas	range
contract	illustrate	label	principal	relax
derive	image	lecture	project	symbol
equipment	injury	likewise	psychological	uniform

_____ 1. most important

_____ 2. a piece of paper with information about the thing attached to it

_____ 3. a carefully planned work

_____ 4. a single thing in a group

_____ 5. the way a person or product is presented to the public

_____ 6. different things of the same general type

_____ 7. in the same way

_____ 8. to make the meaning of something clearer by giving examples

_____ 9. a legal written agreement

_____ 10. a word, principle, or instruction about the best way to do something

_____ 11. in a foreign country across the ocean

_____ 12. something that represents an idea

_____ 13. a wound to your body caused by an accident or attack

_____ 14. being the same in all its parts

_____ 15. relating to the way that people's minds work

_____ 16. a long talk given to a group

_____ 17. special things needed for a sport

_____ 18. an opinion that you express

_____ 19. to have its source in (something)

_____ 20. to feel calm and comfortable

Play a Vocabulary Game

Work in small groups, and think of words and phrases that would fit into categories. Challenge another group to a competition—you tell them the words and phrases, and they guess the category. You can use information in this chapter or choose other vocabulary having to do with sports, recreation, health and fitness, diet, television, or computer technology. Here are some suggestions for categories:

> things that have to do with soccer
> (names of) basketball players
> (names of) popular diets
> things relating to culture or the arts
> things you can do on the Internet
> things teenagers like to do
> food that is good for you
> junk food
> things that might happen to a couch potato
> things a couch potato might use
> dangerous leisure activities
> equipment you need for football
> Olympic sports

Classify Words

Work with a partner. Circle the words or phrases that do not belong in each category.

EXAMPLE: **team sports:** football, baseball, hockey, (tennis)

Tennis does not belong because it is an individual sport, not a team sport.

1. **adventure sports:** helicopter skiing, African safaris, white-water rafting, gardening, rock climbing, bungee jumping, skydiving, mountain climbing

2. **things parents worry about:** pornography, explicit sex on TV, strangers on the Internet, gourmet cooking, childhood obesity, shortening of child's attention span, violence

3. **reasons why many Americans are overweight:** fast-food restaurants, larger portions, second helpings, sedentary lifestyle, overseas travel, poor eating habits, lack of exercise

4. **hobbies:** weaving, playing professional football, painting, performing music, bird-watching, making candles, Chinese cooking, learning a foreign language, traveling

5. **things made possible by technology:** wireless networks, handicrafts, laptop computers, accessing the Internet in a Starbucks, cell phones, email, instant messaging, paging, Internet games, walkie-talkies, exchanging digital photos

EXPAND YOUR KNOWLEDGE

Think, Pair, Share

How do you prefer to spend your leisure time? Read this list of leisure-time activities and decide which you enjoy most. Number them in order of importance, with number 1 as your favorite choice. Share your list with a partner and then with another pair of students.

_____ Go on a walk or hike	_____ Go swimming
_____ Read a good book	_____ Listen to music
_____ See a movie	_____ Attend a concert
_____ Play a sport	_____ Have a family picnic
_____ Work out at a gym	_____ See a play
_____ Have dinner at a restaurant	_____ Visit a museum
_____ Watch TV	_____ Go shopping
_____ Go to a friend's house	_____ Watch a game
_____ Have a friend visit you	_____ Other: _____

Ask Yourself / Ask Americans

If possible, ask several Americans the following questions. Then do a poll among your friends or classmates. Compare their responses with the pie chart on page 241 from the Bureau of Labor Statistics, American Time Use Survey.

1. Think about your daily schedule. How much time each day do you spend doing each of these activities:

   Working and related activities

   Leisure and sports

   Household activities

   Eating and drinking

   Caring for others

   Sleeping

   Other activities _____

2. What are your two or three favorite leisure activities?

People Watching

In some countries, lunch is a leisurely meal that may take two or three hours. Some people eat at a nice restaurant with friends or co-workers, while others return home to eat with their families. For many, lunch is the main meal of the day. In contrast, many Americans eat lunch "on the run."

If possible, observe Americans eating lunch. Compare their lunch habits with those of your culture. Record your observations in the chart. Compare your observations with those of your classmates.

Observation Questions	Americans at Lunch	_____ at Lunch
1. Where are they eating?		
2. What are they eating?		
3. What size are the portions?		
4. How long do they stay?		
5. Do they take any food with them when they leave?		

Use the Internet

Choose one of these activities and do research on the Internet with a partner.

1. Work with a partner to learn about popular American diets. Use the Internet and find information on several diets. Decide which one you think is best and why. Then share your diet choice with your classmates. These are some popular diets:

Vegetarian, or vegan	The Zone
Dean Ornish, or low-fat	Weight Watchers
Atkins, or low-carbohydrate	Jenny Craig
South Beach	Mediterranean

2. Reality TV shows have become very popular in the United States and in other countries. Use the Internet to find out how to become a contestant on these shows. Choose one program and write a report about how to apply to appear on the show.

3. Americans have started to move back into cities from the suburbs to live in communities where they can walk to work, shopping, entertainment, etc. At the same time, there is a trend to urbanize the suburbs by building walking communities that are more like small towns, with houses, schools, shopping, and offices close together. Look on the Internet for more information about these walkable, convenient urban and suburban communities. Some examples are: Capital Hill in Seattle, WA; Short North in Columbus, OH; and Ballston, VA (in the Washington, D.C. area). Check out the website www.walkscore.com

Small-Group Projects

Some people say that Americans don't have any culture. By that they probably mean that the United States has not been a country long enough to have developed its own art forms—music, dance, or theater—usually referred to as the *fine arts*. Work in small groups to test that theory or hypothesis. If you are living in the United States, find out about your local community. Are there libraries? Museums? Theaters where concerts and plays are performed? Check the entertainment section of your local newspaper (or a website) and see if any of the following are scheduled:

1. Ballets or other dance performances
2. Art or other exhibitions
3. Symphony concerts
4. Other concerts or musical performances
5. Poetry readings
6. Operas
7. Plays

Dancers from Morphoses perform in Christopher Wheeldon's "Commedia" at New York City Center.

Make a list of these performances or exhibitions, and indicate the nationality of both the artist who is performing the work and the artist who created it. Share your findings with your classmates. Work in small groups and design a cultural-adventure travel brochure. Decide all the details of the trip.

1. What kind of adventure is it?
2. Where will it take place?
3. What are the dates?
4. How much will it cost and what is included?
5. What experiences will the travelers have?

You may wish to include an itinerary and some pictures, if possible. When you have finished, share your brochure with your classmates.

WRITE ABOUT IT

Choose one of the following topics. Then write a short composition about it.

1. Some would say that American homeowners have an obsession with having a beautiful lawn. In the United States, lawns occupy more land than any single crop, including wheat and corn, and in western cities as much as 60 percent of water is used for lawns. Do you think green spaces are important? Write about the use of land for private lawns or public parks, and describe differences between the United States and your country.

2. Write about the problem of protecting children from sex and violence in television programs and movies, on the Internet, and in video games. Use a graphic organizer to plan your essay.

3. Two of the fastest growing sports are NASCAR racing and golf. Write a report about why you think they are so popular, or choose another sport to write about.

4. Many American children are very impressed with sports stars. Do you think sports superstars have a responsibility to be positive role models for young people? Write an essay explaining why or why not, and give examples.

EXPLORE ON YOUR OWN

Books to Read

H. G. Bissinger, *Friday Night Lights: A Town, A Team, and a Dream*—A successful sportswriter, Bissinger spent a year in the Texas town of Odessa writing about their high school football program.

Pat Conroy, *My Losing Season*—In this memoir, fiction-writer Conroy tells about his personal experience as a high school basketball player at the Citadel, a military college.

Michael Mandelbaum, *The Meaning of Sports: Why Americans Watch Baseball, Football, and Basketball and What They See When They Do*—The author, a well-respected foreign policy analyst, explores Americans' fascination with team sports and how they satisfy deep human needs.

George Plimpton, *Paper Lion*—Plimpton recounts his story of being a 36-year-old rookie playing for the Detroit Lions.

Cheryl Strayed, *Wild: From Lost to Found on the Pacific Crest Trail*—A woman's life changes on a 1,100 mile hike alone on the trail from the Mojave Desert to Washington state.

Movies to See

42—This film is based on the true story of Jackie Robinson, the first African American to play in American major league baseball.

The Fighter—A docudrama explores the remarkable rise of a Massachusetts-born, junior welter-weight champion boxer named "Irish" Micky Ward.

Moneyball—Oakland A's general manager Billy Beane assembles a successful baseball team on a lean budget by employing computer-generated analysis to choose new players.

Rudy—A boy who has always been told that he is too small to play college football is determined to overcome the odds and fulfill his dream of playing for Notre Dame.

The Social Network—This film tells the story of how Mark Zuckerberg and a friend started Facebook when they were students at Harvard.

CHAPTER 11

THE AMERICAN FAMILY

The American has fashioned anew the features of his family institutions, as he does everything else about him.

Max Lerner (1902–1992)

Is the changing structure of American families affecting the American Dream?

BEFORE YOU READ

Preview Vocabulary

A. Read the following questions and notice the words in italics. These key AWL words will help you understand the reading. Use context clues to help you figure out the meanings. Then work with a partner and answer the questions.

1. If a *nuclear* family consists of a husband, wife, and their children, what is an extended family?

2. If you had a problem to solve, would you want your family to offer their *insight* into ways to solve it?

3. If you had children, would sending them to private schools be a *priority* for you, or would something else be more important?

4. How does the *location* of your house or apartment affect your lifestyle? Does it matter where you live?

5. Do you think husbands and wives should be equal *partners* in a marriage?

6. If we say that *approximately* one out of every two marriages now ends in divorce, what does that mean? Does it mean "more or less" or "exactly"?

7. Do you think that men and women should be *compensated* equally for doing the same work, or should they be paid different salaries?

8. What might happen if conscientious parents keep their eyes *exclusively focused* on their children, thinking about what the children need instead of what responsibilities and obligations they have?

9. If we say that by the end of the 1970s *considerably* less than half of the women in the United States still believed that they should put their husbands and children ahead of their own careers, does that mean "a little less than half" or "a lot less than half"?

10. Do you think American families are more *stable* or less stable than families in your country, or is divorce common in your country also?

B. Read the following paragraph from the chapter and notice the words in italics. Then use context clues and write the correct word next to its definition.

Juggling career and family responsibilities can be as difficult for men as it is for women, especially if there is truly an equal division of duties. American fathers are often seen dropping the kids off at the babysitter's *or* taking a sick child to the doctor. Some businesses are recognizing the need to *accommodate* families where both parents work. They may open a daycare center in the office building, offer fathers *paternity leave* to stay home with their new babies, or have *flexible* working hours. Unfortunately, these *benefits* are not yet available to all. While young *couples* strive to achieve equality in their careers, their marriages, and their parenting, society at large still lacks many of the *structures* that are needed to support them.

_____ 1. advantages that you get from your job

_____ 2. accept someone's needs and try to do what they want

_____ 3. trying to fit two or more jobs or activities into your life

_____ 4. things arranged in a definite pattern of organization

_____ 5. a period of time away from work that a father of a new baby is allowed

_____ 6. pairs of people who are together

_____ 7. can be changed easily to suit any new situation

Preview Content

A. Discuss these questions with your classmates.

1. Read the quotation by Max Lerner at the beginning of the chapter. What changes do you think Americans have made in the institution of marriage?

2. Look at the photo on page 255. Why do you think the authors chose this family photo to begin the chapter? How do you think this family relates to the basic traditional values presented in this book?

3. Who do you think lives in a typical American household?

4. Compare what you know about American families with typical families in your country. Use a Venn diagram to list how they are the same and how they are different.

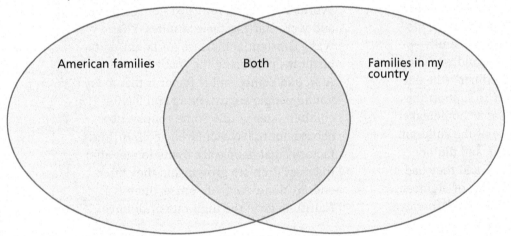

5. Americans often talk about "family values." What do you think they mean?

B. Read the headings in the chapter and look at the illustrations. Write five topics that you predict will be covered in this chapter.

1. _____

2. _____

3. _____

4. _____

5. _____

1   What is the typical American family like? If Americans are asked to name the members of their families, family structure becomes clear. Married American adults will name their husband or wife and their children, if they have any, as their *immediate family*. If they mention their father, mother, sisters, or brothers, they will define them as separate units, usually living in separate households. Aunts, uncles, cousins, and grandparents are considered *extended family*.

2   Traditionally, the American family has been a nuclear family, consisting of a husband, wife, and their children, living in a house or apartment. Grandparents rarely live in the same home with their married sons and daughters, and uncles and aunts almost never do. In the 1950s, the majority of the American households were the classic traditional American family—a husband, wife, and two children. The father was the "breadwinner" (the one who earned the money to support the family), the mother was a "homemaker" (the one who took care of the children, managed the household, and did not work outside the home), and they had two children under the age of eighteen. If you said the word *family* to Americans a generation or two ago, this is the traditional picture that probably came to their minds.

3   Today, however, the reality is much different. A very small percentage of American households consist of a working father, a stay-at-home mother, and children under eighteen. Less than one-quarter of American households now consist of two parents and their children, and the majority of these mothers in these households hold jobs outside the home. The majority of American households today consist of married couples without children, single parents and their children, or unrelated people living together. Perhaps most surprising, 27 percent of Americans live alone. About one-third of those living alone are 65 years or older. Many of them live in small towns in the upper Midwest part of the country, where more people prefer to stay in their own homes as they age. Others who live alone are younger people who move to places such as Atlanta and northern Virginia (the Washington, D.C. area) in search of job opportunities.

4   What has happened to the traditional American family of the 1950s, and why? Some of the explanation is demographic.[1] In the 1950s, men who had fought in World War II had returned home, married, and were starting their families. There was a substantial increase (or boom) in the birthrate, producing the "baby boomers." A second demographic factor is that today young people are marrying and having children later in life. Some couples now choose not to have children at all. A third factor is that people are living longer after their children are grown, and they often end up alone. And, of course, there is a fourth factor—the high rate of divorce.

Less than 25 percent of American families are "traditional"—made up of two parents and their children.

[1] *demographic: related to a part of the population that is considered as a group*

But numbers alone cannot account for the dramatic changes in the family. Understanding the values at work in the family will provide some important insights.

The Emphasis on Individual Freedom

5　Americans view the family as a group whose primary purpose is to advance the happiness of individual members. The result is that the needs of each individual take priority in the life of the family. This means that in contrast to many other cultures, the primary responsibility of the American family member is not to advance the family as a group, either socially or economically. Nor is it to bring honor to the family name. This is partly because the United States is not an aristocratic society.

6　Family name and honor are less important than in aristocratic societies, since equality of opportunity is considered a basic traditional American value. Moreover, there is less emphasis on the family as an economic unit because relatively few families maintain self-supporting family farms or businesses for more than one generation. A farmer's son, for example, is very likely to go on to college, leave the family farm, and take an entirely different job in a different location.

7　The American desire for freedom from outside control clearly extends to the family. Americans do not like to have controls placed on them by other family members. They want to make independent decisions and not be told what to do by grandparents or uncles or aunts. For example, both American men and women expect to decide what job is best for them as individuals. Indeed, young Americans are encouraged by their families to make such independent career decisions. What

would be best for the family is not usually considered to be as important as what would be best for the individual.

Marriage and Divorce

8　Very few marriages are "arranged" in the United States. Traditionally, young people are expected to find a husband or wife on their own; their parents do not usually help them. In fact, parents are frequently not told of marriage plans until the couple has decided to marry. This means that many parents have little control and, generally, not much influence over whom their children marry. Most Americans believe that young people should fall in love and then decide to marry someone they can live happily with, again evidence of the importance of an individual's happiness. Of course, in reality this does not always happen, but it remains the traditional ideal and it shapes the views of courtship[2] and marriage among young Americans.

9　Over the years, the value placed on marriage itself is determined largely by how happy the husband and wife make each other. Happiness is based primarily on companionship. The majority of American women value companionship as the most important part of marriage. Other values, such as having economic support and the opportunity to have children, although important, are seen by many as less important. If the couple is not happy, the individuals may choose to get a divorce. A divorce is relatively easy to obtain in most parts of the United States. Most states have "no-fault" divorce. To obtain a no-fault divorce, a couple states that they can no longer live happily together, that they have irreconcilable differences,[3] and that it is neither partner's fault.

---

[2] courtship: the period of time during which a man and a woman have a romantic relationship before getting married

[3] irreconcilable differences: strong disagreements between two people who are married, given as a legal reason for getting a divorce

10　The divorce rate rose rapidly in the United States from the 1960s through the 1980s and then leveled off. Overall, approximately one out of every two marriages now ends in divorce, but divorce rates vary according to the age of the couple and other factors. The younger people marry, the more likely that they will divorce. The new upper class described by Charles Murray in *Coming Apart: The State of White America* has a much lower divorce rate than the rest of the population (see Chapter 5). They are more likely to get married (usually after they have finished college), stay married, and raise their children in stable homes. These are the very well educated and often super rich, and include many of the nation's leaders. On the other hand, among the poor, there are more children born to single mothers. There are fewer marriages and there is more divorce. Often, children are involved.

11　The majority of adult middle-class Americans believe that unhappy couples should not stay married just because they have children at home, a significant change in attitude since the 1950s. Many people do not believe in sacrificing individual happiness for the sake of the children. They say that children actually may be better off living with one parent than with two who are constantly arguing. Divorce is now so common that it is no longer socially unacceptable, and children are not embarrassed to say that their parents are divorced. However, psychologists and sociologists are still studying the long-term consequences of divorce.

12　Judith Wallerstein has studied the effect of divorce on children as they grow up. In her book *The Unexpected Legacy of Divorce: A 25 Year Landmark Study*, she notes that by the year 2000, almost half of the American adults under the age of forty were children of divorced parents. For twenty-five years she followed a group of children whose parents were divorced and compared their experiences with others whose parents stayed together "for the sake of the children." She found that the key factor was whether or not the parents could set aside their differences enough to focus on the needs of their children, regardless of whether the parents divorced or stayed together. However, even in the best cases, divorce had a lasting effect on children as they grew into adulthood and formed their own relationships. In fact, over half of them said they did not want to have children of their own because they were afraid of causing their children the pain that they had experienced growing up.

The Role of the Child

13　The American emphasis on the individual, rather than the group, affects children in a contradictory way. On the one hand, it may cause them to get more attention and even have more power than they should. On the other hand, because most children have mothers who are working outside the home, they may not get enough attention from either parent. Worse yet, parents who feel guilty for not having enough time with their children may give them more material things to compensate for the lack of attention. Working parents constantly struggle to find enough time to spend with their children.

14　Some American families tend to place more emphasis on the needs and desires of the child than on the child's social and family responsibilities. In the years after World War II, much stress was placed on the psychological needs of children, and the number of experts in this field increased enormously. Child psychologists, counselors,[4] and social workers were employed to help children with problems

---

[4] counselors: people whose job is to help and support people with personal problems

Ready to go trick-or-treating on Halloween

at school or in the family. Many books on how to raise children became best-sellers. Sometimes these books offered conflicting advice, but almost all of them shared the American emphasis on the development of the individual as their primary goal.

15 Some Americans believe that the emphasis on the psychological needs of the individual child was carried too far by parents and experts alike. Dr. Benjamin Spock, one of the most famous of the child-rearing experts, eventually came to this conclusion. He said, "What is making the parent's job most difficult is today's child-centered viewpoint." Many conscientious[5] parents, said Spock, tend to "keep their eyes exclusively focused on their child, thinking about what he [or she] needs from them and from the community, instead of thinking about what the world, the neighborhood, the family will be needing from the child and then making sure that he [or she] will grow up to meet such obligations."

16 Today's parents seem more concerned about teaching their children responsibility. Although Americans may not agree on how best to nurture[6] and discipline their children, most still hold the basic belief that the major purpose of the family is the development and welfare of each of its members as individuals.

Equality in the Family

17 Along with the American emphasis on individual freedom, the belief in equality has had a strong effect on the family. Alexis de Tocqueville saw the connection clearly in the 1830s. He said that in aristocratic societies inequality extends into the family, particularly to the father's relationship to his children. The father is accepted as ruler and master. The children's relations with him are very formal, and love for him is always combined with fear. In the United States, however, the democratic idea of equality destroys much of the father's status as ruler of the family and lessens the emotional distance between father and children. There is less formal respect for, and fear of, the father. But there is more affection expressed toward him. "The master and constituted [legal] ruler have vanished,"[7] said Tocqueville; "the father remains."

18 What Tocqueville said of American fathers and children almost two centuries ago applies to relations between parents and children in the United States today. There is much more social equality

---

[5] conscientious: showing a lot of care and attention

[6] nurture: to feed and take care of a child or a plant while it is growing

[7] vanished: disappeared suddenly, especially in a way that cannot easily be explained; stopped existing suddenly

between parents and children than in most aristocratic societies or societies ruled by centuries of tradition. In fact, some Americans worry that there is too much democracy in the home. They would argue that there has been a significant decline in parental authority and children's respect for their parents. This is particularly true of teenagers. Some parents seem to have little control over the behavior of their teenage children, particularly after they turn sixteen and get their driver's licenses. Another problem parents have with teenagers is monitoring their activity online. It is very difficult for parents to know what sites their kids are visiting and even how much time they are spending online. Having a cell phone gives teenagers a special new kind of freedom, since they can talk to their friends and access the Internet almost everywhere.

19   On the other hand, many Americans give their young people a lot of freedom because they want to teach their children to be independent and self-reliant. Traditionally, American children have been expected to "leave the nest" at about age eighteen, after they graduate from high school. At that time they are expected to go on to college (many go to another city) or to get a job and support themselves. By their mid-twenties, if children are still living with their parents, some people will suspect that something is wrong. Traditionally, children have been given a lot of freedom and equality in the family, so that they will grow up to be independent, self-reliant adults. Today, however, a significant number of young people are living with their parents. Some are attending community colleges and living at home to save expenses. Others are unable to find jobs that support the lifestyle they have grown up with, and they continue to live at home or choose

to move back in with their parents for a time. These young people are sometimes called the "boomerang generation," because they have left the nest once but are now back again. During bad economic times, multigenerational living may improve the standard of living for all. As different generations of the family share expenses, everyone may benefit. However, most people still have the expectation that this will not be a permanent living arrangement.

RISING SHARE OF YOUNG ADULTS LIVING IN MULTI-GENERATIONAL HOUSEHOLDS

% of adults ages 25–34 living in a multi-generational household

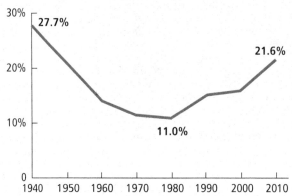

Source: Pew Research Center analysis of U.S. Decennial Census data, 1940–2000 and 2010 American Community Survey (IPUMS).

Four Stages of Marriage Relationships

20   In addition to the relationship between parents and children, the idea of equality affects the family structure in other ways. It has a major impact on the relationships between husbands and wives. Women have witnessed steady progress toward equal status for themselves in the family and in society at large. According to Letha and John Scanzoni, two American sociologists, the institution of marriage in the United States has experienced four stages of development.* In each new stage, wives have increased the degree of

---

*Scanzoni, Letha, and John Scanzoni, Men, Women, and Change. New York: McGraw-Hill, Inc., 1981.

equality with their husbands and have gained more power within the family.

21 **Stage I: Wife as Servant to Husband** During the nineteenth century, American wives were expected to be completely obedient[8] to their husbands. As late as 1850, wife-beating was legal in almost all the states of the United States. Although both husbands and wives had family duties, the wife had no power in family matters other than that which her husband allowed her. Her possessions and any of her earnings belonged to her husband. During the nineteenth century, women were not allowed to vote, a restriction that in part reflected women's status as servant to the family.

22 **Stage II: Husband-Head, Wife-Helper** During the late nineteenth and early twentieth centuries opportunities for women to work outside the household increased. More wives were now able to support themselves, if necessary, and therefore were less likely to accept the traditional idea that wives were servants who must obey their husbands. Even though the great majority of wives chose not to work outside the home, the fact that they might do so increased their power in the marriage. The husband could no longer make family decisions alone and demand that the wife follow them. The wife was freer to disagree with her husband and to insist that her views be taken into account in family decisions.

23 Even though the wife's power increased, the husband remained the head of the family. The wife became his full-time helper by taking care of his house and raising his children. She might argue with him and sometimes change his mind, but his decision on family matters was usually final.

24 This increase in equality of women in marriages reflected increased status for women in the society at large and led to women gaining the right to vote in the early twentieth century. Today, the husband-head, wife-helper marriage is still found in the United States. Economic conditions in the twentieth century, however, carried most marriages into different stages.

25 **Stage III: Husband-Senior Partner, Wife-Junior Partner** During the twentieth century, more and more wives took jobs outside the home. In 1940, for example, only 14 percent of married women in the United States held jobs outside the home. By the 2000s, more than 60 percent were employed. When married women take this step, according to the Scanzonis, their power relative to that of their husbands increases still further. The wife's income becomes important in maintaining the family's standard of living. Her power to affect the outcome of family decisions is greater than when her duties were entirely in the home.

26 Although she has become a partner, however, in this stage the wife is still not an equal partner with her husband, since in these marriages the husband's job or career still provides more of the family income. He sees himself as the senior partner, and she is the junior partner of the family enterprise. Even though she has a job, it has a lower priority than her husband's. If, for example, the husband is asked to move to advance his career, she will give up her job and seek another in a new location.

27 In the United States today, there are still a number of marriages that are the senior-partner/junior-partner type. However, the majority of women have jobs outside the home and some of them earn more money

---

[8] *obedient: always doing what you are told to do by your parents or by someone in authority*

than their husbands do. More and more marriages are what the Scanzonis call Stage IV marriages.

28 **Stage IV: Husband-Wife Equal Partners** Beginning in the late 1960s, a growing number of women expressed a strong dissatisfaction with any marriage arrangement where the husband and his career were the primary considerations in the marriage. By the end of the 1970s, for example, considerably less than half of the women in the United States still believed that they should put their husbands and children ahead of their own careers. In the 2000s, most American women believe that they should be equal partners in their marriages and that their husbands should have equal responsibility for childcare and household chores.

29 In an equal-partnership marriage, the wife pursues a full-time job or career that has equal or greater importance to her husband's. The long-standing division of labor between husband and wife comes to an end. The husband is no longer the main provider of family income, and the wife no longer has the main responsibilities for household duties and raising children. Husband and wife share all these duties equally. Power over family decisions is also shared equally.

30 The reality of life in the United States is that although most American women now have an equal say in the decisions affecting the family, they sometimes earn less than men for the same work, an average of 77 cents for every dollar. Also, although women make up 49 percent of the workforce, most women still spend more time taking care of the children, cooking, and cleaning than their husbands do. Many women are resentful[9] because they feel like they have two full-time jobs—the one at work and the one at home. In the 1980s, women were told they could "have it all"—fast-track career, husband, children, and a clean house. Now, some women are finding that lifestyle exhausting[10] and unrewarding. Some young women are now choosing to stay at home until their children start school, but many others who would like to stay home cannot afford to do so.

In dual-income households with children, average number of hours spent each week on . . .

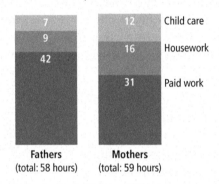

Fathers (total: 58 hours) | Mothers (total: 59 hours)

Source: Pew Research Center, 2013.

31 On the other hand, many women are still striving[11] for true equality in the workplace. Sheryl Sandberg, author of *Lean In: Women, Work, and the Will to Lead,* believes that women should actively seek more leadership roles. She notes that for the last 30 years more American women have graduated from college than men, but men still dominate politics and the corporate world. Today only 4.2 percent of the Fortune 500 companies have female Chief Operating Officers. Sandberg herself is the COO of Facebook, and she is offering advice to women to help them reach their potential. She says, "I believe women can lead more in the workplace. I believe men can contribute more in the home. And I believe that this will create a better world, one where half

[9] resentful: feeling angry and upset about something that you think is unfair

[10] exhausting: making someone very tired

[11] striving: making a great effort to achieve something

In an equal-partnership marriage, husbands share household duties such as cooking.

our institutions are run by women and half our homes are run by men."

32 Juggling two careers and family responsibilities can be as difficult for men as it is for women, especially if there is truly an equal division of duties. American fathers are often seen dropping the kids off at the babysitter's or taking a sick child to the doctor. Some businesses are recognizing the need to accommodate families where both parents work. They may open a daycare center in the office building, offer fathers paternity leave to stay home with their new babies, or have flexible working hours. Unfortunately, these benefits are not yet available to all. While young couples strive to achieve equality in their careers, their marriages, and their parenting, society at large still lacks many of the structures that are needed to support them.

The Role of the Family in Society

33 The American ideal of equality has affected not only marriage, but all forms of relationships between men and women. Americans gain a number of benefits by placing so much importance on achieving individual freedom and equality within the context of the family. The needs and desires of each member are given a great deal of attention and importance. However, a price is paid for these benefits. American families may be less stable and lasting than those of some other cultures. The high rate of divorce in American families is perhaps the most important indicator of this instability.

34 The American attitude toward the family contains many contradictions. On the one hand, Americans will tolerate a good deal of instability in their families, including divorce, in order to protect such values as freedom and equality. On the other hand, they are strongly attached to the idea of the family as the best of all lifestyles. In fact, the great majority of persons who get divorced find a new partner and remarry. Studies show consistently that the vast majority of Americans believe that family life is an important value.

35 What is family life? We have seen that fewer than one in four households consists of a traditional family—a father, mother, and their children. Many of these are actually *stepfamilies* or *blended families*. Since most divorced people remarry, many children are living with a stepmother or stepfather. In a blended family, the parents may each have children from a previous marriage, and then have one or more children together—producing "yours," "mine," and "ours." Such families often result in very complicated and often stressful relationships. A child may have four sets of grandparents instead of two, for example. Blending families is not easy, and, sadly, many second marriages fail.

Three generations of a traditional family

36 In addition to traditional families and blended families, there are a number of single parents, both mothers and fathers (more mothers), raising their children alone. Many of the single mothers are divorced, but some have never married. Indeed, by 2012 almost one half of all new babies were born to single mothers, and this trend continues. Sometimes single parents and their children live with the children's grandparents for economic and emotional support. There are all sorts of living arrangements. In recent years, a number of gay and lesbian couples have created family units, sometimes adopting children and sometimes arranging to have their own biological children. Some states now recognize same-sex marriages, and others may recognize them as *civil unions*. The majority of Americans are now in favor of same-sex marriages and legal recognition is growing. There is no doubt that the definition of *family* has become much broader in the 2000s. The majority of Americans would now define a family as "people who live together and love and support each other."

Challenges to the American Family

37 Along with the problems of divorce, single parenting, and balancing family and career, there are other challenges that many Americans face. Because the general population is getting older and living longer, many middle-aged Americans are finding themselves in the *sandwich generation.* That is, they are "sandwiched" between taking care of their children, and taking care of their aging parents. The Pew Research Center reports that almost half of middle-aged Americans in their 40s and 50s have a parent age 65 or older, and they are either raising a young child or are giving significant support to a grown child (age 18 or over). For many, having to take care of adult children is a result of the last recession, which hit young people harder than other groups in the population. Members of the sandwich generation are pulled in many directions as they try to provide care, financial support, and emotional support to both their aging parents and their children.

38 Raising children in the digital age offers more challenges to sandwich generation parents. The use of digital devices that connect people to the Internet is having a profound effect on the family. Sociologists and psychologists tell us that the family is the best place for children to learn social skills, moral values, and a sense of responsibility. But in order to teach children, parents have to have face-to-face time with their kids. Increasingly, both parents and their children may be on separate digital devices visiting different Internet sites or sending email or text messages. It is not uncommon to see parents and their teenagers sitting at a restaurant using their smartphones and not talking to each other. In a *New York Times* article entitled "The Flight from Conversation" psychologist Sherry Turkle says that Americans have sacrificed conversation for connection:

> We've become accustomed to a new way of being "alone together." Technology-enabled, we are able to be with one

another, and also elsewhere, connected to wherever we want to be. We want to customize our lives. We want to move in and out of where we are because the thing we value most is control over where we focus our attention.

39　In reality, people cannot truly customize their lives. Successful adults must be able to respond to a variety of people in a variety of unpredictable situations that require good social skills. And developing good communication and social skills should start in the family. Unfortunately, children may find that their parents are unavailable to guide them, and parents may not understand what help kids need. For example, parents may not realize that their teenagers are not learning some important social skills while they are spending time in virtual reality. Increasingly, teenagers are using their smartphones for texting instead of talking. Consequently, kids are not learning the social skills that conversation teaches: understanding non-verbal cues, figuring out emotions, having the patience needed for a conversation to develop, and how to make "small talk." Surprisingly, New York University recently offered incoming students a class in how to make small talk. The students knew each other on Facebook but had no idea how to talk to start a conversation and get to know each other in person.

40　Today, the state of the American family is frequently discussed, not only by the experts, but also by the press, elected officials, and the general public. Some Americans believe that the institution of the family and family values are both in trouble. But if you ask Americans how their own families are, most will tell you they are generally happy with their family life. In *Values and Public Policy*, Daniel Yankelovich reports on surveys done on family values. There are eleven points that a majority of Americans agree are family values. Yankelovich classifies six of them as "clearly traditional":

- Respecting one's parents
- Being responsible for one's actions
- Having faith in God
- Respecting authority
- Remaining married to the same person for life
- Leaving the world in better shape

The other five are "a blend of traditional and newer, more expressive values":

- Giving emotional support to other members of the family
- Respecting people for themselves
- Developing greater skill in communicating one's feelings
- Respecting one's children
- Living up to one's potential as an individual

41　The ideal of the American family is group cooperation to help achieve the fulfillment of each individual member and shared affection to renew each member's emotional strength. Families can be viewed as similar to churches in this regard. Both are seen by Americans as places where the human spirit can find refuge from the highly competitive world outside and gain renewed resources to continue the effort. Although in a number of cases families do not succeed in the task of providing mutual support and renewing the spirit, for many Americans this remains the ideal of family life.

AFTER YOU READ

Understand Main Ideas

Working with a partner, discuss how the six traditional basic American values affect the American family. Fill in the chart with the value, the advantages and disadvantages to the individual, and the advantages and disadvantages to the family.

Value: _____

Advantage to the Individual	Disadvantage to the Individual
_____	_____
_____	_____
_____	_____
_____	_____

Advantage to the Family	Disadvantage to the Family
_____	_____
_____	_____
_____	_____
_____	_____

Value: _____

Advantage to the Individual	Disadvantage to the Individual
_____	_____
_____	_____
_____	_____
_____	_____

Advantage to the Family	Disadvantage to the Family
_____	_____
_____	_____
_____	_____
_____	_____

Understand Details

Write **T** if the statement is true and **F** if it is false according to information in the chapter.

_____ 1. One American household in four now consists of someone living alone.

_____ 2. "Baby boomers" are young people who are in their twenties.

_____ 3. Americans usually consider what is best for the whole family first and what is best for them as individuals second.

_____ 4. Americans believe that the family exists primarily to serve the needs of its individual family members.

_____ 5. Most Americans believe that marriages should make both individuals happy and that if they cannot live together happily, it is better for them to get a divorce.

_____ 6. American parents generally think more about the individual needs of their children than they do about what responsibilities the child will have to society as a whole.

_____ 7. Although Americans believe in democracy for society, they generally exercise strict control over their children, particularly teenagers.

_____ 8. The amount of equality between husbands and wives has remained pretty much the same since Tocqueville visited the United States in the 1830s.

_____ 9. If an American wife works outside the home, she is likely to have more power in the family than a married woman who does not work.

_____ 10. In the husband-senior partner, wife-junior partner type of marriage, the husband and wife both work, have equal power and influence in making family decisions, and divide the family duties equally.

_____ 11. In most American families, the father does just as much housework and child care as the mother.

_____ 12. Having faith in God and respecting authority are two of the traditional American family values.

_____ 13. Although one out of every two marriages ends in divorce, Americans still believe strongly in the importance of marriage and the family.

Talk About It

Work in small groups and choose one or more of these questions to discuss.

1. What do you think is the ideal number of children to have? Why? What responsibilities should children have in the family?

2. What type of parenting do you think is most effective? How would you discipline and parent your children? Would you give your teenagers the same amount of freedom as you had as a teenager? Why or why not?

3. Which type of marriage is most common in your country? Which of the four types do you think is ideal? Why?

4. How is divorce viewed in your country? If two people are unhappy, should they get a divorce? What if they have children? Under what circumstances would you get divorced?

5. Should husbands be able to choose to stay at home while their wives go to work? In the United States, these men are sometimes called "househusbands." Are there househusbands in your country?

6. In your country, who takes care of the children if both parents are working? Would you leave your child in a daycare center?

SKILL BUILDING

Develop Your Critical Thinking Skills

Analyzing Polls and Expressing Your Opinion

In most American families, both parents are employed. While they are at work, the children have to be cared for by another family member, a paid babysitter, or workers at a daycare center. Many American parents would say that it is the quality of time they spend with their children and not the quantity. About half of all working mothers and fathers say that it is difficult to balance the responsibilities of their job and their family.

Analyze these polls and answer the questions that follow.

Percentage of **general public** who say the ideal situation **for young children** is to have a mother who works . . .

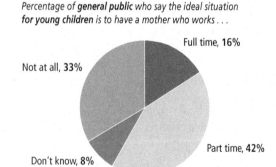

Full time, **16%**

Not at all, **33%**

Don't know, **8%**

Part time, **42%**

Percentage with children who say they spend . . . time with their children

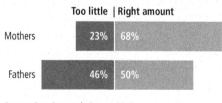

Source: Pew Research Center, 2013.

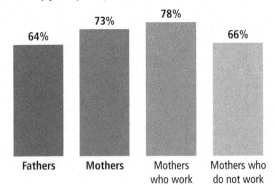

Percentage with children saying they are doing an "excellent" or "very good" job as parents

- Fathers: 64%
- Mothers: 73%
- Mothers who work: 78%
- Mothers who do not work: 66%

Percentage with children who say . . . is extremely important to them

	Working mothers	Working fathers
Job security	78%	80%
A job they enjoy	74%	69%
A flexible schedule	70%	48%
A high-paying job	30%	40%

Source: Pew Research Center, 2013.

1. How do Americans feel about mothers who work? Do most people think the ideal would be for mothers to stay home with their children and not work at all? What percentages can you cite to support your conclusion?

2. Are there any differences in how American men and women feel about the time they have to spend with their children? Cite percentages.

3. Do mothers who work feel that they are not doing a good job parenting? Cite percentages. Why do you think they feel that way?

4. What generalizations can you make about how men and women view their jobs? Cite percentages.

5. Do you personally think it's important for one parent to stay home with the children? Why or why not? If these polls reflected the situation in your country, what would they reveal?

Improve Your Reading Skills: Highlighting and Summarizing

In the American education system, there is a great deal of emphasis on recognizing and remembering main ideas. Highlighting main ideas as you read helps you remember them. In previous chapters, we discussed identifying topic sentences and how they usually contain the main idea of a paragraph. Remember that most topic sentences are the first sentence of the paragraph. Therefore, if you just focus on the first sentence of the paragraph in an academic reading, you should have an understanding of many of the main ideas of the reading.

Work with a partner, and go back through the reading and highlight the main ideas. How many sentences did you highlight that were the first sentence of the paragraph? Compare your highlighting with another pair of students. Then work with your group to make an oral summary of the reading in your own words.

Build Your Vocabulary

Vocabulary Check

Use the words in the box to complete the sentences.

blended	courtship	juggling	refuge
compensate	demographic	nurture	stable
conscientious	exhausting	priority	vanish

1. Many _____ American mothers would like to stay at home

   with their young children, but they have to work to make ends meet.

2. _____ a career and family responsibilities is very stressful.

3. Many young mothers who work have an _____ lifestyle—they

   work all day at their jobs and then take care of their families and homes.

4. Most Americans would probably agree that fathers, as well as mothers,

   should be able to _____ their children.

5. Parents who do not have enough time for their children may feel guilty and

   then try to _____ by giving their children material gifts.

6. Sometimes a demanding career can be a _____ even though a

   parent would like to have more time to spend with the children.

7. _____ families may be a source of stress, as parents try to cope

   with raising each other's children, plus their own.

8. In the United States, _____ is the time that young people in

   love get to know each other and decide if they want to get married.

9. Although marriages are not very _____ in the United States,

   most Americans still believe that it is an important institution in society.

10. Families have traditionally provided an important _____

    from the competitive stresses of American society.

11. _____ studies show that young Americans are now waiting

    longer to get married and have children.

12. In spite of all its problems, the institutions of marriage and the family will

    certainly never _____.

More AWL Words

Test your knowledge of these AWL words by matching the words and their definitions. Write the correct word in the blank next to its definition.

accommodate	emphasis	flexible	license	potential	restriction
consist	expert	generation	obtain	previous	role
contradictory	factor	institution	policy	primary	trend
dramatic	final	labor			

_____ 1. most important

_____ 2. an official document giving permission

_____ 3. exciting and impressive

_____ 4. in opposition or disagreement with something else

_____ 5. able to change or be changed easily

_____ 6. the possibility that something will develop in a certain way

_____ 7. to accept someone's needs and try to do what they want

_____ 8. to get something you want

_____ 9. all people of about the same age

_____ 10. principle, procedure, or way of doing something

_____ 11. a rule that limits or controls

_____ 12. someone who has special skill or knowledge

_____ 13. work using physical effort

_____ 14. the last in a series

_____ 15. the part someone plays

_____ 16. an established system in society

_____ 17. a general tendency

_____ 18. one of several things that influence a situation

_____ 19. to be made of

_____ 20. happening or existing before

_____ 21. special attention or importance

EXPAND YOUR KNOWLEDGE

Ask Americans

Interview several Americans of different ages and ask them about their families. Ask each one the following questions and record their answers. (You may want to interview friends or classmates about their families.)

1. Who are the members of your family? Name them and indicate their relationship to you (mother, sister, etc.).

2. Who lives in your household? Where do your other relatives live?

3. How often do you see your parents? Your grandparents? Your sisters and brothers? Your aunts, uncles, and cousins? Do you write, email, text, or telephone any of them regularly?

4. What occasions bring your relatives together (birthdays, holidays, weddings, births, deaths, trips)? Have you ever been to a family reunion?

5. Do you feel you have a close family? Why or why not?

6. Who would you ask for advice if you had a serious personal problem?

7. Who would take care of you if you became ill?

8. What obligations and responsibilities do you feel you have toward your family?

9. What duties and responsibilities do you believe children have toward their family?

10. On a scale of 1 to 10, with 10 as *most important,* how important are the opinions of the members of your immediate family concerning the following decisions?

    _____ Whom you marry

    _____ Where you live

    _____ Where you go to school

    _____ How you spend your money

    _____ What job you take

Ask Yourself / Ask Americans

Do you agree or disagree with each of the following statements? Put a check under the number that indicates how you feel.

+2 = Strongly agree

+1 = Agree

 0 = No opinion

−1 = Disagree

−2 = Strongly disagree

	+2	+1	0	−1	−2
1. Arranged marriages are better than marriages where the couple have met and dated on their own.	___	___	___	___	___
2. It is very important for my family to approve of the person I marry.	___	___	___	___	___
3. If my parents disapproved of my choice, I would still marry that person if we were very much in love.	___	___	___	___	___
4. A woman's place is in the home.	___	___	___	___	___
5. Married women with small children should not work.	___	___	___	___	___
6. Men should be able to stay home and take care of the children while their wives work.	___	___	___	___	___
7. Husbands and wives should share equally the work of taking care of the house and the children.	___	___	___	___	___
8. Unhappy couples should stay married for the sake of the children.	___	___	___	___	___
9. Married couples who choose not to have children are selfish.	___	___	___	___	___
10. Equality between a husband and wife causes divorce.	___	___	___	___	___

Read these statements to several Americans (or your friends) and ask them if they agree or disagree. Compare your answers with theirs.

People Watching

It has been said that in most societies children are often spectators watching adults interact. They are learning what it means to be an adult in their society. In American society, however, the adults are usually the spectators who are watching the children.

Observe American adults interacting with children in the following places:

- In restaurants
- On a playground or at a sports event
- At the movies
- On the street
- At home (If you are unable to visit an American home, watch American TV shows that have children as characters.)

Record your observations in your journal. You may wish to write up these observations as a report and present it to the class. What differences did you observe about how adults interact with children in other countries? (You may choose to observe adults and children in your own community in your country.)

Families often gather for celebrations.

Understand the Role of the Elderly in America

The role of the elderly is one that most foreigners cannot understand about American life. Some have heard that all the elderly are in nursing homes, but this is not true. Actually, only one in four Americans spends any time in a nursing home, and the average stay is two years. It is generally the sick and the disabled who require nursing home care at the end of their lives. Americans generally try to live on their own as long as possible, choosing to be independent and self-reliant. A few Americans (about 12 percent) purchase long-term care insurance that may provide nursing help in their own home. The vast majority of the care of the elderly is done by family members. Members of the "sandwich generation" strive to provide care and support to aging parents and their own children under the age of 18. However, as the baby boomers age, adult children who are taking care of their parents are themselves getting older and older.

A. To try to understand how Americans feel about being old and what they plan to do with their lives when they retire, ask several Americans who are not yet sixty-five the following questions:

1. What do you hope to do when you retire?
2. Where do you plan to live?
3. Would you move in with your children? Under what conditions?
4. What do you think life will be like when you are 65 or older?
5. Are you afraid of growing old? Are you looking forward to growing old?

B. Many retirement communities now have different kinds of living arrangements, from independent living in homes and apartments, to assisted living in buildings with private rooms and meals served in a common dining room, to nursing homes that offer full-time care by doctors and nurses. If you are able to, visit a retirement community for older Americans, or a nursing home. Answer the following questions.

1. Why do you think that many older people choose to live apart from their grown children?
2. Think about the description of the family presented in this chapter. What evidence do you see of the American values of equality in the family and the emphasis on individual freedom?

Proverbs and Sayings

Ask Americans to explain these proverbs and sayings to you. Then ask them for other examples of sayings about men, women, children, or the family. What sayings like these do you have in your language?

1. The hand that rocks the cradle rules the world.
2. As the twig is bent, so grows the tree.
3. That child is a chip off the old block.
4. A man may work from sun to sun, but a woman's work is never done.
5. Behind every successful man, there is a woman.
6. Blood is thicker than water.

Think, Pair, Share

Working mothers often feel that they have two full-time jobs—one outside the home, for which they get paid, and the other inside the home, for which they do not get paid. Most working American women still have the major responsibility for managing the household—cooking, cleaning, shopping, and seeing that the children are cared for— although American husbands are increasingly sharing more of these responsibilities. (See the illustration on page 264.) What do you think husbands with working wives should do around the house?

Write your answer, and then discuss it with your partner. Then share your answer with another pair of students.

Use the Internet

Many people have difficulty meeting others because of their busy lifestyles. Computer dating is becoming increasingly popular and more acceptable in the United States. People can find dates or even a potential husband or wife on the Internet. Men and women answer questions about themselves—their interests, hobbies, likes and dislikes—and they also indicate the qualities they are looking for in a date. Couples are then matched by the computer, and each person receives a list of names of people to contact.

Work with a partner and look at two popular websites, www.match.com and www.eharmony.com. Spend a few minutes learning about each website and how people meet others there. You may want to take the personality quiz on eharmony.

Read some of the profiles that people have written to introduce themselves. Imagine putting an ad on one of the websites. What would be your "catchphrase," and how would you introduce yourself? Write your ad without your name on it. Collect all the ads from the class and put them in a box. Have each person pick an ad, read it aloud, and guess who wrote it.

WRITE ABOUT IT

A. Choose one of the following topics. Then write a short composition about it.

1. Imagine that a foreign exchange student will be living with you for a year. Write a letter to him or her explaining how your family *is* or *is not* a typical family in your country.

2. Write about the person in your immediate or extended family whom you admire the most. Tell what makes the person special and what you admire.

B. Choose one of these Internet topics to write about.

1. Many Americans have pets that they consider to be part of the family. Some studies have shown that owning a pet lowers a person's blood pressure and helps to reduce stress. There are also dogs that are specially trained to comfort people or to help those who are sight or hearing impaired. Learn more about Americans and their pets. Find information on the Internet, and write a report about what you find. Or write about a pet you have or have had, or what would be your ideal pet.

2. What kind of companies are good places for working mothers? Search the Internet and write a report about how some American businesses accommodate working mothers.

Americans often have pets that are part of the family.

EXPLORE ON YOUR OWN

Books to Read

Andrew Cherlin, *The Marriage-Go-Round: The State of Marriage and the Family in America Today*—A sociologist discusses why Americans marry more and divorce more frequently than in other countries.

Dave Issay, *All There Is: Love Stories from StoryCorps*—Stories of love and marriage come from the national oral history project, StoryCorps, in which Americans across the country talk about their lives.

Sheryl Sandberg, *Lean In: Women, Work, and the Will to Lead*—A powerful business executive believes that women should actively seek more leadership roles.

Judith Wallerstein, *The Unexpected Legacy of Divorce: A 25 Year Landmark Study*—Wallerstein reports on a long-term study of the effect of divorce on children as they grow up.

Laura Ingalls Wilder, *Little House on the Prairie*—The author tells of growing up on the frontier in Kansas with her family.

Movies to See

Cheaper by the Dozen—While a wife is away publicizing her book, her husband must juggle his new job and take care of their twelve children.

Father of the Bride—In this comedy, a remake of the Spencer Tracy classic, a family plans the wedding of their daughter.

My Big Fat Greek Wedding—A young Greek-American woman falls in love with a non-Greek and struggles to get her family to accept him while she comes to terms with her heritage and cultural identity.

My Family, Mi Familia—This film traces the struggles, joys, and successes of an immigrant family over three generations.

Parental Guidance—A traditional grandfather and his eager-to-please wife agree to babysit their three grandchildren.

When Harry Met Sally—This romantic comedy tells about two friends who have known each other for years but are afraid that love would ruin their friendship.

AMERICAN VALUES AT THE CROSSROADS

The sole certainty is that tomorrow will surprise us all.

Alvin Toffler (1928–)

Is there a change in the balance between the values representing benefits or rights and the values representing the prices to be paid or responsibilities for these rights?

BEFORE YOU READ

Preview Vocabulary

A. Read the following sentences from the chapter and notice the words in italics. These key AWL words will help you understand the chapter reading. Use context clues to help you figure out the meanings. Then choose which definition is best for the italicized word.

_____ 1. Throughout our history we have disagreed about the meaning of these rights and how far they should be extended. But at the same time we have all *internalized* these rights as our own.
   a. made a belief or attitude become part of your character
   b. rejected a belief or attitude as not important

_____ 2. Since the 1960s and the Great Society programs, the government has continued to *undertake* new responsibilities.
   a. start or agree to do something
   b. decide not to do something

_____ 3. In Chapter 6, we explored the ways that business has traditionally exemplified the ideal of competition and some of the problems that business has *encountered*.
   a. experienced for the first time
   b. succeeded in overcoming

_____ 4. "Our celebration of *initiative* and enterprise; our insistence on hard work and personal responsibility, are constants in our character."
   a. trying to finish something that you don't want to do
   b. making decisions and taking action without waiting for someone to tell you what to do

_____ 5. Hard America creates wealth; Soft America *reassigns* it.
   a. makes better products
   b. gives something to someone else

_____ 6. "Once they have paid the mortgage, payments on two cars, taxes, health insurance, and day care, these apparently prosperous two-income families have less *discretionary* income today and less money to save for a rainy day than a single-income family of a generation ago."
   a. money that you can spend in any way you want
   b. money that earns you a great profit

_____ 7. White says that those on either side of the values divide live in "two *parallel* universes. Each side seeks to reinforce its thinking by associating with like-minded people."
   a. unrelated
   b. similar

_____ 8. Many potential voters are not *registered* members of either party, and both parties must try to persuade them to vote for their party's candidate.
   a. recorded
   b. opposed

_____ 9. "*Oddly* enough for a nation that conducts, reads, argues over, and bashes polls, we still have difficulty understanding who we really are."
   a. obviously, or naturally
   b. strangely, or surprisingly

_____ 10. Democrats and Republicans seem to make decisions more on the basis of *ideology* and less on the best interests of the nation.
   a. a set of ideas on which a political system is based
   b. the rules for conducting an election

_____ 11. In spite of the current image of the United States and some of the actions the government has taken, there has been a long historical tradition of *isolationism.*
   a. belief that your country should not be involved in the affairs of other countries
   b. belief that your country should act as a "World Policeman"

_____ 12. Many Americans are very *reluctant* to see the United States become involved in international military actions unless they are convinced that there is some national interest to be protected.
   a. fast and enthusiastic
   b. slow and unwilling

B. Read this quotation from the chapter and notice the words in italics. Then use context clues and write the correct word next to its definition.

"Millions of middle-class Americans are living from *paycheck* to paycheck, struggling to pay their bills, having to borrow money and go into debt. Many families are just one *layoff* or one medical *emergency* away from going into *bankruptcy.*"

_____ 1. a dangerous situation that you must deal with immediately

_____ 2. inability to pay your debts

_____ 3. check that pays someone's salary

_____ 4. stopping a worker's employment because there is not enough work

Preview Content

A. Read the quotation by Alvin Toffler at the beginning of the chapter. Do you agree with it? Why or why not? What surprising world events have taken place in recent years?

B. Discuss these questions with your classmates.

1. What impact do you think the traditional American values have on Americans today?

2. What are some of the problems Americans face now?

3. What status does the United States have in the world today?

4. What do you think will happen to American values in the twenty-first century?

C. Read the headings in the chapter and look at the illustrations. Write five topics that you predict will be covered in this chapter.

1. _____

2. _____

3. _____

4. _____

5. _____

1   John J. Zogby, an American pollster, says that Americans really know very little about themselves. "Oddly enough for a nation that conducts, reads, argues over, and bashes[1] polls, we still have difficulty understanding who we really are." He notes that the same question is asked by every generation—What really makes us "American"? What is it that we all share? The nation has survived the American Revolution, the Civil War, the Great Depression, the civil rights struggle, assassinations, and several attempts to impeach[2] presidents. "The reason for this survival is simple—we all share a common set of values that make us Americans." Zogby agrees with Ben Wattenberg, an expert on American culture who believes that "values matter most." These values give Americans a unique identity, and whichever political candidate or party can best represent these values wins an election. The values are the basic rights first stated in the Declaration of Independence:

> We hold these truths to be self-evident, that all men are created equal, that they are endowed by their Creator with certain unalienable rights, that among these are Life, Liberty and the pursuit of Happiness. That to secure these rights, Governments are instituted among Men, deriving their just powers from the consent of the governed.

2   The rights were then described in the Constitution and in the first ten amendments to the Constitution, the Bill of Rights, written to protect the freedom and the rights of the American people. Zogby believes that "unlike any other nation or people, we are defined by the rights we have, not by geography, by the arts and letters, not by our cuisine[3] or sensibilities,[4] not religion or civilization, not by war. . . . Throughout our history we have disagreed about the meaning of these rights and how far they should be extended. But at the same time we have all internalized these rights as our own."

3   The six traditional basic values we have discussed in this book (individual freedom, self-reliance, equality of opportunity, competition, material wealth, and hard work) are still a major force in American society. In this chapter, we will review the six traditional basic values and what challenges they now face.

Individual Freedom and Self-Reliance

4   As has been noted earlier in this book, freedom (sometimes referred to as the "rights of the individual") is the most precious and the most popular of the six basic traditional values of the United States. The traditional ideas of freedom held by the founding fathers and written into the Constitution and the Bill of Rights were dominant until the 1930s. These freedoms included guarantees of the freedom of speech, freedom of the press, and freedom of religion. There were also freedoms guaranteeing a fair criminal trial—that is, the right to a speedy and public trial, the right to a trial by jury, and the right to a defense attorney. In the 1930s, during the Great Depression, the New Deal greatly increased the size and responsibilities of government. Since the 1960s and the Great Society programs, the government has continued to undertake new responsibilities. This has led to a new category of freedoms or rights that

[1] bashes: criticizes someone or something a lot

[2] impeach: to formally accuse a government official of a serious crime in a special government court

[3] cuisine: a particular style of cooking

[4] sensibilities: ways that people react to particular subjects or types of behavior

are economic in nature. For example, the Supreme Court ruled in 1963 that if a person on trial (for a crime) could not afford a defense attorney, the government must provide one for him or her.

5   Almost all Americans believe that their country should strive for a prosperity[5] shared by all. However, the idea of economic rights has a broader meaning. It means that government should (in one way or another) provide economic benefits for U.S. citizens. It is on this point that Americans differ. Indeed, this difference has been called the *values divide*. On the one hand, conservative, mostly Republican, Americans believe that the government has gone too far in creating and guaranteeing these economic benefits. They argue that the more the government makes itself responsible for providing economic benefits, the more it makes the American people dependent on the government for their standard of living. This, in turn, takes away the self-reliance of the people—a basic national value that has helped to make the country great.

6   On the other hand, liberal (or progressive), mostly Democratic, Americans believe that the guarantee of economic rights by the government broadens and improves the traditional idea of freedom. The process of expanding economic rights should, they believe, continue in the twenty-first century. The possible economic rights that are being proposed include the right to medical treatment and basic health insurance; the right to a college education; the right to have a job that provides a standard of living above the poverty level; and, when people are unemployed, the right to receive government assistance (especially for women and children). The debate about the proper balance between self-reliance on the one hand and government-provided economic security on the other will surely continue to be an important debate in the coming years.

Equality of Opportunity and Competition

7   As mentioned before, the American ideal of equality of opportunity can be simply stated—all Americans should have an equal opportunity to succeed in life, to gain prosperity, and to pursue happiness. The United States has sometimes failed to honor this value of equality of opportunity, particularly in the case of African Americans who were subjected to slavery and then to segregation and discrimination. But the nation eventually freed the slaves in the 1860s and then addressed segregation and discrimination with the Civil Rights Acts of the 1960s. Affirmative action programs were an important effort to deal with discrimination. Employers had to seek African-American workers, and colleges had to recruit African-American students, as well as other minorities. The philosophy of the affirmative action programs was that because of years of discrimination, many blacks did not have the skills they needed to successfully compete with members of the white majority. At first, standards of admission were

Courtroom trial in session

[5] *prosperity: when people have money and everything needed for a good life*

The U.S. Supreme Court building in Washington, D.C.

adjusted, in some cases, in order to allow black students to enter school.

8   Traditionally, equality of opportunity has not meant equality of results or attainment. If a number of people have the same opportunity to succeed, some may succeed more than others. It is not up to society or the government to make sure that every person ends up with the same amount of wealth or prestige. This traditional interpretation was challenged by affirmative action programs giving racial and ethnic preferences to blacks, Hispanics, and other minorities. Those who support affirmative action argue that it has helped make up for past discrimination against minorities and that it increases the racial and ethnic diversity on college campuses. Supreme Court Justice Sonia Sotomayor, the first Hispanic justice, is an example of someone who was helped by affirmative action. An excellent student from a poor background, she was offered scholarships from many top universities. She has written about the benefits she received from affirmative action in *My Beloved World.* On the other hand, there are those who argue against the policies of affirmative action. Those who oppose what they see as preferential treatment believe that everyone should have the same educational opportunities and that no one should get any special advantages. They defend the traditional idea of equality of opportunity and say that they believe in the natural diversity of the United States, not diversity mandated[6]

[6] *mandated: required by an official command*

by the government. There have also been claims of reverse discrimination, where qualified white students were denied admission to make room for a minority student.

9 The ultimate expression of equality of opportunity is the election of Barack Obama, the first African-American president. The columnist Ezra Klein writes, "The United States of America—a land where slaves were kept 150 years ago and bathrooms were segregated as recently as 50 years ago—elected and reelected its first black president." It is remarkable to see a black president in the White House, a man whose mother was white and whose father was from Kenya, a president who is married to a woman who is herself descended from slaves. But Barack and Michelle Obama are very mindful of what they represent—the evidence that a qualified individual from any minority background can potentially rise to the highest office in the land. In a very moving photograph, the president is leaning over to let a little black boy touch his hair, to see if Obama's hair feels like his. The message of this popular photo is that black children can now say, "Maybe one day I'll grow up to be president, too."

10 The nation often struggles for a balance between the values of equality of opportunity and competition. The value of competition is most clearly represented by the institution of American business. In Chapter 6, we explored the ways that business has traditionally exemplified the ideal of competition, as well as some of the problems that business has encountered. One of the biggest challenges facing the United States today is deciding what the role of government versus the role of the free enterprise system should be. How far should the government go to ensure the right of equality of opportunity for all? And should it be the right of "opportunity" or the right of "attainment"?

11 In his book *Hard America, Soft America: Competition vs. Coddling*[7] *and the Battle for the Nation's Future*, Michael Barone (a conservative) has written about this need for balance. He thinks that there should be a space in the middle, with a government "that saves people from undeserved social disaster, while preserving the will to achieve." This middle ground is between the conservative "hard" culture and the liberal "soft" culture. Noemie Emery, a conservative columnist, describes Barone's explanation of the division in the United States this way:

> Hard America values risk, innovation, effort, and enterprise. Soft America values security and equality. Hard America is ruled by the market, while Soft America is directed by government planning. Hard America creates wealth; Soft America reassigns it. Hard America causes undeserved suffering by making no distinction between poverty caused by sickness and poverty caused by laziness. Soft America causes its own suffering by making no distinctions between poverty caused by bad luck and poverty caused by bad habits. . . . But the problem is really striking a balance that gets people to strive without making them desperate—that gives them support without sapping[8] their will.

12 President Obama (a liberal) would probably agree that the will to compete is healthy and important. In his second Inaugural Address, Obama said that throughout our more than 200-year history, we have always been suspicious of a strong federal government, and we have understood that not all of society's problems can be solved through government alone. Free enterprise has

[7] coddle: to treat someone in a way that is too kind and gentle and that protects them from pain or difficulty

[8] sapping: gradually taking away something, such as strength or energy

always played an important role. "Our celebration of initiative and enterprise; our insistence on hard work and personal responsibility, are constants in our character." Indeed, liberals and conservatives would probably agree that all of the six values explained in this book are important. However, liberals would probably argue that there are some Americans who are so poor and disadvantaged that they cannot be expected to be completely self-reliant or competitive. They need special help from the government and others to bring them up to the starting line of the race for success, so that they can compete on a more equal basis for the benefits of equality of opportunity and the American Dream.

Material Wealth and Hard Work

13 Material wealth has traditionally been seen as the reward for hard work. Although most people still believe in the ideal of the American Dream, many are now having a difficult time attaining or maintaining it. Middle-class families are under great financial stress. Mortimer Zuckerman wrote in *U.S. News & World Report*, "Millions of middle-class Americans are living from paycheck to paycheck, struggling to pay their bills, having to borrow money and go into debt. Many families are just one layoff or one medical emergency away from going into bankruptcy." Many young people believe that they will not have as good a financial future lifestyle as their parents, and one in four under age 30 feel that they are "downwardly mobile" rather than "upwardly mobile."

14 There are other signs that American families are falling behind: The middle class is smaller, making up only 51 percent of the population, down from 61 percent in the 1960s. Since 2000, their incomes have declined by 5 percent, and their net

worth has shrunk by 28 percent. One-third of them are having trouble paying their bills. The distance between the middle class and the richest Americans is now enormous. As the recession was getting better, in 2011 the top 5 percent of the population (who earn more than $186,000 a year) saw their incomes rise by 5 percent. According to the Economic Policy Institute, households in the wealthiest 1 percent now have 288 times the amount of wealth as the average middle-class family. The Great Recession that began in 2008 hit middle-class families hardest, but it greatly increased the wealth of the richest 1 percent.

15 Several factors have caused this stress on the middle class. First, there has been a huge decline in the number of well-paying jobs that do not require a college degree. Back in the 1970s, there were still good jobs in the manufacturing sector, with about 25 percent of Americans (mostly men) employed in factories. Another significant percentage were employed in other sectors that required little formal education, like construction, mining, or utilities. These were jobs that men held until retirement, when they received a comfortable pension. Now these well-paying blue collar jobs are gone. Much of American manufacturing went overseas in the 1990s, and, although it is coming back, these new manufacturing jobs generally require education beyond the high school level.

16 The second factor affecting the middle class is the need for higher education, and, in fact, the numbers of students graduating from high school and taking some college courses has gone up. One reason is that the recession hit young people harder than other age groups, with unemployment rates as high as 24 percent. Many young people chose to stay in school because there weren't jobs available. Entry-level

Even two-income middle-class families may struggle to pay their bills.

jobs usually taken by young people were often filled by older, more experienced workers who had lost their own jobs. A significant problem that many Americans face is the incredibly high cost of a college education. The spread of community college programs has helped cut costs greatly. However, the United States really has a need for good vocational programs in fields such as informational technology and advanced manufacturing. Many believe that the United States should develop programs like some European countries have that would prepare students to take jobs that now go unfilled, even during the recession. This would require education and industry leaders to work together to develop the training programs and help put students on the pathway to these well-paying jobs.

17   In most middle-class families, both the husband and wife are working. Their combined family income is much larger than that of the single-income family a generation ago, but they are still struggling. Zuckerman says, "Once they have paid the mortgage, payments on two cars, taxes, health insurance, and day care, these apparently prosperous two-income families have less discretionary income today and less money to save for a rainy day than a single-income family of a generation ago. . . . Many feel they are falling further and further behind, no matter how hard they work." Health care and health insurance have become more and more expensive, taking a larger percentage of a worker's paycheck. Many in the middle class bought homes when the prices were going up, and they lost much of the value of their homes when the housing bubble burst. Their net worth has fallen, and they are not saving enough for retirement. Only 25 percent of the baby boomers who are nearing retirement have enough saved to allow them to stop working. Their Social

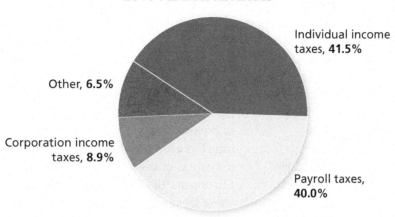

2010 Federal Revenues

Individual income taxes, **41.5%**

Other, **6.5%**

Corporation income taxes, **8.9%**

Payroll taxes, **40.0%**

Source: Data from Office of Management and Budget

Security benefits will not be enough to support them in retirement. The plight of the middle class is one reason why some are now calling for the government to extend rights to include a right to health care, a right to a college education, and a right to a decent-paying job. It is also why there is so much concern over the mounting costs of Social Security and Medicare.

The Values Divide

18 The disagreement about what rights the government should guarantee has caused the "values divide" or the "culture wars" that began in the early 2000s. John Kenneth White has written about the split in *The Values Divide: American Politics and Culture in Transition,* with an introduction by John Zogby. White discusses the fact that Republican conservatives and Democratic liberals disagree strongly about the role of the government in solving the country's problems. He says that those on either side of the values divide live in "two parallel universes. Each side seeks to reinforce its thinking by associating with like-minded people." In a series of articles in *The Washington Post* titled "America in Red and Blue: A Nation Divided," David

Von Drehle explored the political split. "This split is nurtured by the marketing efforts of the major parties, which increasingly aim pinpoint messages to certain demographic groups, rather than seeking broadly appealing new themes."

19 Why have the parties targeted certain groups for various political messages? First of all, the use of computers and demographic studies has made it possible to do so. Second, many Americans are only interested in one or two political issues. They respond well to targeted political messages about specific issues that concern them. Third, many potential voters are not registered members of either party, and both parties must try to persuade them to vote for their party's candidate. Neither party can win without securing some of the Independent votes. Increasingly, however, most Independents tend to lean toward one party or the other. Indeed, the country has become more and more polarized, to the point that the government seems to have difficulty functioning. Democrats and Republicans seem to make decisions more on the basis of ideology and less on the best interests of the nation. There is too often gridlock[9] and too seldom compromise, many would say.

[9] *gridlock: a situation in which nothing can happen, usually because people disagree strongly*

20　It is clear that the United States now faces many challenges. One of the most serious is the need to deal with the ongoing deficits and the growing national debt. Democrats believe it is an income problem—the government needs more money to run the programs that they want. Taxes should be raised, and the wealthiest should pay a higher rate. Republicans believe it is a spending problem—the government should lower taxes and reduce spending by cutting programs. The private sector—business—should take over programs now run by the government. Zogby says this split reveals more than a question about the role of government. "This is about how Americans define responsibility, citizenship and values they want their government to express."

21　CNN's chief political analyst Gloria Borger says that Americans have a love/hate relationship with their government:

> Americans want the government to fix our problems, but they don't trust the government to do it. We want health care to be fixed, Medicare and Social Security to stay intact, emergencies to be handled. We also want lower taxes along with a smaller—yet more responsive—government. All in all, we would like to spend less and get more . . . The public distrusts government because its leaders haven't been able to work together to produce much of anything. . . . Ronald Reagan [a popular Republican president] understood the public's skepticism[10] about government. He often joked that the scariest sentence in America is "I'm from the government and I'm here to help."

22　This suspicion of government is not new. Tocqueville noted that Americans loved both freedom and equality. Throughout their history, Americans have lived with a tension between preserving freedom and promoting equality. Tocqueville believed that, in a democracy, Americans would eventually choose equality over freedom because of the material benefits that equality could bring. However, political scientists have disagreed, recognizing that Americans strongly value freedom, possibly more than any other country. A recent Pew poll asked Americans and Europeans to choose between "freedom to pursue life's goals without state interference" and the "state guarantees nobody is in need." In contrast to the Europeans, the majority of Americans chose freedom. (See page 158.)

The United States in the World

23　In spite of the current image of the United States and some of the actions the government has taken, there has been a long historical tradition of isolationism. President George Washington declared in 1796, "It is our true policy to steer clear of permanent alliances with any portion of the foreign world." The spirit of isolationism persists even today as Americans continue to debate their place in the world community. Many Americans are very reluctant to see the United States become involved in international military actions unless they are convinced that there is some national interest to be protected. Americans are also skeptical about international economic alliances and global agreements, wanting to be sure that their self-interests are protected before commitments are made to other countries. Many Americans are more interested in what is happening close to home than what is happening in the rest of the world. They want to know how events, national or international, will affect them personally.

24　Today, it would be impossible for the United States to isolate itself from the rest of the world even if it tried. While some scholars would say that the United

---

[10] *skepticism: an attitude of doubt about whether something is true, right, or good*

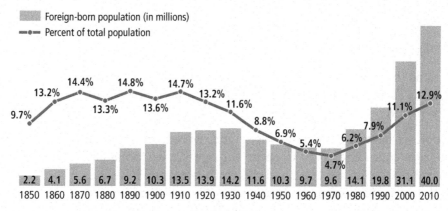

Foreign-born population (in millions)

Percent of total population

| 9.7% | 13.2% | 14.4% | 13.3% | 14.8% | 13.6% | 14.7% | 13.2% | 11.6% | 8.8% | 6.9% | 5.4% | 4.7% | 6.2% | 7.9% | 11.1% | 12.9% |

| 2.2 | 4.1 | 5.6 | 6.7 | 9.2 | 10.3 | 13.5 | 13.9 | 14.2 | 11.6 | 10.3 | 9.7 | 9.6 | 14.1 | 19.8 | 31.1 | 40.0 |
| 1850 | 1860 | 1870 | 1880 | 1890 | 1900 | 1910 | 1920 | 1930 | 1940 | 1950 | 1960 | 1970 | 1980 | 1990 | 2000 | 2010 |

Source: U.S. Census Bureau, American Community Survey, 2010.

States and its culture played a dominant role in the twentieth century, its role in the twenty-first is unclear. However, the rest of the world will certainly continue to have a great impact on the United States, particularly on its economy. A continuing concern for Americans will be protecting themselves from potential terrorist threats, both overseas and at home. There will be more consideration of how much power to give the government in exchange for this protection. In a free and open society, it is impossible to guarantee that terrorist attacks will never happen, and Americans must weigh how much freedom and privacy they will give up in order to be secure.

25 Finally, there is the question of immigration. The levels of legal and illegal immigration are high, and some Americans are worried about the assimilation of all these people from different countries. What will happen to the traditional American values as the population of the United States becomes increasingly diverse? On the other hand, many recognize that all these new immigrants bring new life and energy to the United States. They often come with a stronger belief in the six basic cultural values than many Americans have. As the baby boomers get older, immigrants are an important source of youth and vitality for the nation. A number of them are coming with the technical skills and STEM degrees (science, technology, engineering, mathematics) that the United States needs in industry.

26 Perhaps most importantly, the diversity of ideas and cultures in the United States is one of its greatest sources of strength in the twenty-first century. Ben Wattenberg, an expert in American culture, believes that the United States is becoming a microcosm of the world—it may be the first *universal* nation, where people from every race, religion, culture, and ethnic background live together in freedom, under one government.

27 The American people and their values have reached another historic crossroads. Will these traditional values endure through this century? One hundred years from now, will Americans still have a sense of national identity—of "being American"? What new challenges will this century bring? As Alvin Toffler said, "The sole certainty is that tomorrow will surprise us all."

AFTER YOU READ

Understand Main Ideas

A. Review the predictions that you made on page 284 before reading the chapter. Were your predictions correct? Write the number of the paragraph where you found the information next to your predictions.

B. Throughout the book we have discussed the importance of recognizing main ideas when reading academic material. In Chapter 1, (page 12) we looked at the relationship between the introduction and the conclusion, and how the headings signaled the main ideas. Chapter 2 (pages 38–39) explained how to do a simple outline of main ideas. Chapter 3 (pages 63–64) presented topic sentences and their relationship to main ideas. Chapters 5 (page 113) and 11 (page 271) had exercises on highlighting. Review these explanations. Then work with a partner and answer these questions:

1. What is the relationship between the opening quotation by Toffler, the introduction, and the conclusion of the chapter reading?

2. What is the purpose of the last paragraph in the first section, *The Role of Values in the National Identity,* paragraph 3, on page 285?

3. What is the main idea of the section *Individual Freedom and Self-Reliance*?

4. What is the main idea in the section *Equality of Opportunity and Competition*?

5. What words in the last sentence of paragraph 12 tie that section to the next one?

6. In the section *Material Wealth and Hard Work,* what is the relationship between these two values?

7. In the section *The Values Divide,* how would you describe the two groups on the opposite sides of the values divide?

8. What are the three reasons why the Republicans and Democrats try to target Independent voters with specific issues?

9. In the section *The United States in the World,* what positive contributions do immigrants bring to the United States?

Understand Details

Write *T* if the statement is true and *F* if it is false according to information in the chapter.

_____ 1. John J. Zogby believes that Americans have a clear understanding of their national identity.

_____ 2. Today, if you cannot afford a defense attorney, you will have to represent yourself in an American court of law.

_____ 3. In some ways Americans love their government, but in other ways they hate it.

_____ 4. Everyone agrees that economic rights should be expanded to include health care, a college education, and a good job.

_____ 5. One reason why Americans increasingly worry about their financial security is because there are not many jobs that pay well that do not require a college education.

_____ 6. In most American families today, only one spouse is working outside the home.

_____ 7. There is a split in the way liberals and conservatives view the role of government.

_____ 8. During the recession that started in 2008, the middle class and the upper class did not suffer—it was the low-income earners that were hit hardest.

_____ 9. The spirit of isolationism began when the United States first became a nation.

_____ 10. In contrast to some European countries, the United States does not have a problem with a large financial debt.

Talk About It

Work in small groups and choose one or more of the following questions to discuss.

1. What are the core values in your country? Are they similar to those of Americans?

2. How has your country changed in your lifetime? What changes do you think you will see in the future?

3. What do you think will happen to the balance of power in the world during the next ten years? What role do you think your country will have in this century?

4. How does your country view the United States?

5. Are you basically optimistic or pessimistic about the future? Why?

SKILL BUILDING

Improve Your Reading Skills: Scanning

Read the following quotations and scan the chapter to find who said each quote. Write the name next to each quotation. (Note: Several sources are quoted more than once.)

_____ 1. "Millions of middle-class Americans are living from paycheck to paycheck, struggling to pay their bills, having to borrow money and go into debt."

_____ 2. "The sole certainty is that tomorrow will surprise us all."

_____ 3. "The scariest sentence in America is 'I'm from the government and I'm here to help you.'"

_____ 4. "Unlike any other nation or people, we are defined by the rights we have, not by geography, by the arts and letters, not by our cuisine or sensibilities, not religion or civilization, not by war."

_____ 5. The people on either side of the values divide live in "two parallel universes. Each side seeks to reinforce its thinking by associating with like-minded people."

_____ 6. "Our celebration of initiative and enterprise; our insistence on hard work and personal responsibility, are constants in our character."

_____ 7. "This split is nurtured by the marketing efforts of the major parties, which increasingly aim pinpoint messages to certain demographic groups, rather than seeking broadly appealing new themes."

_____ 8. "It is our true policy to steer clear of permanent alliances with any portion of the foreign world."

_____ 9. "Hard America values risk, innovation, effort, and enterprise. Soft America values security and equality. Hard America is ruled by the market, while Soft America is directed by government planning. Hard America creates wealth; Soft America reassigns it."

_____ 10. "All in all, we would like to spend less and get more."

Develop Your Critical Thinking Skills

This chapter has information about two conflicting views of the role of government. Americans are divided about what role their government should have. Sometimes, it is difficult to know how a government should respond to social issues. For example, what should the government do to protect children from the effects of poverty?

Work with a partner to learn more about this important issue now facing Americans, and then come to your own conclusions. Gather information from several sources, and then answer the questions that follow. Read the information in the box about a major cause of childhood poverty. Reread paragraphs 5, 6, 10, 11 (and the quote), 12, 15, 16, and 17 in the reading.

More and more young Americans are separating marriage from child bearing—a personal decision that is having an impact on society at large. Recent studies show that 48 percent of all first births are now to single mothers, most of whom are high school graduates in their 20s and who may also have a year or two of college. College graduates tend to have their first child two years after marriage. However, the median age of all American women having their first baby is now lower than the median age of marriage. The median age for women to marry is 27 and for men it is 29. Many middle class women are living with their boyfriends and postponing marriage. By the time they are 25, almost half of them have a baby, and about half of those babies were "unplanned."

The problem is that many couples have not made a commitment to raise the child together, and almost 40 percent of them break up before their child is five years old. More than two-thirds of the fathers have little or no contact with their children and provide little or no financial assistance. Consequently, more than half of American single mothers are on some sort of government assistance. Nearly three out of four poor families with children are headed by single mothers. A family with two parents is 82 percent less likely to be poor. Children of single mothers are more likely to have health and emotional problems, do poorly in school, get into trouble with the law, live in poverty, be physically abused, and not graduate from college, which limits their future earning ability. They are also more likely to become single parents and repeat the cycle.

1. One of the reasons why middle-class women are postponing marriage is financial. Without a college degree, potential husbands are not earning enough money to pay for the married life that both want. Is having a baby before marriage a good financial decision? Why, or why not?

2. Another reason why unmarried women in their twenties are having babies is cultural. They do not believe that it is wrong to have a baby without getting married first. Where are they getting this message? What do you think?

3. The practice of single women having children began with low-income women. This started in the 1960s with the "Great Society" welfare programs. Aid to Families with Dependent Children gave government assistance to single mothers who were poor. Unmarried mothers needed more financial help, and they got more money from the government if they weren't married to, or receiving money from, the child's father. How do you think this affected the marriage rate?

4. Now that this practice has spread to the middle class, what do you think will happen? What are the consequences for a child born to parents who have no legal commitment to each other or to the child, particularly the father?

5. What is the responsibility of government to take care of children living in poverty? How is this best done? The federal and state governments now spend about $300 billion a year on payments to single parents with children, about $30,000 per household per year.

6. The government has campaigns against smoking, obesity, and teenage pregnancy. The teenage birth rate is now the lowest it's been since the 1940s, around seven percent. Should the government have a campaign to discourage single women in their twenties from having children? Why, or why not?

7. What role do the six American values play in this situation? What do you think liberals (or progressives) believe should be done? What do you think conservatives believe should be done? What is the basis for your conclusions?

8. How are these issues handled in your country? What are the similarities and differences? What do you think the answers are?

Build Your Vocabulary

Scrambled Words

Review words used frequently throughout the text. Read these definitions, and unscramble the vocabulary words that they define.

_____ 1. **ruectlu**—the ideas, beliefs, and customs that are shared and accepted by people in a society

_____ 2. **oefmred**—the right to do what you want without being controlled or restricted by the government, police, etc.

_____ 3. **drah kwro**—the price you pay for having a high standard of living

_____ 4. **auqytiel**—the state of having the same rights, opportunities, etc., as everyone else

_____ 5. **aaeilmtr thawel**—money and possessions

_____ 6. **lefs-lenaicre**—the state of being dependent on yourself

_____ 7. **pmctioetnio**—a situation in which people or organizations try to be more successful than others

Vocabulary Check

This chapter has several words that have to do with the criminal justice system. Circle the six words and phrases that are related to crime and punishment. Use them to complete the sentences.

court   justice

defense attorney   tension

jury   global

criminals   microcosm

discretionary spending   trial

1. There were also freedoms guaranteeing the right to a speedy and public

   _____.

2. Americans also have the right to a trial by _____ and the right

   to a _____ _____.

3. If someone cannot afford an attorney, one will be appointed by the

   _____.

4. The administration of _____ may be very difficult, but it must

   be fair.

5. People who are found guilty of breaking the law are _____.

More AWL Words

Test your knowledge of these AWL words by matching the words with their definitions. Write the word in the blank next to the correct definition.

category	define	identity	reveal	sole	survive
challenge	distinction	military	sector	stress	target
commitment	evidence	respond	security		

_____ 1. things done to keep a place, person, or thing safe

_____ 2. the qualities of a person or group that make them different from others

_____ 3. continuous feelings of worry about your work or personal life

_____ 4. a promise to do something or behave in a particular way

_____ 5. relating to or used by the army, navy, etc.

_____ 6. a clear difference between things

_____ 7. facts, objects, or signs that make you believe something is true

_____ 8. to continue to exist in spite of difficulties and dangers

_____ 9. to describe something correctly and thoroughly

_____ 10. a part of an area of activity, especially business or trade

_____ 11. to aim an idea or plan at a limited group of people

_____ 12. something that tests strength, skill, or ability

_____ 13. to react to something that has been said or done

_____ 14. a group of people or things that are all of the same type

_____ 15. the only one

_____ 16. to show something that was hidden

EXPAND YOUR KNOWLEDGE

Think, Pair, Share

Review paragraphs 5–8, 11, and the section The Values Divide. _Look for the differences between liberal and conservative views mentioned there. Would you say that your own views are more liberal or conservative? Are you liberal on some issues and conservative on others?_

Write a list of issues in the chart. You may wish to add social issues such as abortion, babies born outside of marriage, and same-sex marriage. Then write the liberal and conservative views in the chart, and your own view. (An example has been done for you.) Share your list with a partner, and then with another pair of students.

Issue	Liberal View	Conservative View	My View Liberal / Conservative (choose)
Government spending for the poor and middle class	Government should support needy people	People should be self-reliant and not have government support	

Ask Yourself / Ask Americans

Do you agree or disagree with these statements? Circle your answers. Then ask an American for his or her opinion. Compare your answers with the American's answers.

1. Single women having children is not a problem.   agree   disagree

2. Science and technology do more to improve the overall quality of life than do religion and philosophy.   agree   disagree

3. Governments should pass laws to help stop global warming.   agree   disagree

4. Governments should provide free health care for all the citizens of the country.   agree   disagree

5. Governments should provide a free college education for all the citizens of the country.   agree   disagree

6. I expect to have more material possessions than my parents do now.   agree   disagree

7. I am confident that my children will have as good a life as mine, or better.   agree   disagree

8. I am basically optimistic about the future.   agree   disagree

Small-Group Project

Work in small groups. Make three predictions about what you think will happen in the future, during your lifetime. Be specific.

Write your predictions on a piece of paper and give them to your teacher. As your teacher reads the predictions aloud, a classmate can write the predictions on a chart or on the chalkboard. Then the class can vote on which predictions they think are most likely to come true.

Use the Internet

Choose one of these and do research on the Internet with a partner. Then report your findings to your classmates.

1. The year 2000 caused many people to think about what life would be like in the future. How would life be different? A number of organizations prepared *time capsules* to be opened sometime in the future. A time capsule is a container filled with objects from a particular time, so that people in the future will know what life was like then. Do research on the Internet about time capsules. Then work in small groups to decide what you would put in a time capsule to be opened in 2100 or another year. Prepare a poster with a collage of photos, or bring in actual items for your time capsule. Present your ideas to the rest of the class and explain your reasons for your choices.

2. There is a summer festival in Chautauqua, NY, where people from all over the country come to discuss important issues; listen to lectures by experts on many topics; hear concerts; watch ballet, opera, and theater performances; participate in art activities; attend interfaith worship services and programs; take courses on a variety of topics; and enjoy outdoor recreation in a walking community by a lake. Chautauqua has had a summer program since 1874, and David McCullough, a noted historian and author, says that it is a treasure trove of Americana. Visit Chautauqua's website www.ciweb.org and learn more about this very special place. See what the theme weeks are for the coming summer. You can click on their YouTube link and watch short videos, and you can watch Chautauqua lectures at www.fora.tv

3. Some commentators think that the new generation of Americans coming of age now—the Millennials—will bring many positive qualities to the country. Do research on the Millennial generation. Who are they? What do they believe? What goals and plans do they have for the future?

WRITE ABOUT IT

Choose one of the final projects to write about.

1. Write about some aspect of American culture. Analyze an American movie, a TV show, commercials on TV, advertisements in newspapers or magazines, some current event in the news, the results of interviews or conversations you have had with Americans about their beliefs, or observations you have made about how Americans behave. Choose any aspect of life in the United States that you have observed. Be sure to mention at least two or three of the six values: individual freedom, self-reliance, equality of opportunity, competition, material wealth, and hard work.

2. Or approach the assignment from a different direction. Choose a value, and then give specific examples of how you have observed that value existing in American life. Contrast this value with your own culture and how things are done differently. When you have finished writing your analysis, prepare a short speech to report your findings to the rest of the class. Now that you have finished this text, what do you think the American Dream is? How can Americans protect it for future generations? How much can and should a nation do to ensure equality of opportunity for its people?

3. Read the following and write an essay in response.

Theodore H. White, a well-known political analyst, has said that the United States's problem is "trying to do everything for everybody." Ever since the early 1960s, he says, Americans have been making promises—

. . . promises to save the cities, promises to take care of the sick, the old, the universities. . . . Many of our problems flow out of American goodwill, trying to do everything for everybody. . . . In the 1960s we exploded with goodwill as blacks, who had been denied equality, rightfully demanded it. We could afford it, and we should have done what we did. But we have ended up pushing equality and other ideas to absurd limits as we sought perfect equality rather than realistic equality of opportunity. . . . We have to choose what we can do; we have to discipline our goodwill.*

Contrast Theodore H. White's view with that expressed by Barack Obama in his second Inaugural Address on January 21, 2013, and the famous "I Have a Dream Speech" of Martin Luther King, Jr.

Martin Luther King, Jr., gave his famous "I Have a Dream" speech at the Lincoln Memorial, at the opposite end of the mall where Obama was inaugurated at the Capitol building. In 1963, on the 100th anniversary of the Emancipation Proclamation that freed the slaves in the southern states that had left the Union, there was a huge civil rights march in Washington, D.C. Martin Luther King, Jr., delivered his famous speech on the steps of the Lincoln Memorial to several hundred thousand marchers. In the speech, he spoke of the journey of African Americans from slavery into freedom, and the need to continue the journey so that they could one day have equality with whites and be truly free from prejudice and discrimination.

The "I Have a Dream" speech is one of the finest in the English language and one that you should hear. You can listen to the speech on the King website www.kinginstititute.info. During the speech, you can hear people speaking out agreeing with him, which is a custom in the African-American church. In the speech, King says that he has a dream "deeply rooted in the American dream . . . that my four little children will one day live in a nation where they will not be judged by the color of their skin, but by the content of their character." The speech concludes with a quote from the Declaration of Independence and an old African-American spiritual (religious song), "Free at last! Free at last! Thank God Almighty. We are free at last."

Dr. Martin Luther King, Jr., giving his famous "I Have a Dream" speech, August 28, 1963.

* *America's Problem: "Trying to Do Everything for Everybody,"* U.S. News & World Report *(July 5, 1982).*

Obama's Second Inauguration, January 21, 2013, was held on the holiday honoring King's birthday, and many Americans thought about how Obama's presidency was in some ways a fulfillment of King's dreams. Here are some excerpts from Obama's speech:

Each time we gather to inaugurate a president, we bear witness to the enduring strength of our Constitution. We affirm the promise of our democracy. We recall that what binds this nation together is not the colors of our skin or the tenets of our faith or the origins of our names. What makes us exceptional—what makes us American—is our allegiance to an idea, articulated in a declaration made more than two centuries ago:

"We hold these truths to be self-evident, that all men are created equal, that they are endowed by their Creator with certain unalienable rights, that among these are Life, Liberty, and the pursuit of Happiness."

Today we continue a never-ending journey to bridge the meaning of those words with the realities of our time. For history tells us that while these truths may be self-evident, they have never been self-executing; that while freedom is a gift from God, it must be secured by His people here on Earth. The patriots of 1776 did not fight to replace the tyranny of a king with the privileges of a few or the rule of a mob. They gave to us a Republic, a government of, and by, and for the people, entrusting each generation to keep safe our founding creed. . . .

That is our generation's task—to make these words, these rights, these values—of Life, and Liberty, and the pursuit of Happiness—real for every American. Being true to our founding documents does not require us to agree on every contour of life; it does not mean we will all define liberty in exactly the same way, or follow the same precise path to happiness. Progress does not compel us to settle centuries-long debates about the role of government for all time—but it does require us to act in our time. . . .

Let each of us now embrace, with solemn duty and awesome joy, what is our lasting birthright. With common effort and common purpose, with passion and dedication, let us answer the call of history, and carry into an uncertain future that precious light of freedom.

Thank you, God Bless you, and may He forever bless these United States of America.

EXPLORE ON YOUR OWN

Books to Read

Margaret Hoover, *American Individualism: How a New Generation of Conservatives Can Save the Republican Party*—The great-granddaughter of President Hoover writes about how Republicans need to emphasize individual freedom in both economic and social policies to appeal to a new generation of voters.

Jeanne Marie Laskas, *Hidden America: From Coal Miners to Cowboys, an Extraordinary Exploration of the Unseen People Who Make This Country Work*—Laskas presents stories about the people who make our lives run every day, but whom we barely think of.

Thomas E. Mann and Norman J. Ornstein, *It's even Worse Than It Looks: How the American Constitutional System Collided with the New Politics of Extremism*—Congressional scholars from Washington "think tanks" representing both Republicans and Democrats discuss government gridlock.

Michelle Obama, *American Grown: The Story of the White House Kitchen Garden and Gardens Across America*—The First Lady shares her own experiences and encourages Americans to start planting their own gardens and eat healthy food.

Joseph E. Stiglitz, *The Price of Inequality: How Today's Divided Society Endangers Our Future*—A winner of the Nobel Prize for Economics examines the consequences of America's growing inequality and argues that there are ways to change it.

Movies to See

The Butler—Filmmaker Lee Daniels tells the story of the life of an African-American butler who served eight presidents through the civil rights era of the 1950s and 1960s and the decades of the 1970s and 1980s.

Hackers—A young boy is arrested by the Secret Service for writing a computer virus, and years later he and his friends try to stop a dangerous computer virus while being watched by the Secret Service.

The Namesake—American-born Gogol, the son of Indian immigrants, wants to fit in among his fellow New Yorkers, despite his family's unwillingness to let go of their traditional ways.

Chasing Ice—National Geographic photographer James Balog filmed this documentary about the melting of glaciers.

Supersize Me—In this documentary, a man eats nothing but fast food for a month.

ACADEMIC WORD LIST

The reading material in each chapter has been analyzed by comparing it to several vocabulary lists: the 2,000 Most Frequent Word Family List and the Academic Word List. Vocabulary words used in exercises (1) are from the Academic Word List or (2) are not from either of the two lists but are important to the context of the reading and are useful to know for academic reading in general.

The Academic Word List (AWL) was developed by Averil Coxhead. The list contains 570 word families that were selected by examining academic texts from a variety of subject areas. The list does not include words that are among the most frequent 2,000 words of English. Each word family has a headword (the stem form) and a list of other word forms (or parts of speech) for that headword.

AWL WORDS USED IN CHAPTER READINGS

The number after each AWL headword indicates all the chapters in which the words are used. (Note: Another form of the word may have been used, not the stem form.)

abandon 3, 5, 6, 7, 9
academy 5, 9, 10
access 4, 5, 6, 7, 10, 11
accommodate 8, 11
accompany 5
accumulate 2, 6
accuracy 5, 8
achieve 2, 3, 6, 7, 8, 9, 10, 11, 12
acquire 2, 4, 5, 6, 9
adapt 3, 6
adequate 4, 5, 6
adjust 5, 6, 7, 9, 12
administrate 6
adult 1, 2, 3, 4, 5, 8, 9, 10, 11
advocate 10
affect 2, 3, 5, 7, 9, 10, 11, 12
aid 6, 7, 9
alternative 6, 10
amendment 3, 4, 12
analyze 5, 8, 12
annual 6, 9
apparent 12
approach 1
approximate 11
area 3, 4, 5, 6, 7, 8, 9, 11
aspect 1, 2, 3, 4, 5, 6
assemble 5, 7
assess 9
assign 10, 12
assist 2, 9, 12
assume 5, 7
attach 2, 3, 11
attain 9, 12
attribute 10
attitude 3, 5, 7, 10, 11

author 11
authority 2, 3, 5, 6, 7, 11
automate 4, 5, 7
available 5, 9, 11, 12
aware 4, 5, 6, 7

benefit 2, 5, 6, 7, 8, 9, 11, 12
bias 8
bond 10

capable 4, 6
capacity 3
category 1, 12
challenge 2, 4, 5, 7, 9, 10, 11, 12
channel 5
chapter 1, 2, 3, 6, 7, 8, 9, 10, 11, 12
chart 1
circumstance 4, 7, 9
cite 3
civil 4, 7, 8, 11, 12
classic 1, 4, 11
codes 9
collapse 6
comment 3, 6, 10
commit 6, 7, 10, 12
communicate 5, 10, 11
community 1, 2, 3, 4, 6, 7, 8, 9, 10, 11, 12
compensate 11
complex 4, 6
compute 5, 10, 12
concentrate 9
concept 1, 2, 5, 9
conclude 5, 6, 7, 10, 11
conduct 3, 6, 8, 12

confine 4
conflict 5, 7, 9, 11
consent 7, 12
consequent 3, 5, 11
considerable 7, 11
consist 2, 4, 7, 10, 11
constant 2, 3, 4, 6, 10, 11, 12
constitute 1, 2, 3, 4, 7, 9, 11, 12
construct 4, 5, 8, 12
consume 5, 6, 7, 9, 10
contemporary 3
context 2, 3, 11
contract 10
contradict 3, 8, 10, 11
contrary 10
contrast 3, 6, 7, 9, 10, 11, 12
contribute 1, 3, 5, 6, 7, 10, 11
controversy 4, 5, 6, 7, 9
convene 7
convert 2
convince 1, 5, 7, 12
cooperate 4, 6, 7, 11
core 7, 9
corporate 6, 7, 11
couple 11
create 1, 2, 3, 4, 5, 6, 7, 8, 9, 11, 12
credit 3, 5, 6, 9
criteria 9
culture 1, 2, 3, 4, 5, 6, 7, 8, 9, 10, 11, 12
cycle 6, 7, 8, 10

data 1, 5, 6
debate 1, 3, 4, 5, 6, 9, 12
decade 1, 4, 6, 7

decline 1, 2, 3, 6, 11, 12
deduct 3
define 1, 2, 3, 5, 6, 8, 9, 11, 12
demonstrate 4, 6, 7, 8, 9
deny 4, 8, 9, 10, 12
depress 6, 7, 12
derive 2, 10, 12
design 3, 6, 7, 9
despite 8, 9
detect 4
device 5, 11
devote 3, 6
diminish 2
discretionary 12
discriminate 8, 9, 12
display 3
displace 9
distinct 1, 7, 8, 9, 12
distribute 6
diverse 1, 2, 3, 6, 8, 9, 12
document 8
dominate 1, 4, 5, 7, 8, 12
drama 2, 3, 4, 5, 6, 8, 9, 10, 11
dynamic 3

economy 1, 2, 6, 7, 8, 9, 10, 11, 12
edit 5, 6
element 10
eliminate 2, 5, 6, 7, 8, 10
emerge 1, 2, 6
emphasis 2, 3 4, 5, 7, 9, 11
enable 2, 4, 5, 6, 7, 11
encounter 12
energy 2, 5, 6, 10
enforce 5, 10
enhance 10
enormous 1, 2, 6, 7, 8, 9, 10, 11, 12
ensure 2, 6, 7, 9, 12
environment 5, 6, 7
equip 9, 10
establish 1, 2, 3, 4, 6, 7, 8, 9, 10
estimate 1, 3, 4, 10 5, 6
ethic 2, 3, 10
ethnic 1, 2, 3, 7, 8, 9, 12
evaluate 5, 9
eventual 1, 2, 4, 6, 8, 9, 11, 12
evident 1, 2, 4, 10, 11, 12
evolve 2, 3
exclude 1, 11
expand 5, 7, 8, 9, 12
expert 5, 7, 8, 10, 11, 12
export 5
expose 10

facilitate 8, 9, 10
factor 1, 2, 4, 5, 6, 9, 10, 11, 12
feature 4, 10

federal 7, 8, 9, 10, 12
fee 5
final 2, 4, 6, 8, 9, 11
finance 2, 6, 7, 8, 9, 12
flexible 6, 9, 11
focus 5, 7, 9, 10, 11
found 4, 6, 7, 8, 12
foundation 2, 3, 4, 5, 10
framework 2
function 3, 8, 12
fund 5, 6, 7, 9, 10
fundamental 2, 3
furthermore 6, 7, 10

gender 2, 5
generate 5, 10
generation 1, 2, 5, 6, 8, 9, 11, 12
globe 2, 12
goal 2, 3, 6, 7, 8, 9, 10, 11, 12
grade 7, 9
grant 3, 5, 9
guarantee 3, 4, 5, 6, 7, 9, 12
guideline 10

hypothesis 1

identify 1, 2, 5, 8, 10, 12
ideology 7, 12
illustrate 3, 7, 10
image 4, 5, 6, 10, 12
immigrate 1, 2, 3, 5, 6, 8, 9
impact 1, 4, 6 7, 9, 10, 11
implement 6, 7, 10
impose 3
income 9, 11, 12
incentive 5
incidence 1, 4, 8, 10
incline 8
income 5, 6, 7, 8, 9
index 6
indicate 9, 11
individual 2, 3, 4, 5, 6, 7, 8, 9, 10, 11, 12
infinite 5
infrastructure 7
injure 10
innovate 5, 6, 12
insight 11
initiative 12
instance 4, 7, 10
institute 1, 4, 5, 6, 7, 9, 11, 12
instruct 8, 9
interact 6, 7
integrate 8, 9
intelligence 2, 4
intense 6, 10
internal 12

interpret 5, 7, 12
invest 3, 5, 6
involve 2, 9, 10, 11, 12
isolate 9, 12
issue 1, 2, 4, 6, 9, 10, 12
item 4, 10

job 1, 2, 6 7, 8, 9, 11, 12
justify 9

label 10
labor 2, 5, 7, 8, 10, 11
lecture 9, 10
legal 1, 3, 7, 8, 9, 11
legislate 4, 7, 10
liberal 3, 7, 9, 12
license 1, 11
likewise 10
link 6
locate 5, 6, 11

maintain 1, 2, 5, 6, 8, 9, 10, 11, 12
major 1, 2, 3, 4, 5, 6, 7, 8, 9, 10, 11, 12
mature 9
maximum 9
measure 5
media 1, 5, 9, 10
medical 5, 6, 7, 8, 12
mental
method 6, 7, 9
migration 8
military 4, 6, 7, 8, 10, 12
minimum 9
minor 1, 7, 8, 9, 12
monitor 11
motive 1, 2, 3, 6, 10

negate 5
network 5, 6
neutral 1
nevertheless 2, 10
normal 4
nuclear 6, 11

obtain 9, 11
obvious 9
occupy 6, 10
occur 3, 4, 8, 9, 10
odd 12
ongoing 12
option 5
orient 3, 6
outcome 7, 11
output 6
overall 6, 10, 11
overseas 6, 7, 10, 12

parallel 12
participate 1, 6, 9, 10
partner 7, 11
perceive 2, 8
percent 1, 3, 4, 5, 6, 7, 8, 9, 10, 11, 12
period 1, 4, 5, 7, 11
persist 3, 6, 7, 10, 12
perspective 9
phase 4
phenomenon 8
philosophy 3, 9, 10, 12
physical 4, 9, 10
plus 6, 7
policy 6, 7, 9, 11, 12
portion 4, 10, 12
positive 5, 6
potential 2, 5, 6, 7, 9, 11, 12
predict 5, 7, 8, 11
predominant 9
previous 3, 7, 9, 11
primary 4, 7, 9, 11
principal 4, 10
principle 7, 9
priority 6, 11
proceed 7, 9
process 1, 5, 6, 7, 8, 9, 10, 12
professional 5, 9, 10
project 5, 7, 8, 10
promote 2, 7, 10, 12
prospective 5, 9
psychology 10, 11
publish 5, 6
purchase 5
pursue 2, 3, 7, 11, 12

range 4, 10
react 4
recover 6
refine 6
region 4, 8, 10
register 8, 12
regulate 4, 6, 7, 10
reinforce 3, 4, 5, 6, 8, 12
reject 2, 8
relax 10

reluctance 12
rely 2, 3, 4, 6, 7, 8, 9, 10, 11, 12
remove 9, 10
require 2, 3, 5, 6, 7, 8, 9, 10, 11, 12
research 3, 5, 6, 7, 10, 11
reside 1, 8, 9
resolve 7
resource 1, 2, 5, 8, 9, 11
respond 5, 6, 11, 12
restore 6
restrain 7
restrict 1, 7, 10, 11
retain 8
reveal 1, 4, 5, 6, 7, 9, 10, 12
revenue 5
reverse 7, 12
revolution 5, 6. 7, 8, 10, 12
role 1, 2, 3, 5, 6, 7, 10, 11, 12

schedule 9, 10
section 5, 8
sector 6, 9, 12
secure 4, 5, 6, 7, 9, 12
seek 2, 3, 4, 6, 8, 9, 10, 11, 12
select 1, 9
series 7, 9, 12
sex 3, 8, 10, 11
shift 2, 6, 7
significant 1, 3, 5, 6, 7, 8, 9, 10, 11, 12
similar 3, 7, 9, 10, 11
site 5, 6, 11
sole 3, 7
somewhat 8
source 2, 4, 5, 6
specific 1, 7, 10, 12
specify 1
stable 11
status 2, 5, 6, 8, 9, 11
strategy 7
stress 5, 10, 11, 12
structure 2, 5, 6, 11
style 6, 7
submit 6
subsidy 5

substitute 3
sum 2, 3, 6, 7
survey 2, 10, 11
survive 1, 4, 6, 10, 12
symbol 5, 7, 10

tape 3
target 4, 5, 7, 12
task 4, 5, 11
team 5, 6, 9, 10
technical 9
technique 5, 6
technology 5, 6, 8, 10, 11, 12
temporary 6, 7
tension 7, 12
text 1, 5, 9
theme 2, 6, 12
theory 6
trace 1, 8, 10
tradition 1, 2, 3, 4, 5, 6, 7, 8, 9, 10, 11, 12
transform 6, 9
transfer 9
transition 12
trend 1, 11

ultimate 6, 7, 8, 12
undergo 6, 7
undertake 12
uniform 2, 10
unique 1, 2, 6, 8, 9, 12
utility 12

vary 1, 7, 9, 10, 11
version 4
via 10
vision 6, 7
violate 9
virtual 1, 8, 11
visible 1
voluntary 3, 9

welfare 2, 7, 11
widespread 2, 7, 9

BIBLIOGRAPHY

PRINT SOURCES

"10 Ideas that are Changing Your Life." *Time,* 12 March 2012, 59–87.

"50 Years After Brown: Unequal Education." *U.S. News & World Report,* 22, 29 March 2004, 64–70.

"A Class of Their Own." *Time,* 31 October 1994, 52–61.

"A New Era of Segregation: Classrooms Still Aren't Colorblind." *Newsweek,* 27 December 1993, 44.

"A Rich Legacy of Preference: Alumni Kids Get a Big Break on Admissions." *Newsweek,* 24 June 1991, 59.

Aaron, Henry J., Thomas E. Mann, and Timothy Taylor, eds. "Introduction." *Values and Public Policy.* Washington, D.C.: The Brookings Institution, 1994.

Adelman, Larry. "Down the Road from the Michigan Rulings: Right Ruling, Wrong Reason." *Washington Post,* 29 June 2003, Outlook section B3.

Alger, Horatio. *Mark the Match Boy, or Richard Hunter's Ward.* Philadelphia: John C. Winston Company, 1897.

Alger, Horatio. *Tony the Tramp, or Right Is Might.* New York: The New York Book Company, 1909.

"America's Immigrant Challenge." *Time,* Special Issue, Fall 1993, 3–12.

Anthony, Ted. "America innovates, expands—digitally now." *Daily News,* 20 May 2012, A, 9.

Asnes, Marion. "The Affluent American: A Money Survey Delves into the Changing Definition of 'the Good Life.'" *Money.* December 2003, 40, 43.

Bacon, Perry, Jr. "How Much Diversity Do You Want from Me?" *Time,* 7 July 2003, 108.

Barlett, Donald L. and James B. Steele. *The Betrayal of the American Dream.* New York: PublicAffairs, 2012.

Barone, Michael. "A Tale of Two Nations: Why Coddled Kids Grow Up to Become Supercompetent Adults." *U.S. News & World Report,* 12 May 2003, 24.

Becker, Carl L. *The Declaration of Independence: A Study in the History of Political Ideas.* New York: Vantage Books, 1958.

"Been There, Done That" [Adventure Travel]. *Newsweek,* 19 July 1993, 42–49.

Begley, Sharon. "I Can't Think! The Twitterization of our culture has revolutionized our lives, but with an unintended consequence—our overloaded brains freeze when we have to make decisions." *Newsweek,* 7 March 2011, 28–33.

"Best Columns: The U.S.: American Culture: A Dwindling Export." *The Week,* 4 April 2003.

"Best Columns: The U.S.: Orange Alert: Why We're Laughing; Peace Protests: Giving Naivete a Chance; Bush: A Third Kind of President; Affirmative Action: What's Really at Stake. *The Week,* 7 March 2003, 12.

Bohr, Peter. "In the Age of Super-Sizing, Is There Room in America for the Small Car?" *AAA World,* January/February 2003, 30–36.

Bono. "The Resource Miracle: The rock star and activist explains why Africa could be this century's success story." *Time,* 28 May 2012, 28.

Boorstein, Michelle. "Delving into the study of secularism: Georgetown University course is part of a nascent field trying to define itself." *The Washington Post,* 17 December 2011, B 2.

Bowman, Karlyn, ed. "Men Today/Guy Talk." *The American Enterprise.* September 2003, 60–61.

Bradley, Bill. "Citizens United: Monied interests increasingly run the government. Only voters can reverse that." *Time,* 14 May 2012, 23.

Brascoupe, Jeremy. "My World: Young Native Americans Today." *Smithsonian National Museum of the American Indian.* Spring 2003, 9.

Bremmer, Ian. "5 Myths about America's Decline." *The Washington Post,* 6 May 2012, B, 2.

Brogan, D. W. *The American Character.* New York: Alfred A. Knopf, 1944.

Brogan, Hugh. *Tocqueville.* London: Fontana, 1973.

Brookheser, Richard. "We Can All Share American Culture." *Time*, 31 August 1992, 74.

Burns, James MacGregor. *Cobblestone Leadership: Majority Rule, Minority Power.* Norman: University of Oklahoma Press, 1990.

Burns, James MacGregor. *Deadlock of Democracy: Far-Party Politics in America.* Englewood Cliffs, N.J.: Prentice-Hall, 1963.

"Campaign Finance Reform: Opinions of People of Faith and the Clergy." A survey by the Gallup Organization for The Interfaith Alliance Foundation August 2001 in *Call for Reform,* published by The Interfaith Alliance Foundation.

Carlson, Margaret. "And Now, Obesity Rights." *Time*, 6 December 1993, 96.

Carnegie, Andrew. *Autobiography of Andrew Carnegie.* Boston: Houghton Mifflin, 1920.

Carnegie, Andrew. *The Gospel of Wealth and Other Timely Essays.* Cambridge: Harvard University, Belknap Press, 1962.

Cash, W. J. *The Mind of the South.* New York: Alfred A. Knopf, 1960.

Cater, Douglass, ed. *Television as a Social Force: New Approaches to TV Criticism.* New York: Praeger, 1975.

Chinni, Dante. "Inequality is bad for all of us. Even those at the top." *The Washington Post,* 26 August 2012, B1, 4.

Cloud, John. "Why the SUV Is All the Rage." *Time*, 24 February 2003, 35–42.

CNN/*USA Today*/Gallup Poll, 2–4 Sept. 2002. "How Important Would You Say Religion Is in Your Own Life: Very Important, Fairly Important, or Not Very Important?"

Cohen, Richard. "Intolerance Swaddled in Faith." *Washington Post,* 1 May 2003, A27.

Cohn, D'Vera, and Sarah Cohen. "Statistics Portray Settled, Affluent Mideast Community." *Washington Post,* 20 November 2001, A4.

Cohn, D'Vera. "Hispanics Declared Largest Minority: Blacks Overtaken in Census Update." *Washington Post,* 19 June 2003, A1, 46.

"Controversy of the week: The American Dream: What went wrong" *The Week,* 12 October 2012, 6.

Corliss, Richard, Jeffrey Ressner, and James Inverne. "Ladies' Night Out" [Movies]. *Time,* March 2003, 73–75.

Cose, Ellis. "The Black Gender Gap." *Newsweek,* 3 March 2003, 46–55

Counts, George S. *Education and American Civilization.* New York: Bureau of Publications, Teachers College, Columbia University, 1952.

Counts, George S. *Education and the Foundations of Human Freedom.* Pittsburgh: University of Pittsburgh Press, 1962.

Coy, Peter. "Right Place, Right Time." *Business Week,* 13 October 2003.

Cullen, Bob. "New Kids on the Block: As Affluent Schools in the Suburbs Grow More Diverse, They Face the Test That City Schools Failed: Can They Keep Everyone Happy?" *The Washingtonian.* April 2003, 29–34.

Cullen, Lisa Takeuchi. "Now Hiring!" *Time*, 24 November 2004.

"Daughters of Murphy Brown" [Single Motherhood]. *Newsweek,* 2 August 1993, 58–59.

Diamandis, Peter H., and Steven Kotler. *Abundance: The Future Is Better Than You Think.* New York: Free Press, 2012.

Dionne, E. J. Jr. *Our Divided Political Heart: The Battle for the American Idea in an Age of Discontent.* New York: Bloomsbury, 2012.

"Diversity or Division On Campus: Minority Graduation Galas Highlight a Timely Issue." *Washington Post,* 19 May 2003, A1, 8.

Dobbs, David. "Restless Genes: The compulsion to see what lies beyond that far ridge or that ocean—or this planet—is a defining part of human identity and success." *National Geographic,* January 2013, 44–57.

Dokoupil, Tony. "Tweets, Texts, Email, Posts: Is the Onslaught Making Us Crazy?" *Newsweek,* 16 July 2012, 24–30.

"Domesticated Bliss: New Laws Are Making It Official for Gay or Live-In Straight Couples." *Newsweek,* 23 March 1992, 62–63.

Douthat, Ross. "Divided by God: As the religious center erodes, it becomes tough to pull together as a nation." *The New York Times,* 8 April 2012, Sunday Review, 1, 6.

Duhigg, Charles. *The Power of Habit: Why We Do What We Do in Life and Business.* New York: Random House, 2012.

Elliott, Philip. "Schools shift from textbooks to tablets." *Daily News,* 10 March 2013, C, 11.

Ellison, Christopher G., and W. Allen Martin, eds. *Race and Ethnic Relations in the United States: Readings for the 21st Century.* University of Florida, 1998.

Ellwood, Robert S. "East Asian Religions in Today's America." *World Religions in America: An Introduction,* ed. Jacob Neusner. Louisville, Ky.: Westminster/John Knox Press, 1994.

Emery, Noemie. "America in the Middle: Michael Barone Seeks a Balance." *Weekly Standard.* 17 May 2004, 31–33.

Entine, John, Gary Salles, and Jay T. Kearney. *Taboo: Why Black Athletes Dominate Sports and Why We're Afraid to Talk About It.* New York: Public Affairs, 2001.

Esposito, John L. "Islam in the World and in America." *World Religions in America: An Introduction,* ed. Jacob Neusner. Louisville, Ky.: Westminster/John Knox Press, 1994.

Farrand, Max. *The Framing of the Constitution of the United States.* New Haven: Yale University Press, 1913.

Ferguson, Niall. "Rich America, Poor America." *Newsweek,* 23 January 2012, 42–47.

Fetto, John. "Reader Request: Your Questions Answered: Not Only Are Americans Going to School in Record Numbers, They're Also Staying in School Longer." *American Demographics.* April 2003, 8–9.

Fineman, Howard, and Tamara Lipper. "Do We Still Need Affirmative Action? Affirmative Action: Race in the Spin Cycle." *Newsweek,* 27 January 2003, 26–29.

Fineman, Howard. "Bush and God: A Higher Calling: How Faith Changed His Life and Shapes His Presidency." *Newsweek,* 10 March 2003, 22–30.

Finlely, Bill. "Women's Game Is Looking Good, and Fans Notice." *New York Times,* 20 July 2003, Sports section: 5.

Florida, Richard. *The Rise of the Creative Class: and how it's transforming work, leisure, community, & everyday life.* New York: Basic Books, 2003.

Ford, Michael F. "5 Myths about the American Dream." *The Washington Post,* 8 January 2012, B, 2.

Fox-Genovese, Elizabeth. "Religion and Women in America." *World Religions in America: An Introduction,* ed. Jacob Neusner. Louisville, Ky: Westminster/John Knox Press, 1994.

"Fractured Family Ties: Television's New Theme Is Single Parenting." *Newsweek,* 30 August 1993, 50–52.

Friedan, Betty. *The Feminine Mystique.* New York: W.W. Norton, 1963.

Friedan, Betty. *The Second Stage.* New York: Summit Books, 1981.

Galbraith, John Kenneth. *American Capitalism: The Concept of Countervailing Power.* Classics in Economics Series. Boston: Houghton Mifflin, 1956.

Galbraith, John Kenneth. *The Affluent Society.* Boston: Houghton Mifflin, 1976.

Galbraith, John Kenneth. *The Culture of Contentment.* Boston: Houghton Mifflin, 1992.

Garreau, Joel. *The Nine Nations of North America.* New York: Houghton Mifflin, 1981.

Gibbs, Nancy. "The Vicious Cycle." *Time,* 20 June 1994, 24–33.

Gill, Sam. "Native Americans and Their Religions." *World Religions in America: An Introduction,* ed. Jacob Neusner. Louisville, Ky.: Westminster/John Knox Press, 1994.

Gladwell, Malcolm. "Big and Bad: How the S.U.V. Ran Over Automotive Safety." *The New Yorker,* 12 January 2004, 28–33.

Glazer, Nathan, and Daniel P. Moynihan. *Beyond the Melting Pot: The Negroes, Puerto Ricans, Jews, Italians, and Irish of NYC.* Publications of the Joint Center for Urban Studies. Cambridge: M.I.T. Press, 1963.

Glazer, Nathan. "Multiculturalism and Public Policy." *Values and Public Policy,* ed. Henry J. Aaron, Thomas E. Mann, and Timothy Taylor. Washington, D.C.: The Brookings Institution, 1994.

Goldsborough, James O. "The American Political Landscape in 2004." *San Diego Union,* 1 January 2004.

Gonzalez, David. "What's the Problem with 'Hispanic'? Just Ask a 'Latino.'" *New York Times,* 15 November 1992.

Gonzalez, Justo L. "The Religious World of Hispanic Americans." *World Religions in America: An Introduction,* ed. Jacob Neusner. Louisville, Ky.: Westminster/John Knox Press, 1994.

Graham, Ruth. "Religion returns to New England: Evangelists focusing on area that has become nation's most secular." *Daily News,* 30 November 2012, B, 1, 3.

Greeley, Andrew M. "Religion and Politics in America." *World Religions in America: An Introduction,* ed. Jacob Neusner. Louisville, Ky. Westminster/John Knox Press, 1994.

Greeley, Andrew M. "The Catholics in the World and in America." *World Religions in America: An Introduction,* ed. Jacob Neusner. Louisville, Ky.: Westminster/John Knox Press, 1994.

Green, William Scott. "Religion and Society in America." *World Religions in America: An Introduction,* ed. Jacob Neusner. Louisville, Ky.: Westminster/John Knox Press, 1994.

Grossman, Lev. "Drone Home: They Fight and Spy for American Abroad. But What Happens When Drones Return Home?" *Time,* 11 February 2013, 26–33.

Grossman, Lev. "The Beast with a Billion Eyes: In just seven years, YouTube has become the most rapidly growing force in human history. Where does it go from here?" *Time,* 30 January 2012, 38–43.

Grunwald, Michael. "Immigrant Son: Marco Rubio wants to sell the GOP on a path to citizenship for undocumented Americans. So why is his mom calling?" *Time,* 18 February 2013, 24–30.

Hamilton, Anita. "Your Time: Find It on Craig's List." *Time,* 3 March 2003, 76.

Handlin, Oscar. *Race and Nationality in American Life.* Boston: Little, Brown, 1957.

"Happily Unmarried: How-to from a Guidebook for Couples Living Together Without Saying 'I Do.'" *Time,* Bonus Section, March 2003, A10.

Harris Interactive. *The Harris Poll* ® #30, 21 May 2003. "Americans Are Far More Optimistic and Have Much Higher Life Satisfaction Than Europeans" by Humphrey Taylor.

Henderson, Neil. "Greenspan Calls for Better-Educated Workforce." *Washington Post,* 21 February 2004, Business E3: 1, 3.

Henry, W. A. "Pride and Prejudice." *Time,* 28 February 1994.

Hertsguard, Mark. "The Pasta Crisis: Temperatures are rising. Rainfalls are shifting. Droughts are intensifying. What will we eat when wheat won't grow?" *Newsweek,* 17 December 2012, 30–35.

Hinson, Hal. "Life, Liberty and the Pursuit of Cows: How the Western Defines America's View of Itself." *Washington Post,* 3 July 1994, 1(G), 6(G).

Hofstadter, Richard. *Social Darwinism in American Thought.* New York: G. Braziller, 1969.

Hofstadter, Richard. *The American Political Tradition and the Men Who Made It.* New York: Vintage Books, 1954.

Huffington, Ariana. *Third World America: How Our Politicians Are Abandoning the Middle Class and Betraying the American Dream.* New York: Broadway, 2011.

Huffington, Arianna. *Pigs at the Trough: How Corporate Greed and Political Corruption are Undermining America.* New York: Crowne Publishing Group, 2003.

"In Search of the Sacred." *Newsweek.* 28 November 1994, 52–55.

"Income Report: The Near-Affluent, the Affluent, the Upper Echelon: Generosity and Income." *American Demographics.* December 2002/January 2003, 40–47.

Issenberg, Sasha. "A More Perfect Union: How President Obama's Campaign Used Big Data to Rally Individual Voters." *MIT Technology Review.* January/February 2013.

Jones, Malcolm. "The New Turf Wars: A Plague of Critics Bushwhacks the Venerable American Lawn." *Newsweek,* 21 June 1993, 62–63.

Joyce, Amy. "Balancing Their Personal Goals: Younger Employees Value Family Time as Highly as Career Advancement." *Washington Post,* 24 October 2004, F5.

Kanag, Cecilia. "Survey finds e-reader devices fuel book consumption overall." *The Washington Post,* 4 April 2012, A, 11.

Kantrowitz, Barbara, and Pat Wingert. "Education: What's at Stake." *Newsweek,* 27 January 2003, 30–38.

Kegley, Charles, and Eugene Wittkopf. *World Politics: Trend and Transformations,* 3d ed. New York: St. Martin's, 1989.

Kennedy, John F. *A Nation of Immigrants.* New York: Harper & Row, 1958.

Kenworthy, Lane. "5 Myths about the Middle Class." *The Washington Post,* 5 August 2012, B, 2.

Kids Who Care: Everybody Wins When Students Volunteer to Help Out." *Better Homes and Gardens,* March 1992, 37–39.

Killian, Linda. "5 Myths about independent voters." *The Washington Post,* 30 May 2012, B, 2.

King, Martin Luther, Jr. *I Have a Dream.* Littleton, Mass.: Sundance Publications, 1991.

Klein, Ezra. "A remarkable, historic period of change." *The Washington Post,* 13 November 2012, A, 2.

Klein, Ezra. "America in decline? Not likely." *The Washington Post,* 18 May 2012, A, 2.

Klein, Joe. "The Education of Berenice Belizaire." *Time,* 9 August 1993, 26.

Klein, Joe. "Whose Family? Whose Values? Who Makes the Choices?" *Newsweek,* 8 June 1992, 18–22.

Konigsberg, Ruth Davis. "Chore Wars: Men are now pulling their weight—at work and at home. So why do women still think they're slacking off?" *Time,* 8 August 2011, 45–49.

Korte, Gregory. "Immigrants shine on U.S. civics lessons: But survey finds native citizens need to study up." *USA Today,* 27 April 2012.

Kristol, Irving. "The Rise of the Neocons." *The Week,* 23 May 2003, 13.

Langley, Alison. "It's a Fat World, After All: U.S. Food Companies Face Scrutiny Abroad." *New York Times,* 20 July 2003, Money & Business: section 3: 1, 11.

Lasch, Christopher. *The Culture of Narcissism: American Life in an Age of Diminishing Expectations.* New York: W. W. Norton, 1978.

Leinberger, Christopher B. "Now Coveted: A Walkable, Convenient Place." *The New York Times,* 27 May 2012, Sunday Review, 6–7.

Lemann, Nicholas. "Best columns: The U.S.: Viewpoint." *The Week,* 1 June 2012, 12.

Leo, John. "On Society: Pushing the Bias Button." *U.S. News & World Report,* 9 June 2003, 37.

Levy, Steven, and Pat Wingert. "The Next Frontiers [Series]: Spielberg Nation: With Digital Camcorders, PCs and Easy-to-use Software, Anyone Can Become a Film Auteur." *Newsweek,* 25 November 2003, 56–58.

Lewin, Tamar. "One Course, 150,000 Students." *The New York Times,* 22 July 2-12, Education Life, 33.

Lipset, Seymour Martin. *American Exceptionalism: A Double-Edged Sword.* New York: W. W. Norton, 1996.

Lipset, Seymour Martin. Continental Divide: *The Values and Institutions of the United States and Canada.* New York: Routledge, 1990.

Lowi, Theodore, and Benjamin Ginsberg. *American Government: Freedom and Power.* New York: W. W. Norton, 1994.

Lowi, Theodore. *The End of Liberalism: Republic of the United States.* New York: W. W. Norton, 1969.

Lowry, Rich. "The time-wasting network: Facebook might be fun for some people, but there is more to life." *Daily News,* 19 May 2012, A, 4.

Luscombe, Belinda. "Confidence Woman: Facebook's Sheryl Sandberg in on a mission to change the balance of power. Why she just might pull it off." *Time,* 18 March 2013, 34–42.

Macbay, Harvey. *Swim with the Sharks Without Being Eaten Alive.* New York: William Morrow Company, 1988.

Madrigal, Alexis. "The Last Word: My digital shadow: Who's following my every move on the web, asks Alexis Madrigal, and what do they want from me?" *The Week,* 20 April 2012, 40–41.

Malcolm X." *Newsweek,* 16 November 1992, 66–71.

Malcom X and Alex Haley. *The Autobiography of Malcolm X.* New York: Grove Publishers, 1966.

Mansbridge, Jane. "Public Spirit in Political Systems." *Values and Public Policy,* ed. Henry J. Aaron, Thomas E. Mann, and Timothy Taylor. Washington, D.C.: The Brookings Institution, 1994.

Marklein, Mary Beth. "Higher Education: Tribal Colleges Bridge Culture Gap to Future." *USA Today,* 13 April 1998, 4D.

Markon, Jerry. "Virginia Colleges May Bar Illegal Immigrants: Judge's Ruling Is Said to Be U.S. First." *Washington Post,* 26 February 2004, B1.

Marty, Martin E. "Protestant Christianity in the World and in America." *World Religions in America: An Introduction,* ed. Jacob Neusner. Louisville, Ky.: Westminster/John Knox Press, 1994.

Marty, Martin E. "The Sin of Pride: Vision Thing: Why His 'God Talk' Worries Friends and Foes." *Newsweek,* 10 March 2003, 32–33.

Mason, Alpheus T. *In Quest of Freedom: American Political Thought and Practice.* Englewood Cliffs, N.J.: Prentice-Hall, 1959.

Mason, Alpheus T., and Gordon E. Baker, eds. *Free Government in the Making: Readings in American Political Thought.* New York: Oxford University Press, 1949.

Meacham, Jon. "The American Dream: A Biography: It has seen better days, but it's an idea that has shaped the nation's destiny from the beginning—and can point the way to the future." *Time,* 2 July 2012, 26–39.

Michaud, Anne. "City Population Hits 8.1 Million, Keeps Growing: Reasons: Immigrants, New Housing." *Crain's New York Business.* 29 March–4 April 2004, 1, 24.

Morello, Carol. "Caroline County's Loving Revolution: Interracial couple fought Va. Law and pioneered a new sense of identity." *The Washington Post,* 12 February 2012, C, 1, 10.

Morello, Carol. "Interracial marriage rates soar as attitudes change: Virginia has highest percentage of unions between blacks, whites." *The Washington Post,* 16 February 2012, B 1, 5.

Morganthau, Tom. "America: Still a Melting Pot?" *Newsweek,* 9 August 1993, 16–23.

Morin, Richard. "Misperceptions Cloud Whites' View of Blacks." *Washington Post,* 11 July 2001, A1.

Morin, Richard. "Unconventional Wisdom: New Facts and Hot Stats from the Social Sciences: Church Givers vs. Church Goers." *Washington Post,* 4 April 2004, Outlook section: B5.

Morrow, Lance. "Family Values." *Time,* 31 August 1992, 22–27.

Murray, Charles. *Coming Apart: The State of White America 1960–2010.* New York: Crown Forum, 2012.

"National Endowment Campaign Launched to Spearhead Native Language Revitalization." *Native Language Network, Newsletter of the Indigenous Language Institute.* Winter/Spring 2002.

Naughton, Keith and Marc Peyser. "The World According to Trump." *Newsweek,* 1 March 2004, 48–57.

Nelan, Bruce W. "Not So Welcome Anymore." *Time,* Special Issue, Fall 1993, 10–12.

"Networks Under the Gun." *Newsweek,* 12 July 1993, 14–15.

Neusner, Jacob, ed. "Introduction." *World Religions in America: An Introduction.* Louisville, Ky.: Westminster/John Knox Press, 1994.

Nevins, Allan, and Henry Steele Commager. *America: The Story of a Free People.* Boston: Little, Brown, 1942.

Nielsen, Michael. *Reinventing Discovery: The New Era of Networked Science.* Princeton: Princeton University Press, 2012.

Noonan, Peggy. "The Working Spirit: Why We Work So Hard." *O* [Oprah]. May/June 2000, 90.

O'Keefe, Ed. "House freshmen thrown right in." *The Washington Post,* 13 November 2012, A, 6.

O'Neill, Helen. "Young illegal immigrants 'coming out:' States vary wildly on how to treat children of families who are living in country illegally." *Daily News,* 20 May 2012, C, 10.

Obama, Barack. *Dreams from My Father: A Story of Race and Inheritance.* New York: Three Rivers Press, 1995.

Obama, Barack. *The Audacity of Hope: Thoughts on Reclaiming the American Dream.* New York: Crown Publishing Group, 2006.

Obama, Michelle. *American Grown: The Story of the White House Kitchen Garden and Gardens Across America.* New York: Crown, 2012.

Page, Clarence. "GOP needs to listen: Voters spoke their minds before and after election; Republicans' minds were elsewhere." *Daily News,* 13 November 2012, A, 4.

Paris, Peter J. "The Religious World of African Americans." *World Religions in America: An Introduction.* ed. Jacob Neusner. Louisville, Ky.: Westminster/John Knox Press, 1994.

Park, Alice. "Health & Science: The Reason for Recess. Children who are more physically active may do better in school." *Time,* 16 January 2012.

"Partnership or Peril? Faith-Based Initiatives and the First Amendment" by Oliver Thomas, First Reports, vol. 2. no. 1, May 2001, A First Amendment Center Publication, First Amendment Center, Funded by the Freedom Forum (an affiliate of the Newseum).

Pearlstein, Steven. "Washington is broken, just as intended." *The Washington Post,* 22 April 2012, B, 1, 7.

Peterson, Karen S. "Stay Close By, for the Sake of the Kids: Children of Divorce Suffer When a Parent Moves Away, Study Says." *USA Today,* 7 July 2003, Health & Behavior section: 7D.

Peterson, Peter. *Facing Up: How to Rescue the Economy from Crushing Debt and Restore the American Dream.* New York: Simon & Schuster, 1993.

Pink, Daniel H. *A Whole New Mind: Moving from the Information Age to the Conceptual Age.* New York: Riverhead Books, 2005.

Poniewozik, James, "Has the Mainstream Run Dry? What Does Mass Culture Without the Masses Look Like?" *Time,* 29 December 2003–5 January 2004, 148–152.

Popenoe, David. "The Family Condition of America: Cultural Change and Public Policy." *Values and Public Policy,* ed. Henry J. Aaron, Thomas E. Mann, and Timothy Taylor. Washington, D.C.: The Brookings Institution, 1994.

Potter, David M. *People of Plenty: Economic Abundance and the American Character.* Chicago: University of Chicago Press, 1969.

"Profile of General Demographic Characteristics for the United States: 2000 Census."

Putnam, Robert D., and David E. Campbell, with the assistance of Shaylyn Romney Garrett. *American Grace: How Religion Divides and Unites Us.* New York: Simon and Schuster, 2010.

Quinn, Jane Bryant. "Retire Early? Think Again." *Newsweek,* 21 July 2003, 43.

Rainie, Lee. "In the Know Opinion: Seniors' Moment in a Digital World: Fully 60 percent of Internet user 65-plus now get news online." *AARP Bulletin,* November 2012, 36.

Ravitch, Diane. *The Death and Life of the Great American School System: How Testing and Choice Are Undermining Education.* New York: Basic Books, 2010.

Reeves, Richard. *American Journey: Travelling with Tocqueville in Search of Democracy in America.* New York: Simon & Schuster, 1982.

Reich, Charles A. *The Greening of America.* New York: Random House, 1970.

Reich, Robert. *The Work of Nations: Preparing Ourselves for 21st-Century Capitalism.* New York: Alfred A. Knopf, 1991.

Relin, David Oliver. "More Than 13 million Children in America Are Struggling to Survive: Won't You Help Feed Them?" *Parade,* 4 April 2004, 7–9.

Riesman, David. *Individualism Reconsidered and Other Essays.* Glencoe, Ill.: The Free Press, 1954.

Riesman, David. *The Lonely Crowd: A Study on the Changing American Character.* New Haven: Yale University Press, 1950.

Roberts, David. "Points of Interest: Whose Rock Is It Anyway?" *Smithsonian.* March 2003, pp. 26, 29.

Roberts, Johnnie L. "Rethinking Black Leadership: The Race to the Top." *Newsweek,* 28 January 2002, 42–45.

Roberts, Sam. *Who We Are: A Portrait of America Based on the Latest U.S. Census.* New York: Times Books, 1993.

Robinson, Joe. "Ahh, Free at la-Oops! Time's Up." *Washington Post,* 27 July 2003, Outlook section: B1–3.

Robinson, Joe. *Work to Live: Reclaim Your Life, Health, Family, and Sanity.* New York: Perigee Trade, 2003.

Rosenberg, Debra. "Justice: 25 Years After Bakke: Not Just Black and White." *Newsweek.* 30 June 2003, 37.

Sabato, Larry J., ed. *Barack Obama and the New America: The 2012 Election and the Changing Face of Politics.* Lanham: Rowman & Littlefield Publishers, Inc., 2013.

Samuel, Terrence. "Born-Again Agenda: The Peak of Political Power." *U.S. News & World Report,* 23 December 2002, 42–43.

Samuelson, Robert J. "Divided by our love of country." *The Washington Post,* 4 July 2012, A, 21.

Samuelson, Robert J. "Globalization Goes to War." *Newsweek.* 24 February 2003, 41.

Samuelson, Robert J. "We're not 'Coming Apart,'" *The Washington Post,* 26 February 2012, A, 15.

Sandberg, Sheryl, with Nell Scovell. *Lean In: Women, Work, and the Will to Lead.* New York: Alfred A. Knopf, 2013.

"Saving Youth from Violence." *Carnegie Quarterly.* Winter 1994, 1–15.

Scanzoni, John. *Opportunity and the Family.* New York: The Free Press, 1970.

Scanzoni, John. *Sex Roles, Lifestyles, and Childbearing: Changing Patterns in Marriage and the Family.* New York: The Free Press, 1975.

Schickel, Richard. "Ladies Who Lunge." *Time,* 7 July 2003, 96.

Schlesinger, Arthur M., Jr. *The Disuniting of America: Reflections on a Multicultural Society.* New York: W.W. Norton, 1992.

"Sexism in the Schoolhouse: A Report Charges That Schools Favor Boys Over Girls." *Newsweek,* 24 February 1992, 62.

Shapiro, Gary, Foreword by Mark Cuban. *The Comeback: How Innovation Will Restore The American Dream.* New York: Beaufort Books, 2011.

Sheler, Jeffery L. "All in the Family: As Billy Graham Steps Down, Will His Kids Shape the Future of American Evangelicalism?" *U.S. News & World Report,* 23 December 2002, 36–43.

Sides, Hampton. "Connecting the Dots: Shattered Faith: What the fall of Greg Mortenson tells us about America's irrepressible longing for heroes." *Newsweek,* 2 May 2011, 5–6.

Siegel, Lee. "The Kids Aren't Alright: The perils of parenting in the digital age." *Newsweek,* 15 October 2012, 18–20.

Singer, Audrey "At Home in the Nation's Capital: Immigrant Trends in Metropolitan Washington." A report by the Brookings Institution Center on Urban and Metropolitan Policy, June 2003.

Smolan, Rick, and Jennifer Erwitt, eds., *The Human Face of Big Data.* Sausalito: Against All Odds Productions, 2012.

Solomon, Andrew. "Meet My Real Modern Family: As a gay man, the author never expected to have children. Now he and his husband have four between them." *Newsweek,* 7 February 2011, 32–37.

Sotomayor, Sonia. *My Beloved World.* New York: Alfred A. Knopf, 2013.

Span, Paula. "Marriage at First Sight." *The Washington Post* Magazine, 23 February 2003, 16–23, 32–38.

Squires, Sally. "Food Labels Must List Trans Fats: Starting in 2006, Rule Targets Risk Factor for Heart Disease." *The Washington Post,* 10 July 2003. A3.

Stampp, Kenneth. *The Peculiar Institution: Slavery in the Ante-bellum South.* New York: Vintage Books, 1956.

Stein, Joel. "Your Data, Yourself: Every detail of your life—what you buy, where you go, whom you love—is being extracted from the Internet, bundled and traded by data-mining companies. What's in it for you?" *Time,* 21 March 2011, 40–46.

Stiglitz, Joseph E. *The Price of Inequality: How Today's Divided Society Endangers Our Future.* New York: W. W. Norton & Company, 2013.

Summers, Lawrence. "Our inequality of opportunity." *The Washington Post,* 16 July 2012, A 15.

Suro, Roberto. "Study of Immigrants Finds Asians at Top in Science and Medicine." *The Washington Post,* 18 April 1994, 6(A).

"Survey of the attitudes of the American people on highway and auto safety: Wave five of a periodic tracking survey." Louis Harris and Pete Harris Research Group, Inc., June 2004.

Takaki, Ronald. *A Different Mirror: A History of Multicultural America.* Boston: Little, Brown, 1993.

"Talking Points: Evangelicals: The Hidden Mainstream." *The Week,* 21 March 2003, 16.

"Talking Points: Retro-sexism: The Return of the Real Man." *The Week,* 21 March 2003, 17.

"The Dawn of Online Home Schooling." *Newsweek,* 10 October 1994, 67.

"The Fight to Bear Arms." *U.S. News & World Report,* 22 May 1995, 28–37.

"The Grid: Mapping Consumer Markets: Sweat Equity: Where Today's Do-it-yourselfers Are Most Likely to Stake a Claim." *American Demographics,* April 2003, 18–19

"The Simple Life." *Time,* 8 April 1991, 58–63.

"The War for the West." *Newsweek,* 30 September 1991, 18–32.

Tocqueville, Alexis de. *Democracy in America.* New York: J. & H. G. Langley, 1845.

Toffler, Alvin. *Power Shift: Knowledge, Wealth, and Violence at the Edge of the 21st Century.* New York: Bantam Books, 1991.

Treuer, David. "Warren says she's Native American. So she is. American Indian author David Treuer says self-identity is thicker than blood." *The Washington Post,* 6 May 2012, B, 6.

"Trouble at the Top: A U.S. Survey Says a 'Glass Ceiling' Blocks Women from Corporate Heights." *U.S. News & World Report,* 17 June 1991, 40–48.

Tumulty, Karen. "Female candidates make history, head for the Hill." *The Washington Post,* 8 November 2012, A, 42.

Turkle, Sherry. "The Flight From Conversation: We think that our sips of online connection add up to a gulp. They don't." *The New York Times,* 22 April 2012, Sunday Review, 1, 8.

Turner, Frederick Jackson. *The Rise of the New West.* New York: Harper & Brothers, 1906.

Tyrangiel, Josh. "The Center of Attention" [Yao Ming]. *Time,* 10 February 2003, 68–71.

Tyre, Peg and Daniel McGinn. "She Works, He Doesn't." *Newsweek,* 12 May 2003, 44–53.

Tyre, Peg. "Getting Physical: A New Fitness Philosophy Puts Gym Teachers on the Front Lines in the Battle Against Childhood Obesity." *Newsweek,* 3 February 2003, 46–47.

U.S. Department of Education, National Center for Education Statistics, *The Condition of Education 2003,* NCES 2003–067, Washington, D.C.: U.S. Government Printing Office, 2003.

Vargas, Jose Antonio. "The Last Word: My undocumented life: I came here illegally at 12, says Jose Antonio Vargas, but I've earned the right to be called an American." *The Week,* 19–26 August 2011, 44–45.

Von Drehle, David. "America in Red and Blue: A Nation Divided [Series]: Political Split Is Pervasive: Clash of Cultures Is Driven by Targeted Appeals and Reinforced Geography." *Washington Post,* A1, 10.

Waldman, Steven. "Benefits 'R' Us." *Newsweek,* 10 August 1992, 56–58.

Wallerstein, Judith. *The Unexpected Legacy of Divorce: A 25 Year Landmark Study.* New York: Hyperion, 2000.

"Washington Area School Superintendents Demand Changes in Testing Regulations Affecting LEP and Special Education Students." 2 February 2004, a press release by the Washington Area School Study Council.

Waters, Harry F. "On the Trail of Tears: Ted Turner's Massive, Compelling Chronicle of the Native American Order." *Newsweek,* 10 October 1994, 56–58.

Wattenberg, Ben J. *The First Universal Nation: Leading Indicators and Ideas about the Surge of America in the 1990s.* New York: The Free Press, 1991.

Wattenberg, Ben J. *The Good News Is the Bad News Is Wrong.* New York: Simon & Schuster, 1984.

Wattenberg, Ben J. *The Real America: A Surprising Examination of the State of the Union.* New York: Doubleday, 1974.

Wattenberg, Ben J. *Values Matter Most: How Republicans or Democrats or a Third Party Can Win and Renew the American Way of Life.* New York: The Free Press, 1995.

Weil, Andrew. "Don't Let Chaos get You Down: You aren't depressed; our brains just aren't equipped for 21st-century life." *Newsweek,* 7 & 14 November 2011, 9.

Weiss, Michael. *Latitudes & Attitudes: An Atlas of Tastes, Trends, Politics and Passions.* Boston: Little, Brown, 1994.

Whelan, David. "In a Fog about Blogs." *American Demographics,* July/August 2003, Media Channels: 22–23.

"When America Went to the Moon." *U.S. News & World Report,* 11 July 1994, 50–60.

White, John Kenneth. *The Values Divide: American Politics and Culture in Transition,* with forward by John Zogby. New York: Chatham House Publishers of Seven Bridges Press, LLC, 2003.

Will, George. "Land of entitlements: What once was a small portion of the U.S. budget now dominant spending category." *Daily News,* 28 October 2012, C, 2.

Wilson, James Q. "Culture, Incentives, and the Underclass." *Values and Public Policy,* ed. Henry J. Aaron, Thomas E. Mann, and Timothy Taylor. Washington, D.C.: The Brookings Institution, 1994.

Woodward, Kenneth L. "Gospel on the Potomac." *Newsweek,* 10 March 2003, 29.

Woodward, Kenneth. "Angels: Hark! America's Latest Search for Spiritual Meaning Has a Halo Effect." *Newsweek,* 27 December 1993, 52–57.

Woodward, Kenneth. "Dead End for the Mainline: The Mightiest Protestants Are Running Out of Money, Members and Meaning." *Newsweek,* 9 August 1993, 46–48.

Yankelovich, Daniel. "How Changes in the Economy Are Reshaping American Values." *Values and Public Policy,* ed. Henry J. Aaron, Thomas E. Mann, and Timothy Taylor. Washington, D.C.: The Brookings Institution, 1994.

Yankelovich, Daniel. *New Rules: Searching for Self-Fulfillment in a World Turned Upside Down.* New York: Random House, 1981.

Yen, Hope. "Census shows 1 in 3 U.S. counties are dying." *Daily News,* 17 March 2013, C, 9.

Zakaria, Fareed. "Bush, Rice and the 9-11 Shift." *Newsweek,* 16 December 2002, 35.

Zakaria, Fareed. "The Arrogant Empire: Part Three: America's Global Reach: Where Bush Went Wrong." *Newsweek,* 23 June 2004, 18–33.

Zoll, Rachel. "U.S. Protestants lose majority status, study finds: While the category of no religious affiliation as defined by Pew researchers includes atheists, it also encompasses majorities of people who say they believe in God, and a notable minority who pray daily or consider themselves 'spiritual' but not 'religious.'" *Daily News,* 12 October 2012, B, 1.

Zuckerman, Mortimer B. "A Truly Cruel College Squeeze." *U.S. News &World Report,* 8 March 2004, 80.

Zuckerman, Mortimer B. "America's High Anxiety." *U.S. News &World Report,* 15 March 2004, 83–84.

WEB SOURCES

"A history of mass shootings in the US since Columbine." *Telegraph Media Group Limited,* 24 August 2012. Telegraph website.

"A Third of Americans Now Say They are in the Lower Classes." *Pew Research Center: Pew Social & Demographic Trends,* 10 September 2012. Pew Social Trends website.

Alcorn, Shelly, and Mark Alcorn. "Benefit Corporations: A New Formula for Social Change." *ASAE [American Society of Association Executives] The Center for Association Leadership: Associations Now,* June 2012. ASAE Center website.

Alphonse, Lylah M. "Michelle Obama's White Heritage: New Book Explores Her Roots, Race." *Shine from Yahoo!* 18 June 2012. Shine Yahoo! website.

"American Schools Still Heavily Segregated By Race, Income: Civil Rights Project Report. *HuffPost Education,* 20 September 2012. Huffington Post website.

"American Time Use Survey." *Bureau of Labor Statistics,* 22 June 2012. Bureau of Labor Statistics website.

"Americans See Inequality as a Major Problem: Division as to who would be best to address it—Republicans or President Obama?" *Harris Interactive: The Harris Poll,* 5 April 2012. Harris Interactive website.

"Annual State of the American Dream Survey." *Center for the Study of the American Dream,* March 2011. Xavier University website.

Armarlo, Christine. "Average cost of four-year university up 15%." *USA Today: Money,* 13 June 2012. USA Today website.

Assessment, "The Globalization of Crime: A Transitional Crime Threat Assessment," Chapter 6 Firearms. *United Nations Office of Drugs and Crime,* 2010. UNODC (United Nations Office of Drugs and Crime) website.

"Back to school statistics: Fast Facts." *Institute of Education Sciences, National Center for Education Statistics.* National Center for Education Statistics website.

Begley, Sharon. "Fat and getting fatter: U.S. obesity rates to soar by 2030." *Reuters,* 18 September 2012. Reuters website.

Bennett, William J. "It's good news that government is stalled." *CNN.com,* 27 September 2012. CNN.com website.

Borger, Gloria. "America's love/hate affair with government." *CNN Opinion,* 29 September 2012. CNN.com website.

Brenner, Joanna. "Commentary: Social Networking." *Pew Internet: Social Networking,* 14 February 2013. Pew Internet website.

Brenner, Joanna. "Pew Internet: Mobile" *Pew Research Center: Pew Internet & American Life Project,* 31 January 2013. Pew Internet website.

Briggs, David. "Diversity Rising: Census Shows Mormons, Nondenominational Churches, Muslims Spreading Out Across U.S." *ARDA Blog,* 1 May 2012. ARDA website.

Burzynski, Andrea. "Hungry Americans get 'A Place at the Table' in new documentary." *Reuters,* 1 March 2013. Reuters website.

Castagnoli, Francesca. "The Giving Workout: Teach Your Kid the Value of Volunteering." *Parents,* November 2012. Parents website.

Chittum, Ryan. "Billionaires made from scratch? Hardly: Forbes spins a bogus Horatio Alger story about its 400 richest list." *Columbia Journalism Review,* 28 September 2012. Columbia journalism Review website.

"Civilian Firearms Ownership." United Nations Organized Crime Threat Assessment, "The Globalization of Crime: A Transitional Crime Threat Assessment," Chapter 6 Firearms. *United Nations Office of Drugs and Crime,* 2010. UNODC (United Nations Office of Drugs and Crime) website.

Cline, Seth. "Are Mass Shootings a Fact of Life in America?" *U.S. News & World Report,* 28 August 2012. U.S. News & World Report website.

CNN Political Unit. "Gun control opinions following shootings." *Political Ticker,* 8 September 2012. Political Ticker Blog CNN website.

Cohen, Aaron M. "The Emergence of a Global Generation: A review of *The Way We'll Be* by John Zogby. *The Futurist: The World Future Society,* January-February 2009. World Future Society website.

Cohn, D'Vera and Rich Morin. "Who Moves? Who Stays Put? Where's Home?" *Pew Research Social & Demographic Trends,* 29 December 2008. Pew social Trends website.

Cohn, D'Vera. "Second-Generation Americans, by the Numbers. *Pew Research Social & Demographic Trends,* 7 February 2013.

Confessore, Nicholas. "Tramps Like Them: Coming Apart: The State of White America, 1960–2012 by Charles Murray." *The New York Times,* 10 February 2012. The New York Times website.

"Daily Chart: Accounting for Time." *The Economist Online,* 25 June 2012. Economist website.

Davis, Jessica. "School Enrollment and Work Status: 2011." *American Community Survey Briefs: United States Census Bureau,* October 2012. U.S. Census Bureau website.

"Declining childhood obesity rates—where are we seeing the most progress?" *Robert Wood Johnson Foundation Health Policy Snapshot: Childhood Obesity Issue Brief,* 1 September 2012. Robert Wood Johnson Foundation website.

Emery, Noemie. "America in the Middle: Michael Barone seeks a balance: *Hard America/Soft America: Competition vs. Coddling.*" *The Weekly Standard,* 17 May 2004, The Weekly Standard website.

"Enrollment: Fast Facts." *Institute of Education Sciences, National Center for Education Statistics.* National Center for Education Statistics website.

"Environment." *Gallup Polls,* 2011–2012. Gallup website.

"Exercise Statistics." *Statistic Brain,* 7 March 2012. Statistic Brain website.

Florida, Richard. "Where to Find a Creative Class Job in 2020." *The Atlantic Cities,* 2 March 2012. The Atlantic Cities website.

"Focus on Prices and Spending: Consumer Expenditures: 2008." *U.S. Bureau of Labor Statistics: Office of Publications & Special Studies,* May 2010. U.S Bureau of Labor Statistics website.

Follman, Mark, Gavin Aronsen, and Deanna Pan. "A Guide to Mass Shootings in America." *Mother Jones,* 20 July 2012. Mother Jones website.

Ford, Michael. "Civic Illiteracy: A Threat to the American Dream." *Huff Post Politics,* 15 May 2012. Huffington Post website.

Francis, David. "Decline of the Middle Class: Behind the Numbers: An Inside Look at the Middle-Class Squeeze: From retirement to health how the struggle plays out in everyday life." *US News Money,* 16 October 2012. Money US News website.

"Frequently Asked Questions." *SBA [Small Business Administration] Office of Advocacy,* January 2011. SBA Office of Advocacy website.

Gabriel, Trip. "Despite Push, Success at Charter Schools Is Mixed." *The New York Times,* 1 May 2010. The New York Times website.

"Gallup Daily: U.S. Life Evaluation: Based on the Gallup-Healthways Well-Being Index." *Gallup Daily Poll,* February 2013. Gallup website.

Gelman, Andrew. "Charles Murray's *Coming Apart* and the measurement of social and political divisions." Written for *Statistics, Politics and Policy* Columbia University Journal, 20 September 2012. Columbia University website.

Gergen, David and Michael Zuckerman. "Is America becoming a house divided against itself?" *CNN Opinion,* 28 September 2011. CNN website.

"Higher Achievements: U.S. High School and College completion Rates Continue to Climb." *Pew Research Social & Demographic Trends,* 5 November 2012. Pew Social Trends website.

"Households and Families: 2010." *U.S. Census Bureau: 2010 Census Briefs,* April 2012. U.S. Census website.

Huffington, Arianna and Mary Matlin. "Author One-to-One." Editorial Reviews *Amazon.com Review.* Amazon.com website, 2011.

Huffington, Arianna. "Real Misery Index: highest level ever in April 2010." Quotation from *Third World America*, p. 55, 2 September 2010. On The Issues website.

"If you had to choose, which of these groups are you in: the haves or the have-nots?" *Pew Research Center/Washington Post Poll*, 22–25 September 2011. Polling Report website.

"In Gun Control Debate, Several Options Draw Majority Support: Gun Rights Proponents More Politically Active." *Pew Research Center for the People & the Press*, 14 January 2013. People-press website.

"Is College Worth It?" *Pew Research Social & Demographic Trends*, 15 May 2011. Pew Social Trends website.

Jackson, Brooks. "Fiscal FactCheck: Does Washington have a spending problem or an income problem? We offer some key facts." *Fact Check*, 15 July 2011. Fact Check website.

Jamrisko, Michelle and Ilan Kolet. "Cost of College Degree in U.S. Soars 12 Fold: Chart of the Day." *Bloomberg*, 15 August 2012. Bloomberg website.

"John Lewis Georgia Congressman." *Time*, 15 January 2009. Time website.

Jones, Jeffrey M. "Nurses Top Honesty and Ethics List for 11th Year: Lobbyists, car salespeople, members of Congress get the lowest ratings." *Gallup Poll*, 3 December 2010. Gallup website.

Kadlec, Dan. "Social Security Now Takes More Than It Gives." *Times: Business and Money*, 7 August 2012. Time Business website.

Kaplan, Karen. "Knot Yet: Getting married later can have economic costs, benefits." *Los Angeles Times*, 15 March 2013. LA Times website.

Klein, Ezra. "Transcript: President Obama 2013 inaugural address." *The Washington Post*, 21 January 2013. Washington Post website.

"Knot Yet: The Benefits and Costs of Delayed Marriage in America." *The National Marriage Project: The University of Virginia*, March 2013. National Marriage Project website.

Kolata, Gina. "Well: Updating the Message to Get Americans Moving." *Personal Best blog The New York Times*, 19 November 2012. The New York Times website.

"Life." *PollingReport.com*, December 2012. PolingReport.com website.

Lindsay, Jay. "Religion And Giving: More Religious States Give More To Charity." *Huffpost*, 20 August 2012. Huffington Post website.

Livingston, Gretchen and D'Vera Cohn. "U.S. Birthrate Falls to a Record Low; Decline Is Greatest Among Immigrants." *Pew Research Social & Demographic Trends*, 29 November 2012. Pew Social Trends website.

Lopez, Mark Hugo. "Latinos and Education: Explaining the Attainment Gap." *Pew Research Center Publications*, 7 October 2009. Pew Research website.

Lowenstein, Roger. "Book Review: *Coming Apart* by Charles Murray. *Bloomberg Businessweek Magazine*, 19 January 2012. Business Week website.

Lynch, Matthew. "It's Tough to Trailblaze: Challenges of First-Generation College Students." *Diverse Education*, 23 January 2013. Diverse Education website.

"Majority of Americans See Connection Between Video Games and Violent Behavior in Teens: Harris Poll Finds One-Third of Those with Young Game Players Do Not Censor Games: Majority of U.S. Adults Admit to Understanding Little or Nothing About Video Game Rating System." *The Harris Poll*, 27 February 2013. Harris Interactive website.

May, Gary S. "Essay on what MOOCs are missing to truly transform higher education." *Inside Higher Education*, 11 September 2012. Inside Higher Ed website.

McColl, Lindsey. "Are Ads Really Following You Online?" *Lindsey McColl Blog*, 21 November 2012. Lindsey McColl website.

"Middle Class America: 5 Sad Charts About The Country's Favorite Demographic." *HuffPost Business*, 1 September 2012. The Huffington Post website.

Morales, Lymari. "U.S. Payroll to Population Rates Higher Among College Grads: Less educated Americans least likely to be employed full time for an employer." *Gallup Poll*, 18 September 2012. Gallup website.

Morello, Carol. "Study: Delaying marriage hurts middle-class most." *The Washington Post*, 15 March 2012. Washington Post website.

Morello, Carol. Census: Middle class shrinks to an all-time low." *The Washington Post Business,* 12 September 2012. Washington Post website.

Morin, Rich, Paul Taylor and Eileen Patten. "A Bipartisan Nation of Beneficiaries." *Pew Research Social & Demographic Trends,* 18 December 2012. Pew Social Trends website.

Morin, Rich. "The Public Renders a Split Verdict On Changes in Family Structure." *Pew Research Social & Demographic Trends,* 16 February 2011. Pew Social Trends website.

"Mother's Day: May 13, 2012." *Profile America Facts for Features: U.S. Census Bureau News,* 19 March 2012. U.S. Census website.

Msnbc.com staff. "Asians are fastest-growing race group in US, Census Bureau says." *US News: NBC News,* 21 March 2012. US News NBC News website.

"Municipal Solid Waste." *United States Environmental Protection Agency,* 15 November 2012. EPA website.

Nasser, Haya El. "Study: Some immigrants assimilate faster." *USA Today,* 13 May 2008.

Navarrette, Ruben Jr. "Are baby boomers to blame for broken government?" CNN Opinion, 29 September 2012. CNN.com website.

"New Immigrants Made Asians Fastest-Growing U.S. Group." *Los Angeles Times,* 19 June 2012. LA Times website.

"New TechNet Survey: Americans Support High-Skilled Immigration Reform." *TechNet,* 14 March 2013. *TechNet* website.

Newport, Frank. "Americans: Economy Takes Precedence Over Environment: First time majority has supported economy in 25 years of asking question." *Gallup Poll,* 19 March 2009. Gallup website.

Newport, Frank. "Mississippi Is Most Religious U.S. State: Vermont and New Hampshire are the least religious states." *Gallup Poll,* 27 March 2012. Gallup Poll website.

Newport, Frank. "Seven in 10 Americans Are Very or Moderately Religious: But Protestant population is shrinking as 'unbranded' religion grows." *Gallup Poll,* 4 December 2012. Gallup Poll website.

Nittle, Nadra Kareem. "Barack Obama's Irish Heritage." *Race Relations About.com,* 28 June 2012. Race Relations About.com website.

"'Nones' on the Rise: One-in-Five Adults Have No Religious Affiliation." *Pew Research Center: The Pew Forum on Religion & Public Life,* 9 October 2012. Pew Forum website.

"Overweight and Obesity: Adult Obesity Facts." *Centers for Disease Control and Prevention,* 13 August 2012. Centers for Disease Control website.

Parker, Kim and Eileen Patten. "The Sandwich Generation: Rising financial Burdens for Middle-Aged Americans." *Pew Research Social & Demographic Trends,* 30 January 2013. Pew Social Trends website.

Parker, Kim and Wendy Wang. "Modern Parenthood: Roles of Moms and Dads Converge as They Balance Work and Family." *Pew Research Social & Demographic Trends,* 14 March 2013. Pew Social Trends website.

Parker, Kim. "The Boomerang Generation: Feeling OK about Living with Mon and Dad." *Pew Research Social & Demographic Trends,* 15 March 2012. Pew Social Trends website.

Plumer, Brad. "Who receives government benefits, in six charts." *The Washington Post,* 18 September 2012. Washington Post website.

"Policy Basics: Top Ten Facts About Social Security." *Center on Budget and Policy Priorities,* 6 November 2012. Center on Budget and Policy Priorities website.

Preston, Jennifer. "Views on Gun Laws Unchanged After Colorado Shooting, Poll Finds." *The New York Times: The Lede, Blogging the News With Robert Mackey,* 30 July 2012. The New York Times website.

Ravitch, Diane. "We Must Out-Educate and Out-Innovate Other Nations." *Bill Moyers Group Think,* 8 February 2013. Bill Moyers website.

Rector, Robert. "Marriage: America's Greatest Weapon Against Child Poverty." *The Heritage Foundation,* 2 September 2012. Heritage Foundation website.

Rich, Motoko. "Segregation Prominent in Schools, Study Finds." *The New York Times,* 19 September 2012. The New York Times website.

Richmond, Emily. "Schools Are More Segregated Today Than During the Late 1960s." *The Atlantic,* 11 June 2012. The Atlantic website.

Roof, Wade Clark. "Religious Kaleidoscope: American Religion in the 1990s." *Temenos* 32, 1996, 183–193. Temenos website.

"School Finance: Federal, State, and Local K–12 School Finance Overview." *New America Foundation: Federal Education Budget Project,* 13 December 2012. New America Foundation website.

Schuessler, Jennifer. "A Lightning Rod in the Storm Over America's Class Divide." *The New York Times,* 5 February 2012. The New York Times website.

Skerry, Peter. "Do We Really Want Immigrants to Assimilate?" *Brookings: Society Article,* March/April 2000. Brookings website.

Smith, Mark S. "Obama Census Choice: African-American." *HuffPost*, 28 June 2012. Huffington Post website.

"Social Security Basic Facts." *Social Security Administration,* 7 February 2013. Social Security Administration website.

"STAND Lesson 1: Understanding your exposure to advertising." *University of Rhode Island, Harrington School of Communication and Media,* n.d. Media Education Lab website.

Story, Louise. "Anywhere the Eye Can See, It's Likely to See an Ad." *The New York Times,* 15 January 2007. The New York Times website.

Strauss, Valerie. "Report Reveals Trend of Segregation in Charter Schools." *CBS Local Detroit,* 10 March 2012. CBS Local website.

Strauss, Valerie. "Whose children have been left behind? Framing the 2012 ed debate." *Washington Post blog The Answer Sheet,* 3 January 2012. Washington Post website.

"Super PAC spending election 2012." *Los Angeles Times Data Desk.* LA Times website, 20 November 2012.

Taylor, Paul and D'Vera Cohn. "A Milestone En Route to a Majority Minority Nation." *Pew Research Social & Demographic Trends,* 7 November 2012. Pew Social Trends website.

Taylor, Paul. "The Growing Electoral Clout of Blacks Is Driven by Turnout, Not Demographics." *Pew Research Social & Demographic Trends,* 26 December 2012. Pew Social Trends website.

"The 2011 Metlife Study of the American Dream: The Do-It-Yourself Dream." *Metlife,* 29 November 2011. Metlife website.

"The American-Western European Values Gap: American Exceptionalism Subsides." *Pew Research Center: Pew Global Attitudes Project,* 29 February 2012. Pew Research Center website.

"The changing face of religious America: Census reveals how number of Muslims in U.S. has DOUBLED since 9/11—while Mormonism has spread to East Coast." *Mail Online,* 2 May 2012. Daily Mail website.

"The Foreign-Born Population in the United States: 2010." *American Community Service Reports,* May 2012. United States Census Bureau website.

"The Rise of Asian Americans." *Pew Research Center: Pew Social & Demographic Trends,* 19 June 2012. Pew Social Trends website.

"The Top 10 Outdoor Activities Based on Money Spent." *Adventure Lab: Outside Online*, 27 June 2012. Outside Online website.

Thompson, Derek. "Your Day in a Chart: 10 Cool Facts About How Americans Spend Our Time." *The Atlantic,* 25 June 2012. The Atlantic website.

Thompson, Krissah. "Michelle Obama to visit three states on 'Let's Move' tour, highlight successes." *The Washington Post,* 26 February 2013. Washington Post website.

"U.S. Religious Landscape Survey: Report 1 Religious Affiliation." *Pew Forum on Religion & Public Life,* 2007. Pew Forum website.

"U.S. Religious Landscape Survey: Report 2 Religious Beliefs & Practices/Social & Political." *Pew Forum on Religion & Public Life,* 2007. Pew Forum website.

"U.S. Travel Answer Sheet: Facts about a Leading American Industry That's More Than Just Fun." *U.S. Travel Association,* January 2013. U.S. Travel website.

"Values." *PollingReport.com,* February 2012. PollingReport.com website.

"Views of Gun Control—A Detailed Demographic Breakdown." *Pew Research Center Publications,* 13 January 2011. Pew Research website.

Wang, Wendy. "The Rise of Intermarriage: Rates, Characteristics Vary by Race and Gender." *Pew Research Social & Demographic Trends,* 16 February 2012. Pew Social Trends website.

Washington, Jesse. "Obama's mixed background raises question of racial categories." *Columbia Missourian,* 13 December 2008. Columbia Missourian website.

Wesley, John. "John Wesley Quotes." *Good Reads.* Good Reads website.

"When Labels Don't Fit: Hispanics and Their Views of Identity." *Pew Research Publications,* 4 April 2012. Pew Research website.

Wike, Richard. "Anti-Americanism Down in Europe, but a Values Gap Persists." *Pew Research Global Attitudes Project,* 4 December 2012. Pew Global website.

Wilbert, Caroline, Reviewed by Louise Chang. "Are Americans Backing Off Exercise? Percentage of Americans Getting Regular Exercise Declines, Survey Finds." *WebMD,* 21 January 2010. WebMD website.

Wilcox, Bradford. "Values Inequality: 'Coming Apart' argues that a large swath of America—poor and working-class whites—is turning away from traditional values and losing ground." *Bookshelf: The Wall Street Journal,* 31 January 2012.

"Youth Sports Statistics." *Statistic Brain,* 26 January 2012. Statistic Brain website.

Zickuhr, Kathryn, and Aaron Smith. "Digital Differences: While increased internet adoption and the rise of mobile connectivity have reduced many gaps in technology access over the past decade, for some groups digital disparities still remain." *Pew Research Center's Internet & American Life Project,* 13 April 2012. Pew Internet website.

Zogby, John. "Drones and Dreams." *Forbes,* 10 February 2013. Forbes website.

Zogby, John. "It's Not Only the Economy, Stupid." *The National Interest,* 17 September 2012. The National Interest website.

Zogby, John. "Zogby: The Values Divide, 2012." *Forbes,* 7 September 2012. Forbes website.

CREDITS

PHOTOS

ILLUSTRATIONS

TEXT

2nd Generation."Data from "Second Generation Americans," Pew Research, Washington D.C. (February 7, 2013). http://www.pewsocialtrends.org/2013/02/07/second-generation-americans.; Pages 208–209: Chart and Graph of tuition rate changes at private and public 4-year colleges. Data are from Trends in College Pricing, 2012. © 2012. The College Board. www.collegeboard.org. Reproduced with permission.; Page 223: "Mean Earnings by Age 2009." From "Is College Worth It?" Pew Research Center, Washington D.C. (May 15, 2011).http://www.pewsocialtrends.org/2011/05/15/is-college-worth-it/6/#chapter-5-the-monetary-value-of-a-college-education?src=prc-number.; Page 241: Cartoon: Peter Steiner, "On the Internet, nobody knows you're a dog." PeterSteiner/The New Yorker Collection/www.cartoonbank.com.; Page 262: Graph: "Rising Share of Young Adults Living in Multi-Generational Households." From Kim Parker, "The Boomerang Generation," Pew Research Center (March 15, 2012). http://www.pewsocialtrends.org/2012/03/15/the-boomerang-generation.; Page 264: Chart: "In dual-income households with children, average number of hours spent each week on…" "Modern Parenthood Slideshow: How it adds up for spouses in dual-income families." Pew Research Center, Washington, D.C. (March 14, 2013). http://www.pewsocialtrends.org/2013/03/14/modern-parenthood-slideshow/modernparenthood-slideshow_003/; Page 270: Graph: "Percentage of general public who say the ideal situation for young children is to have a mother who works." "Modern Parenthood Slideshow: What's the ideal situation for kids?" Pew Research Center, Washington, D.C. (March 14, 2013). http://www.pewsocialtrends.org/2013/03/14/modern-parenthood-slideshow/modernparenthood-slideshow_006/.; Page 270: Graph: "Percentage with children who say they spend . . . time with their children. "Modern Parenthood Slideshow: Most parents give themselves an 'A'." Pew Research Center, Washington D.C. (March 14, 2013). http://www.pewsocialtrends.org/2013/03/14/modern-parenthood-slideshow/modernparenthood-slideshow_010.; Page 271: Graph: "Percentage with children saying they are doing an 'excellent' or 'very good' as parents." "Modern Parenthood Slideshow: What working moms and dads want in a job." Pew Research Center, Washington D.C. (March 14, 2013). http://www.pewsocialtrends.org/2013/03/14/modern-parenthood-slideshow/modernparenthood-slideshow_008.; Page 271: Graph: "Percentage with children who say . . . is extremely important to them."Modern Parenthood Slideshow: What working moms and dads want in a job." Pew Research Center, Washington D.C. (March 14, 2013).http://www.pewsocialtrends.org/2013/03/14/modern-parenthood-slideshow/modernparenthood-slideshow_008.; Page 291: Chart: 2010 Federal Revenues. Data from Office of Management and Budget. http://www.cbo.gov/publication/43153; Page 304: Excerpt from Barack Obama's Second Inaugural Address.